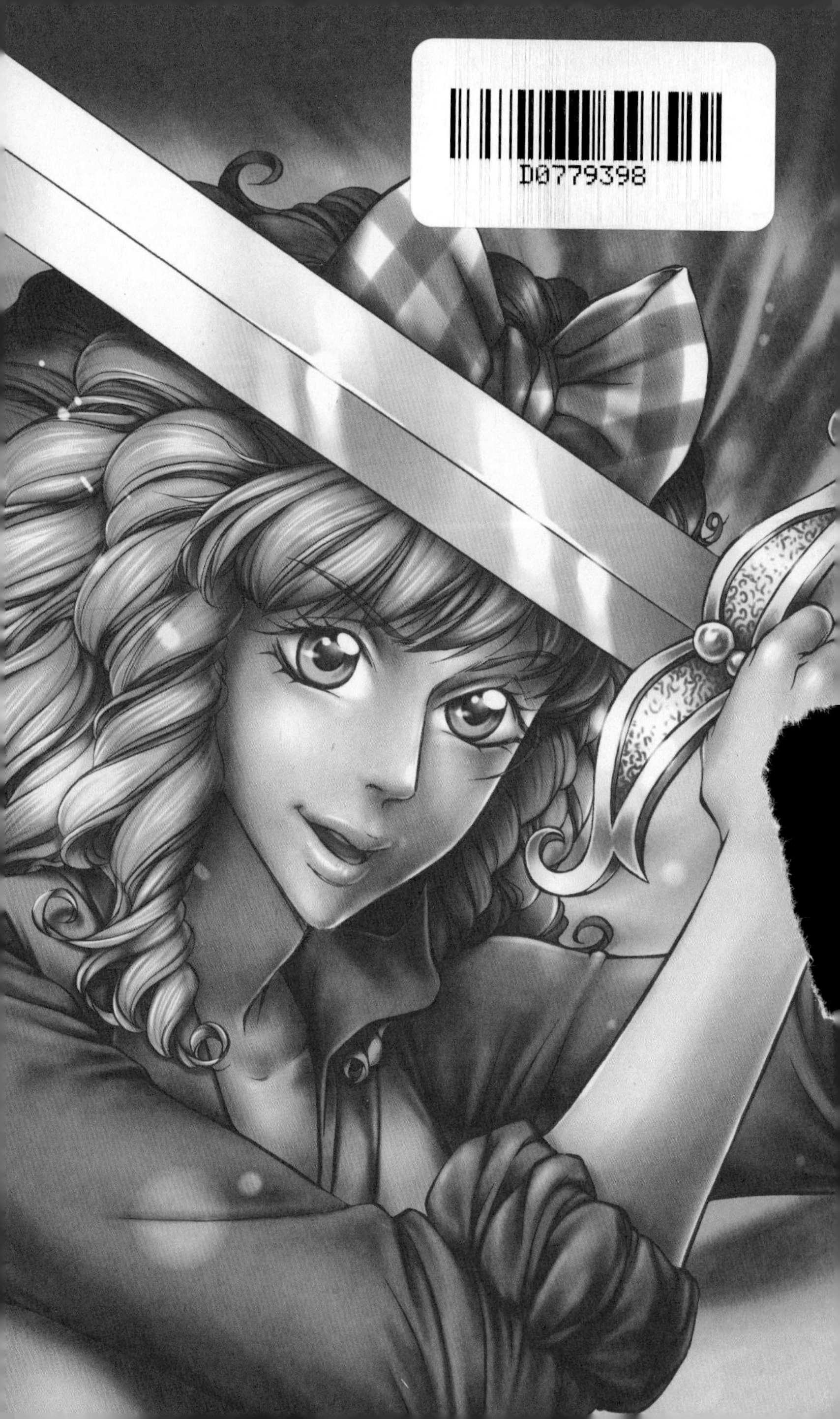

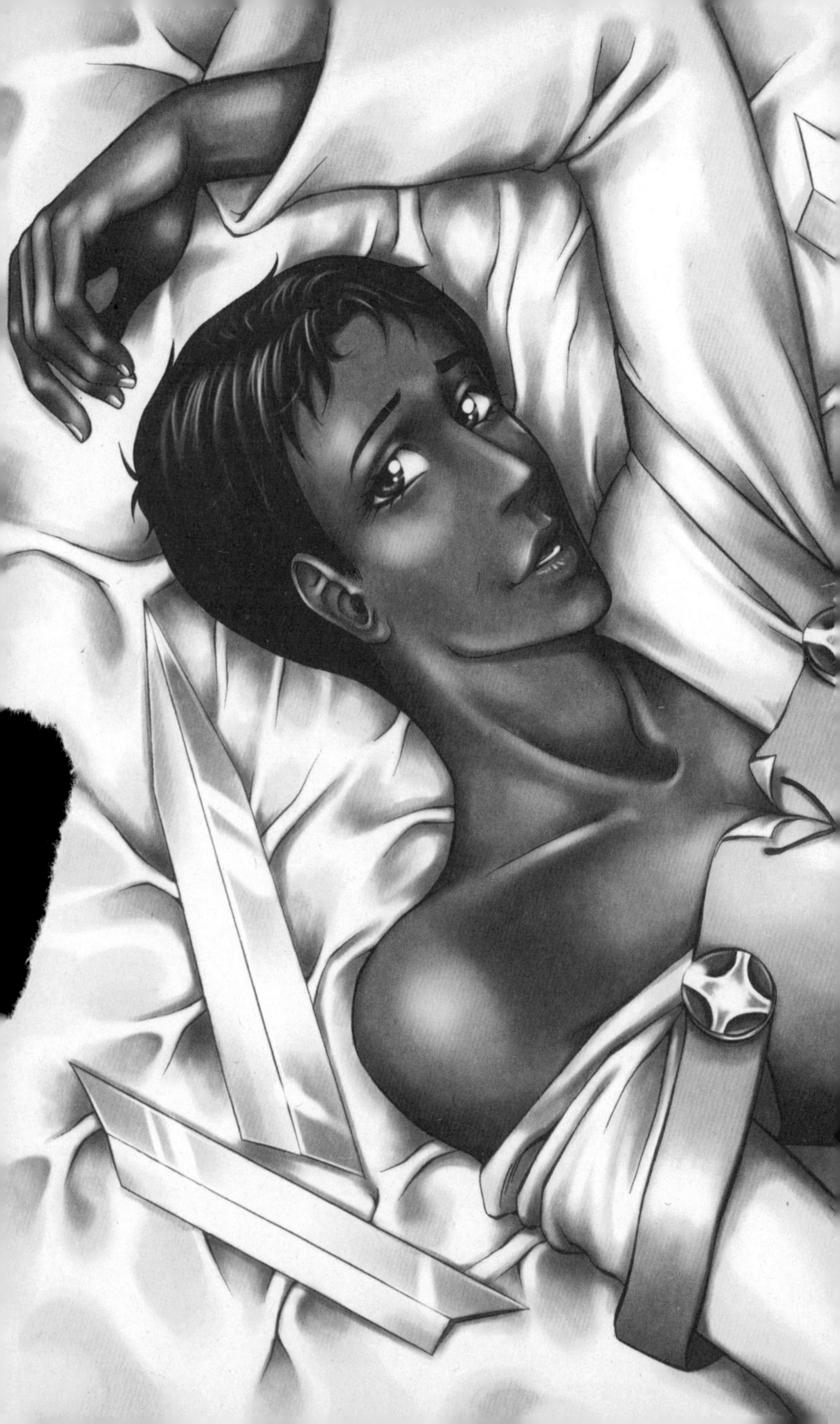

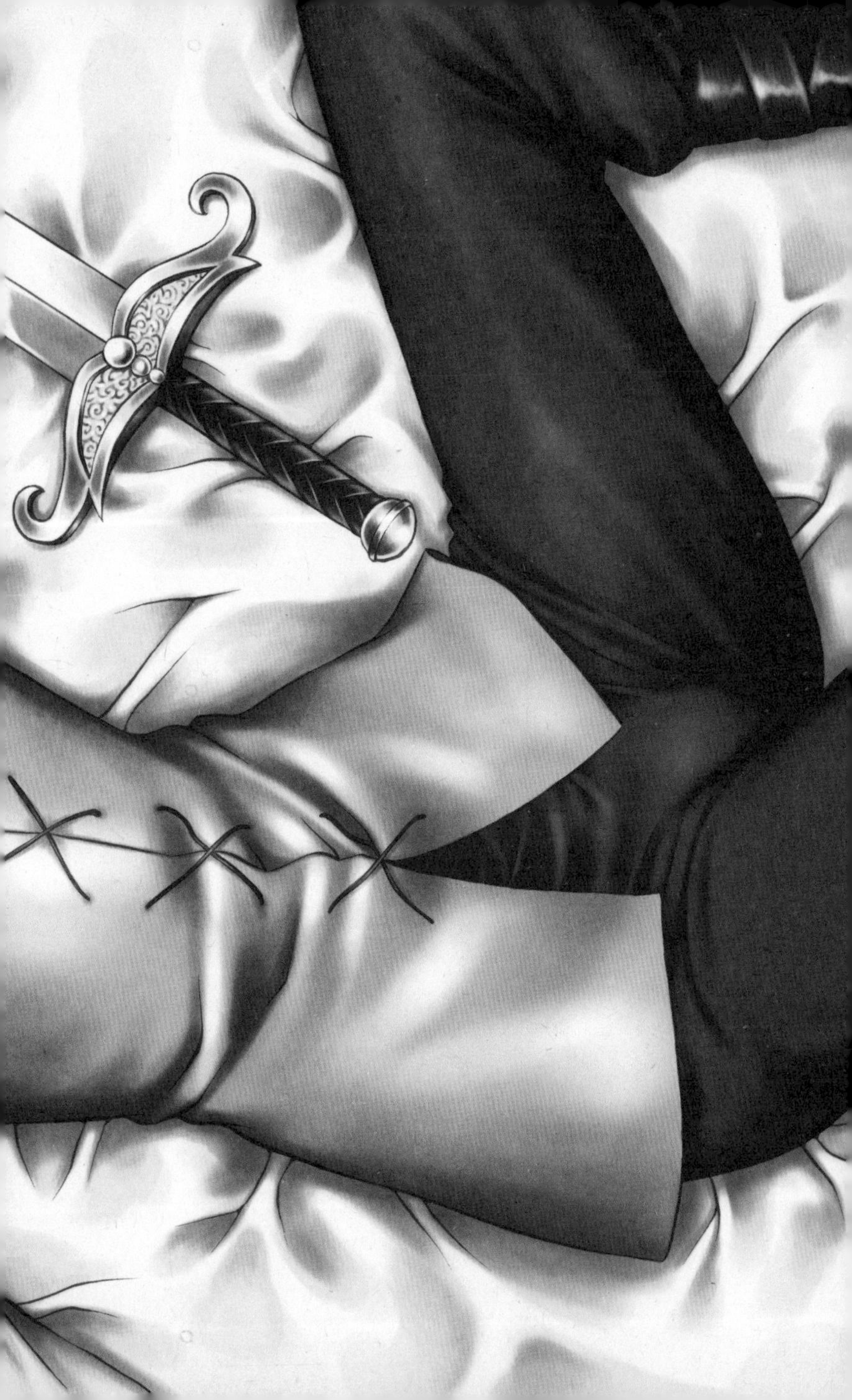

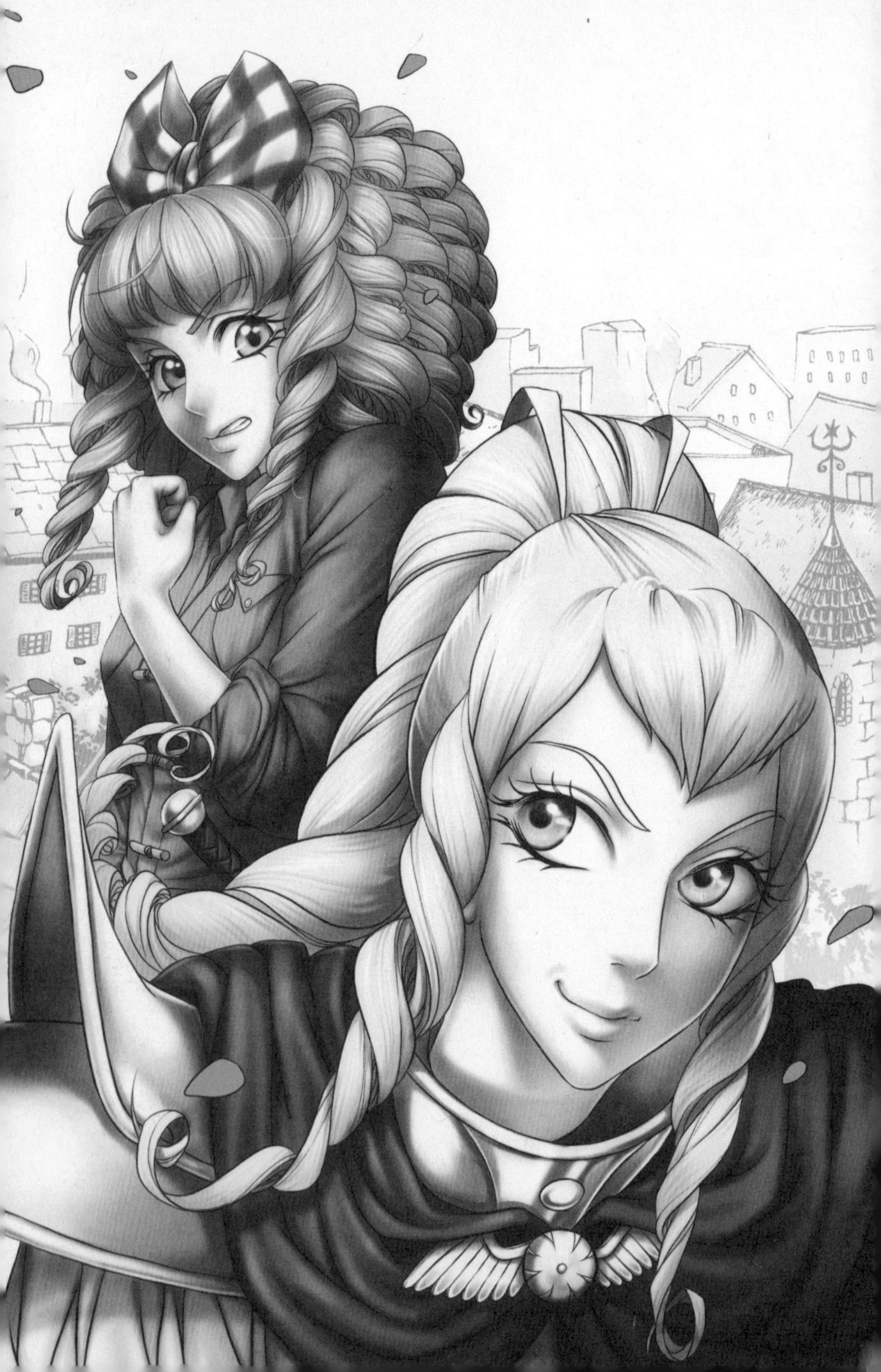

Sword Princess Amaltea

2

Natalia Batista

TOKYOPOP

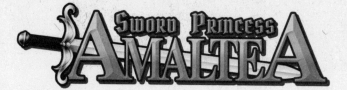

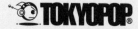

Characters in Book Two:

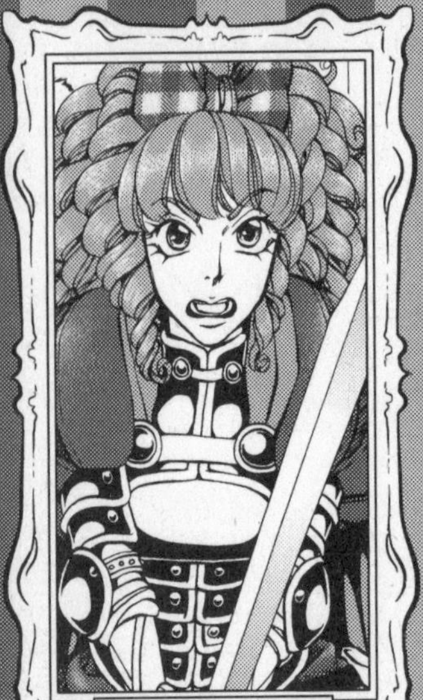
Princess Amaltea

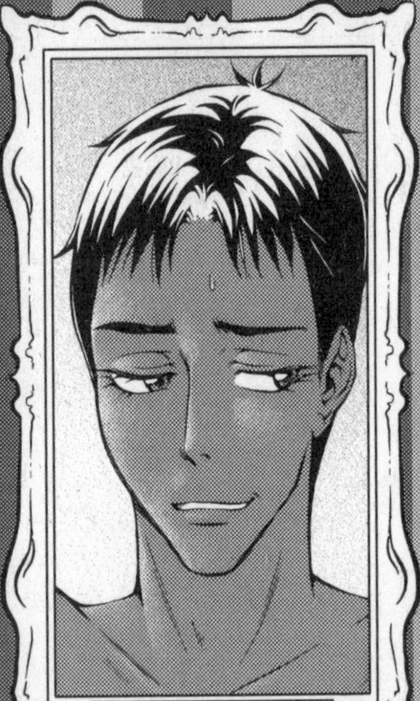
Prince Ossian

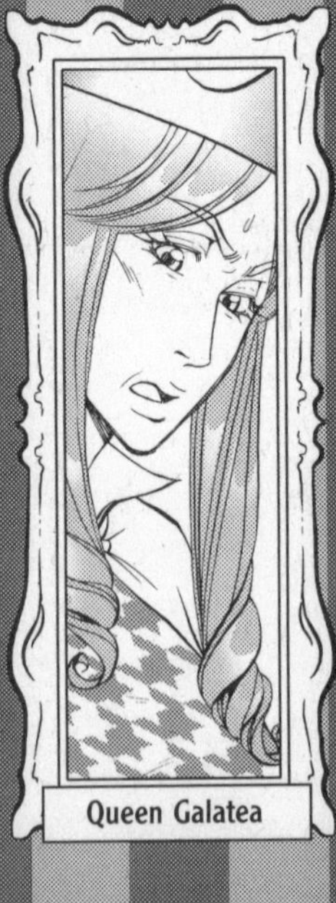
Queen Galatea

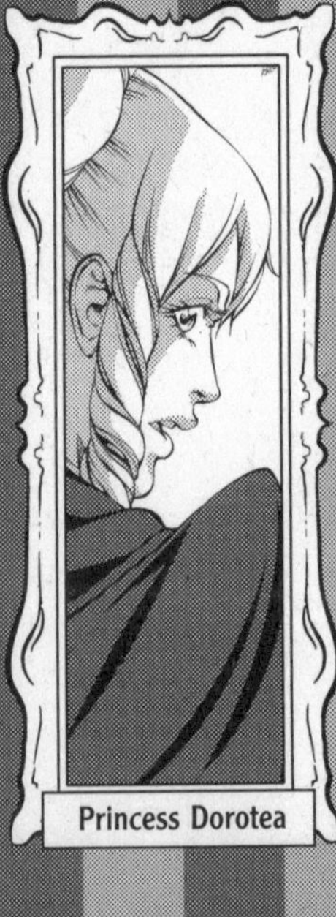
Princess Dorotea

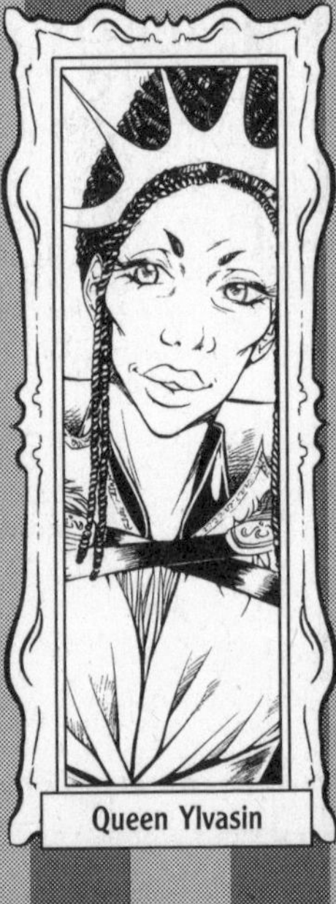
Queen Ylvasin

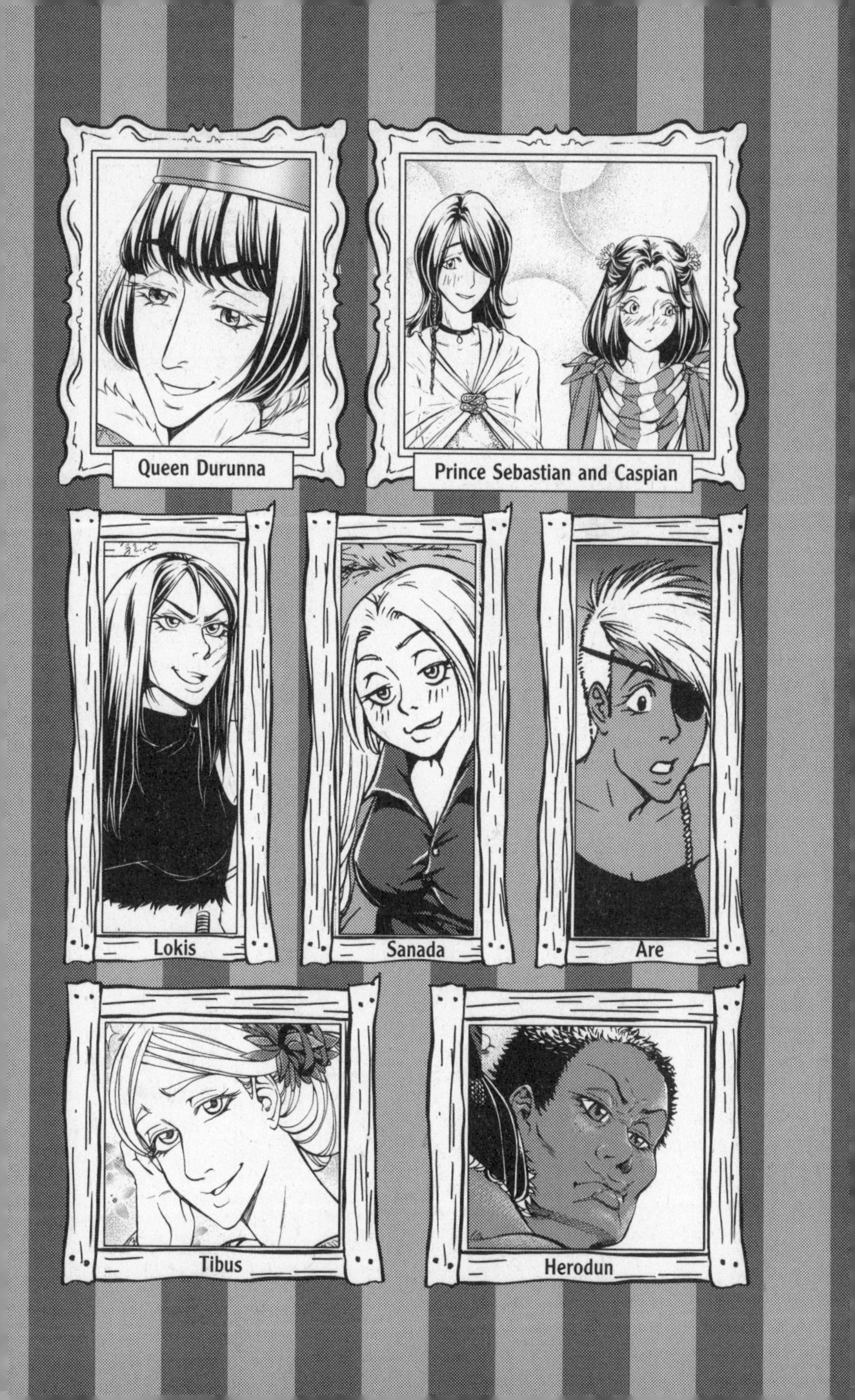
Queen Durunna
Prince Sebastian and Caspian
Lokis
Sanada
Are
Tibus
Herodun

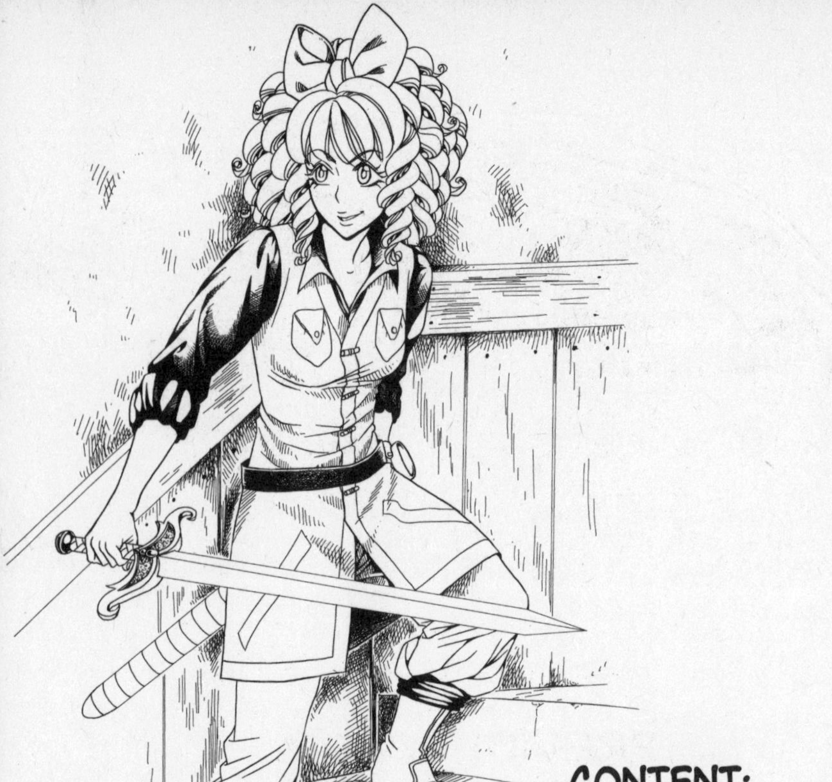

CONTENT:

PREVIOUSLY ON...

SWORD PRINCESS AMALTEA

GOING ON A HEROIC JOURNEY MIGHT BE A RIGHT OF PASSAGE FOR A YOUNG PRINCESS, BUT AMALTEA'S LEARNED THE HARD WAY THAT IT'S NOT NEARLY AS EASY AS IT MIGHT HAVE SEEMED. HER PRINCE — WHOM SHE SO VALIANTLY RESCUED! — WANTS NOTHING TO DO WITH HER, SHE WAS AMBUSHED BY BANDITS AND NOW HER WALLET'S BEEN STOLEN BY A STICKY-FINGERED BAR BOY.

SURELY THINGS CAN'T GET ANY WORSE...

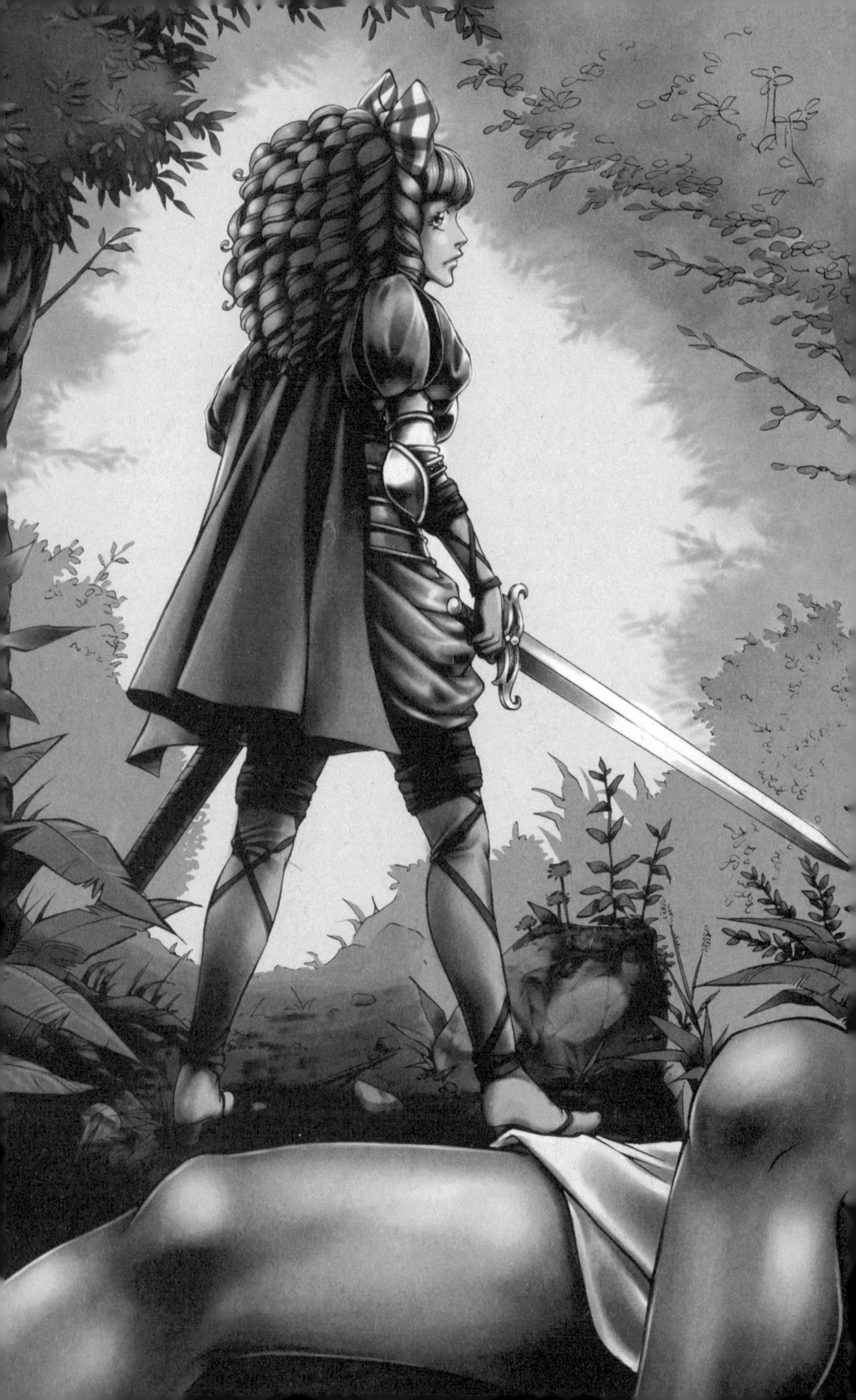

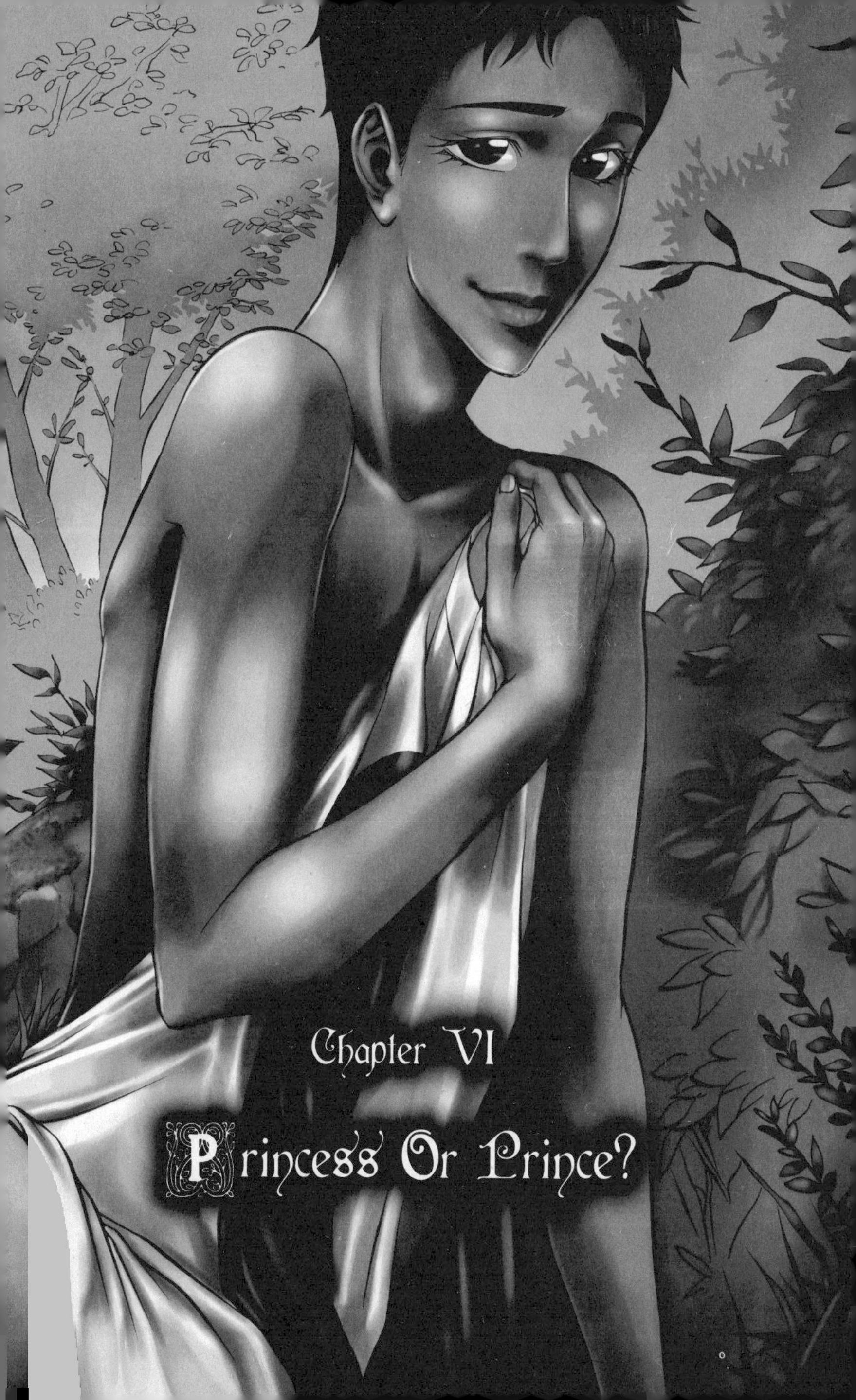
Chapter VI
Princess Or Prince?

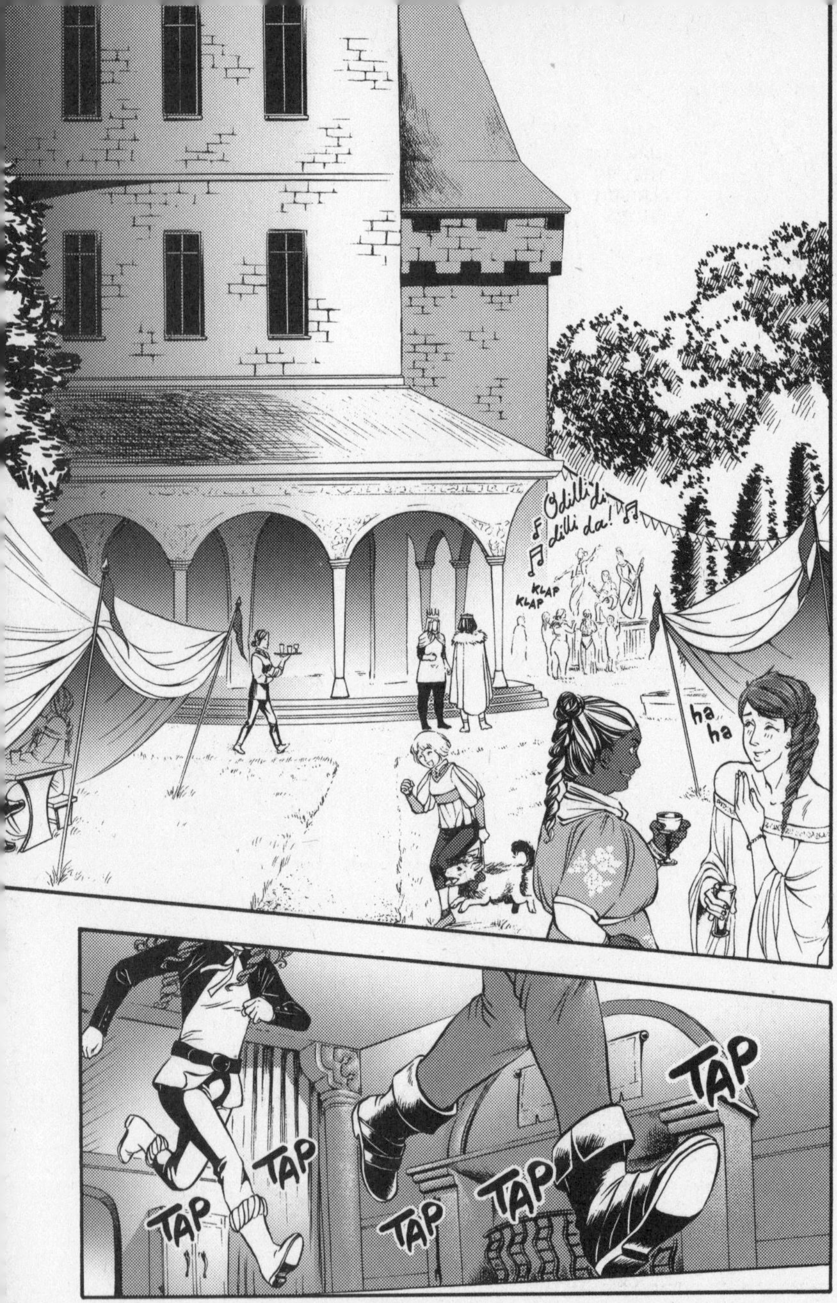
♪ Odilli di dilli da! ♪
KLAP KLAP
ha ha
TAP
TAP
TAP
TAP
TAP

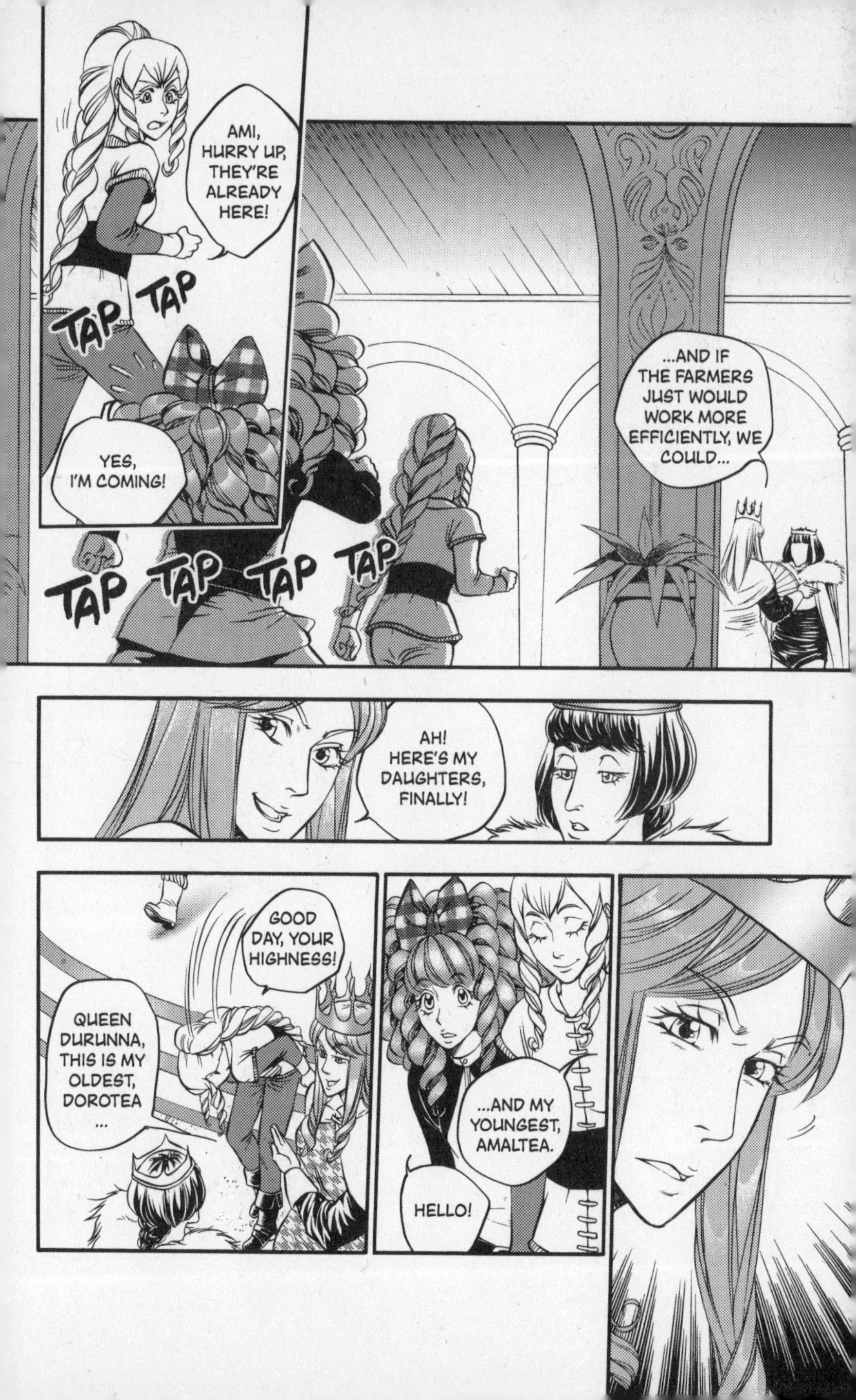
AMI, HURRY UP, THEY'RE ALREADY HERE!
TAP TAP
YES, I'M COMING!
TAP TAP TAP TAP
...AND IF THE FARMERS JUST WOULD WORK MORE EFFICIENTLY, WE COULD...
AH! HERE'S MY DAUGHTERS, FINALLY!
GOOD DAY, YOUR HIGHNESS!
QUEEN DURUNNA, THIS IS MY OLDEST, DOROTEA ...
...AND MY YOUNGEST, AMALTEA.
HELLO!

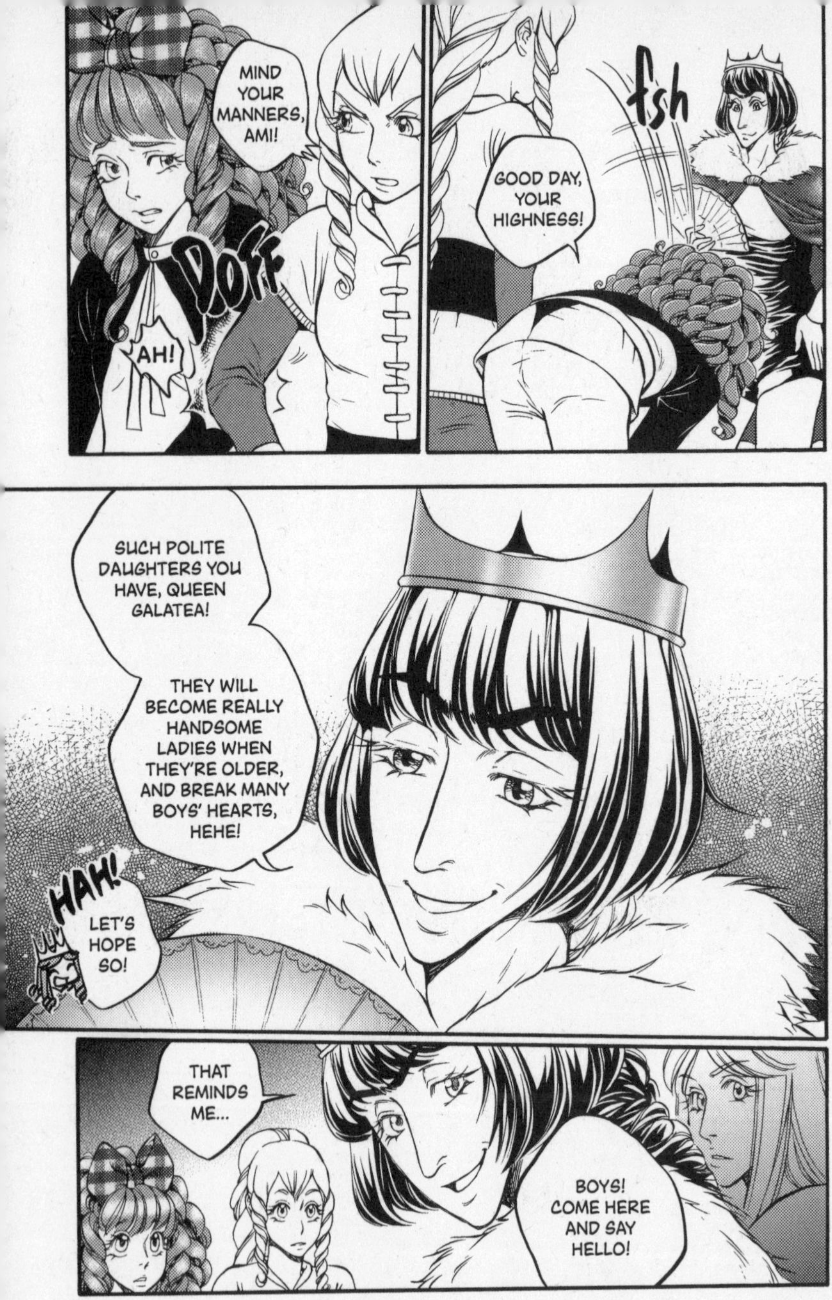
MIND YOUR MANNERS, AMI!
DOFF
AH!
fsh
GOOD DAY, YOUR HIGHNESS!
SUCH POLITE DAUGHTERS YOU HAVE, QUEEN GALATEA!
THEY WILL BECOME REALLY HANDSOME LADIES WHEN THEY'RE OLDER, AND BREAK MANY BOYS' HEARTS, HEHE!
HAH!
LET'S HOPE SO!
THAT REMINDS ME...
BOYS! COME HERE AND SAY HELLO!

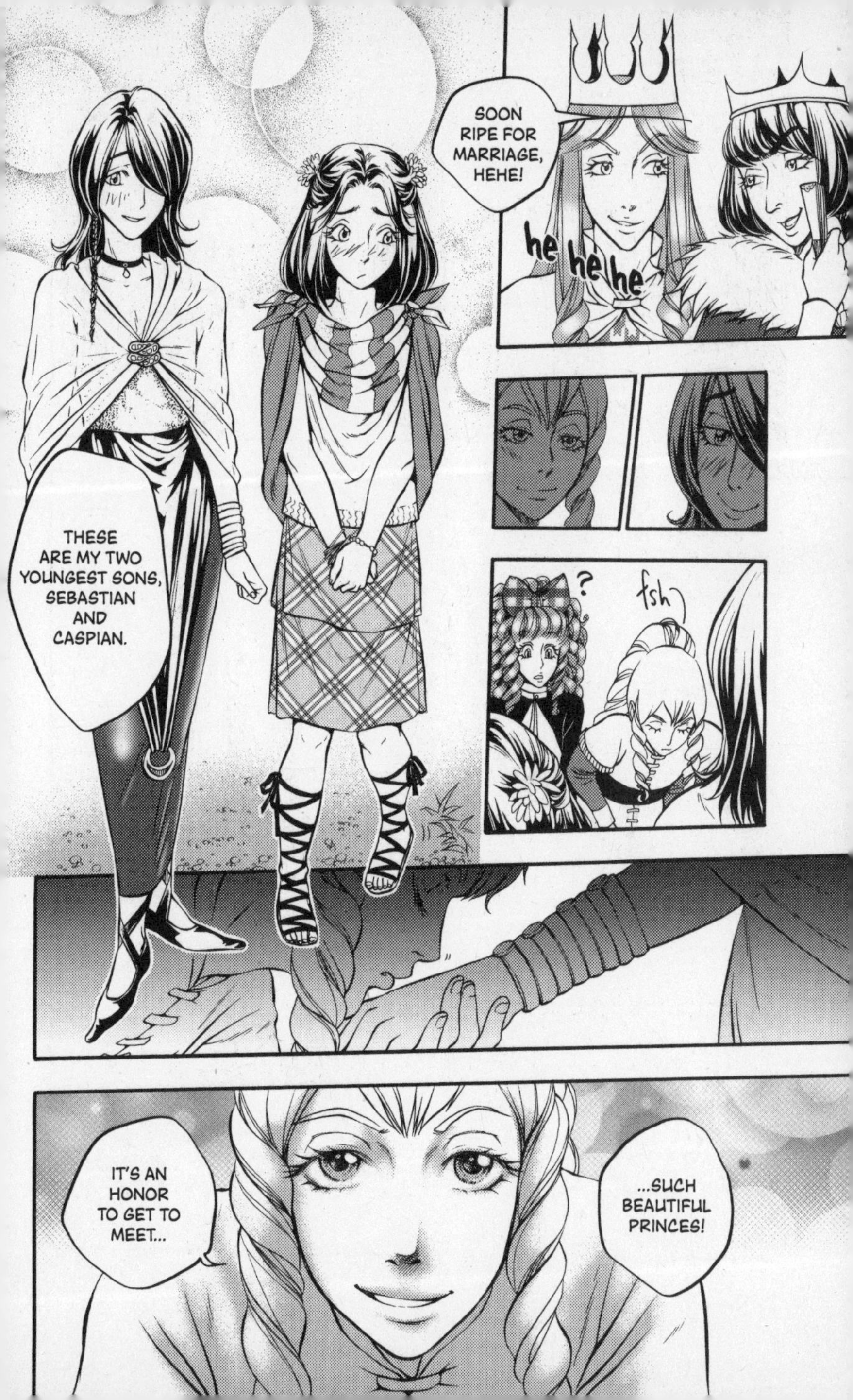
THESE ARE MY TWO YOUNGEST SONS, SEBASTIAN AND CASPIAN.
SOON RIPE FOR MARRIAGE, HEHE!
he he he
?
fsh
IT'S AN HONOR TO GET TO MEET...
...SUCH BEAUTIFUL PRINCES!

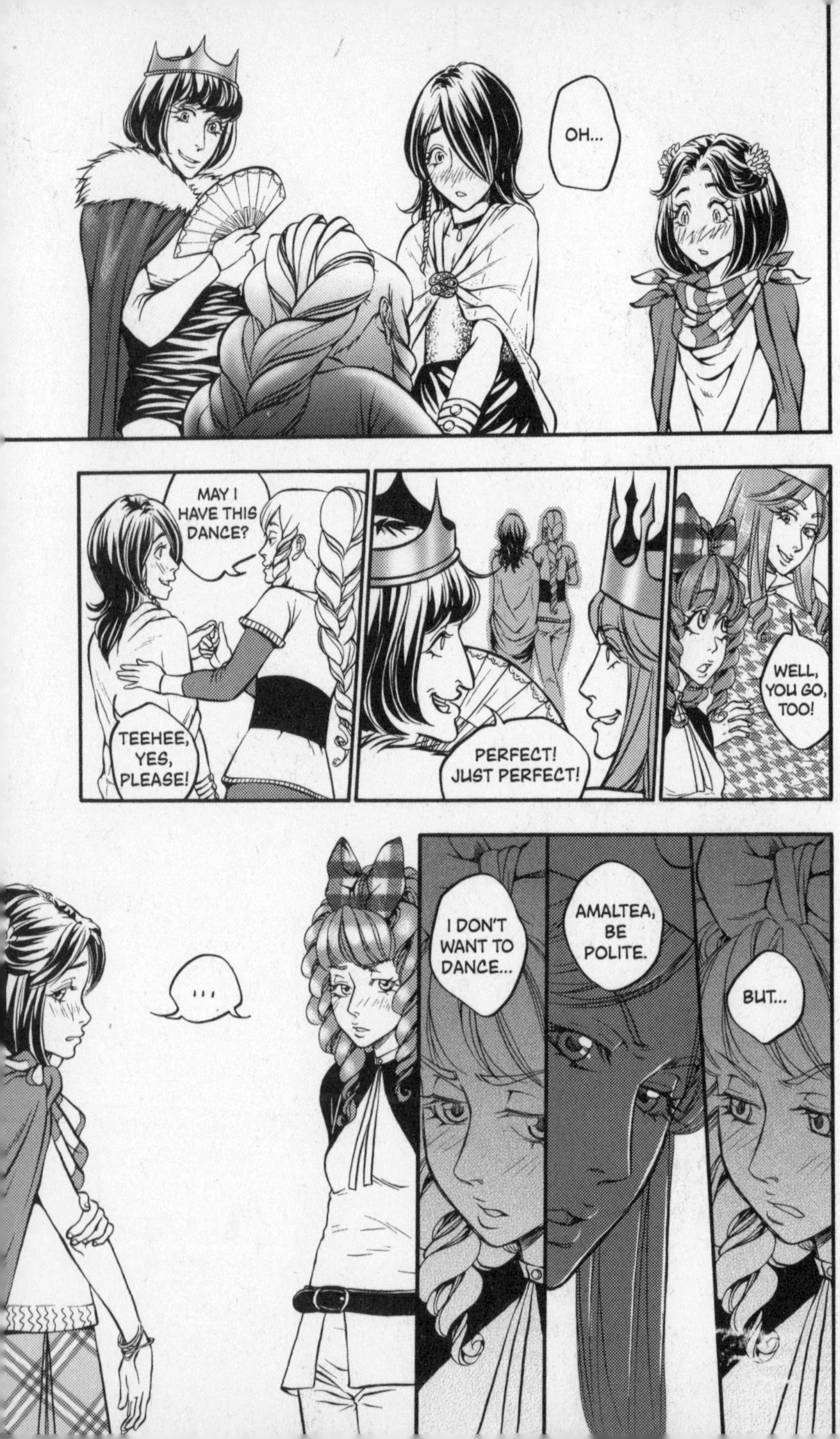
OH...
MAY I HAVE THIS DANCE?
TEEHEE, YES, PLEASE!
PERFECT! JUST PERFECT!
WELL, YOU GO, TOO!
...
I DON'T WANT TO DANCE...
AMALTEA, BE POLITE.
BUT...

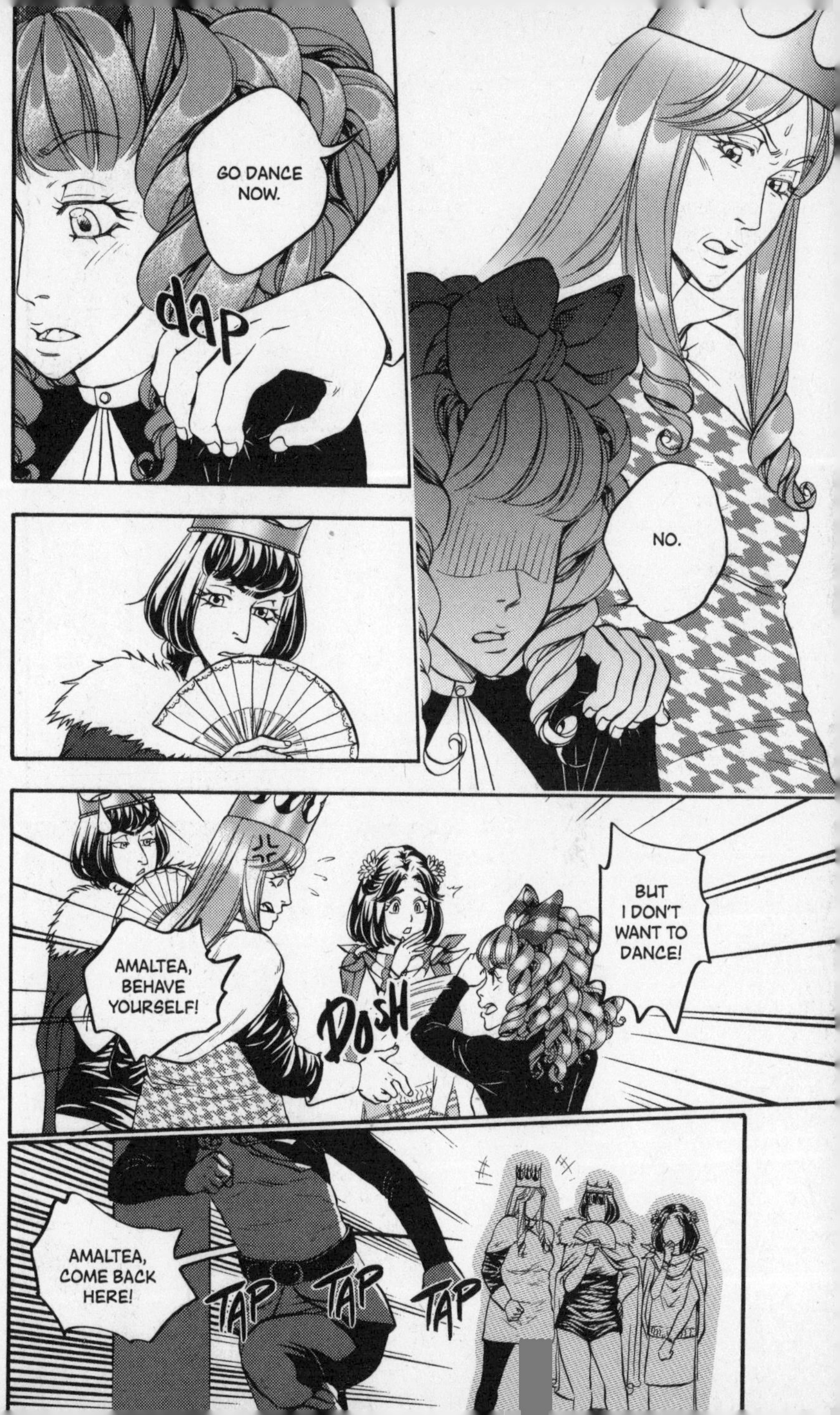
GO DANCE NOW.
dap
NO.
AMALTEA, BEHAVE YOURSELF!
DOSH
BUT I DON'T WANT TO DANCE!
AMALTEA, COME BACK HERE!
TAP
TAP
TAP

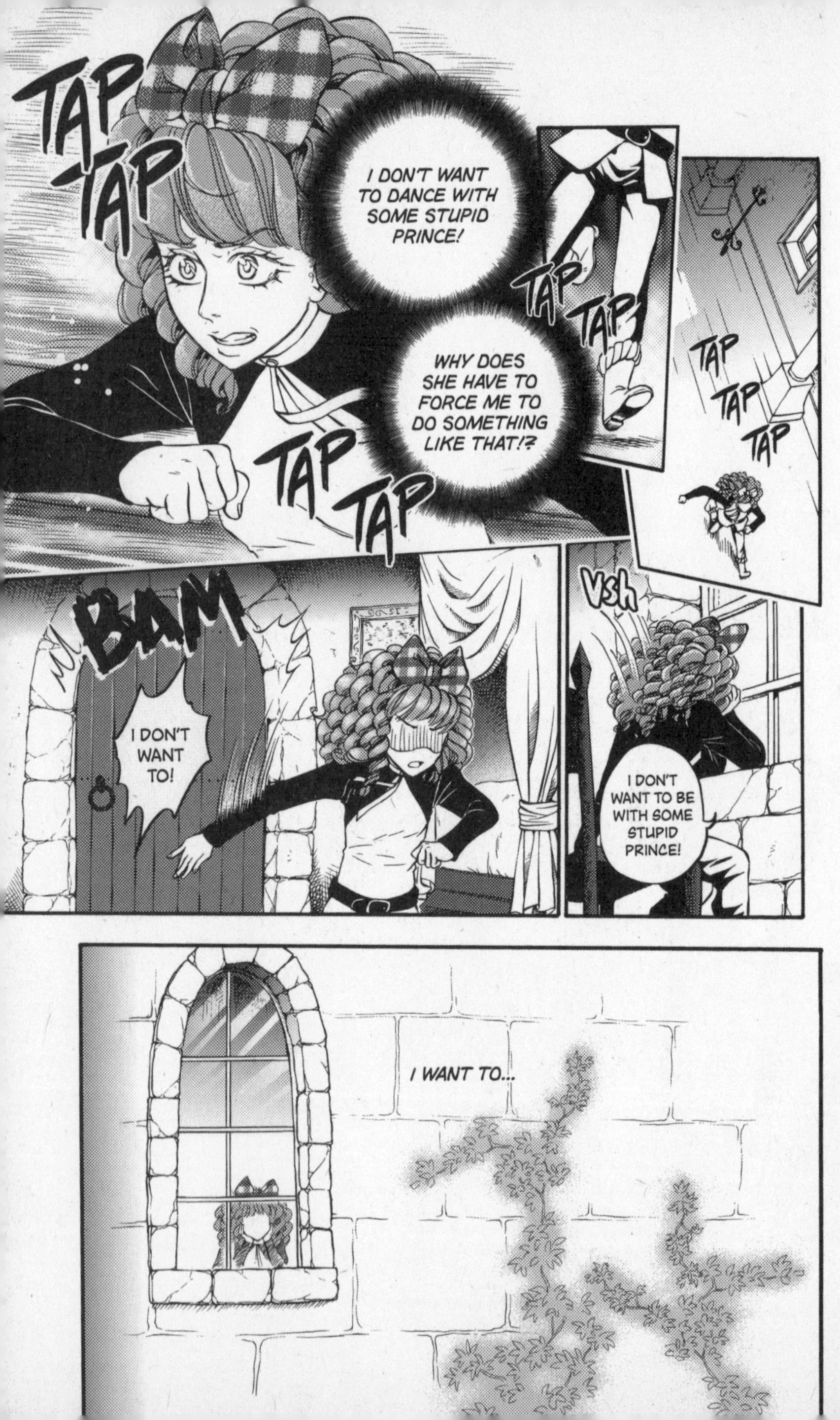
TAP TAP
I DON'T WANT TO DANCE WITH SOME STUPID PRINCE!
WHY DOES SHE HAVE TO FORCE ME TO DO SOMETHING LIKE THAT!?
TAP TAP
TAP TAP
TAP TAP TAP
BAM
I DON'T WANT TO!
Vsh
I DON'T WANT TO BE WITH SOME STUPID PRINCE!
I WANT TO...

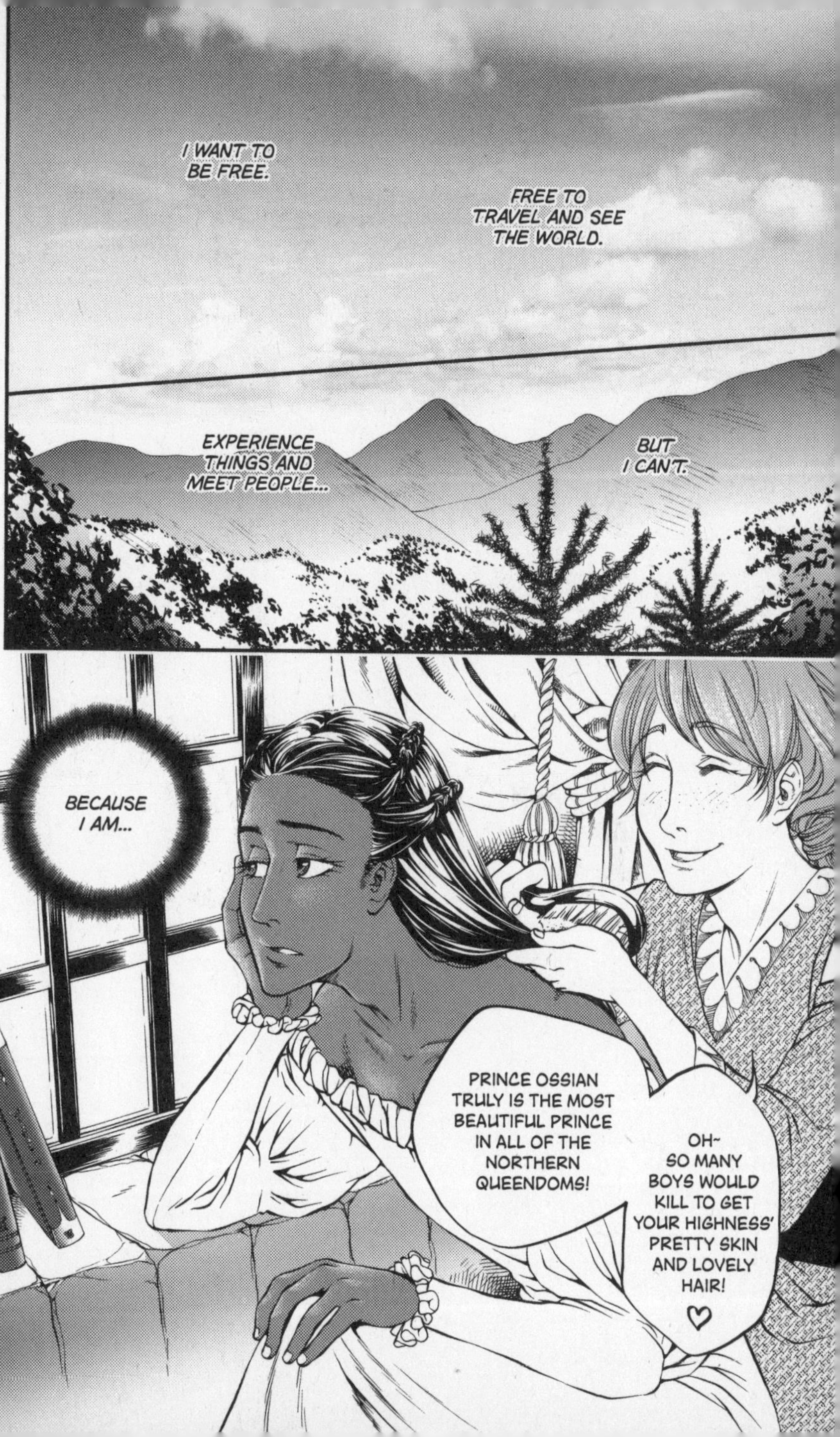
I WANT TO BE FREE.
FREE TO TRAVEL AND SEE THE WORLD.
EXPERIENCE THINGS AND MEET PEOPLE...
BUT I CAN'T.
BECAUSE I AM...
PRINCE OSSIAN TRULY IS THE MOST BEAUTIFUL PRINCE IN ALL OF THE NORTHERN QUEENDOMS!
OH~ SO MANY BOYS WOULD KILL TO GET YOUR HIGHNESS' PRETTY SKIN AND LOVELY HAIR! ♥

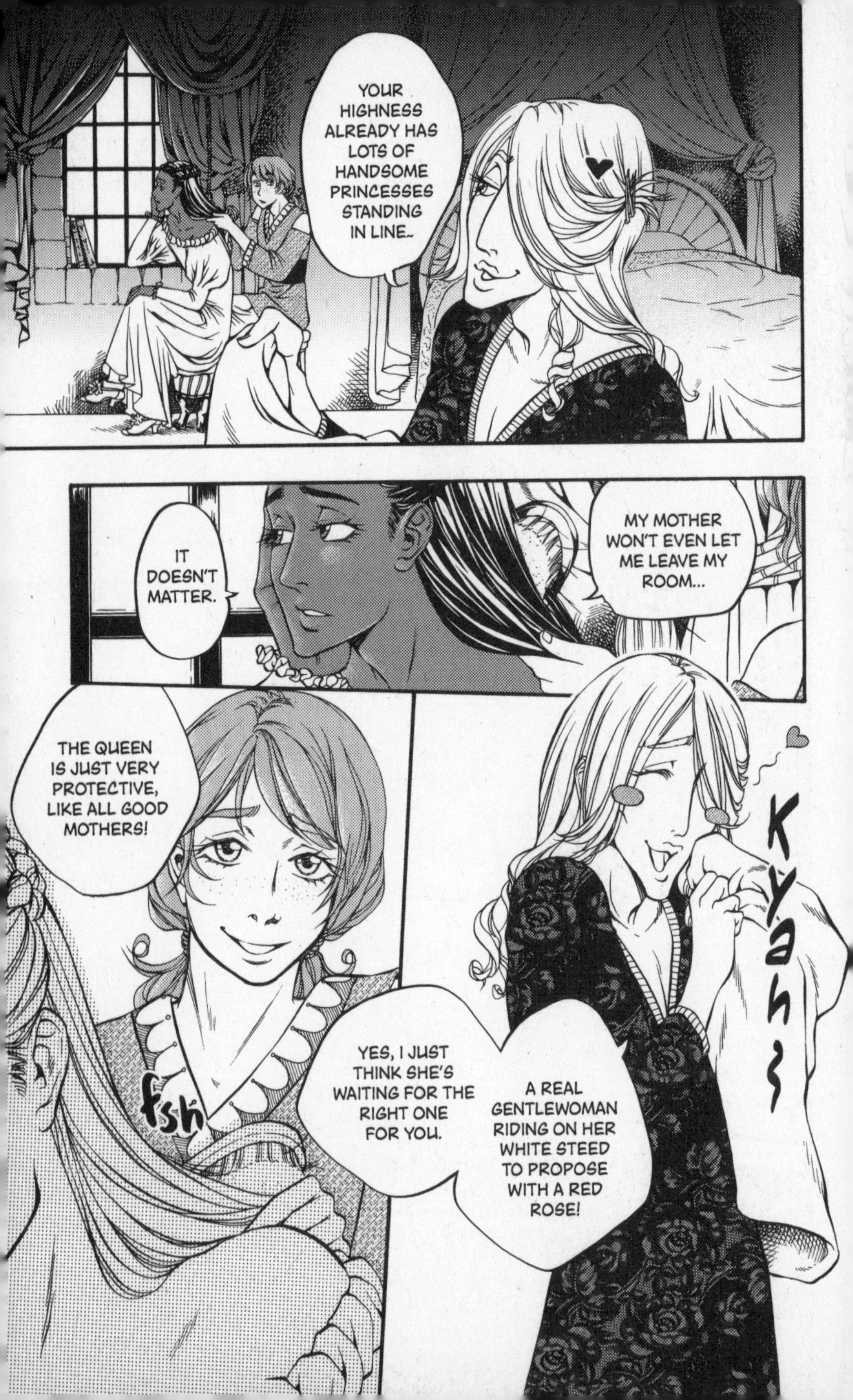
YOUR HIGHNESS ALREADY HAS LOTS OF HANDSOME PRINCESSES STANDING IN LINE~
IT DOESN'T MATTER.
MY MOTHER WON'T EVEN LET ME LEAVE MY ROOM...
THE QUEEN IS JUST VERY PROTECTIVE, LIKE ALL GOOD MOTHERS!
fsh
YES, I JUST THINK SHE'S WAITING FOR THE RIGHT ONE FOR YOU.
A REAL GENTLEWOMAN RIDING ON HER WHITE STEED TO PROPOSE WITH A RED ROSE!
Kyah~

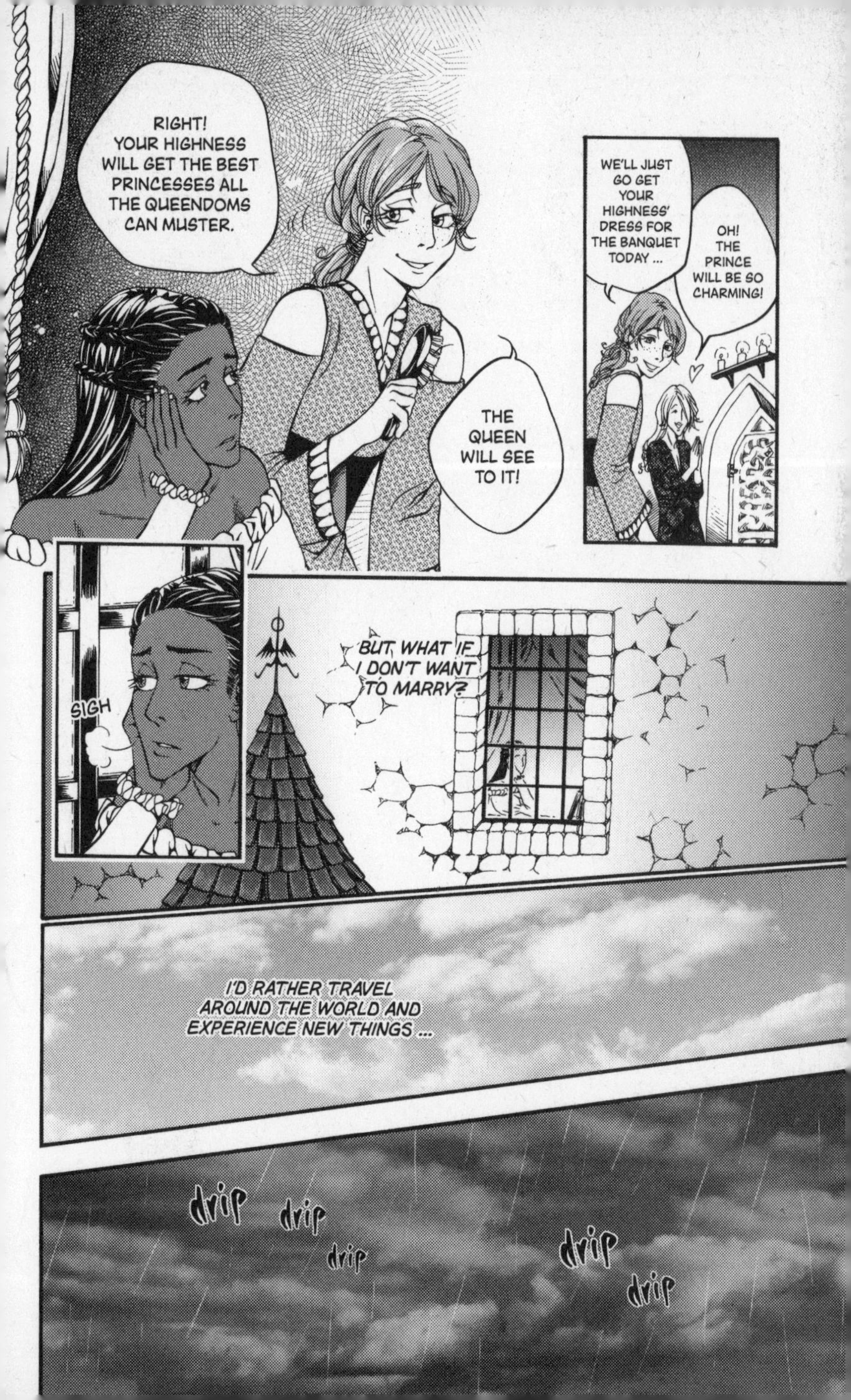
RIGHT! YOUR HIGHNESS WILL GET THE BEST PRINCESSES ALL THE QUEENDOMS CAN MUSTER.
THE QUEEN WILL SEE TO IT!
WE'LL JUST GO GET YOUR HIGHNESS' DRESS FOR THE BANQUET TODAY ...
OH! THE PRINCE WILL BE SO CHARMING!
SIGH
BUT, WHAT IF I DON'T WANT TO MARRY?
I'D RATHER TRAVEL AROUND THE WORLD AND EXPERIENCE NEW THINGS ...
drip
drip
drip
drip
drip

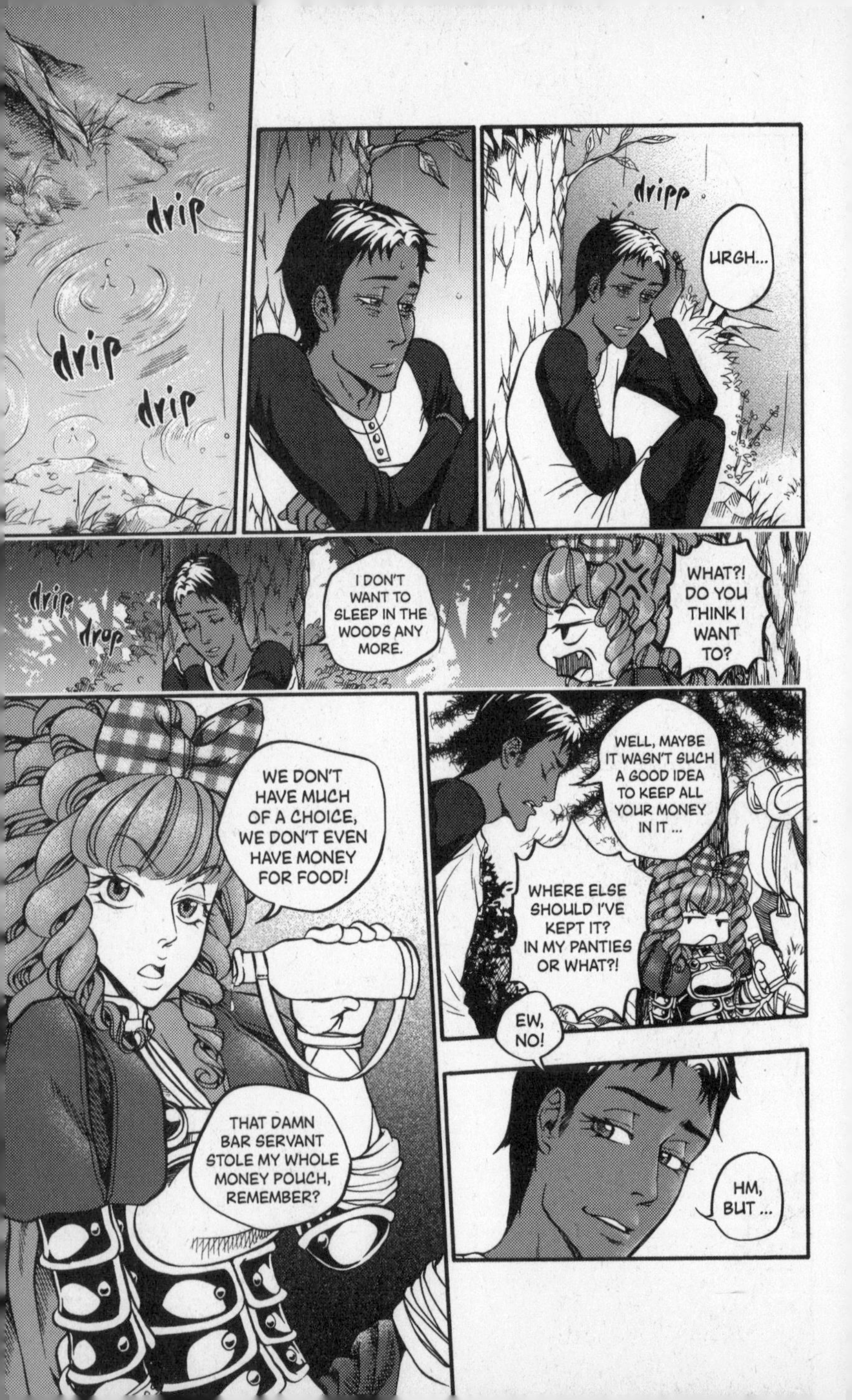
drip
drip
drip
dripp
URGH...
drip
drop
I DON'T WANT TO SLEEP IN THE WOODS ANY MORE.
WHAT?! DO YOU THINK I WANT TO?
WE DON'T HAVE MUCH OF A CHOICE, WE DON'T EVEN HAVE MONEY FOR FOOD!
THAT DAMN BAR SERVANT STOLE MY WHOLE MONEY POUCH, REMEMBER?
WELL, MAYBE IT WASN'T SUCH A GOOD IDEA TO KEEP ALL YOUR MONEY IN IT ...
WHERE ELSE SHOULD I'VE KEPT IT? IN MY PANTIES OR WHAT?!
EW, NO!
HM, BUT ...

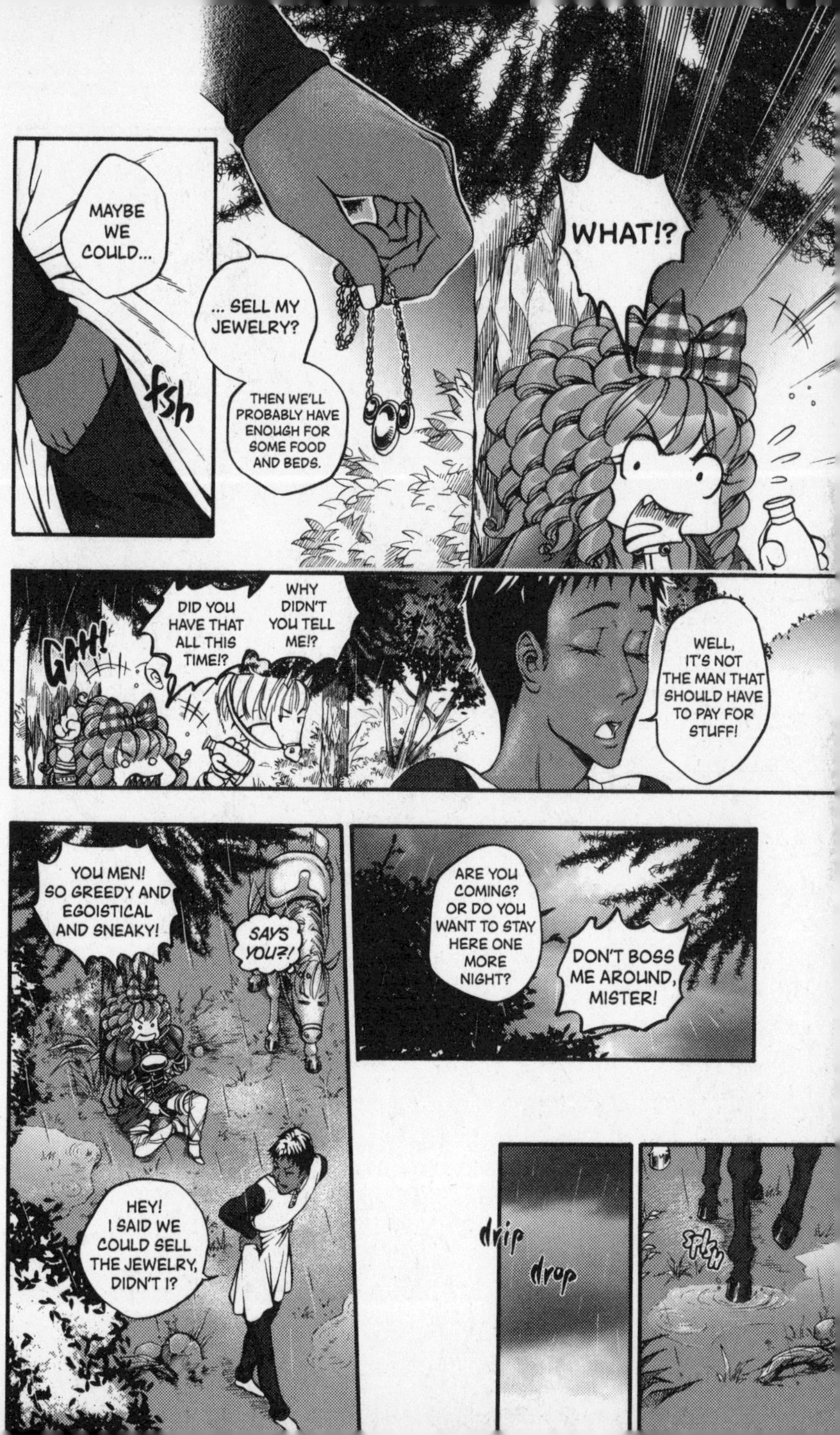
MAYBE WE COULD...
... SELL MY JEWELRY?
THEN WE'LL PROBABLY HAVE ENOUGH FOR SOME FOOD AND BEDS.
fsh
WHAT!?
GAH!
DID YOU HAVE THAT ALL THIS TIME!?
WHY DIDN'T YOU TELL ME!?
WELL, IT'S NOT THE MAN THAT SHOULD HAVE TO PAY FOR STUFF!
YOU MEN! SO GREEDY AND EGOISTICAL AND SNEAKY!
SAYS YOU?!
HEY! I SAID WE COULD SELL THE JEWELRY, DIDN'T I?
ARE YOU COMING? OR DO YOU WANT TO STAY HERE ONE MORE NIGHT?
DON'T BOSS ME AROUND, MISTER!
drip
drop
splsh

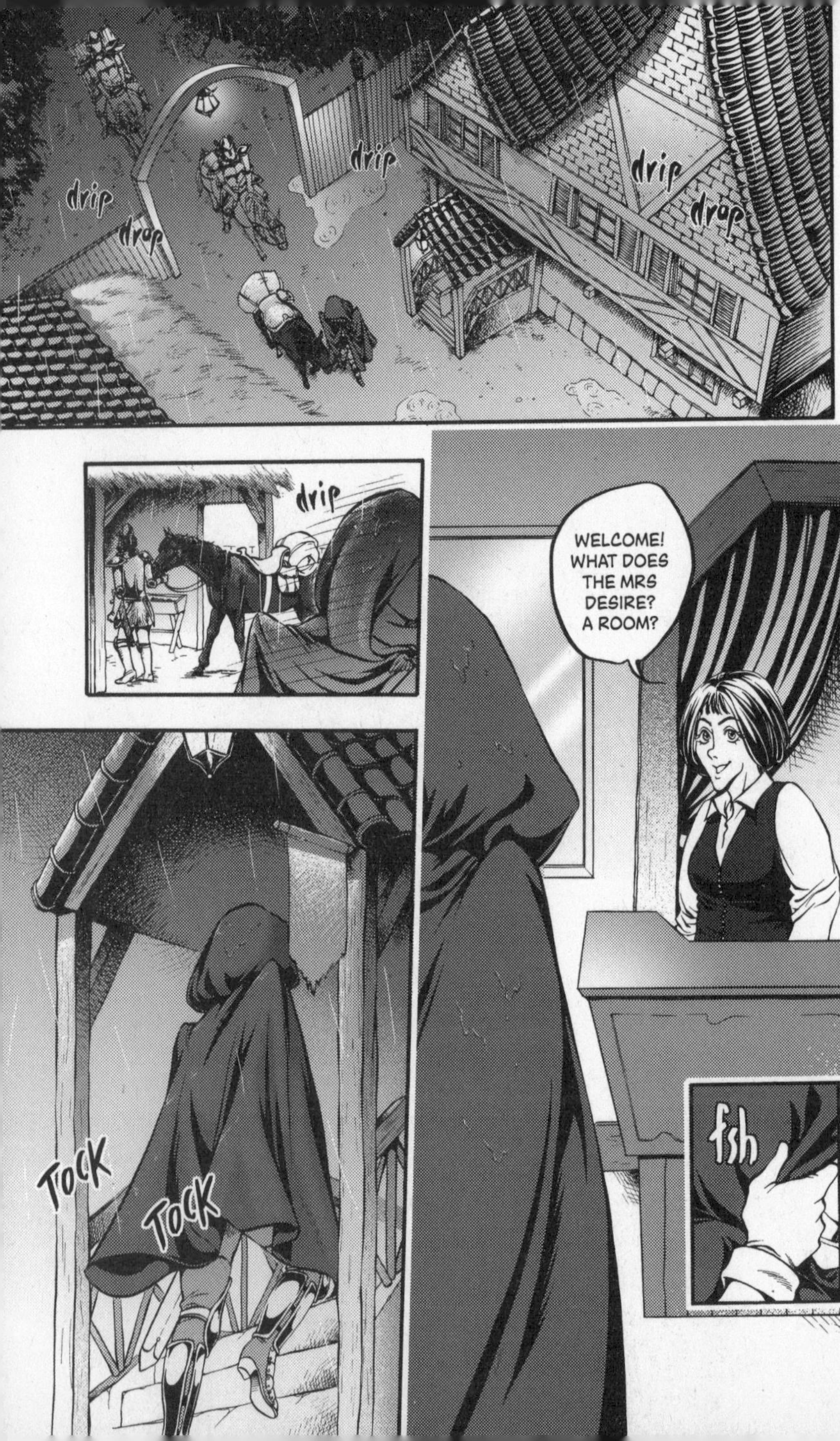
drip
drop
drip
drip
drop
drip
TOCK
TOCK
WELCOME! WHAT DOES THE MRS DESIRE? A ROOM?
fsh

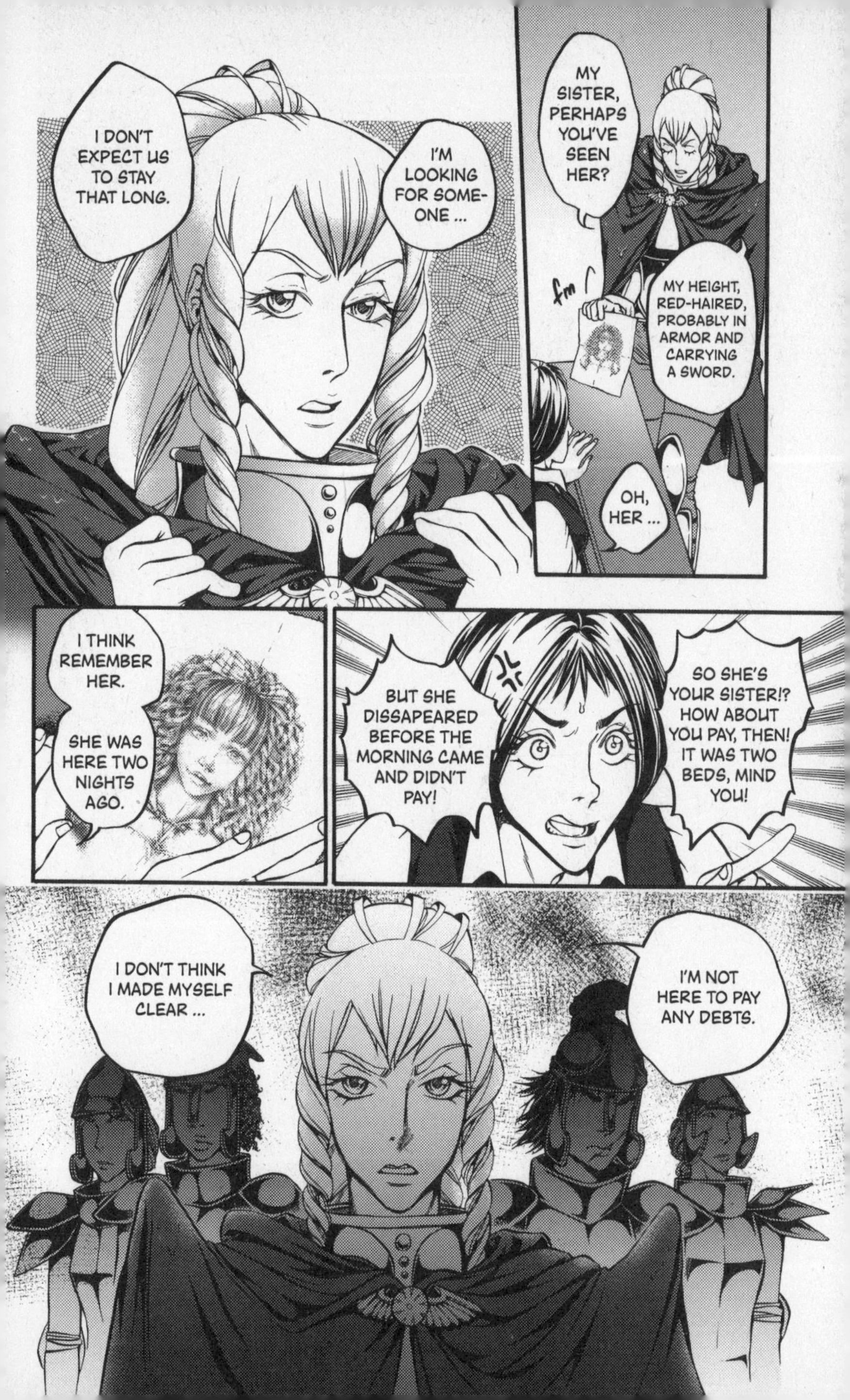
I DON'T EXPECT US TO STAY THAT LONG.
I'M LOOKING FOR SOME-ONE ...
MY SISTER, PERHAPS YOU'VE SEEN HER?
fm
MY HEIGHT, RED-HAIRED, PROBABLY IN ARMOR AND CARRYING A SWORD.
OH, HER ...
I THINK REMEMBER HER.
SHE WAS HERE TWO NIGHTS AGO.
BUT SHE DISSAPEARED BEFORE THE MORNING CAME AND DIDN'T PAY!
SO SHE'S YOUR SISTER!? HOW ABOUT YOU PAY, THEN! IT WAS TWO BEDS, MIND YOU!
I DON'T THINK I MADE MYSELF CLEAR ...
I'M NOT HERE TO PAY ANY DEBTS.

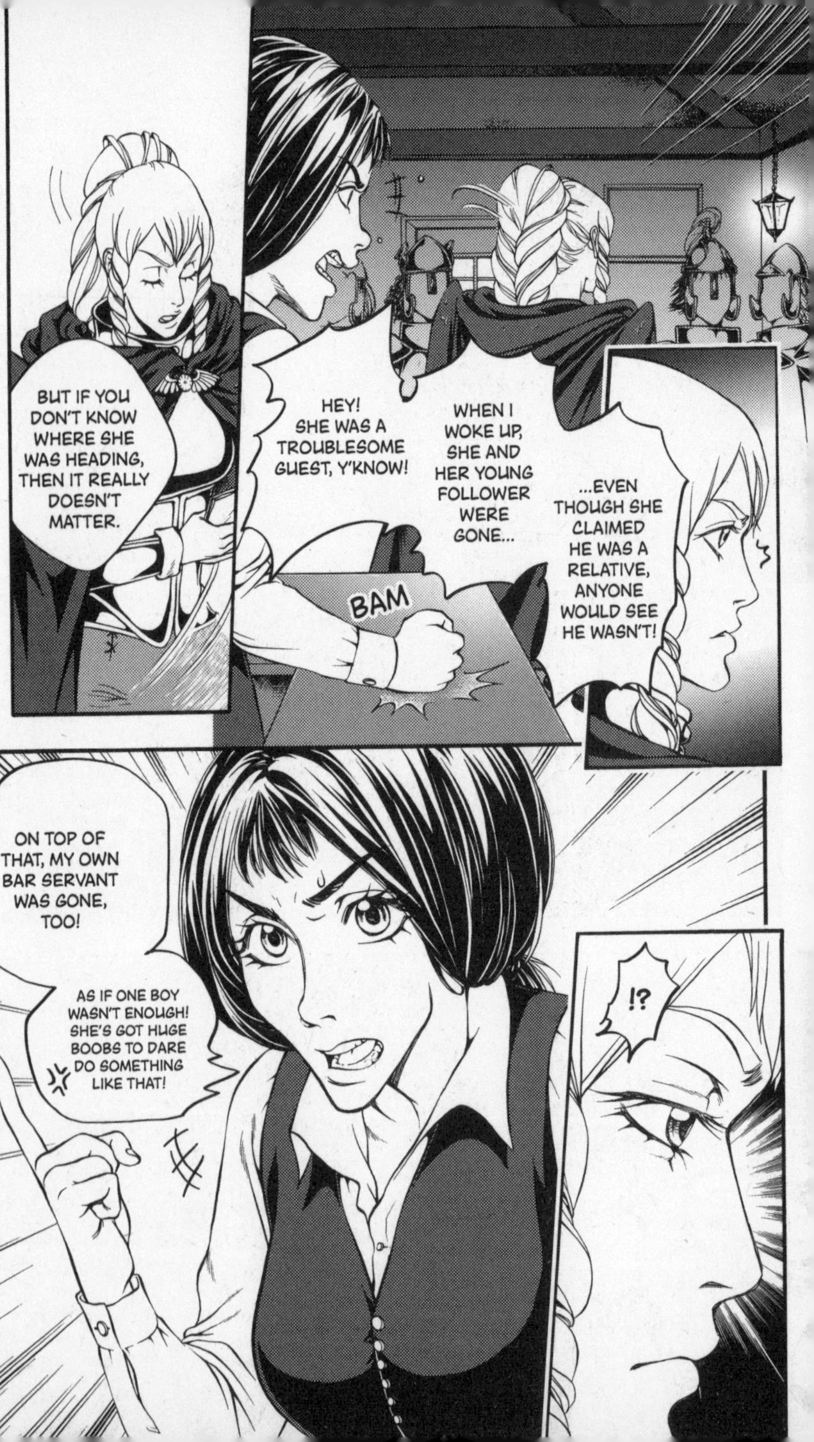
BUT IF YOU DON'T KNOW WHERE SHE WAS HEADING, THEN IT REALLY DOESN'T MATTER.
HEY! SHE WAS A TROUBLESOME GUEST, Y'KNOW!
WHEN I WOKE UP, SHE AND HER YOUNG FOLLOWER WERE GONE...
BAM
...EVEN THOUGH SHE CLAIMED HE WAS A RELATIVE, ANYONE WOULD SEE HE WASN'T!
ON TOP OF THAT, MY OWN BAR SERVANT WAS GONE, TOO!
AS IF ONE BOY WASN'T ENOUGH! SHE'S GOT HUGE BOOBS TO DARE DO SOMETHING LIKE THAT!
!?

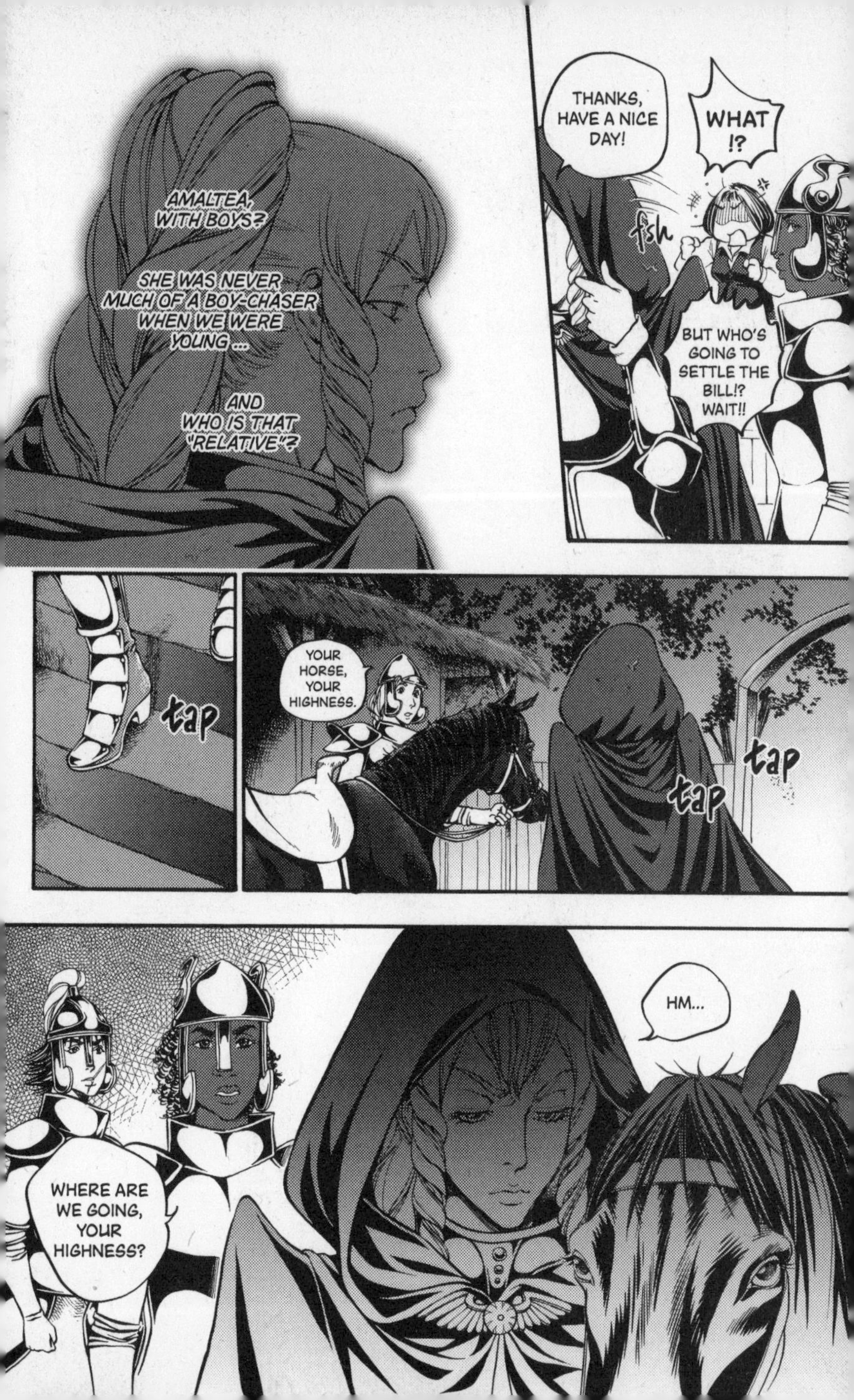
AMALTEA, WITH BOYS?
SHE WAS NEVER MUCH OF A BOY-CHASER WHEN WE WERE YOUNG ...
AND WHO IS THAT "RELATIVE"?
THANKS, HAVE A NICE DAY!
WHAT !?
fsh
BUT WHO'S GOING TO SETTLE THE BILL!? WAIT!!
tap
YOUR HORSE, YOUR HIGHNESS.
tap
tap
WHERE ARE WE GOING, YOUR HIGHNESS?
HM...

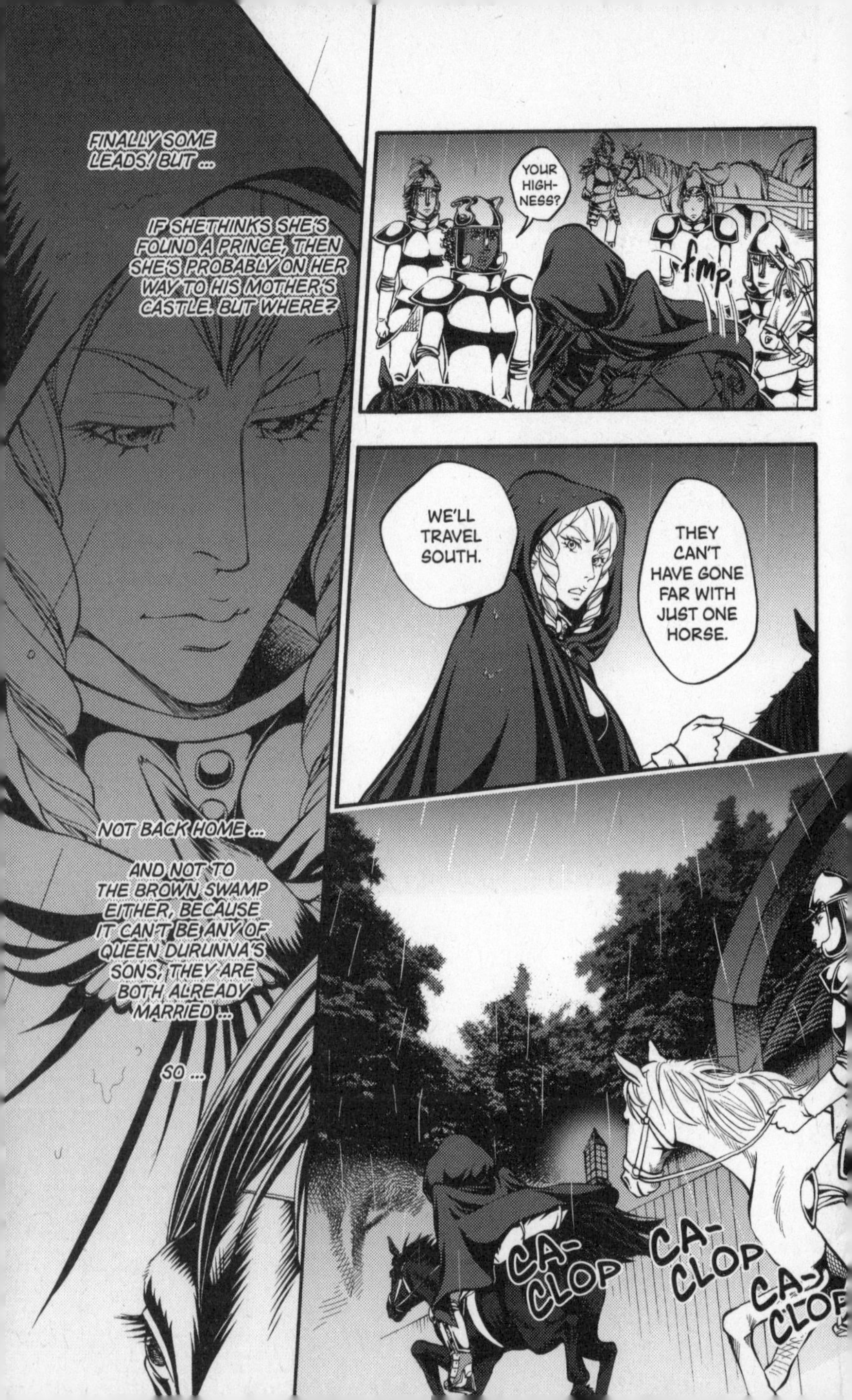
FINALLY SOME LEADS! BUT ...
IF SHETHINKS SHE'S FOUND A PRINCE, THEN SHE'S PROBABLY ON HER WAY TO HIS MOTHER'S CASTLE. BUT WHERE?
NOT BACK HOME ...
AND NOT TO THE BROWN SWAMP EITHER, BECAUSE IT CAN'T BE ANY OF QUEEN DURUNNA'S SONS, THEY ARE BOTH ALREADY MARRIED ...
SO ...
YOUR HIGHNESS?
fmp
WE'LL TRAVEL SOUTH.
THEY CAN'T HAVE GONE FAR WITH JUST ONE HORSE.
CA-CLOP
CA-CLOP
CA-CLOP

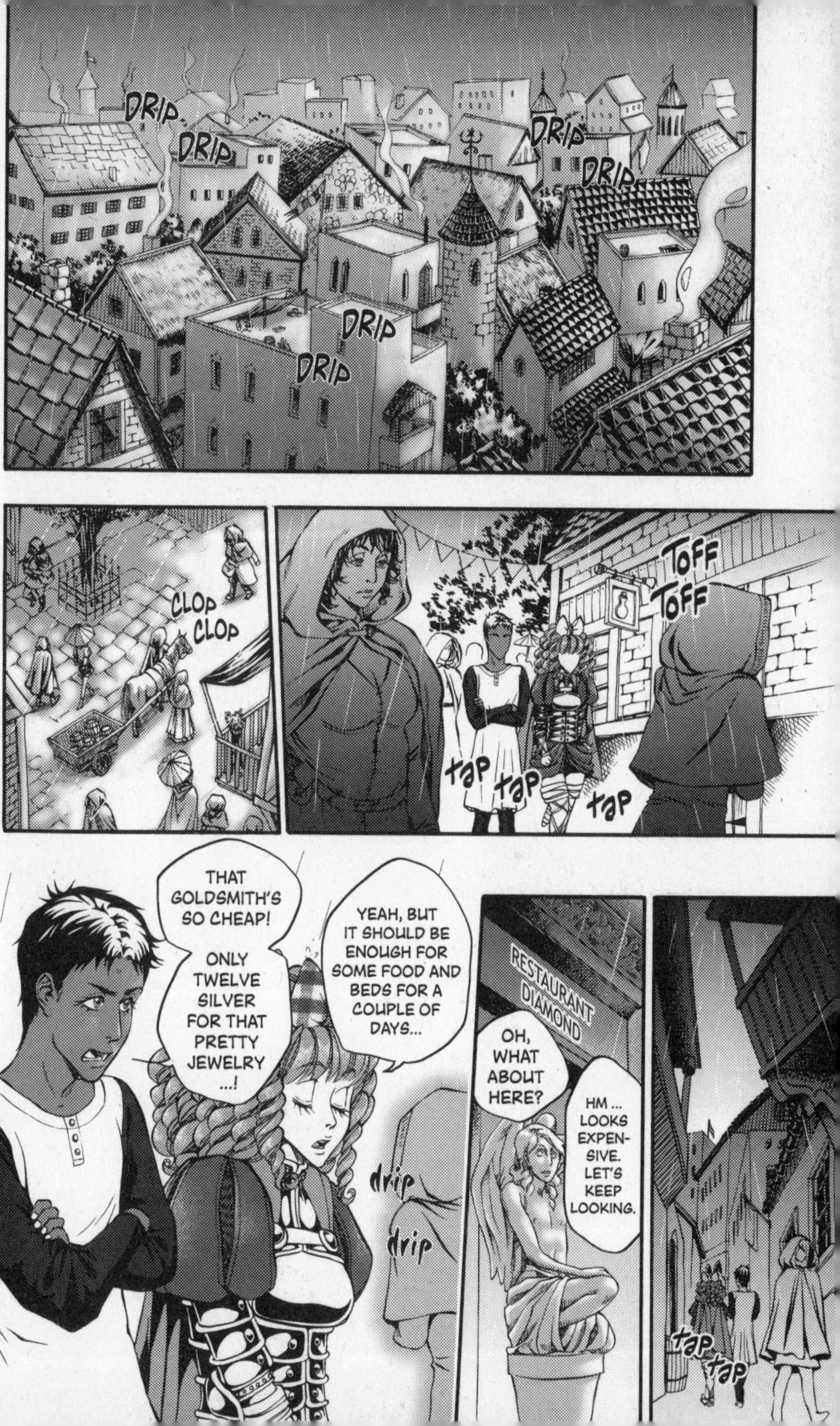
DRIP
DRIP
DRIP
DRIP
DRIP
DRIP
CLOP CLOP
TOFF TOFF
tap tap tap
THAT GOLDSMITH'S SO CHEAP!
ONLY TWELVE SILVER FOR THAT PRETTY JEWELRY ...!
YEAH, BUT IT SHOULD BE ENOUGH FOR SOME FOOD AND BEDS FOR A COUPLE OF DAYS...
drip
drip
RESTAURANT DIAMOND
OH, WHAT ABOUT HERE?
HM ... LOOKS EXPEN-SIVE. LET'S KEEP LOOKING.
tap tap

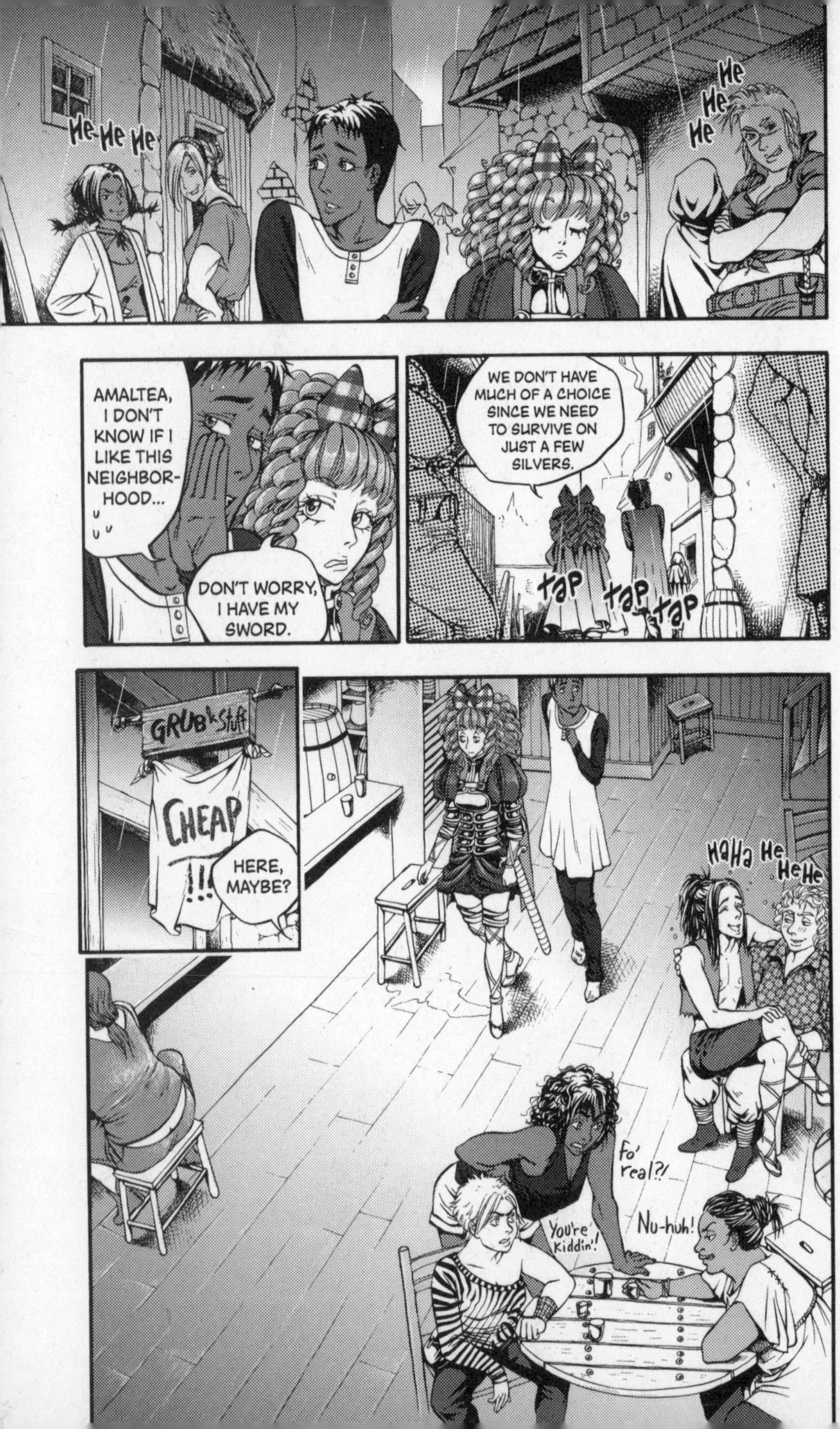
He He He
He He He
AMALTEA, I DON'T KNOW IF I LIKE THIS NEIGHBOR-HOOD...
DON'T WORRY, I HAVE MY SWORD.
WE DON'T HAVE MUCH OF A CHOICE SINCE WE NEED TO SURVIVE ON JUST A FEW SILVERS.
tap tap tap
GRUB Stuff
CHEAP !!!
HERE, MAYBE?
HaHa He HeHe
Fo' real?!
Nu-huh!
You're Kiddin'!

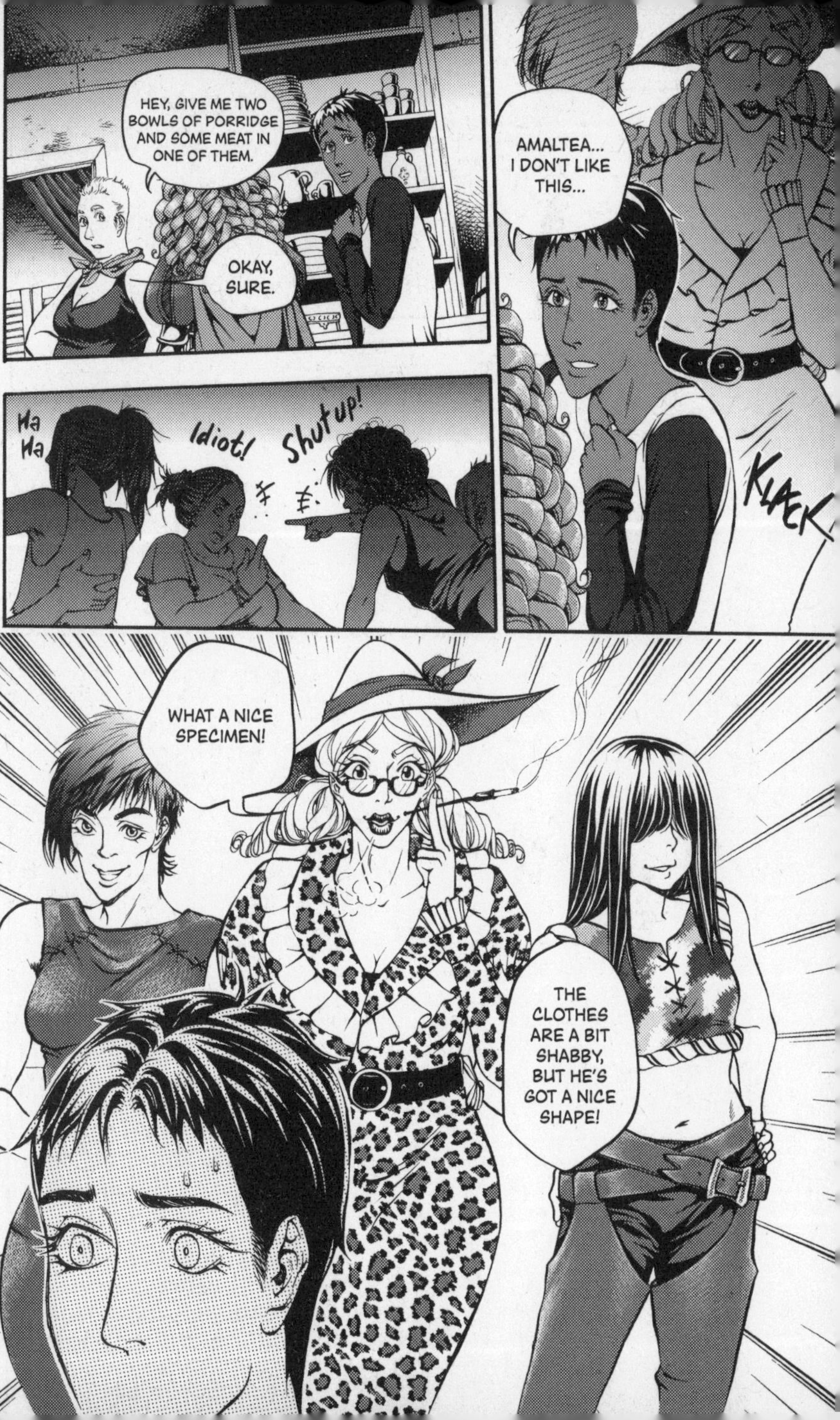
HEY, GIVE ME TWO BOWLS OF PORRIDGE AND SOME MEAT IN ONE OF THEM.
OKAY, SURE.
Ha Ha
Idiot!
Shut up!
AMALTEA... I DON'T LIKE THIS...
KLACK
WHAT A NICE SPECIMEN!
THE CLOTHES ARE A BIT SHABBY, BUT HE'S GOT A NICE SHAPE!

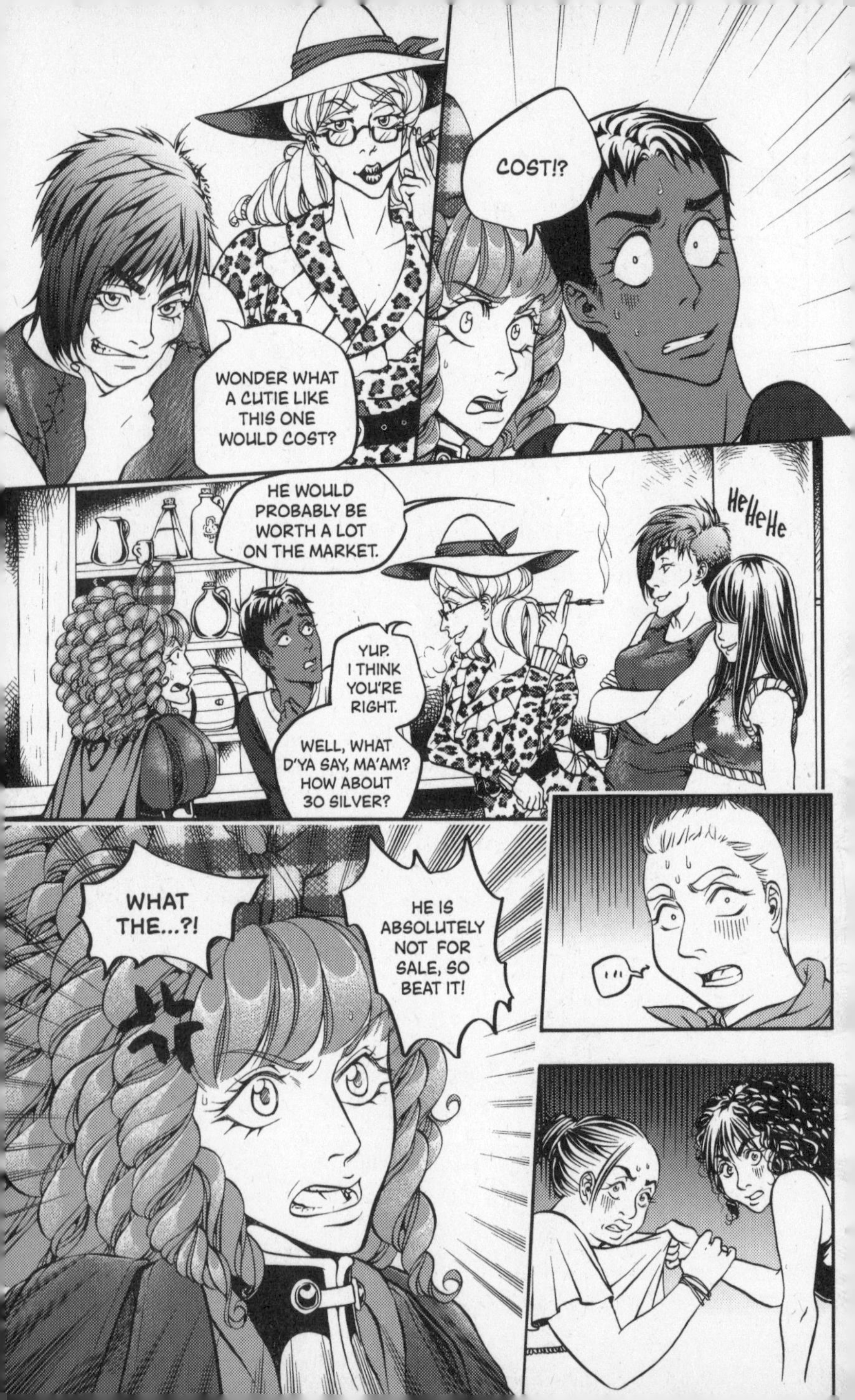
WONDER WHAT A CUTIE LIKE THIS ONE WOULD COST?
COST!?
HE WOULD PROBABLY BE WORTH A LOT ON THE MARKET.
HeHeHe
YUP. I THINK YOU'RE RIGHT.
WELL, WHAT D'YA SAY, MA'AM? HOW ABOUT 30 SILVER?
WHAT THE...?!
HE IS ABSOLUTELY NOT FOR SALE, SO BEAT IT!
...

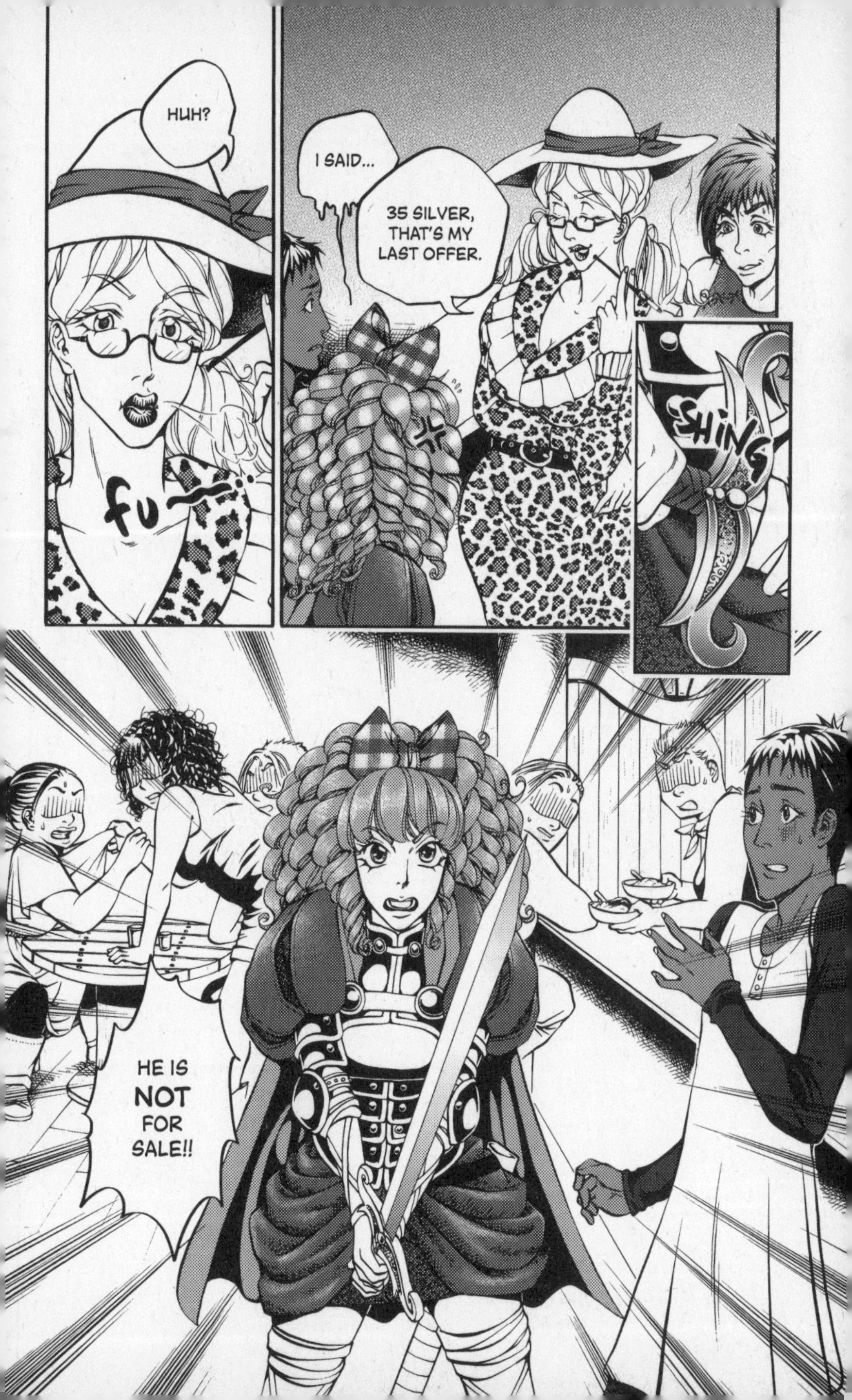
HUH?
fu~~
I SAID...
35 SILVER, THAT'S MY LAST OFFER.
SHING
HE IS NOT FOR SALE!!

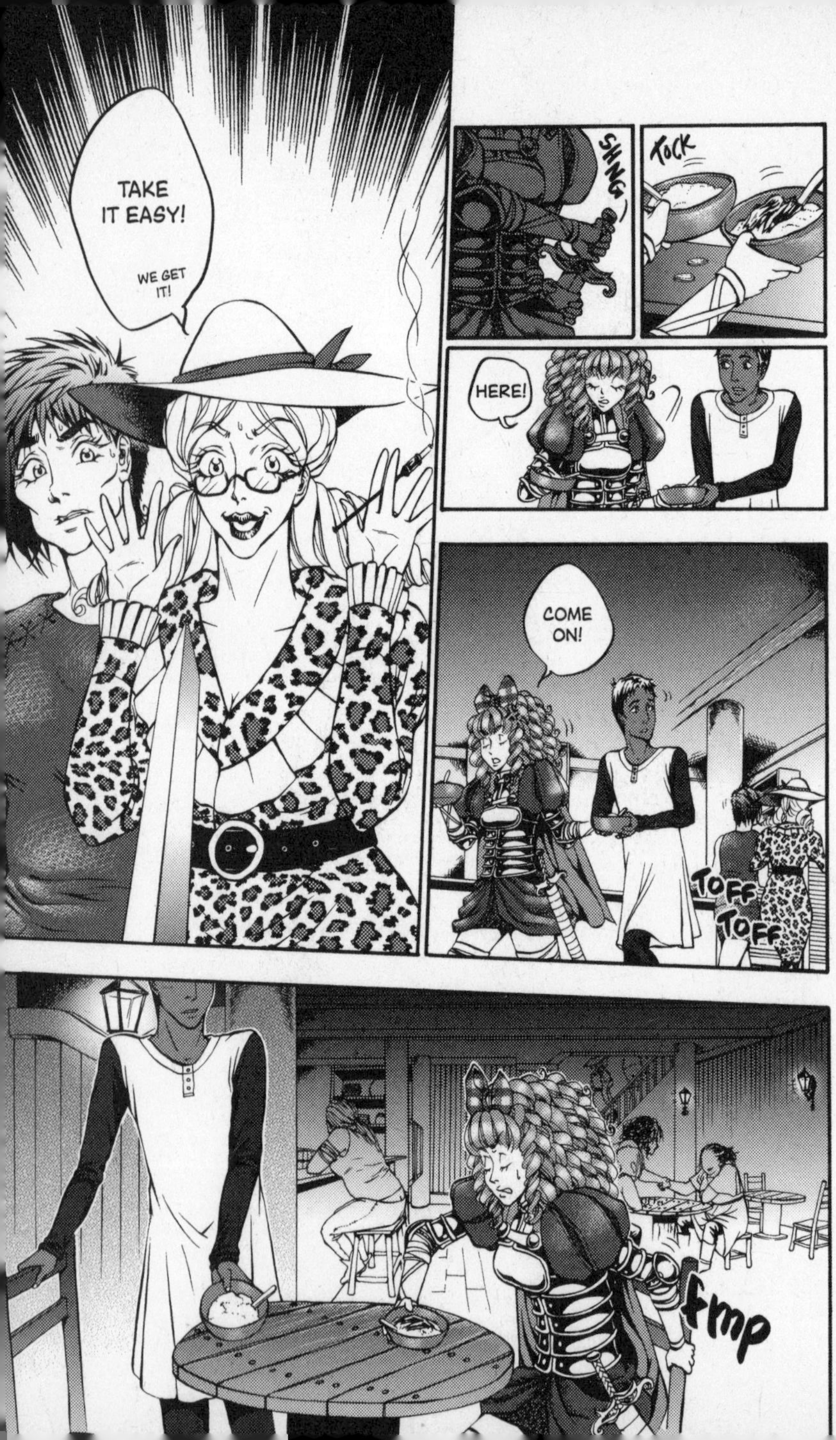
TAKE IT EASY!
WE GET IT!
SHING
TOCK
HERE!
COME ON!
TOFF
TOFF
FMP

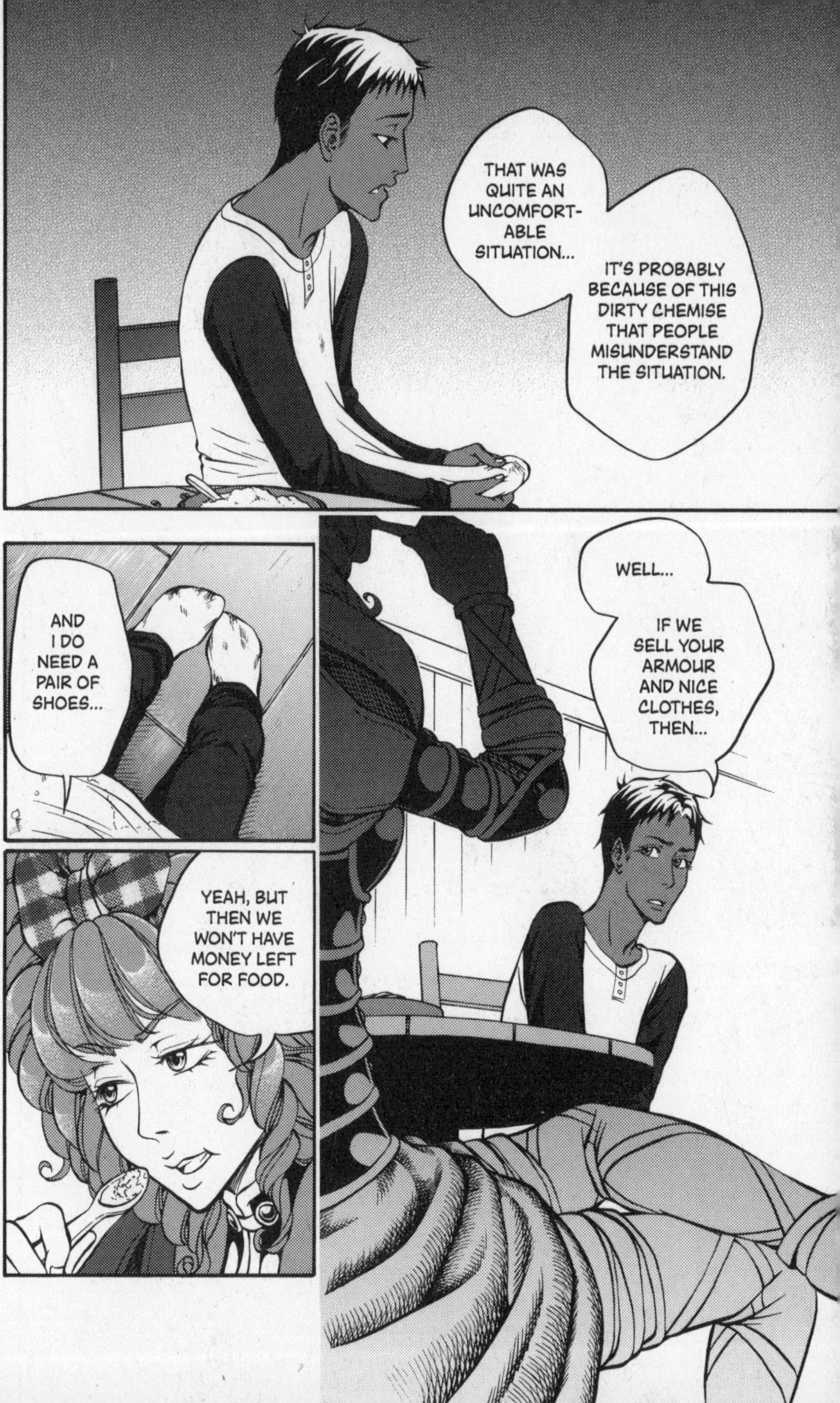

THAT WAS QUITE AN UNCOMFORT-ABLE SITUATION...
IT'S PROBABLY BECAUSE OF THIS DIRTY CHEMISE THAT PEOPLE MISUNDERSTAND THE SITUATION.
AND I DO NEED A PAIR OF SHOES...
YEAH, BUT THEN WE WON'T HAVE MONEY LEFT FOR FOOD.
WELL...
IF WE SELL YOUR ARMOUR AND NICE CLOTHES, THEN...

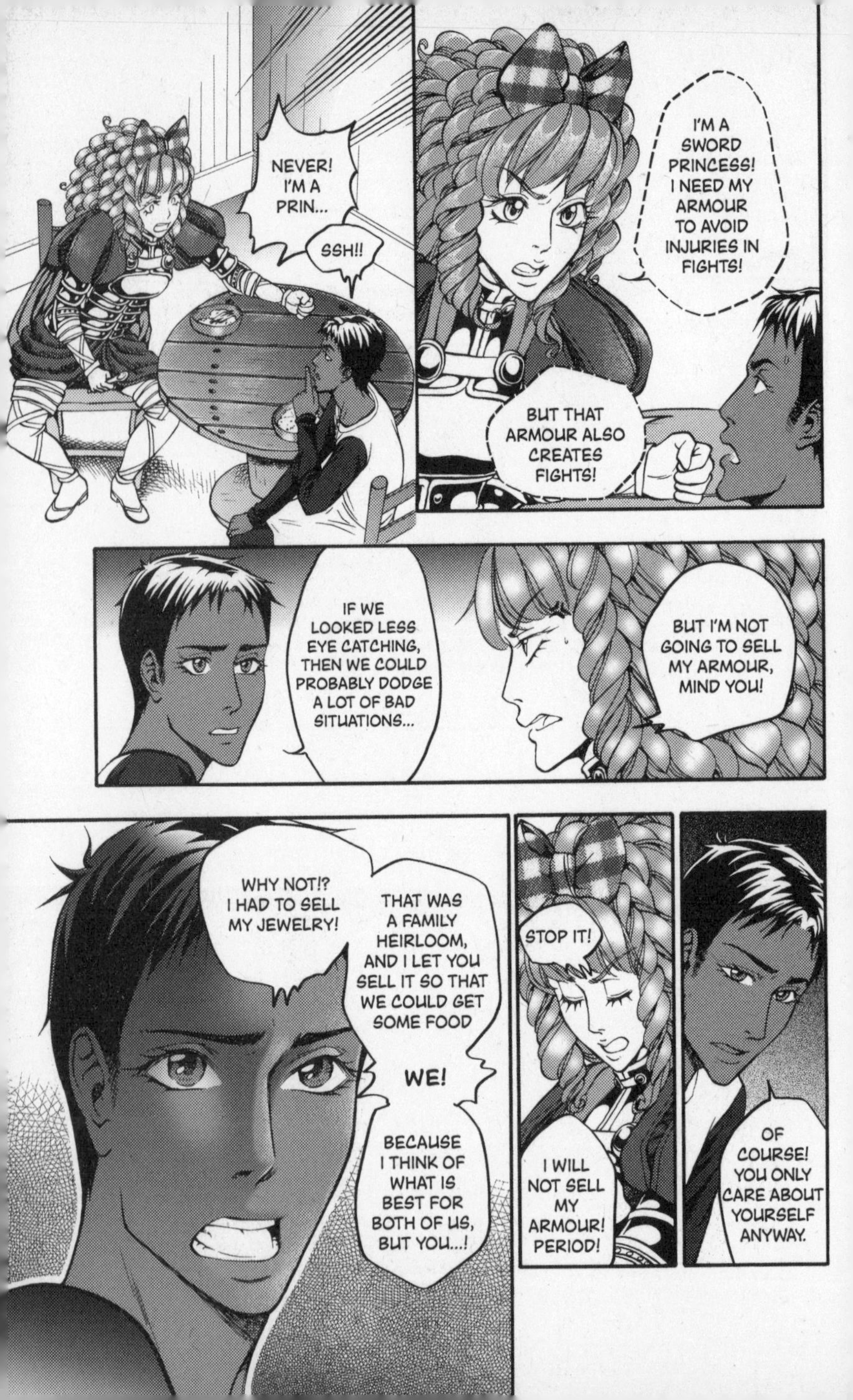

NEVER! I'M A PRIN...
SSH!!
I'M A SWORD PRINCESS! I NEED MY ARMOUR TO AVOID INJURIES IN FIGHTS!
BUT THAT ARMOUR ALSO CREATES FIGHTS!
IF WE LOOKED LESS EYE CATCHING, THEN WE COULD PROBABLY DODGE A LOT OF BAD SITUATIONS...
BUT I'M NOT GOING TO SELL MY ARMOUR, MIND YOU!
WHY NOT!? I HAD TO SELL MY JEWELRY!
THAT WAS A FAMILY HEIRLOOM, AND I LET YOU SELL IT SO THAT WE COULD GET SOME FOOD
WE!
BECAUSE I THINK OF WHAT IS BEST FOR BOTH OF US, BUT YOU...!
STOP IT!
I WILL NOT SELL MY ARMOUR! PERIOD!
OF COURSE! YOU ONLY CARE ABOUT YOURSELF ANYWAY.

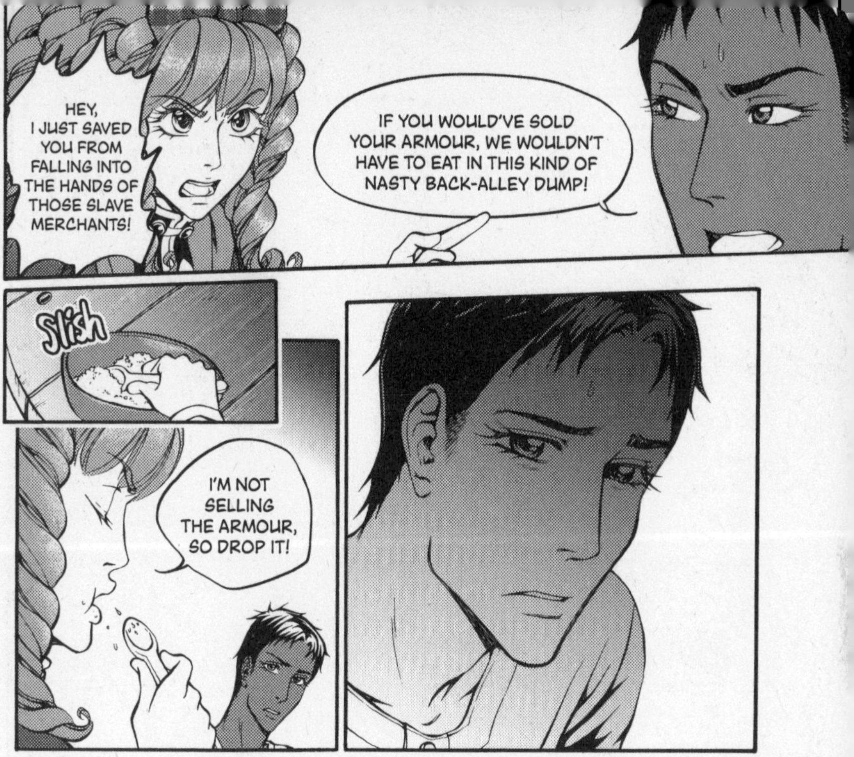
HEY, I JUST SAVED YOU FROM FALLING INTO THE HANDS OF THOSE SLAVE MERCHANTS!
IF YOU WOULD'VE SOLD YOUR ARMOUR, WE WOULDN'T HAVE TO EAT IN THIS KIND OF NASTY BACK-ALLEY DUMP!
Slish
I'M NOT SELLING THE ARMOUR, SO DROP IT!

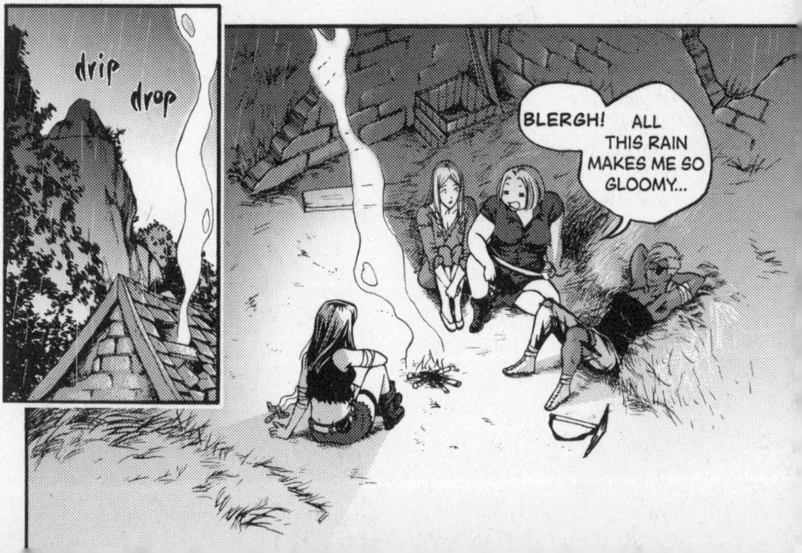
drip
drop
BLERGH! ALL THIS RAIN MAKES ME SO GLOOMY...

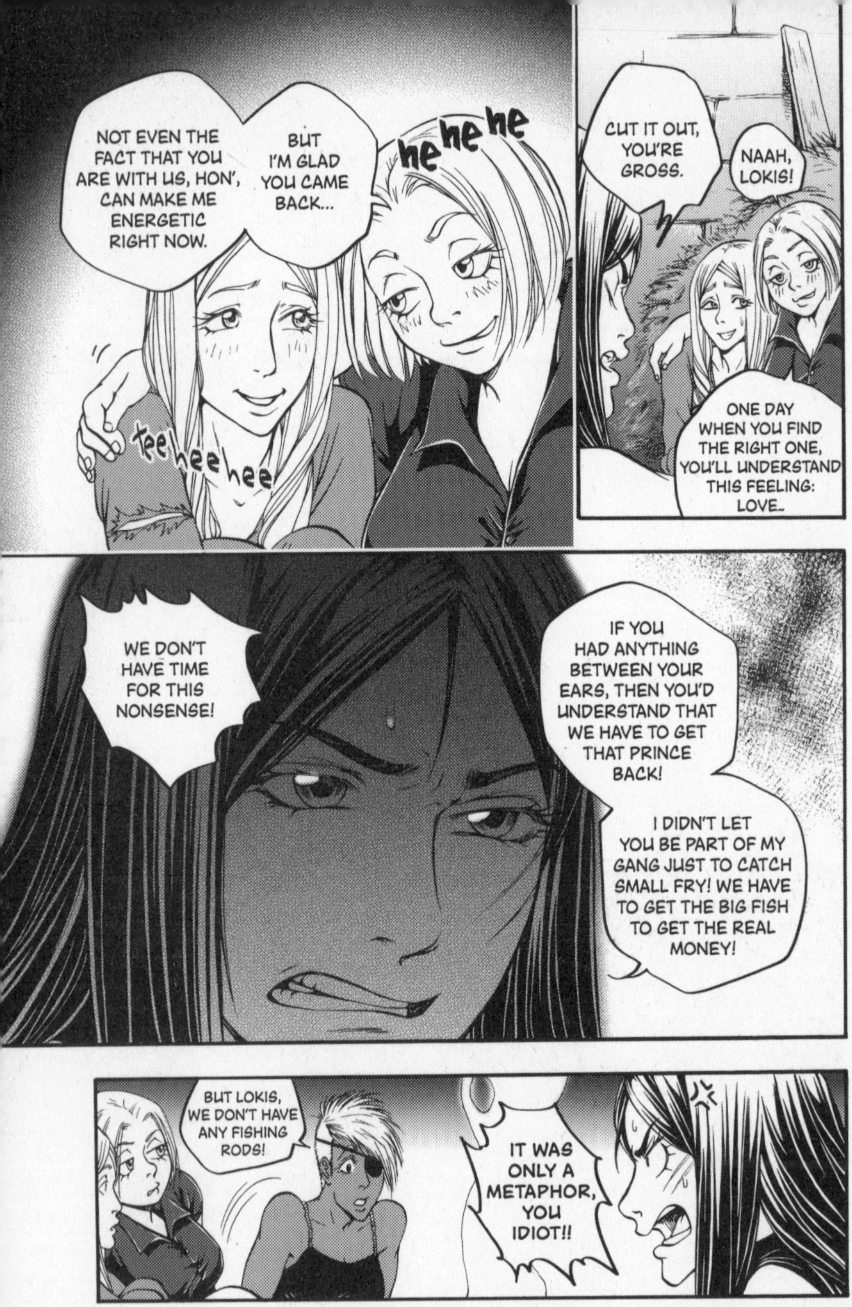
NOT EVEN THE FACT THAT YOU ARE WITH US, HON', CAN MAKE ME ENERGETIC RIGHT NOW.
BUT I'M GLAD YOU CAME BACK...
he he he
tee hee hee
CUT IT OUT, YOU'RE GROSS.
NAAH, LOKIS!
ONE DAY WHEN YOU FIND THE RIGHT ONE, YOU'LL UNDERSTAND THIS FEELING: LOVE~
WE DON'T HAVE TIME FOR THIS NONSENSE!
IF YOU HAD ANYTHING BETWEEN YOUR EARS, THEN YOU'D UNDERSTAND THAT WE HAVE TO GET THAT PRINCE BACK!
I DIDN'T LET YOU BE PART OF MY GANG JUST TO CATCH SMALL FRY! WE HAVE TO GET THE BIG FISH TO GET THE REAL MONEY!
BUT LOKIS, WE DON'T HAVE ANY FISHING RODS!
IT WAS ONLY A METAPHOR, YOU IDIOT!!

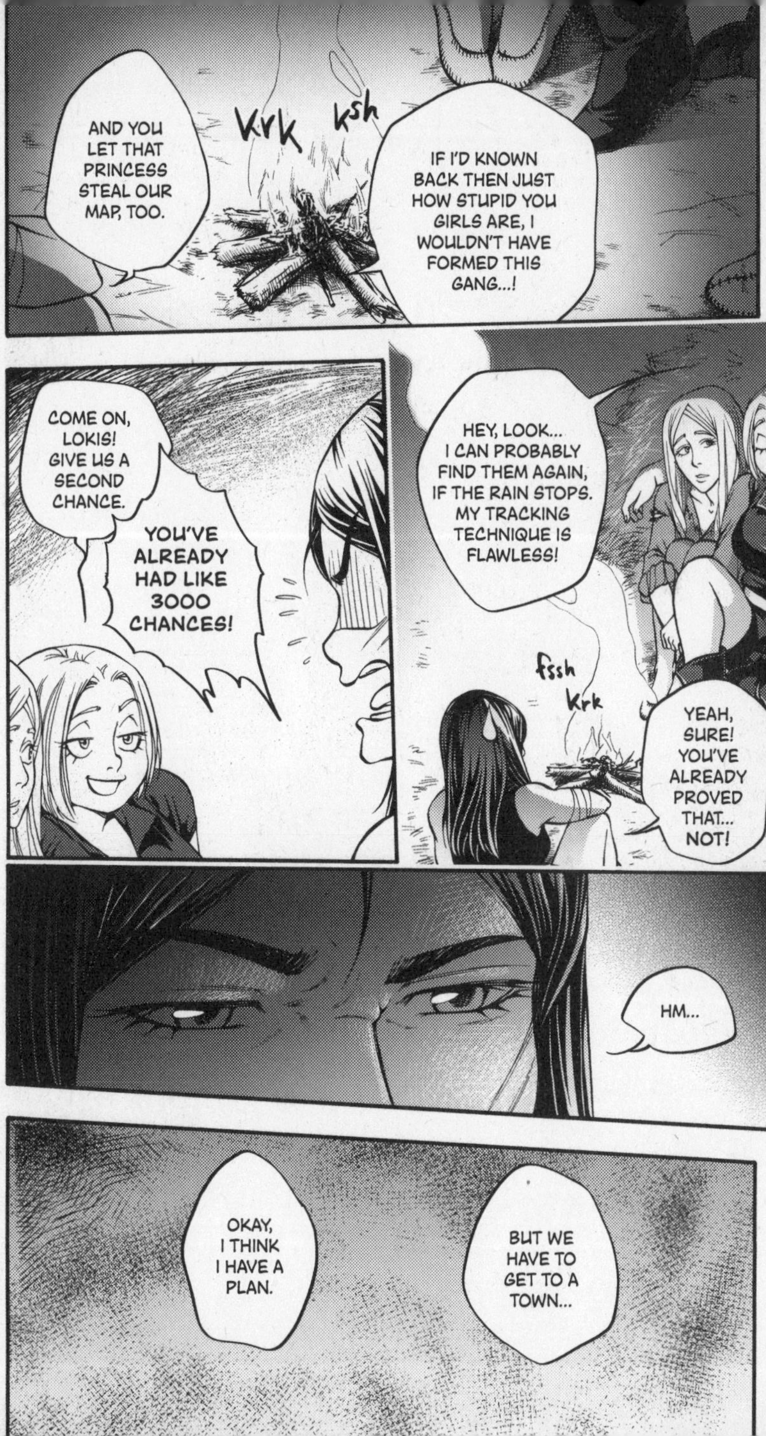
AND YOU LET THAT PRINCESS STEAL OUR MAP, TOO.
Krk
ksh
IF I'D KNOWN BACK THEN JUST HOW STUPID YOU GIRLS ARE, I WOULDN'T HAVE FORMED THIS GANG...!
COME ON, LOKIS! GIVE US A SECOND CHANCE.
YOU'VE ALREADY HAD LIKE 3000 CHANCES!
HEY, LOOK... I CAN PROBABLY FIND THEM AGAIN, IF THE RAIN STOPS. MY TRACKING TECHNIQUE IS FLAWLESS!
fssh
Krk
YEAH, SURE! YOU'VE ALREADY PROVED THAT... NOT!
HM...
OKAY, I THINK I HAVE A PLAN.
BUT WE HAVE TO GET TO A TOWN...

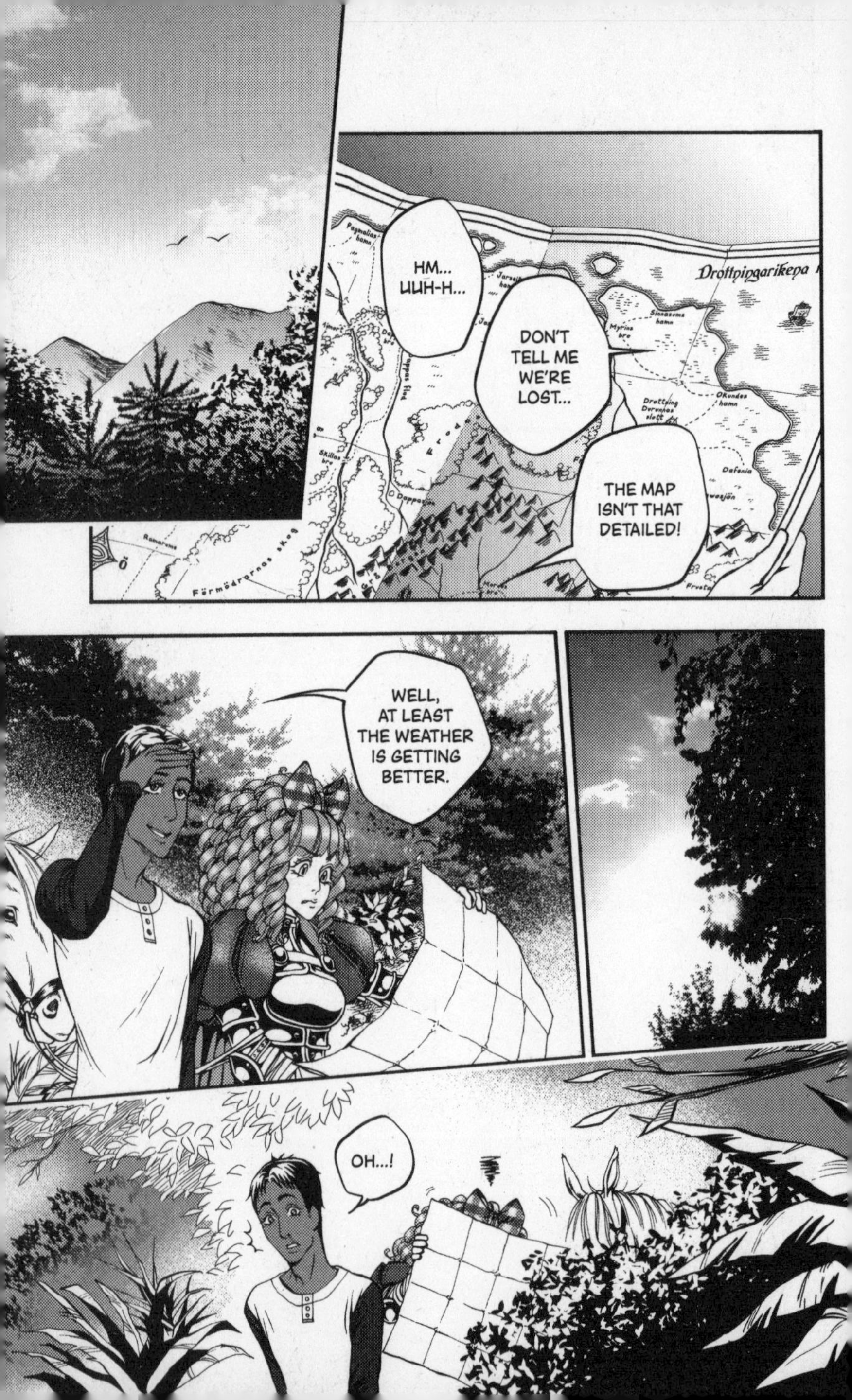
HM... UUH-H...
DON'T TELL ME WE'RE LOST...
THE MAP ISN'T THAT DETAILED!
WELL, AT LEAST THE WEATHER IS GETTING BETTER.
OH...!

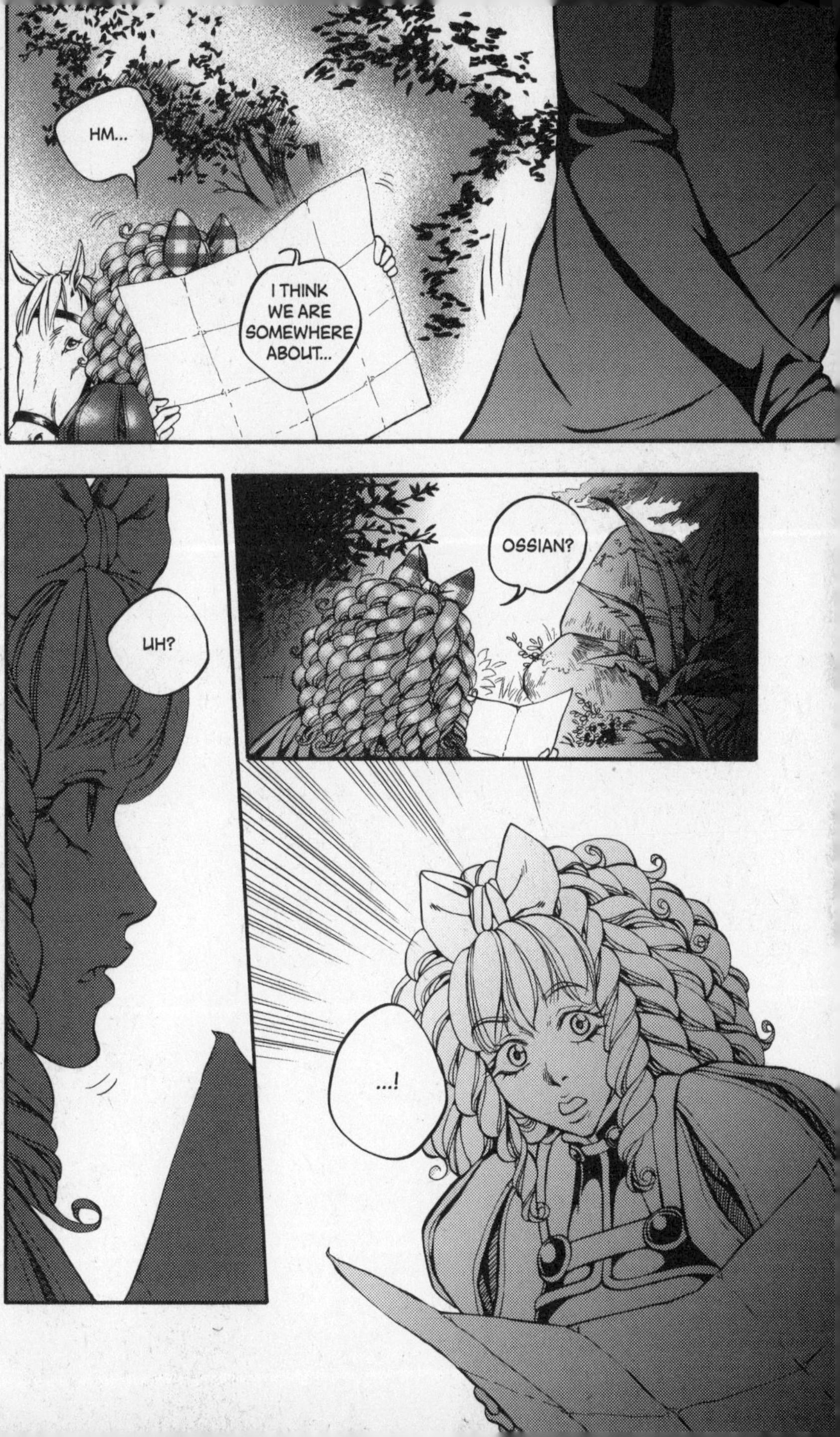
HM...
I THINK WE ARE SOMEWHERE ABOUT...
OSSIAN?
...!
UH?

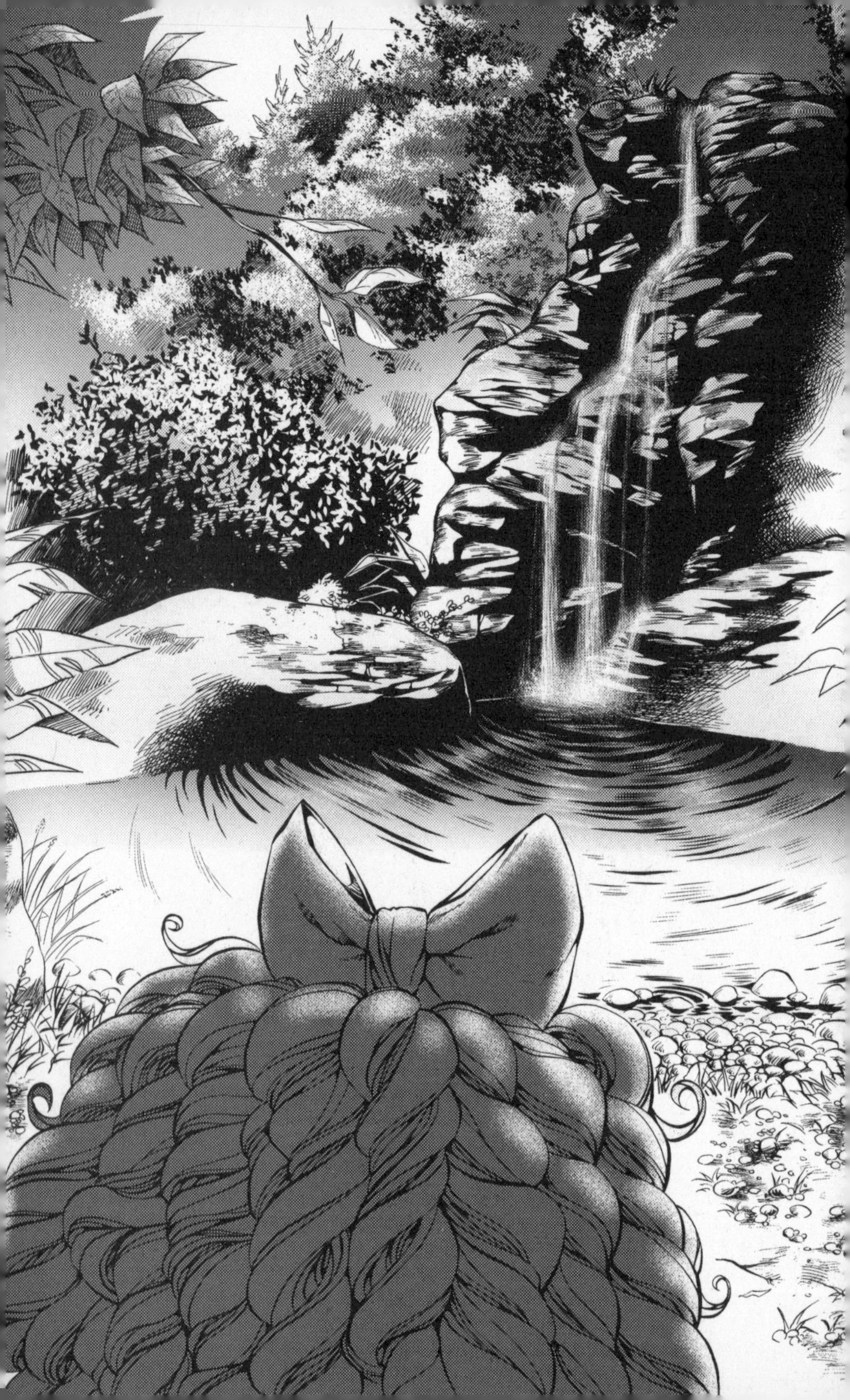

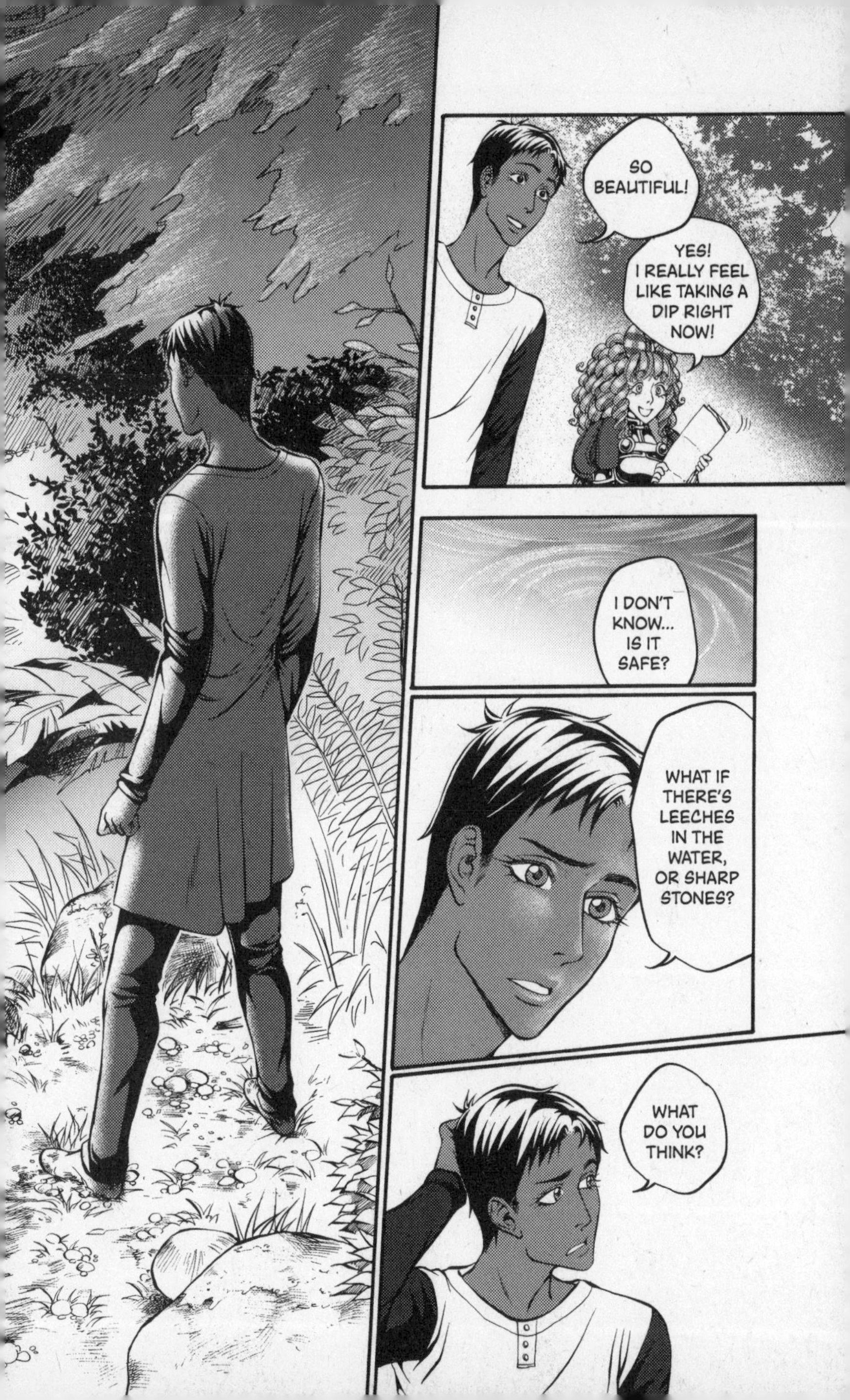
SO BEAUTIFUL!
YES! I REALLY FEEL LIKE TAKING A DIP RIGHT NOW!
I DON'T KNOW... IS IT SAFE?
WHAT IF THERE'S LEECHES IN THE WATER, OR SHARP STONES?
WHAT DO YOU THINK?

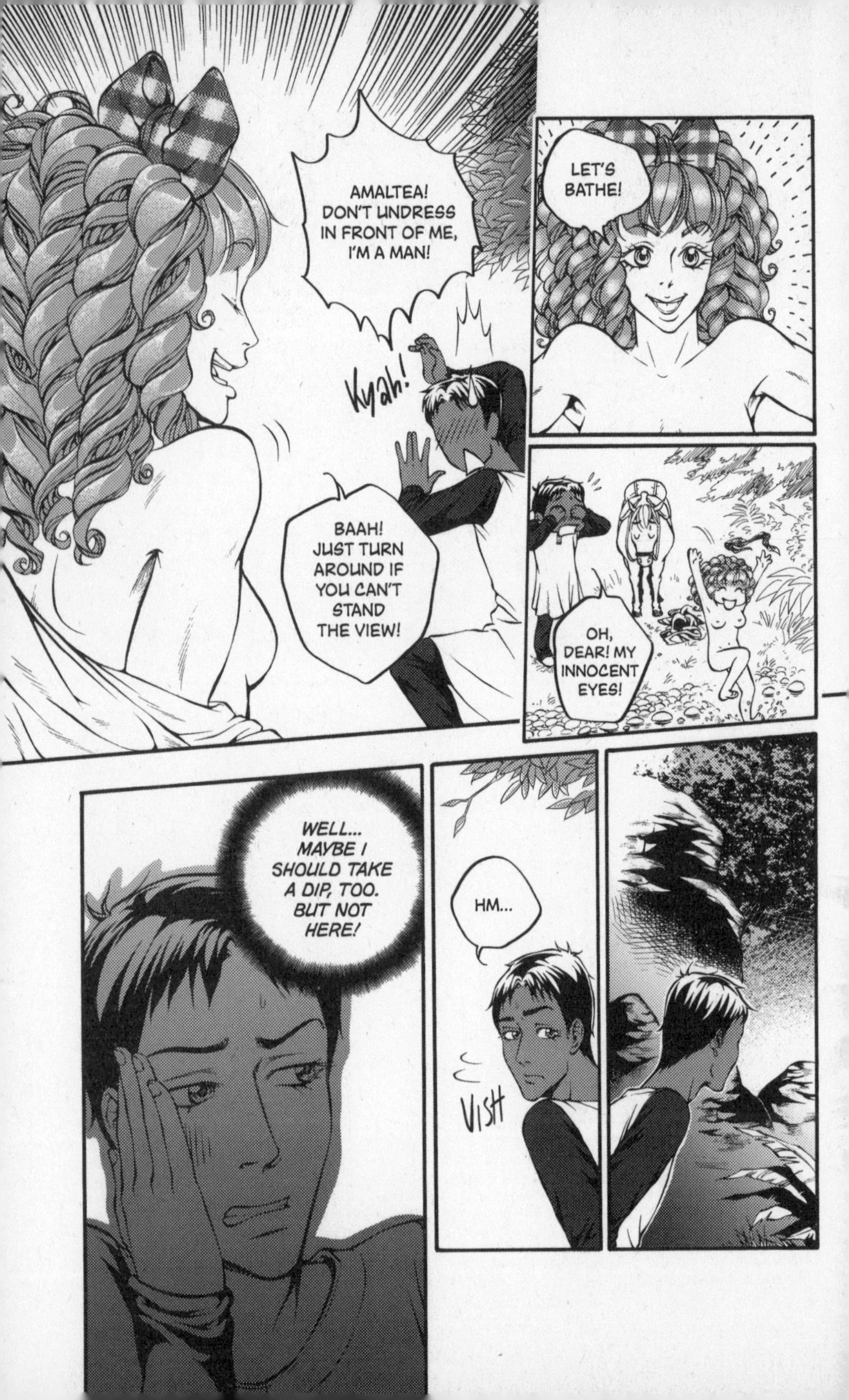
AMALTEA! DON'T UNDRESS IN FRONT OF ME, I'M A MAN!
Kyah!
BAAH! JUST TURN AROUND IF YOU CAN'T STAND THE VIEW!
LET'S BATHE!
OH, DEAR! MY INNOCENT EYES!
WELL... MAYBE I SHOULD TAKE A DIP, TOO. BUT NOT HERE!
HM...
VISH

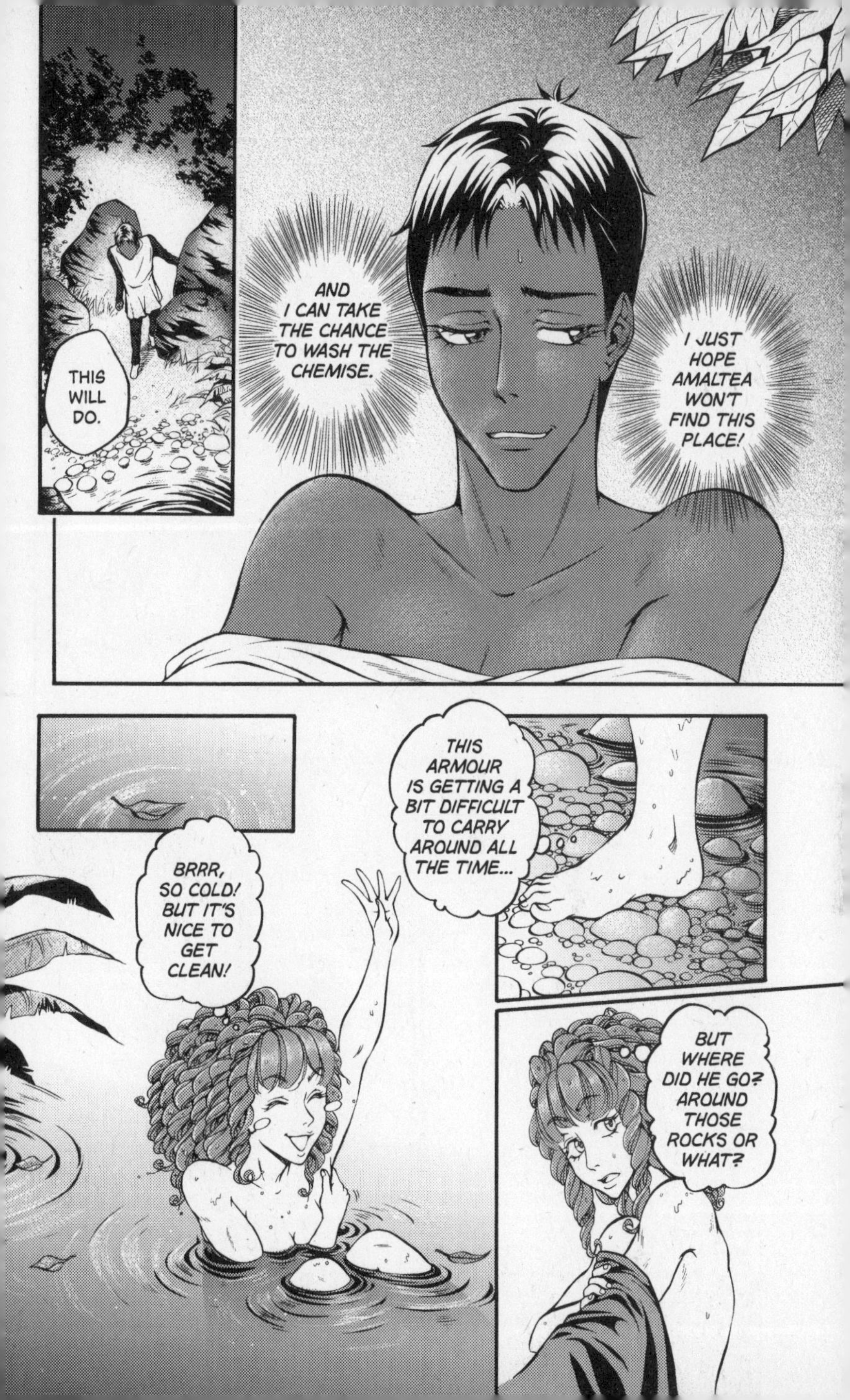
THIS WILL DO.
AND I CAN TAKE THE CHANCE TO WASH THE CHEMISE.
I JUST HOPE AMALTEA WON'T FIND THIS PLACE!
THIS ARMOUR IS GETTING A BIT DIFFICULT TO CARRY AROUND ALL THE TIME...
BRRR, SO COLD! BUT IT'S NICE TO GET CLEAN!
BUT WHERE DID HE GO? AROUND THOSE ROCKS OR WHAT?

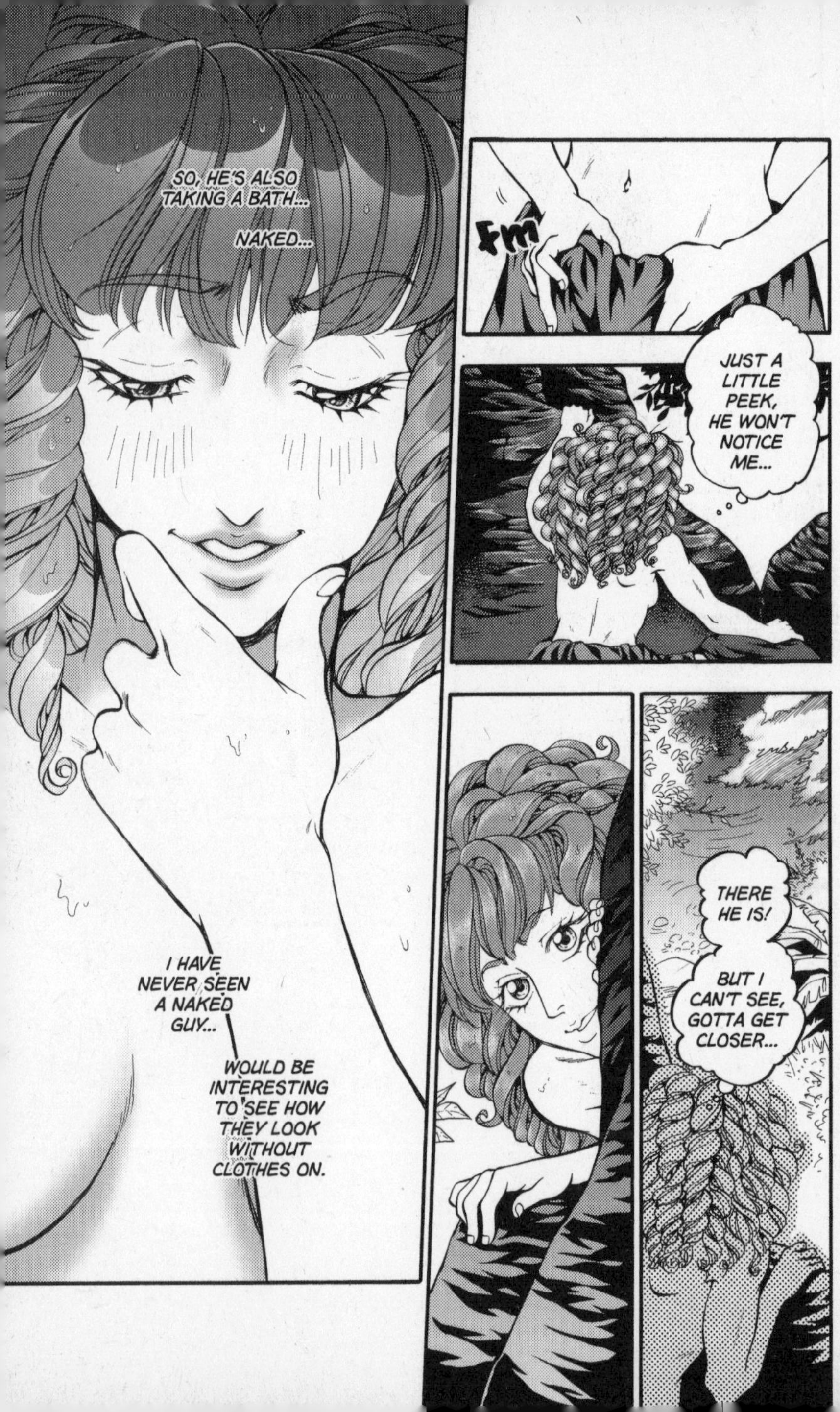

SO, HE'S ALSO TAKING A BATH...
NAKED...
I HAVE NEVER SEEN A NAKED GUY...
WOULD BE INTERESTING TO SEE HOW THEY LOOK WITHOUT CLOTHES ON.
FM
JUST A LITTLE PEEK, HE WON'T NOTICE ME...
THERE HE IS!
BUT I CAN'T SEE, GOTTA GET CLOSER...

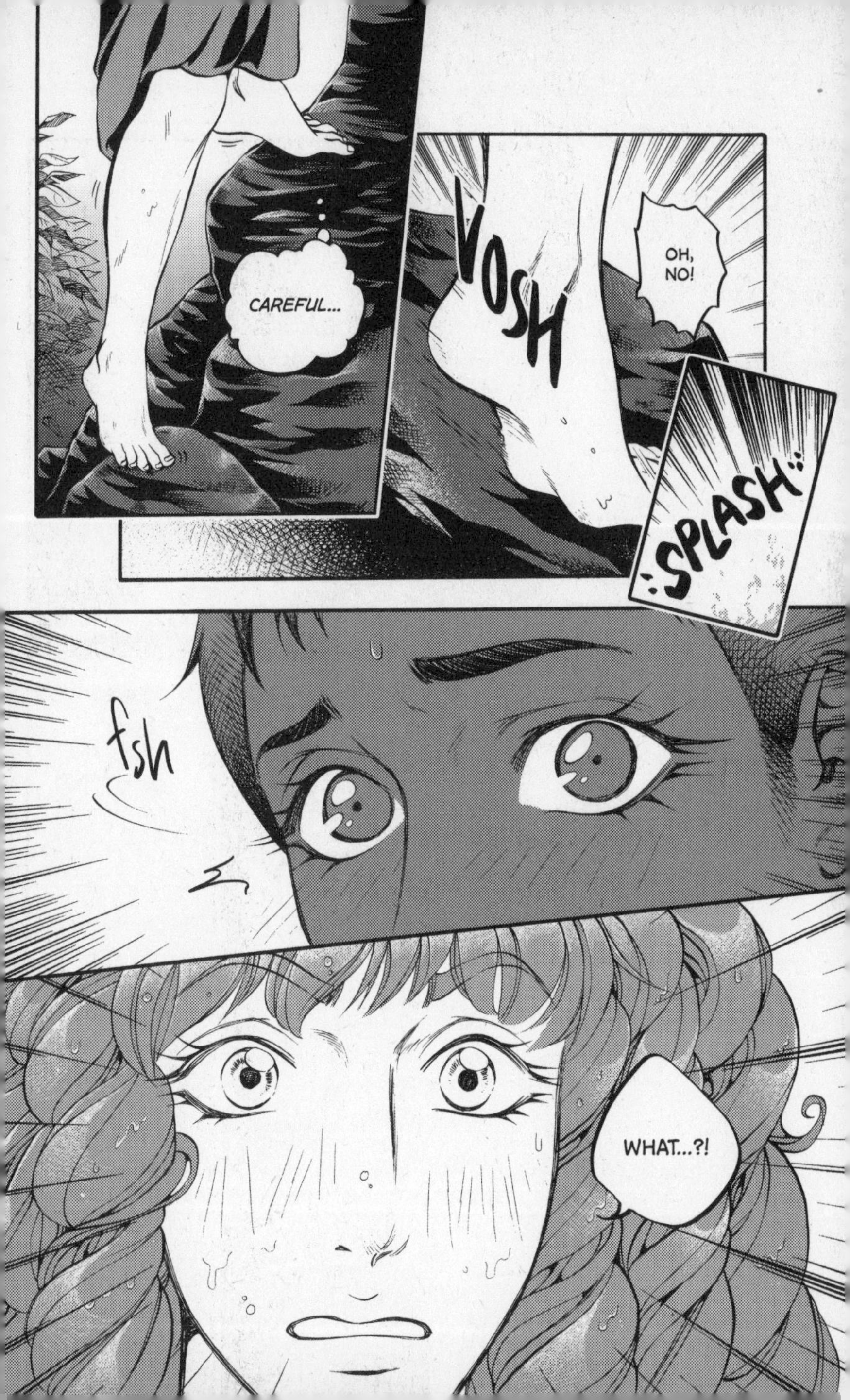
CAREFUL...
VOSH
OH, NO!
SPLASH
fsh
WHAT...?!

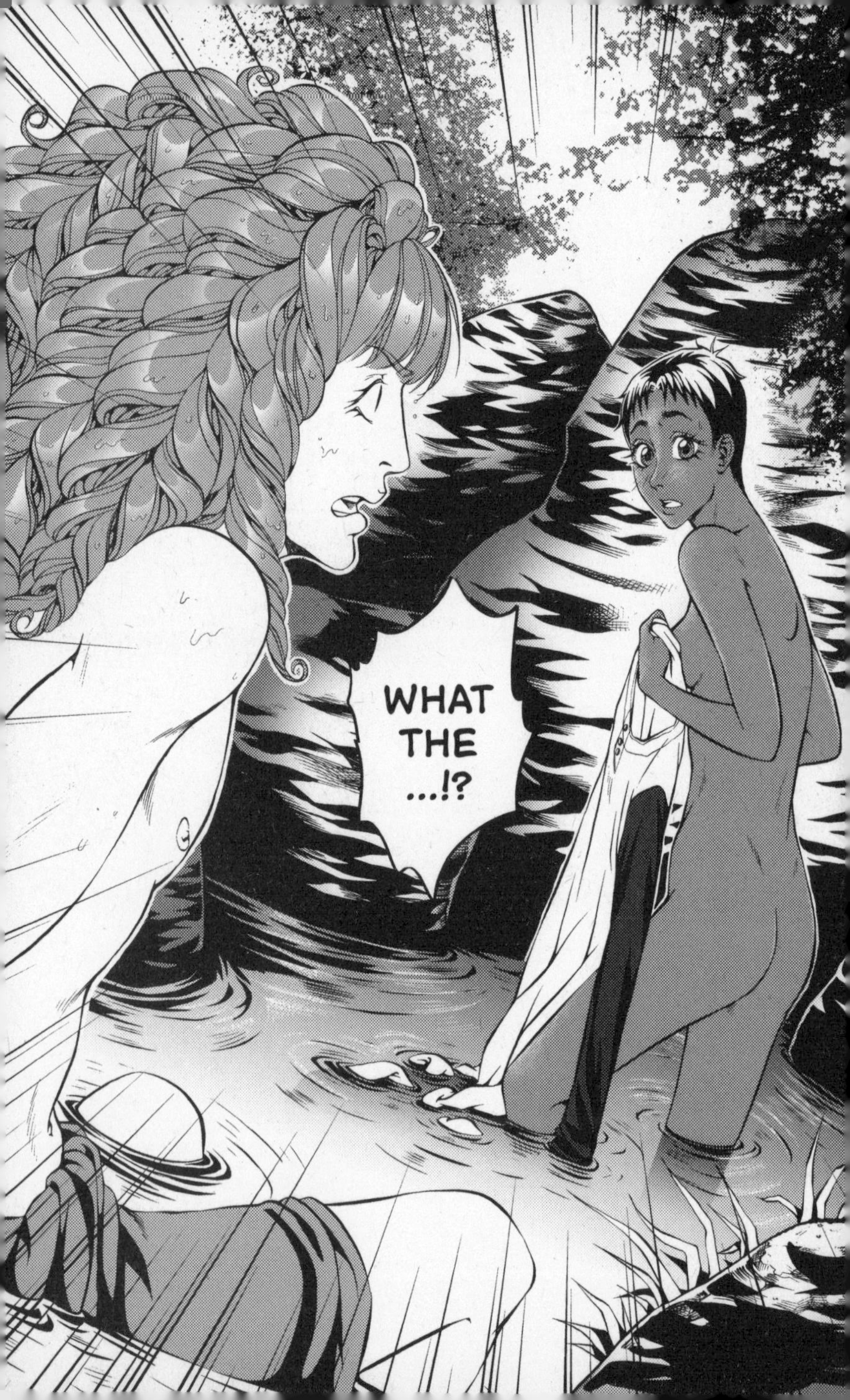
WHAT THE ...!?

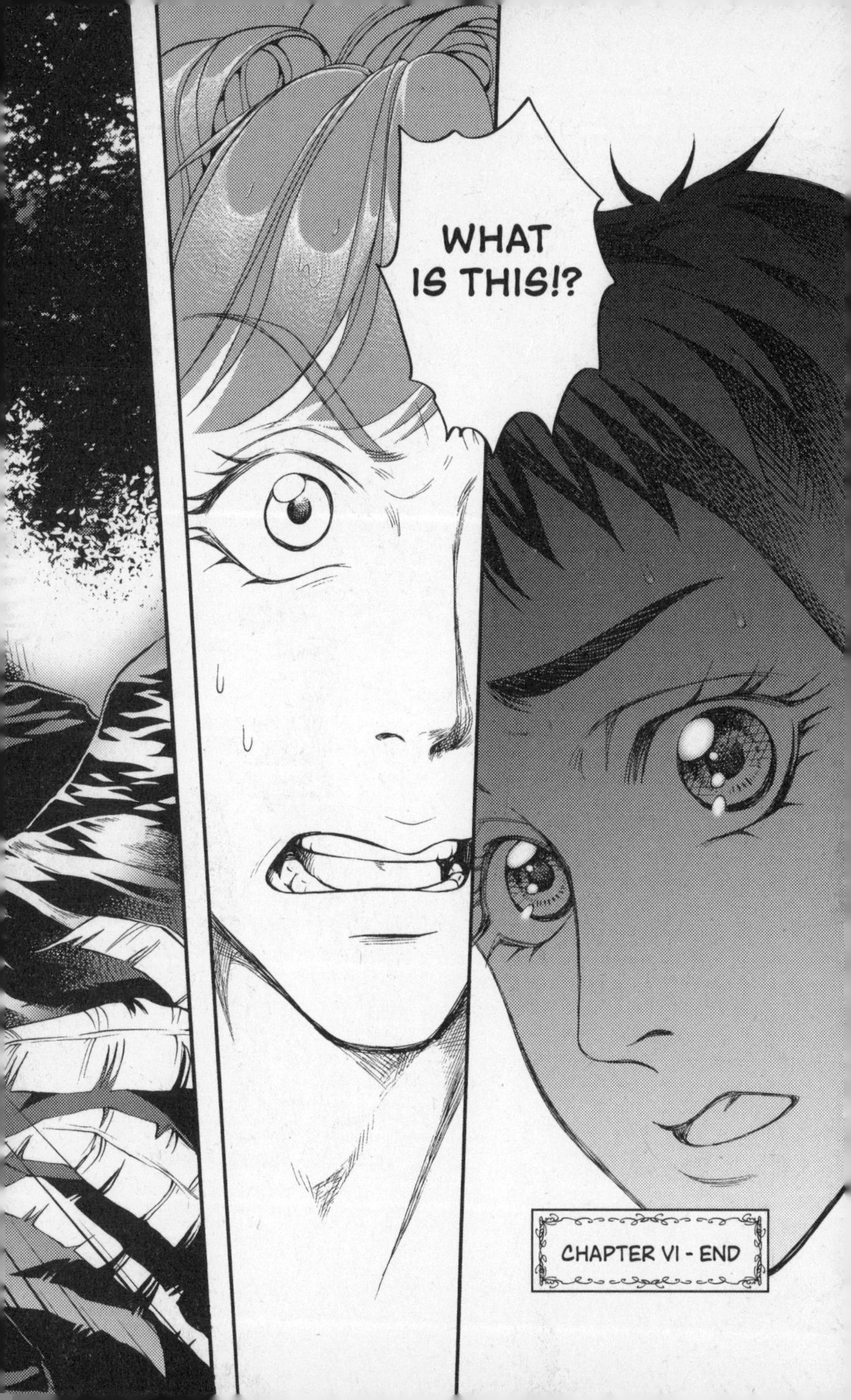
WHAT IS THIS!?
CHAPTER VI - END

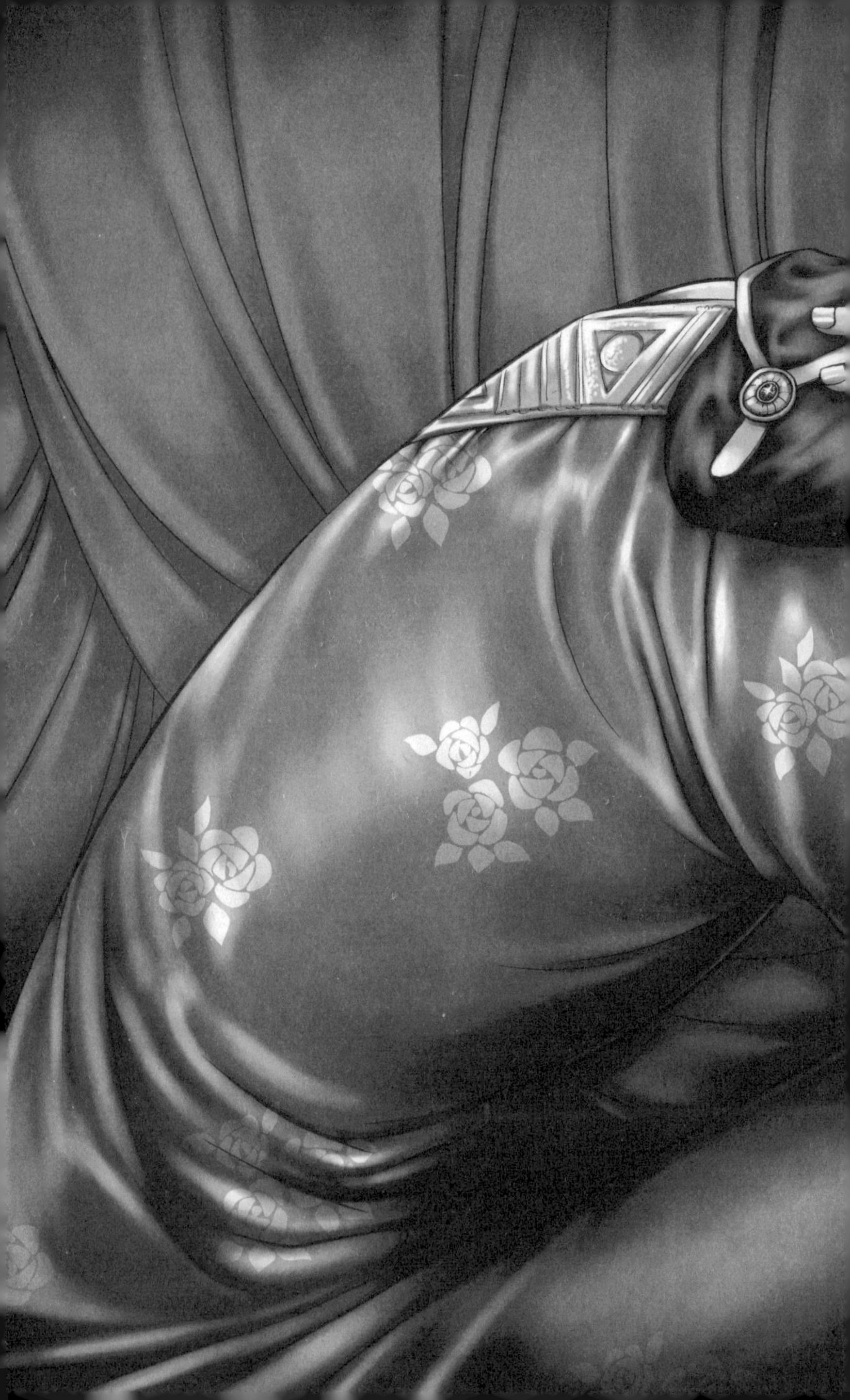

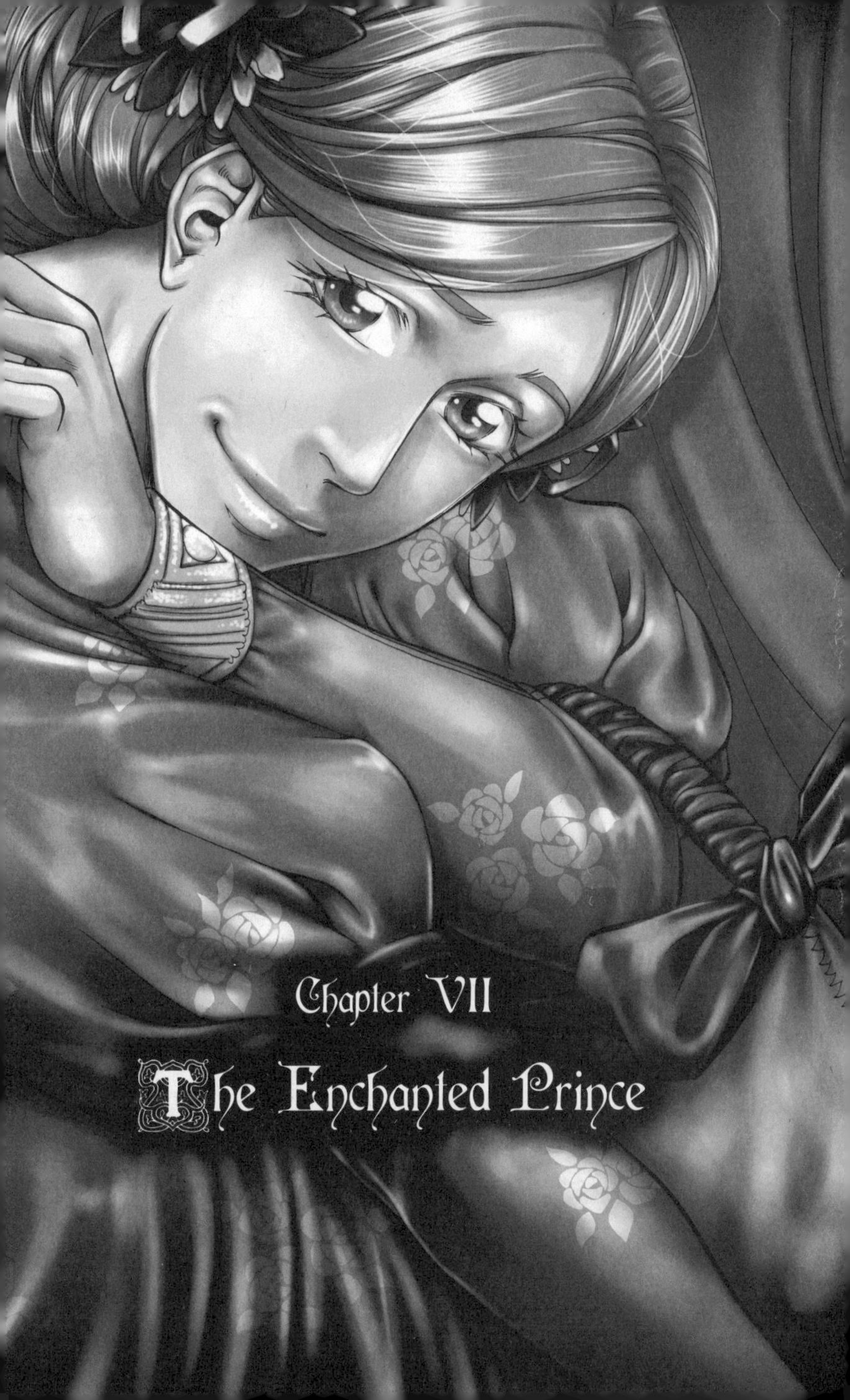
Chapter VII
The Enchanted Prince

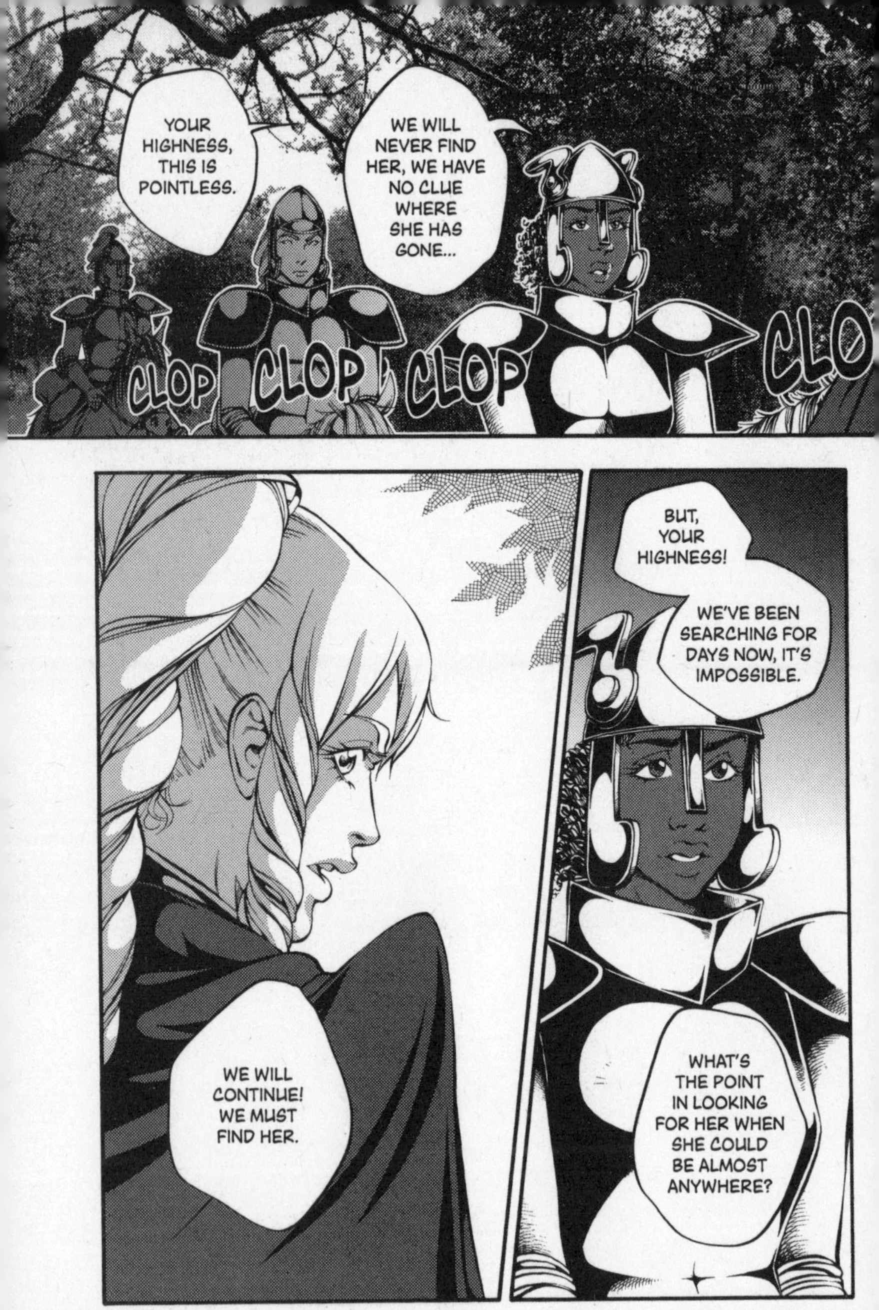
YOUR HIGHNESS, THIS IS POINTLESS.
WE WILL NEVER FIND HER, WE HAVE NO CLUE WHERE SHE HAS GONE...
CLOP
CLOP
CLOP
CLO
WE WILL CONTINUE! WE MUST FIND HER.
BUT, YOUR HIGHNESS!
WE'VE BEEN SEARCHING FOR DAYS NOW, IT'S IMPOSSIBLE.
WHAT'S THE POINT IN LOOKING FOR HER WHEN SHE COULD BE ALMOST ANYWHERE?

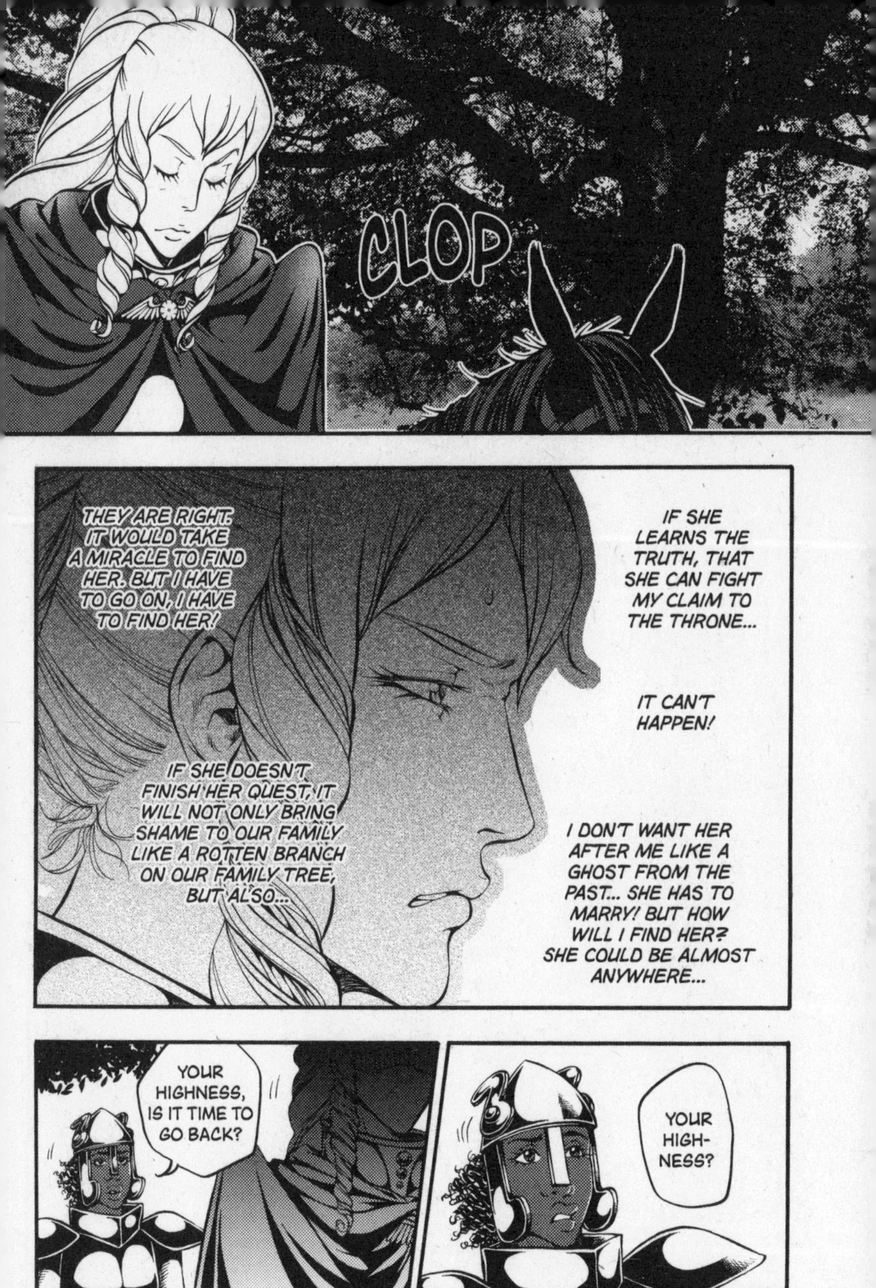
CLOP
THEY ARE RIGHT. IT WOULD TAKE A MIRACLE TO FIND HER. BUT I HAVE TO GO ON, I HAVE TO FIND HER!
IF SHE LEARNS THE TRUTH, THAT SHE CAN FIGHT MY CLAIM TO THE THRONE...
IT CAN'T HAPPEN!
IF SHE DOESN'T FINISH HER QUEST, IT WILL NOT ONLY BRING SHAME TO OUR FAMILY LIKE A ROTTEN BRANCH ON OUR FAMILY TREE, BUT ALSO...
I DON'T WANT HER AFTER ME LIKE A GHOST FROM THE PAST... SHE HAS TO MARRY! BUT HOW WILL I FIND HER? SHE COULD BE ALMOST ANYWHERE...
YOUR HIGHNESS, IS IT TIME TO GO BACK?
YOUR HIGH-NESS?

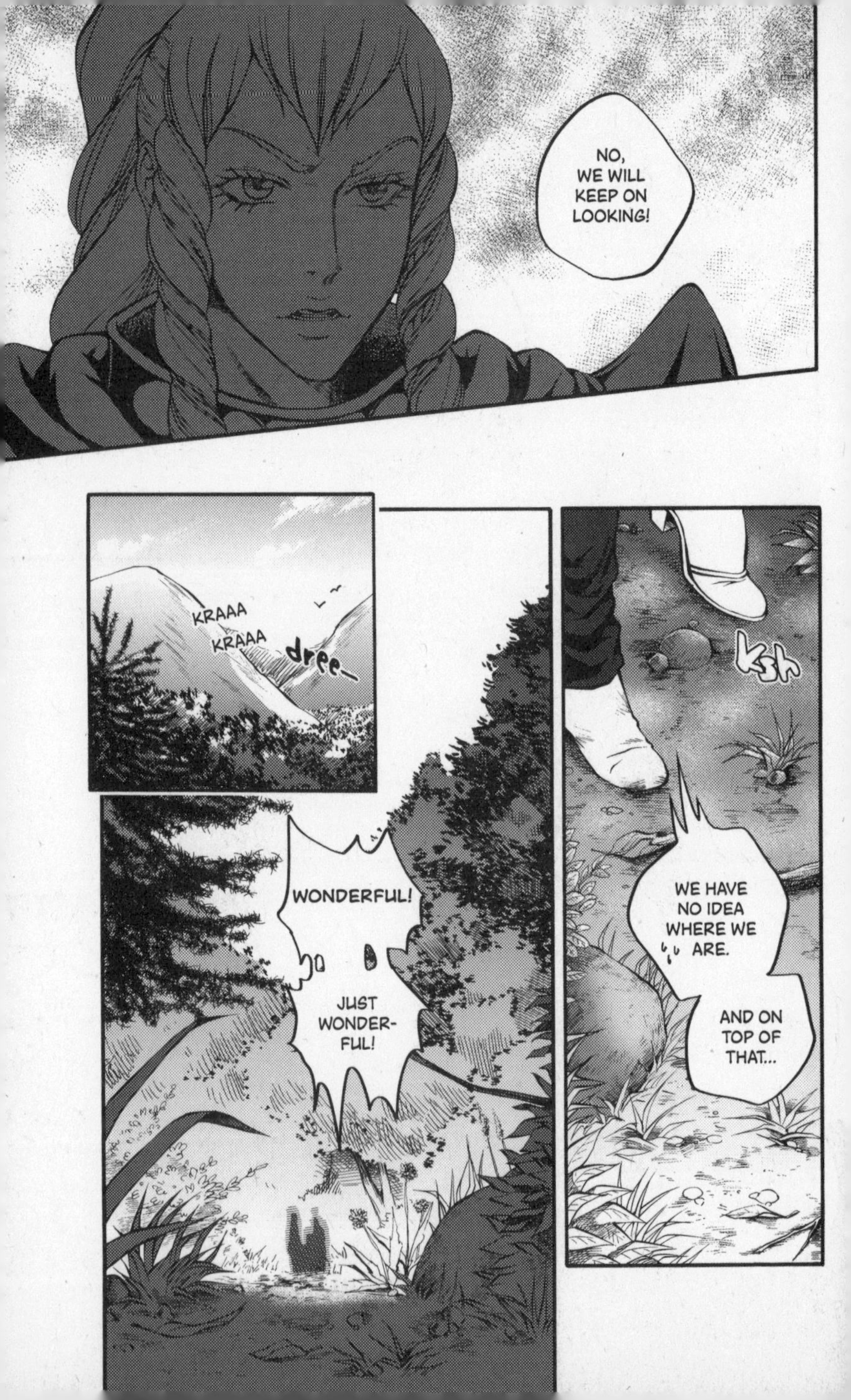
NO, WE WILL KEEP ON LOOKING!
KRAAA
KRAAA
dree-
WONDERFUL!
JUST WONDERFUL!
Ksh
WE HAVE NO IDEA WHERE WE ARE.
AND ON TOP OF THAT...

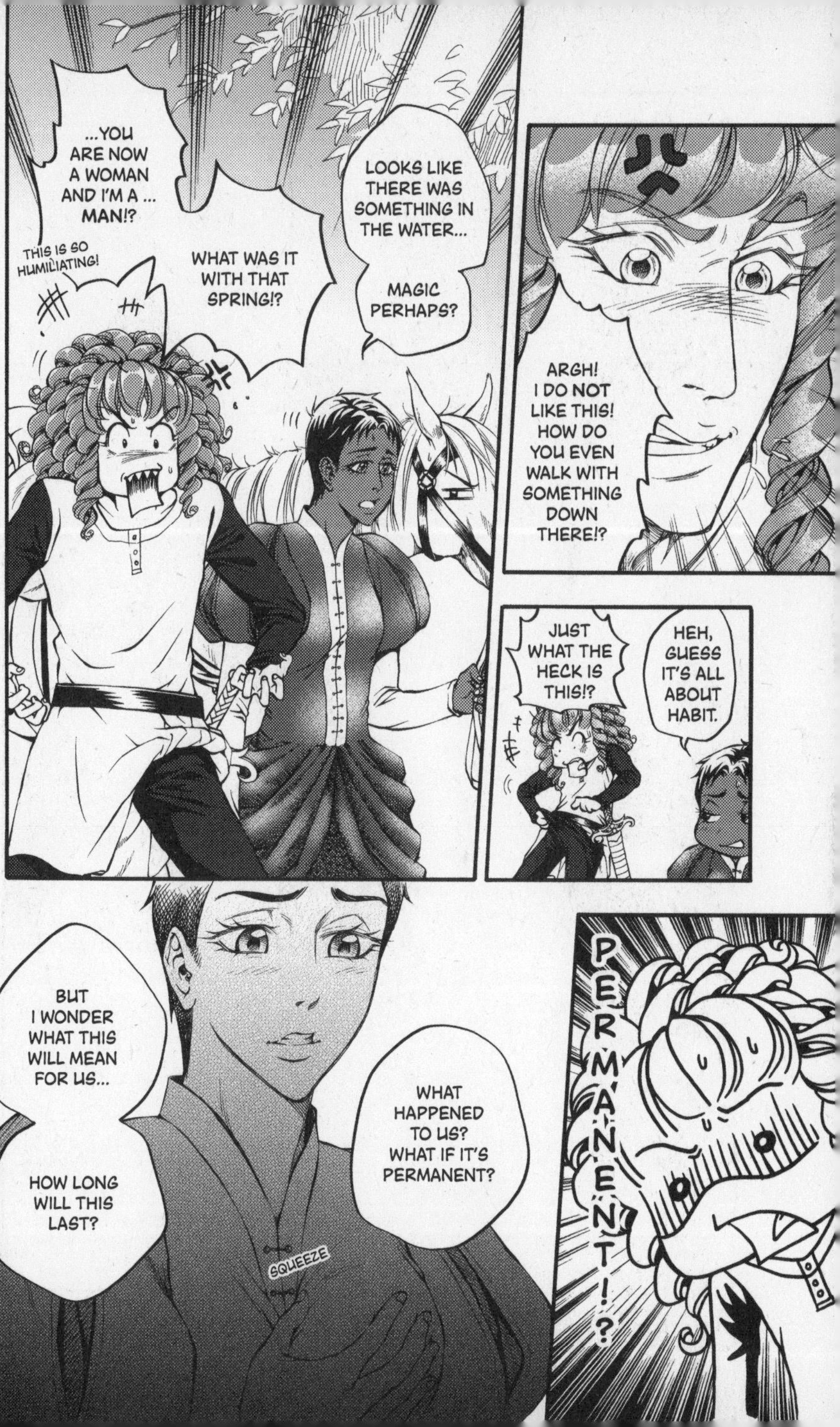
...YOU ARE NOW A WOMAN AND I'M A ... MAN!?
THIS IS SO HUMILIATING!
WHAT WAS IT WITH THAT SPRING!?
LOOKS LIKE THERE WAS SOMETHING IN THE WATER...
MAGIC PERHAPS?
ARGH! I DO NOT LIKE THIS! HOW DO YOU EVEN WALK WITH SOMETHING DOWN THERE!?
JUST WHAT THE HECK IS THIS!?
HEH, GUESS IT'S ALL ABOUT HABIT.
BUT I WONDER WHAT THIS WILL MEAN FOR US...
HOW LONG WILL THIS LAST?
WHAT HAPPENED TO US? WHAT IF IT'S PERMANENT?
SQUEEZE
PERMANENT!?

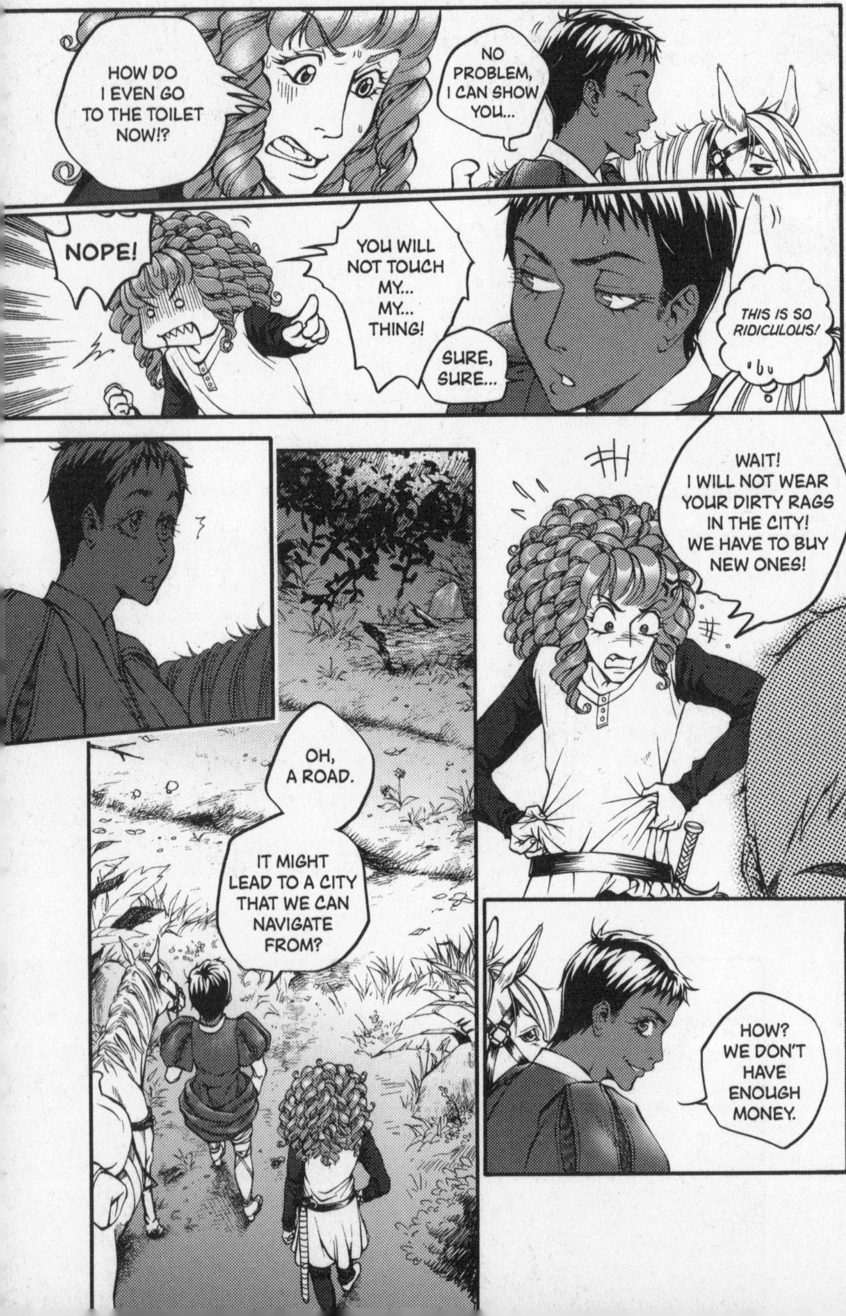
HOW DO I EVEN GO TO THE TOILET NOW!?
NO PROBLEM, I CAN SHOW YOU...
NOPE!
YOU WILL NOT TOUCH MY... MY... THING!
SURE, SURE...
THIS IS SO RIDICULOUS!
OH, A ROAD.
IT MIGHT LEAD TO A CITY THAT WE CAN NAVIGATE FROM?
WAIT! I WILL NOT WEAR YOUR DIRTY RAGS IN THE CITY! WE HAVE TO BUY NEW ONES!
HOW? WE DON'T HAVE ENOUGH MONEY.

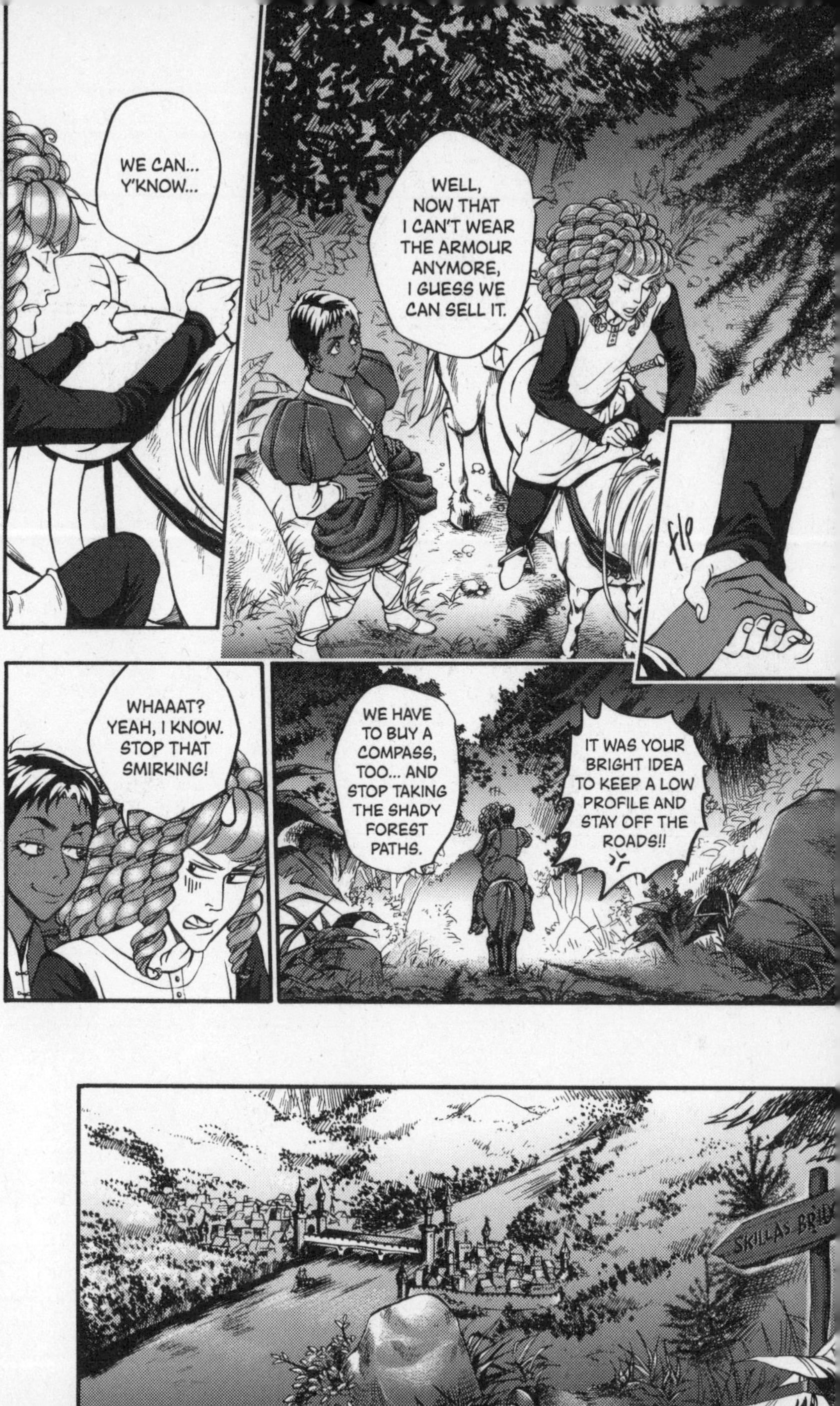
WE CAN... Y'KNOW...
WELL, NOW THAT I CAN'T WEAR THE ARMOUR ANYMORE, I GUESS WE CAN SELL IT.
FLIP
WHAAAT? YEAH, I KNOW. STOP THAT SMIRKING!
WE HAVE TO BUY A COMPASS, TOO... AND STOP TAKING THE SHADY FOREST PATHS.
IT WAS YOUR BRIGHT IDEA TO KEEP A LOW PROFILE AND STAY OFF THE ROADS!!

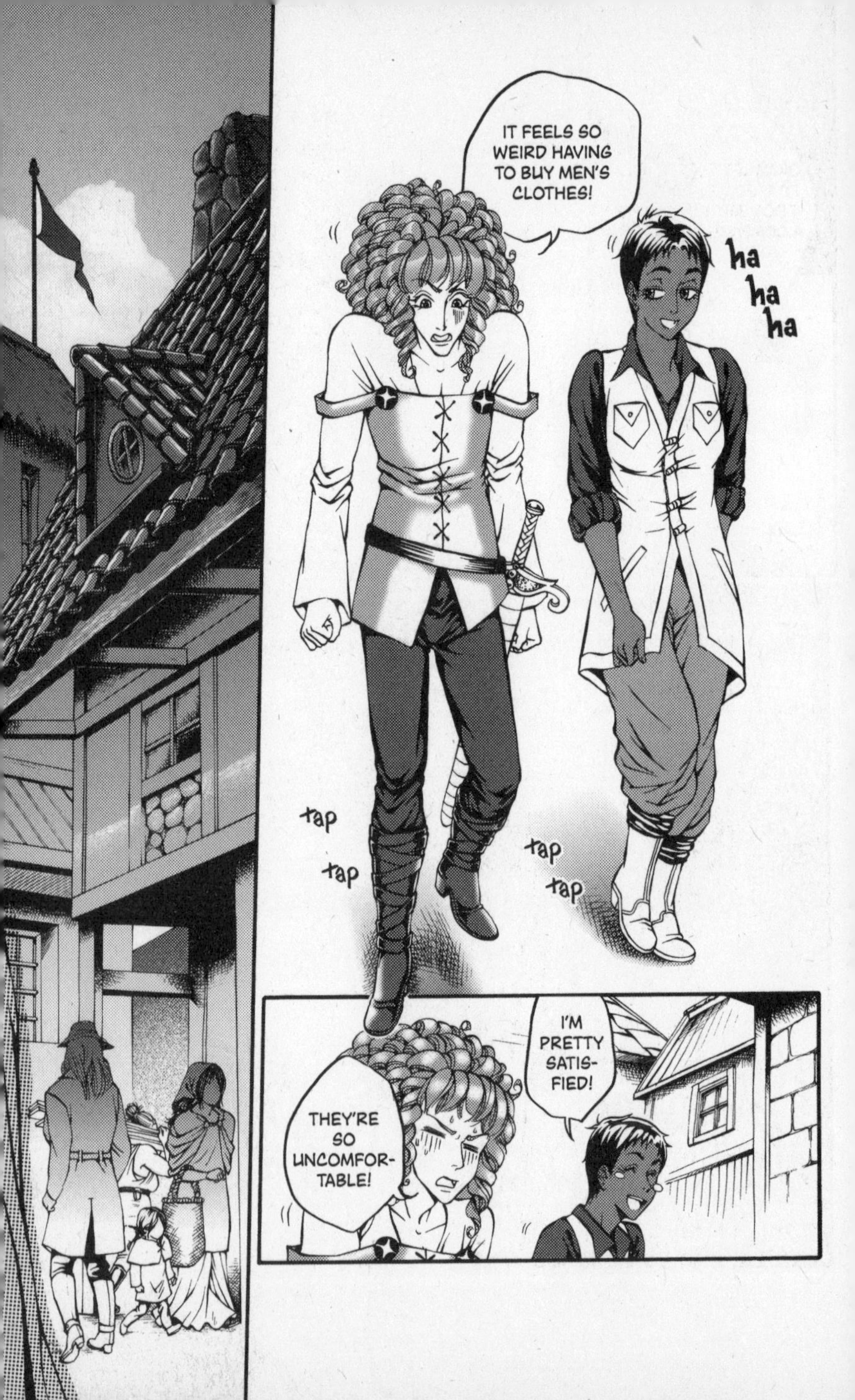
IT FEELS SO WEIRD HAVING TO BUY MEN'S CLOTHES!
ha ha ha
tap
tap
tap
tap
THEY'RE SO UNCOMFOR-TABLE!
I'M PRETTY SATIS-FIED!

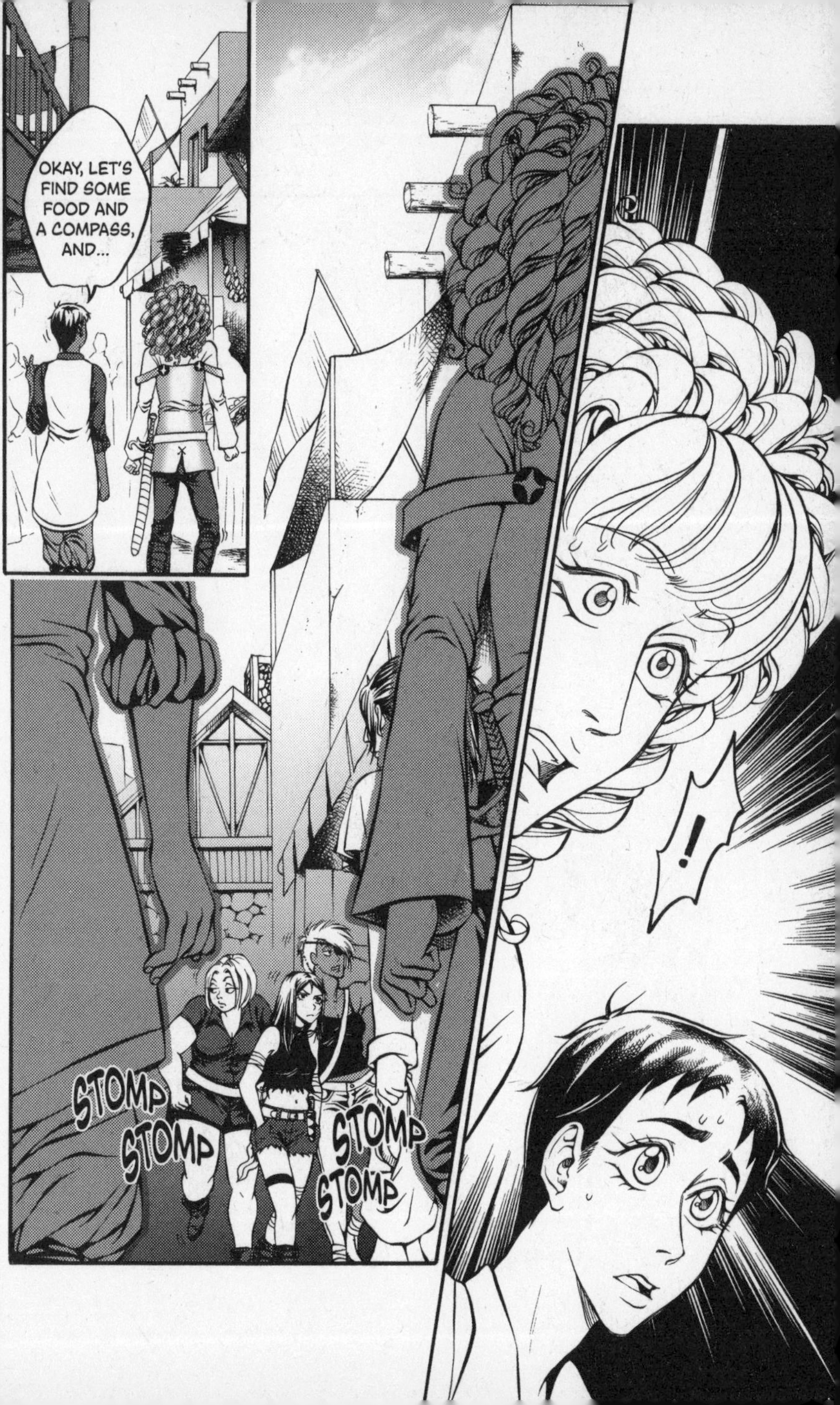
OKAY, LET'S FIND SOME FOOD AND A COMPASS, AND...
STOMP STOMP
STOMP STOMP
!

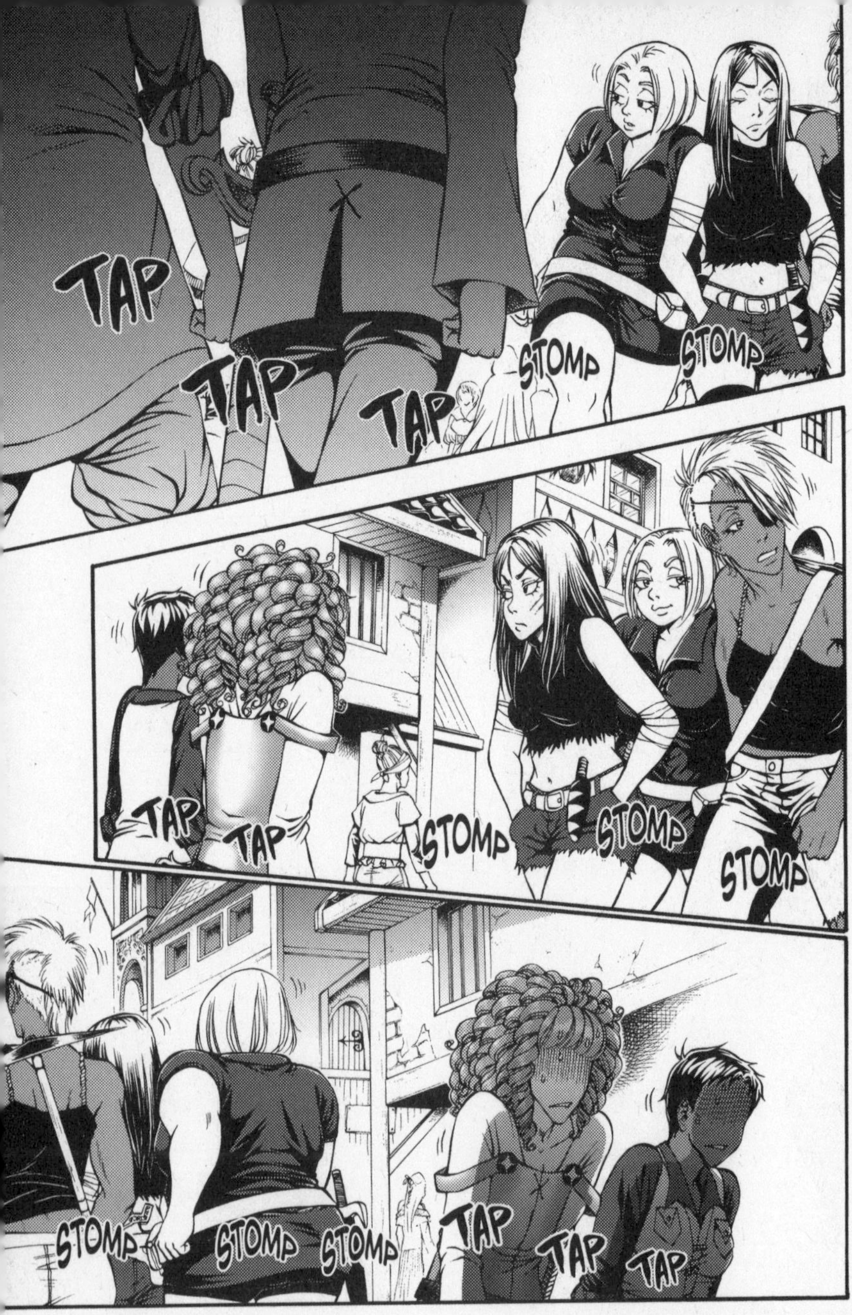
TAP
TAP
TAP
STOMP
STOMP
TAP
TAP
STOMP
STOMP
STOMP
STOMP
STOMP
STOMP
TAP
TAP
TAP

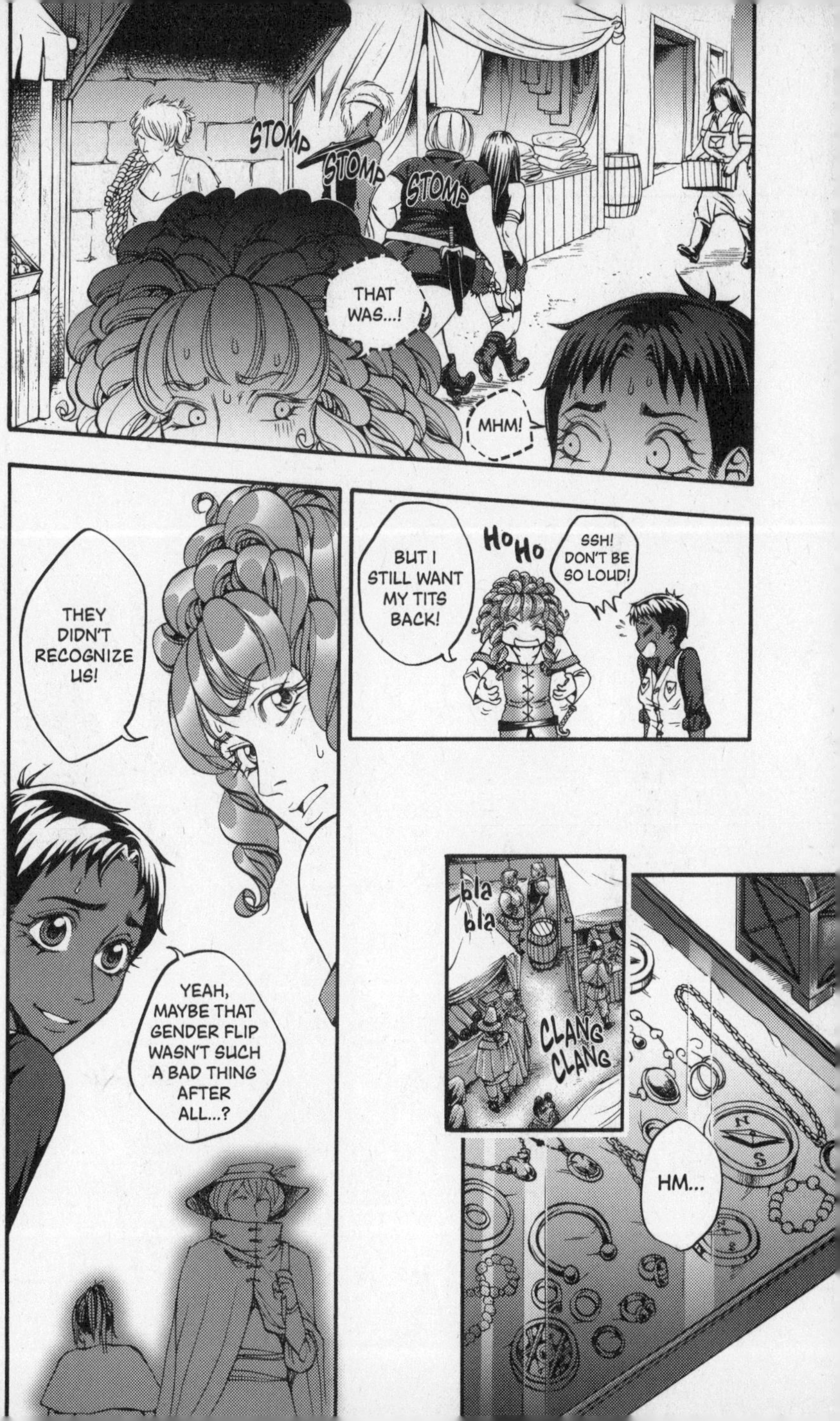
STOMP
STOMP
STOMP
THAT WAS...!
MHM!
THEY DIDN'T RECOGNIZE US!
YEAH, MAYBE THAT GENDER FLIP WASN'T SUCH A BAD THING AFTER ALL...?
BUT I STILL WANT MY TITS BACK!
HO HO
SSH! DON'T BE SO LOUD!
bla bla
CLANG CLANG
HM...

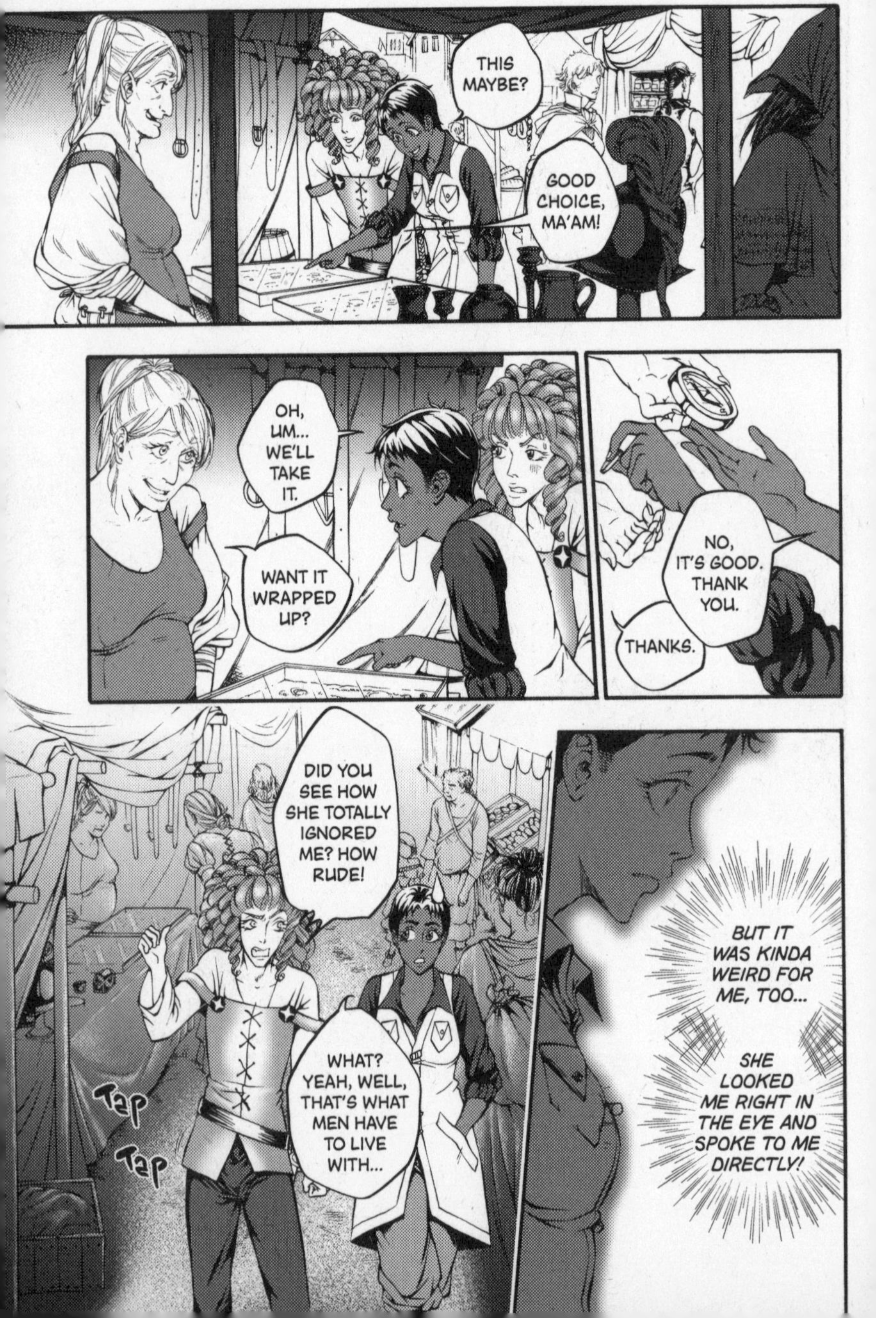
THIS MAYBE?
GOOD CHOICE, MA'AM!
OH, UM... WE'LL TAKE IT.
WANT IT WRAPPED UP?
NO, IT'S GOOD. THANK YOU.
THANKS.
DID YOU SEE HOW SHE TOTALLY IGNORED ME? HOW RUDE!
WHAT? YEAH, WELL, THAT'S WHAT MEN HAVE TO LIVE WITH...
TAP
TAP
BUT IT WAS KINDA WEIRD FOR ME, TOO...
SHE LOOKED ME RIGHT IN THE EYE AND SPOKE TO ME DIRECTLY!

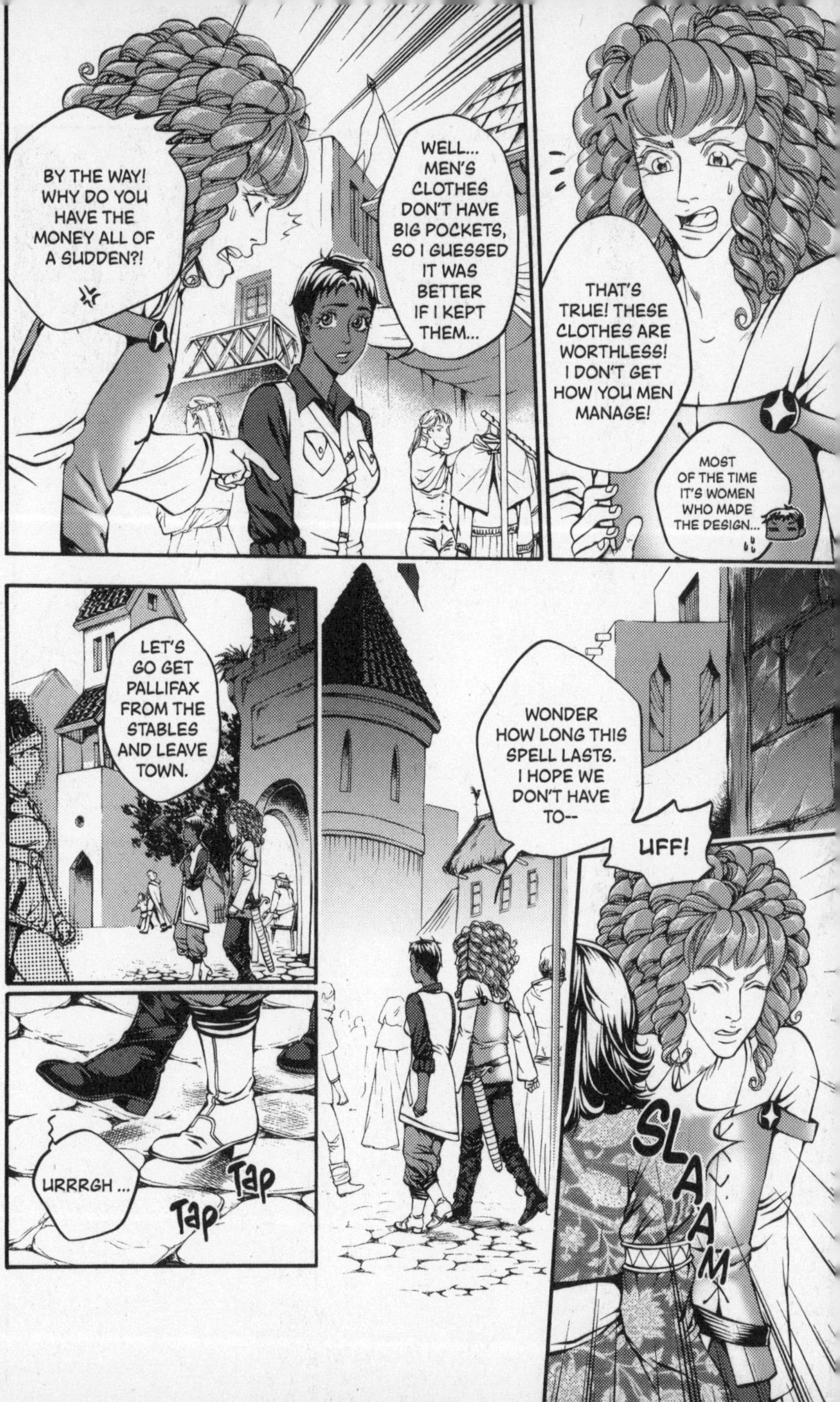
BY THE WAY! WHY DO YOU HAVE THE MONEY ALL OF A SUDDEN?!
WELL... MEN'S CLOTHES DON'T HAVE BIG POCKETS, SO I GUESSED IT WAS BETTER IF I KEPT THEM...
THAT'S TRUE! THESE CLOTHES ARE WORTHLESS! I DON'T GET HOW YOU MEN MANAGE!
MOST OF THE TIME IT'S WOMEN WHO MADE THE DESIGN...
LET'S GO GET PALLIFAX FROM THE STABLES AND LEAVE TOWN.
URRRGH ...
Tap
Tap
WONDER HOW LONG THIS SPELL LASTS. I HOPE WE DON'T HAVE TO--
UFF!
SLAAM

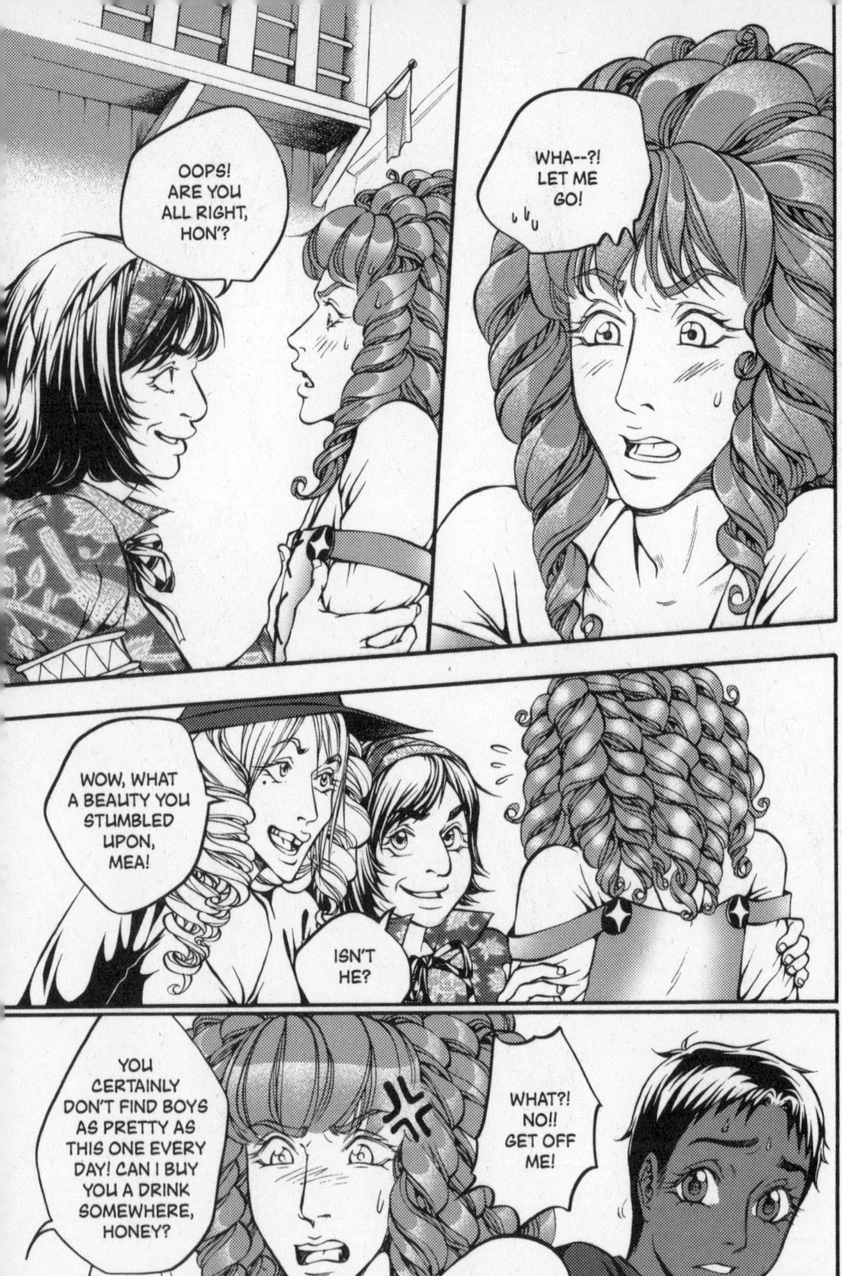
OOPS! ARE YOU ALL RIGHT, HON'?
WHA--?! LET ME GO!
WOW, WHAT A BEAUTY YOU STUMBLED UPON, MEA!
ISN'T HE?
YOU CERTAINLY DON'T FIND BOYS AS PRETTY AS THIS ONE EVERY DAY! CAN I BUY YOU A DRINK SOMEWHERE, HONEY?
WHAT?! NO!! GET OFF ME!

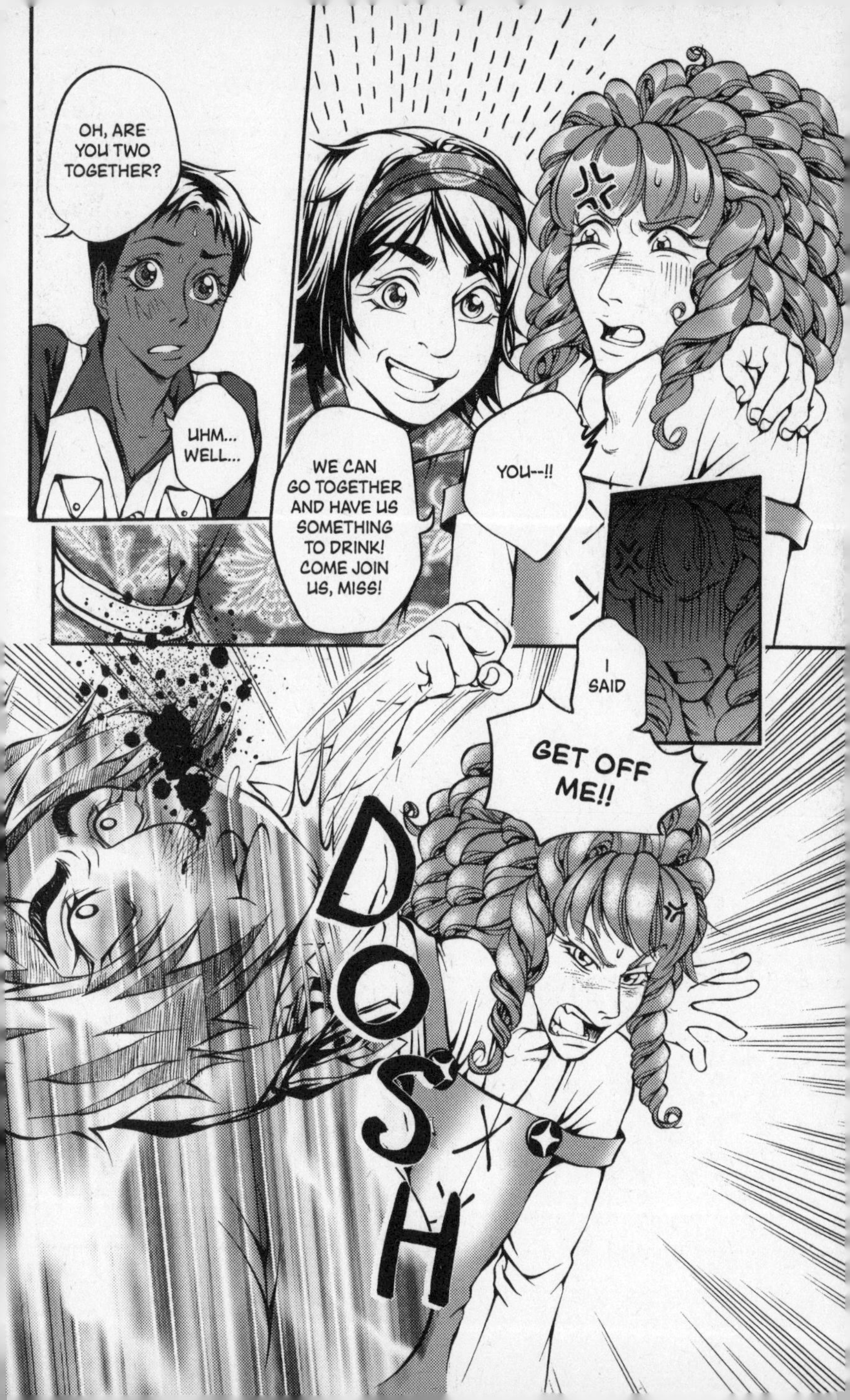
OH, ARE YOU TWO TOGETHER?
UHM... WELL...
WE CAN GO TOGETHER AND HAVE US SOMETHING TO DRINK! COME JOIN US, MISS!
YOU--!!
I SAID
GET OFF ME!!
DOSH

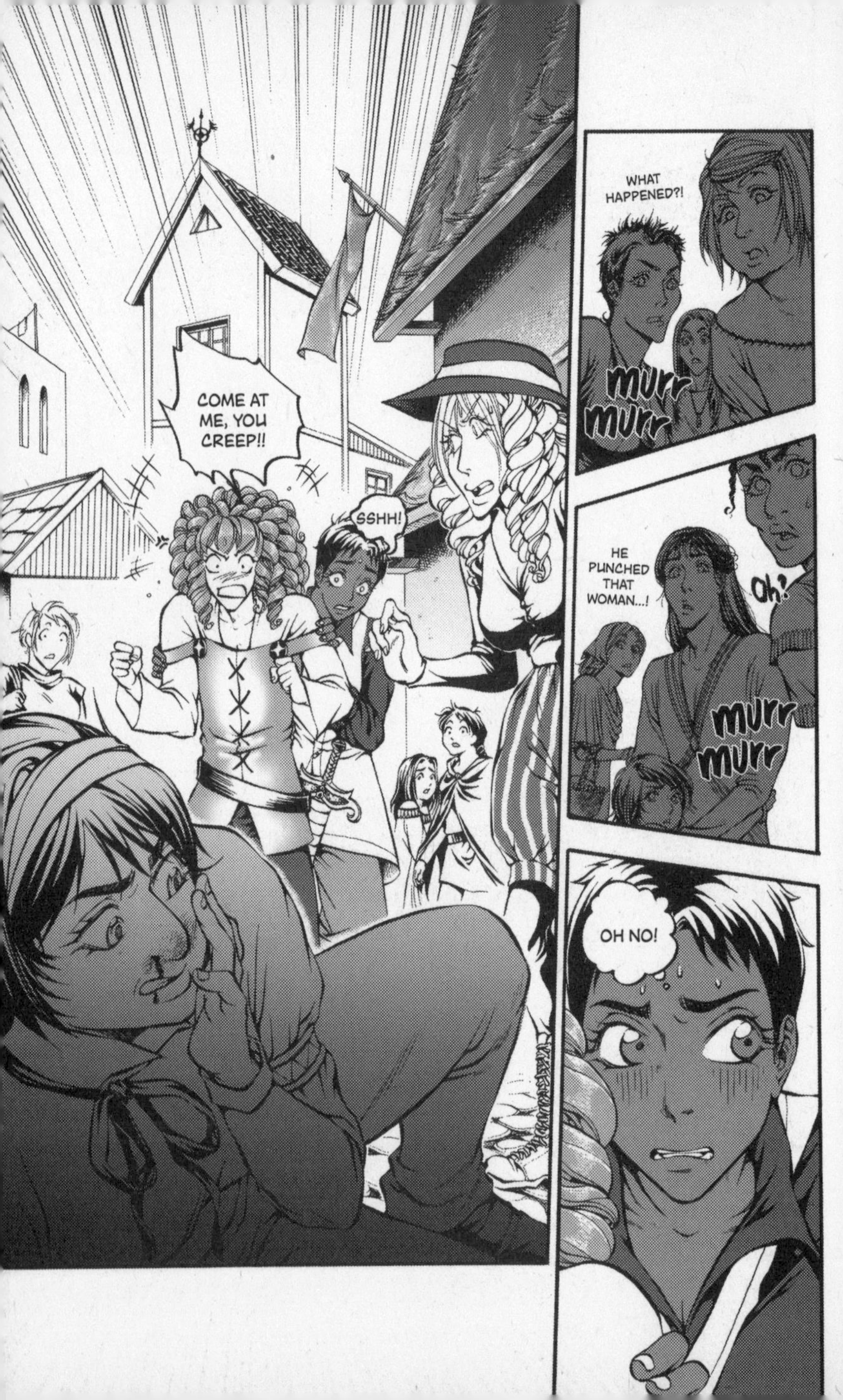
COME AT ME, YOU CREEP!!
SSHH!
WHAT HAPPENED?!
murr murr
HE PUNCHED THAT WOMAN...!
Oh?
murr murr
OH NO!

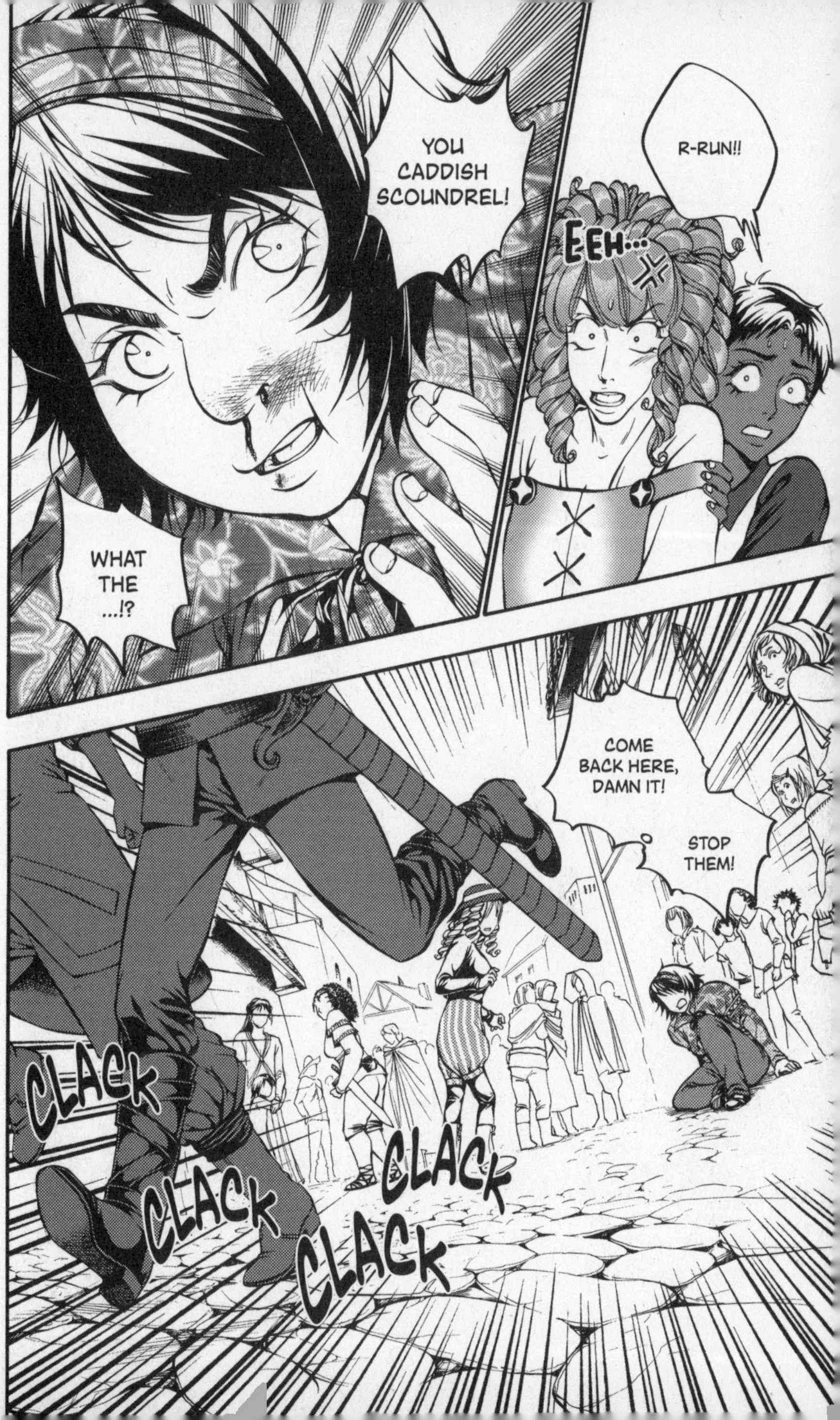

YOU CADDISH SCOUNDREL!
WHAT THE ...!?
R-RUN!!
EEH...
COME BACK HERE, DAMN IT!
STOP THEM!
CLACK
CLACK
CLACK
CLACK

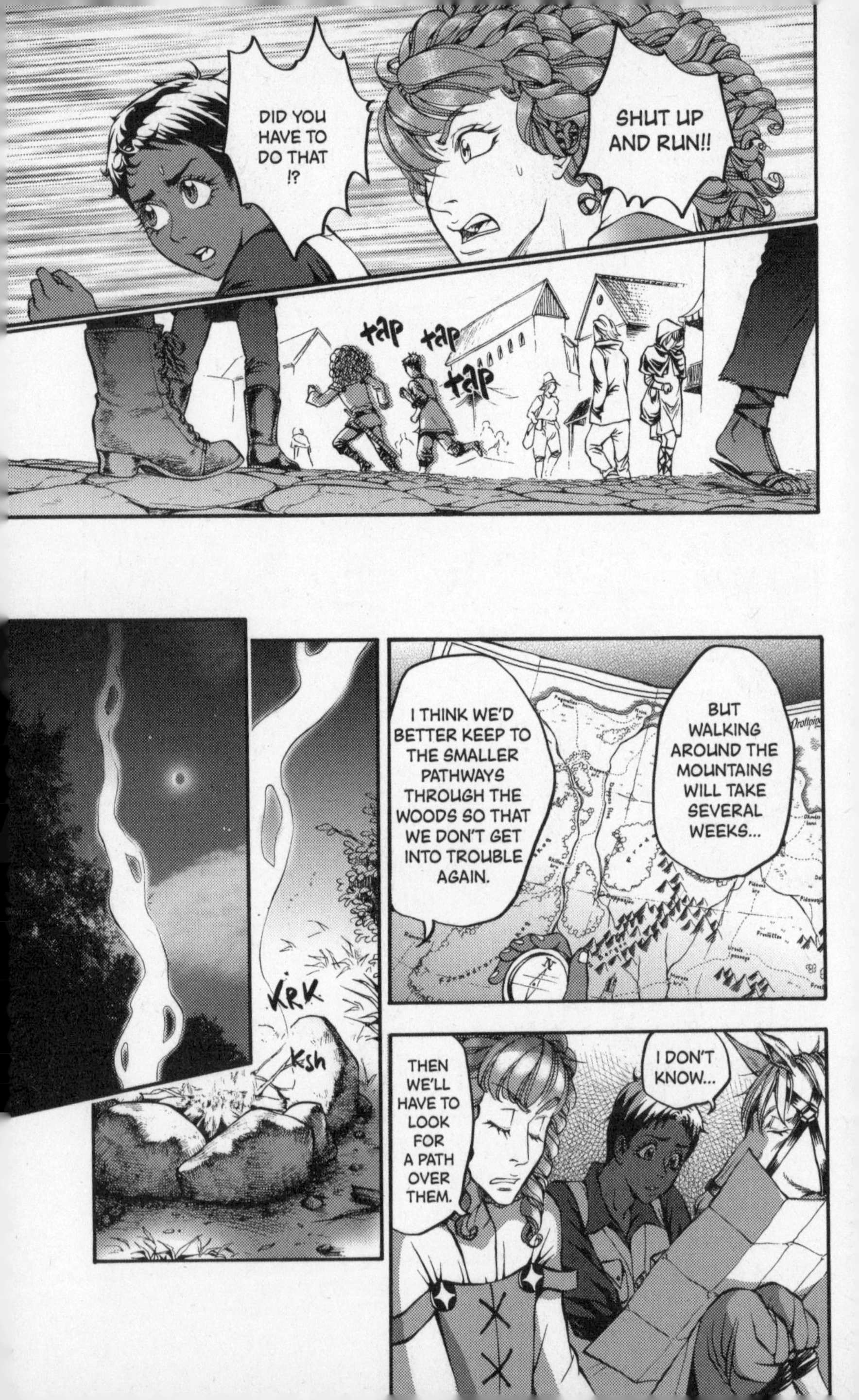
DID YOU HAVE TO DO THAT !?
SHUT UP AND RUN!!
tap tap tap
KRK
Ksh
I THINK WE'D BETTER KEEP TO THE SMALLER PATHWAYS THROUGH THE WOODS SO THAT WE DON'T GET INTO TROUBLE AGAIN.
BUT WALKING AROUND THE MOUNTAINS WILL TAKE SEVERAL WEEKS...
THEN WE'LL HAVE TO LOOK FOR A PATH OVER THEM.
I DON'T KNOW...

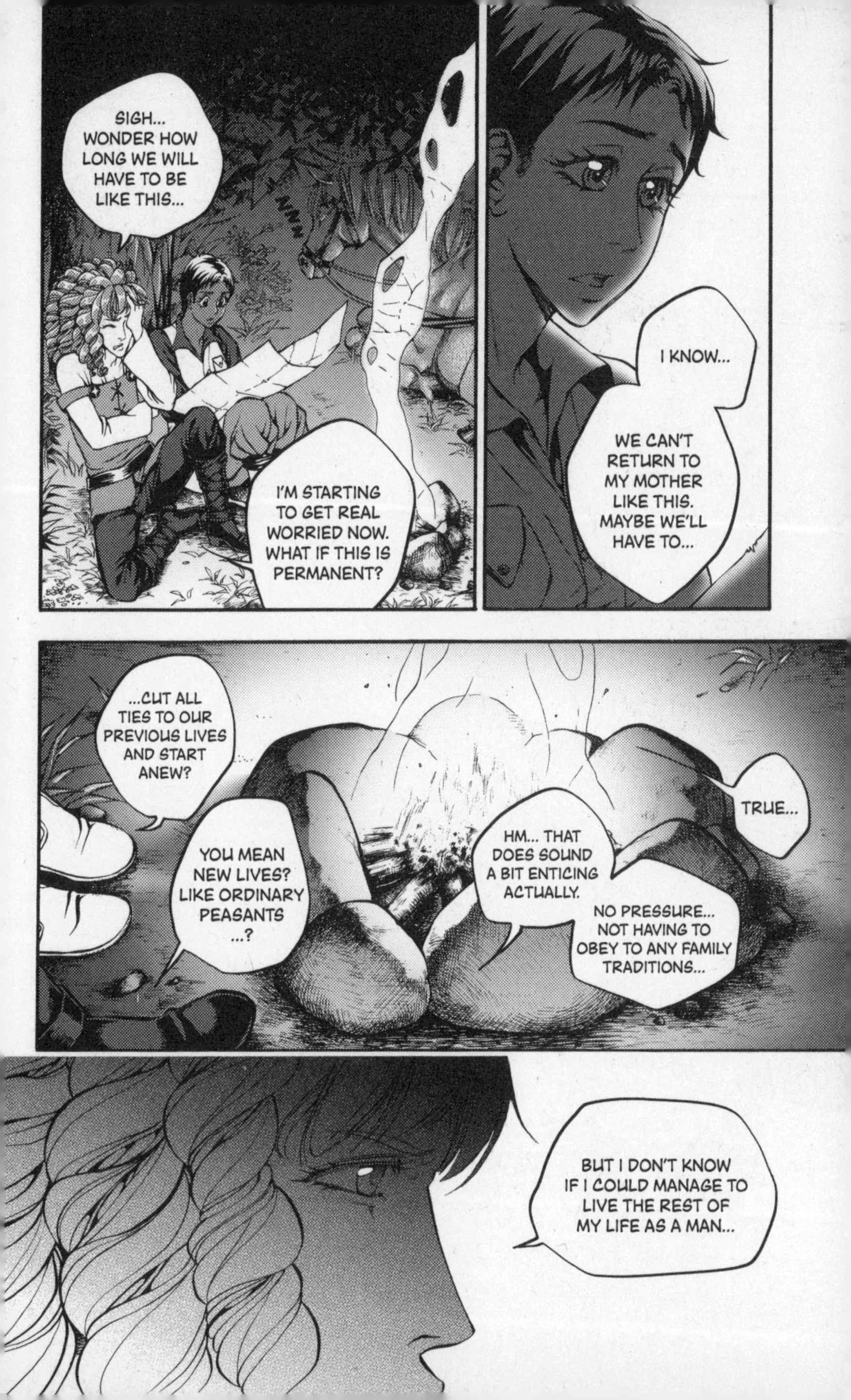
SIGH... WONDER HOW LONG WE WILL HAVE TO BE LIKE THIS...
I'M STARTING TO GET REAL WORRIED NOW. WHAT IF THIS IS PERMANENT?
I KNOW...
WE CAN'T RETURN TO MY MOTHER LIKE THIS. MAYBE WE'LL HAVE TO...
...CUT ALL TIES TO OUR PREVIOUS LIVES AND START ANEW?
YOU MEAN NEW LIVES? LIKE ORDINARY PEASANTS ...?
HM... THAT DOES SOUND A BIT ENTICING ACTUALLY.
TRUE...
NO PRESSURE... NOT HAVING TO OBEY TO ANY FAMILY TRADITIONS...
BUT I DON'T KNOW IF I COULD MANAGE TO LIVE THE REST OF MY LIFE AS A MAN...

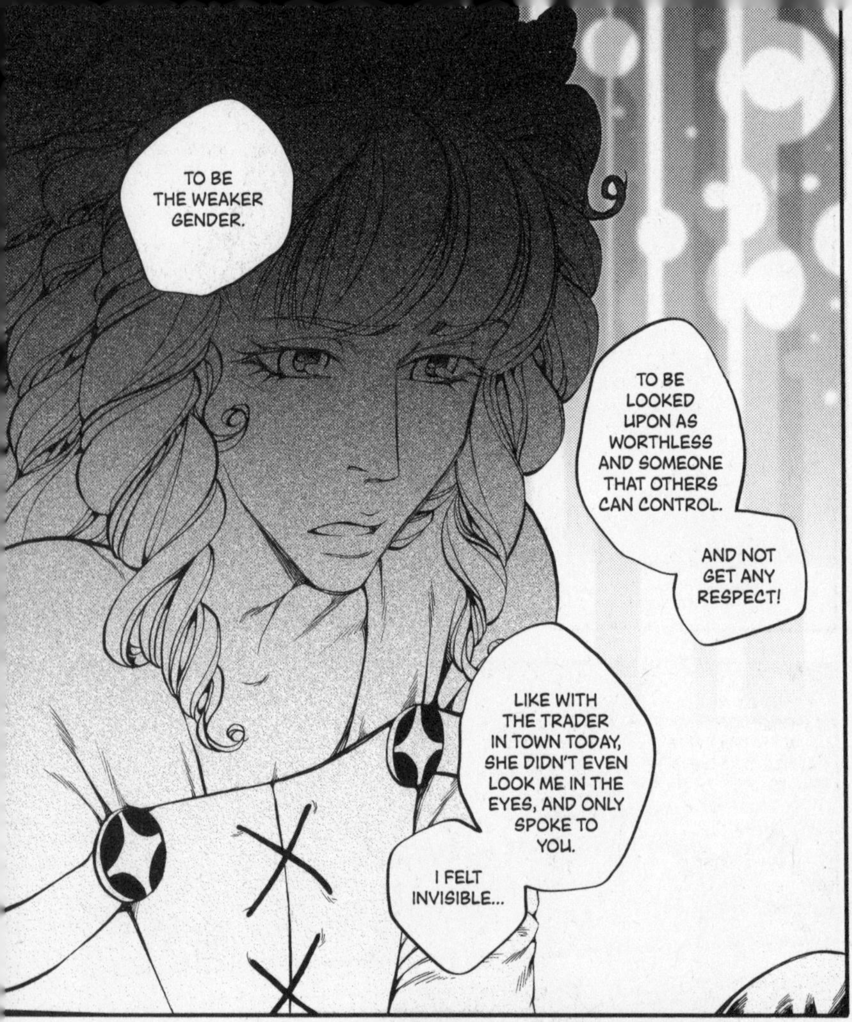
TO BE THE WEAKER GENDER.
TO BE LOOKED UPON AS WORTHLESS AND SOMEONE THAT OTHERS CAN CONTROL.
AND NOT GET ANY RESPECT!
LIKE WITH THE TRADER IN TOWN TODAY, SHE DIDN'T EVEN LOOK ME IN THE EYES, AND ONLY SPOKE TO YOU.
I FELT INVISIBLE...

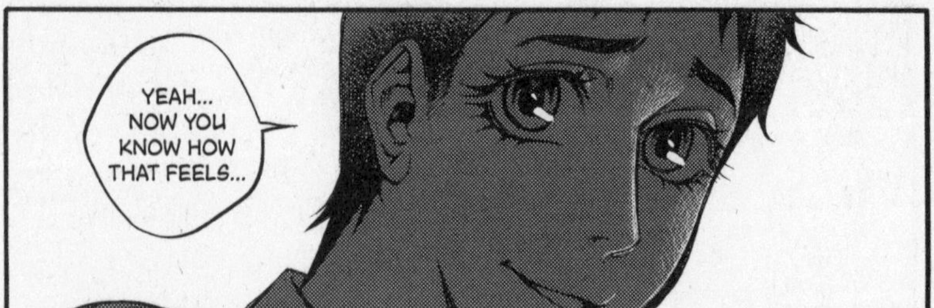
YEAH... NOW YOU KNOW HOW THAT FEELS...

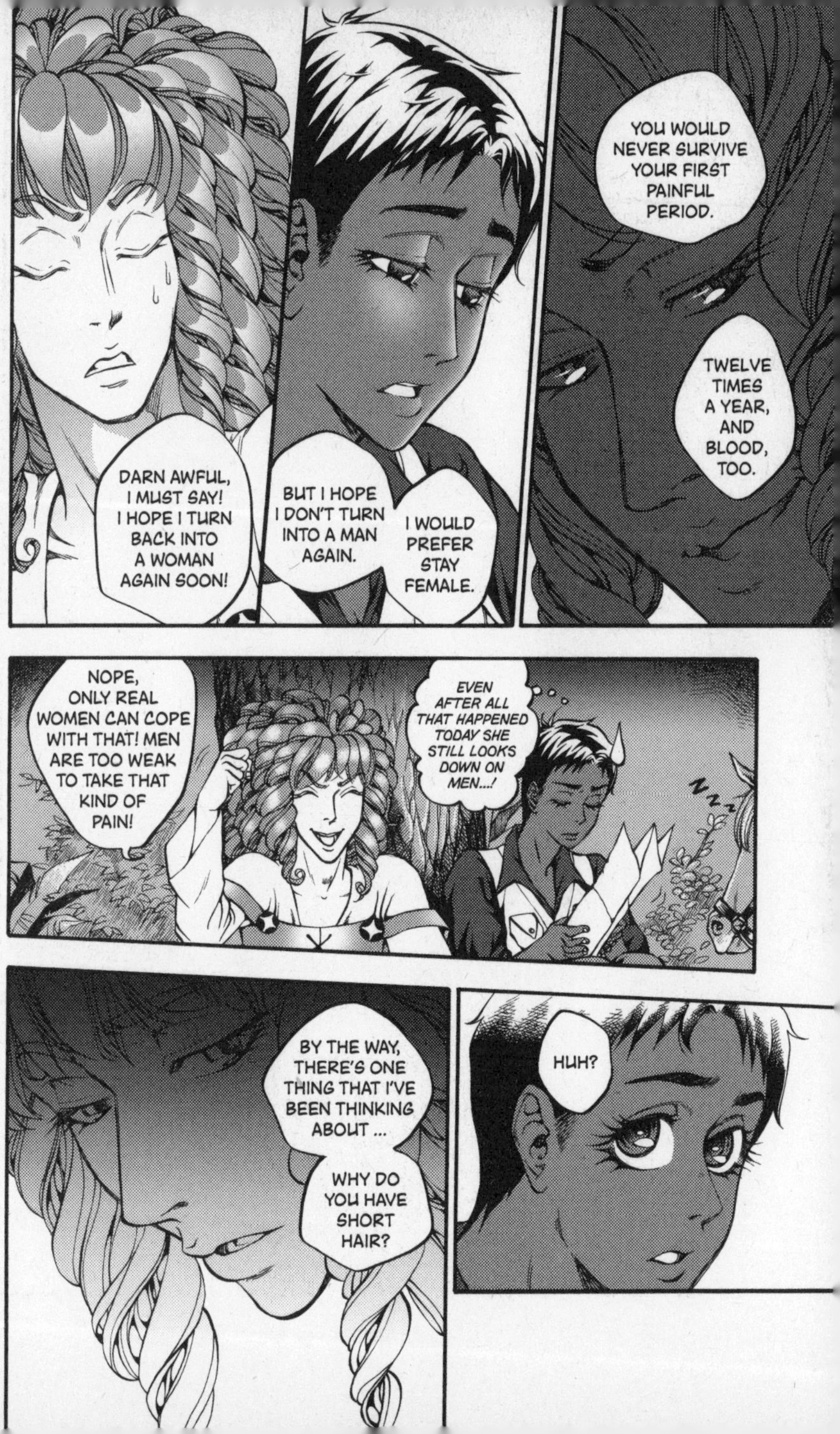
DARN AWFUL, I MUST SAY! I HOPE I TURN BACK INTO A WOMAN AGAIN SOON!
BUT I HOPE I DON'T TURN INTO A MAN AGAIN.
I WOULD PREFER STAY FEMALE.
YOU WOULD NEVER SURVIVE YOUR FIRST PAINFUL PERIOD.
TWELVE TIMES A YEAR, AND BLOOD, TOO.
NOPE, ONLY REAL WOMEN CAN COPE WITH THAT! MEN ARE TOO WEAK TO TAKE THAT KIND OF PAIN!
EVEN AFTER ALL THAT HAPPENED TODAY SHE STILL LOOKS DOWN ON MEN...!
ZZZ
BY THE WAY, THERE'S ONE THING THAT I'VE BEEN THINKING ABOUT ...
WHY DO YOU HAVE SHORT HAIR?
HUH?

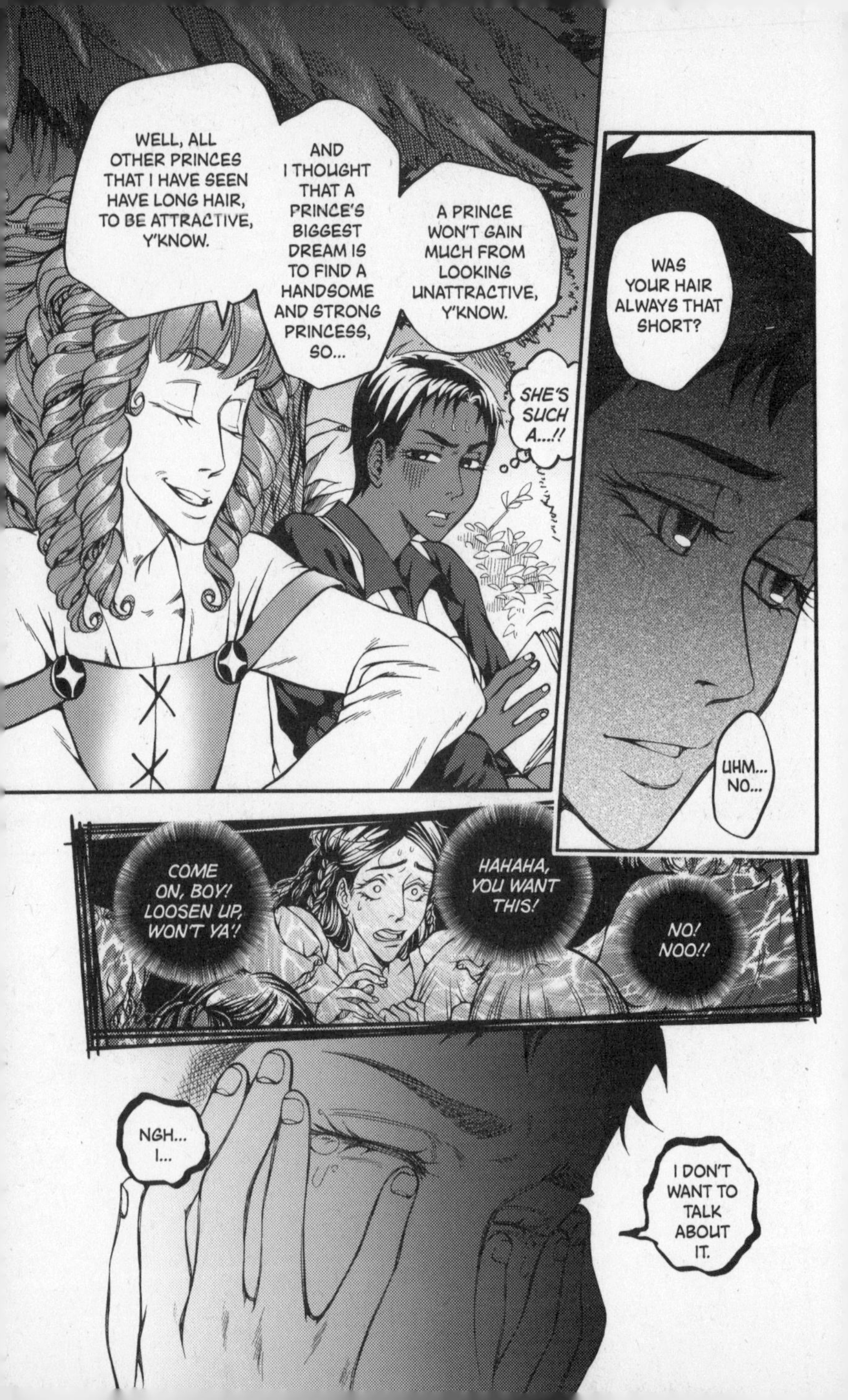
WELL, ALL OTHER PRINCES THAT I HAVE SEEN HAVE LONG HAIR, TO BE ATTRACTIVE, Y'KNOW.
AND I THOUGHT THAT A PRINCE'S BIGGEST DREAM IS TO FIND A HANDSOME AND STRONG PRINCESS, SO...
A PRINCE WON'T GAIN MUCH FROM LOOKING UNATTRACTIVE, Y'KNOW.
SHE'S SUCH A...!!
WAS YOUR HAIR ALWAYS THAT SHORT?
UHM... NO...
COME ON, BOY! LOOSEN UP, WON'T YA'!
HAHAHA, YOU WANT THIS!
NO! NOO!!
NGH... I...
I DON'T WANT TO TALK ABOUT IT.

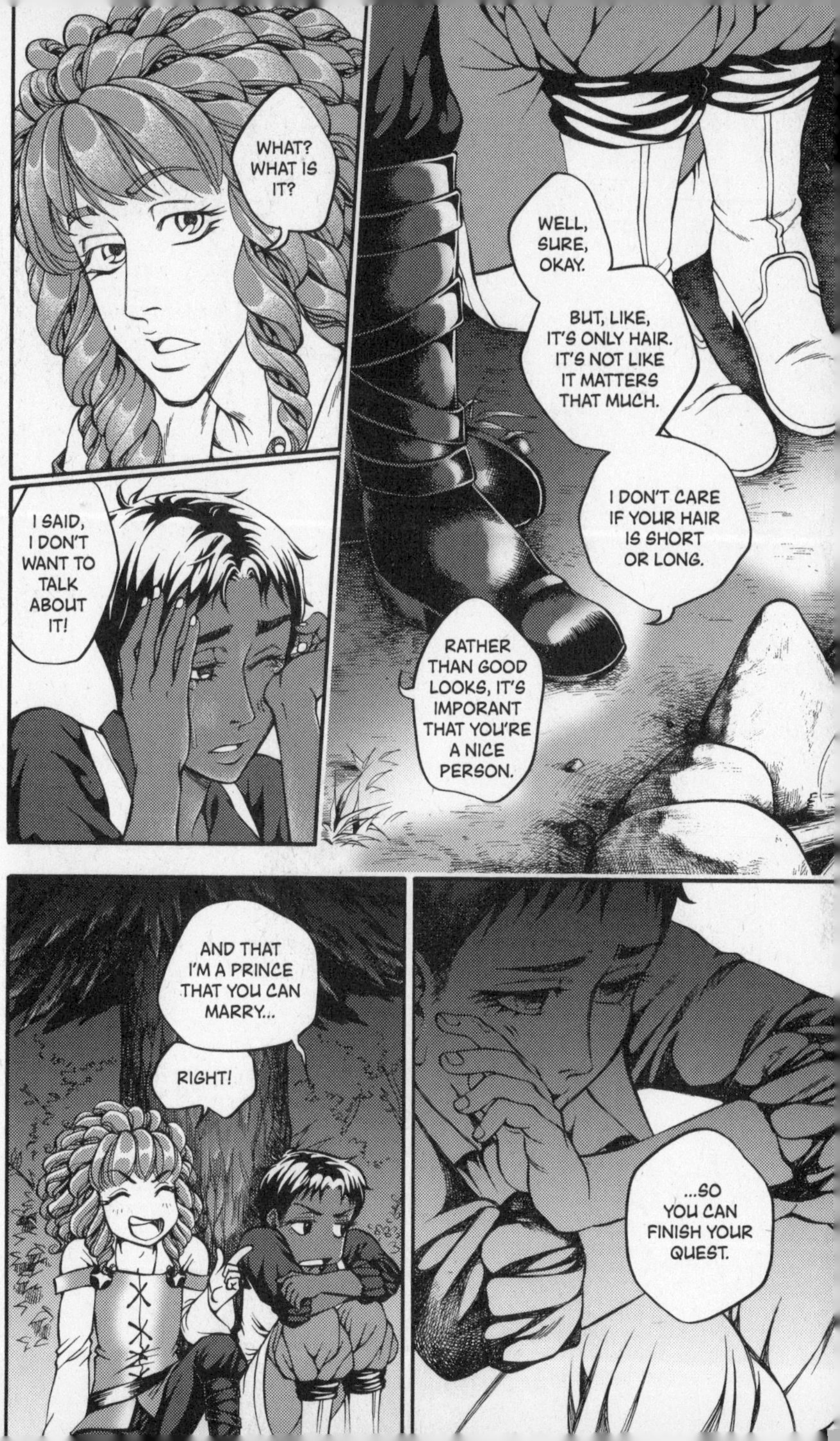
WHAT? WHAT IS IT?
I SAID, I DON'T WANT TO TALK ABOUT IT!
WELL, SURE, OKAY.
BUT, LIKE, IT'S ONLY HAIR. IT'S NOT LIKE IT MATTERS THAT MUCH.
I DON'T CARE IF YOUR HAIR IS SHORT OR LONG.
RATHER THAN GOOD LOOKS, IT'S IMPORANT THAT YOU'RE A NICE PERSON.
AND THAT I'M A PRINCE THAT YOU CAN MARRY...
RIGHT!
...SO YOU CAN FINISH YOUR QUEST.

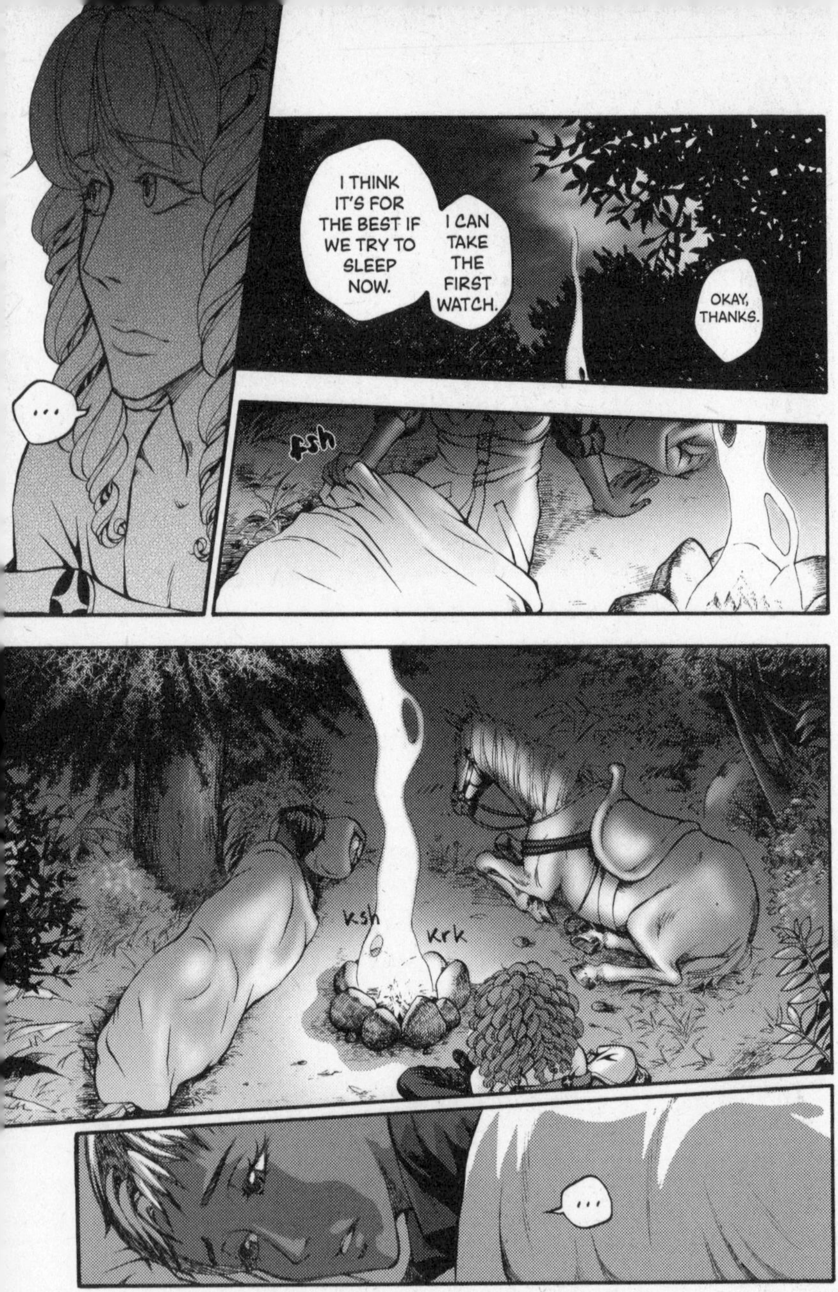
...
I THINK IT'S FOR THE BEST IF WE TRY TO SLEEP NOW.
I CAN TAKE THE FIRST WATCH.
OKAY, THANKS.
fsh
ksh
krk
...

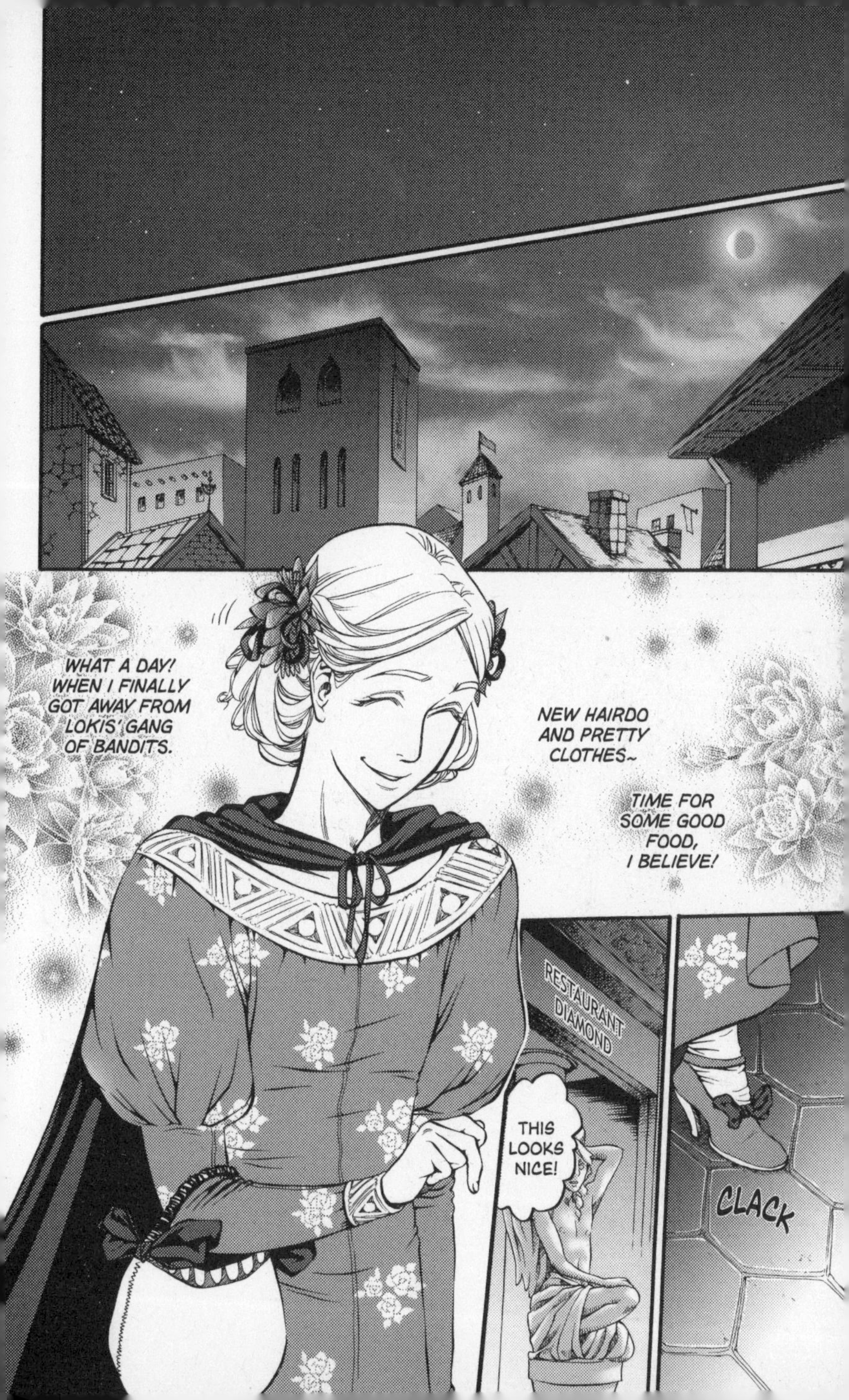
WHAT A DAY! WHEN I FINALLY GOT AWAY FROM LOKIS' GANG OF BANDITS.
NEW HAIRDO AND PRETTY CLOTHES~
TIME FOR SOME GOOD FOOD, I BELIEVE!
RESTAURANT DIAMOND
THIS LOOKS NICE!
CLACK

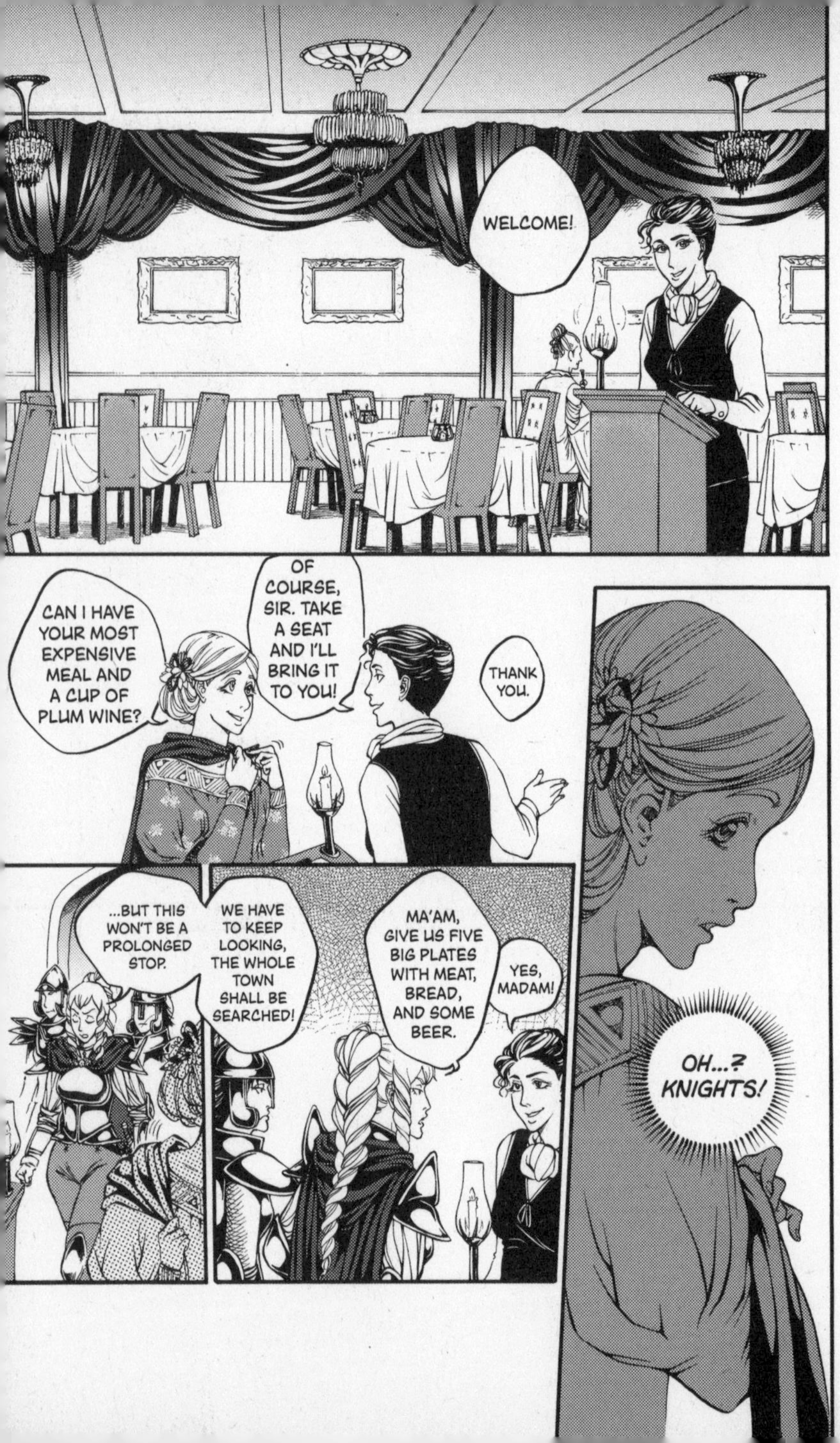
WELCOME!
CAN I HAVE YOUR MOST EXPENSIVE MEAL AND A CUP OF PLUM WINE?
OF COURSE, SIR. TAKE A SEAT AND I'LL BRING IT TO YOU!
THANK YOU.
...BUT THIS WON'T BE A PROLONGED STOP.
WE HAVE TO KEEP LOOKING, THE WHOLE TOWN SHALL BE SEARCHED!
MA'AM, GIVE US FIVE BIG PLATES WITH MEAT, BREAD, AND SOME BEER.
YES, MADAM!
OH...? KNIGHTS!

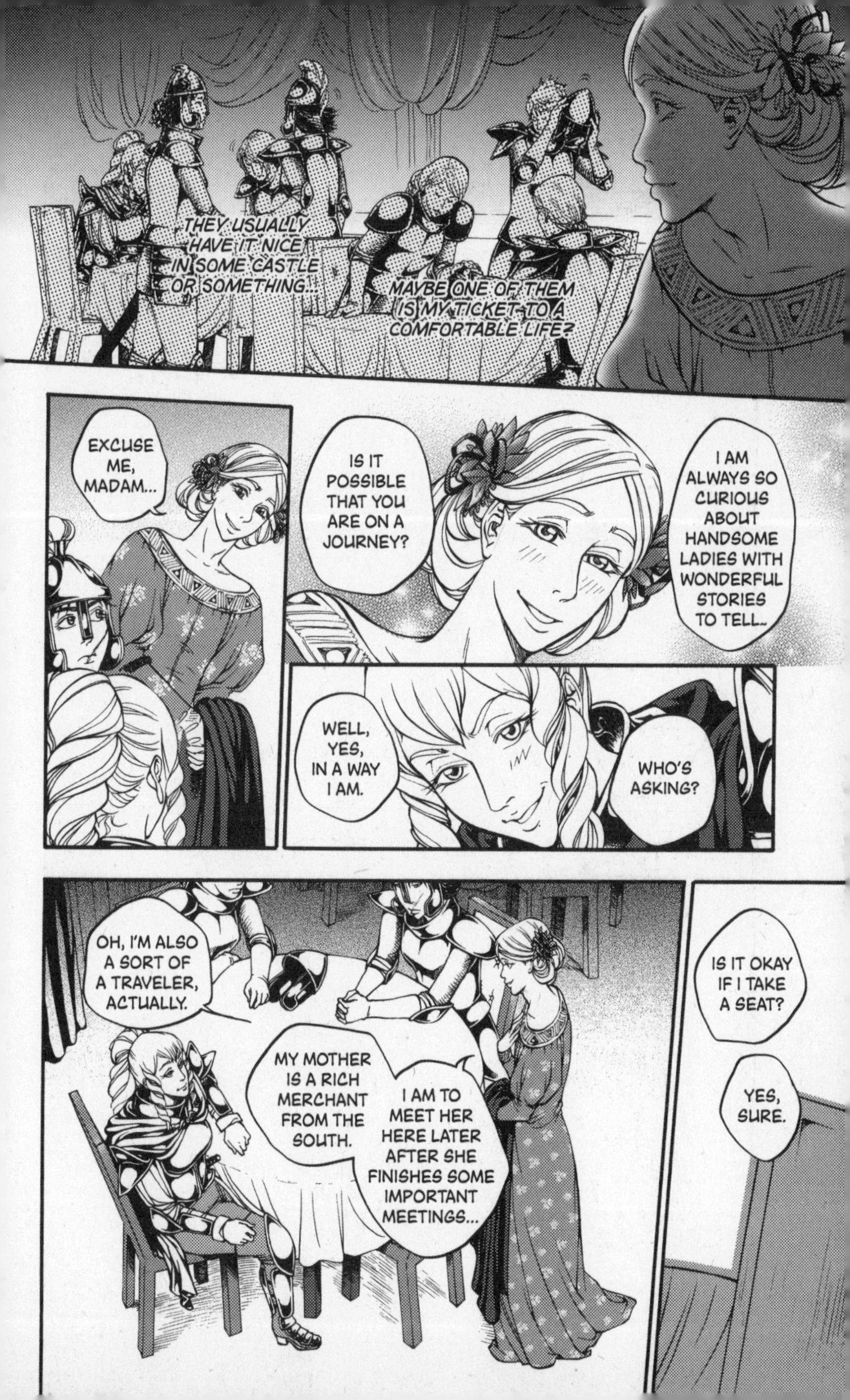
THEY USUALLY HAVE IT NICE IN SOME CASTLE OR SOMETHING...
MAYBE ONE OF THEM IS MY TICKET TO A COMFORTABLE LIFE?
EXCUSE ME, MADAM...
IS IT POSSIBLE THAT YOU ARE ON A JOURNEY?
I AM ALWAYS SO CURIOUS ABOUT HANDSOME LADIES WITH WONDERFUL STORIES TO TELL..
WELL, YES, IN A WAY I AM.
WHO'S ASKING?
OH, I'M ALSO A SORT OF A TRAVELER, ACTUALLY.
MY MOTHER IS A RICH MERCHANT FROM THE SOUTH.
I AM TO MEET HER HERE LATER AFTER SHE FINISHES SOME IMPORTANT MEETINGS...
IS IT OKAY IF I TAKE A SEAT?
YES, SURE.

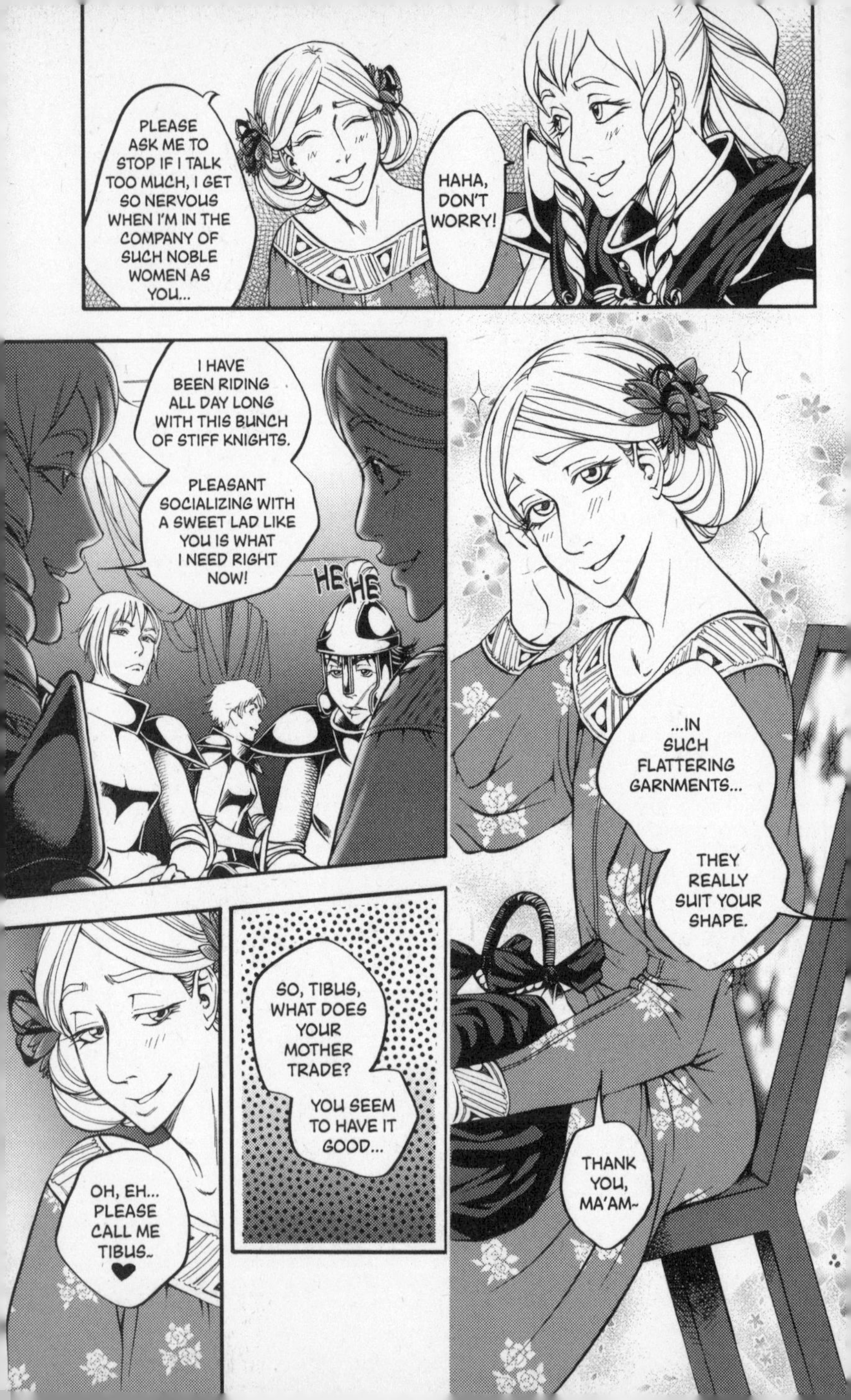
PLEASE ASK ME TO STOP IF I TALK TOO MUCH, I GET SO NERVOUS WHEN I'M IN THE COMPANY OF SUCH NOBLE WOMEN AS YOU...
HAHA, DON'T WORRY!
I HAVE BEEN RIDING ALL DAY LONG WITH THIS BUNCH OF STIFF KNIGHTS.
PLEASANT SOCIALIZING WITH A SWEET LAD LIKE YOU IS WHAT I NEED RIGHT NOW!
HE HE
...IN SUCH FLATTERING GARMENTS...
THEY REALLY SUIT YOUR SHAPE.
THANK YOU, MA'AM~
OH, EH... PLEASE CALL ME TIBUS~ ♥
SO, TIBUS, WHAT DOES YOUR MOTHER TRADE?
YOU SEEM TO HAVE IT GOOD...

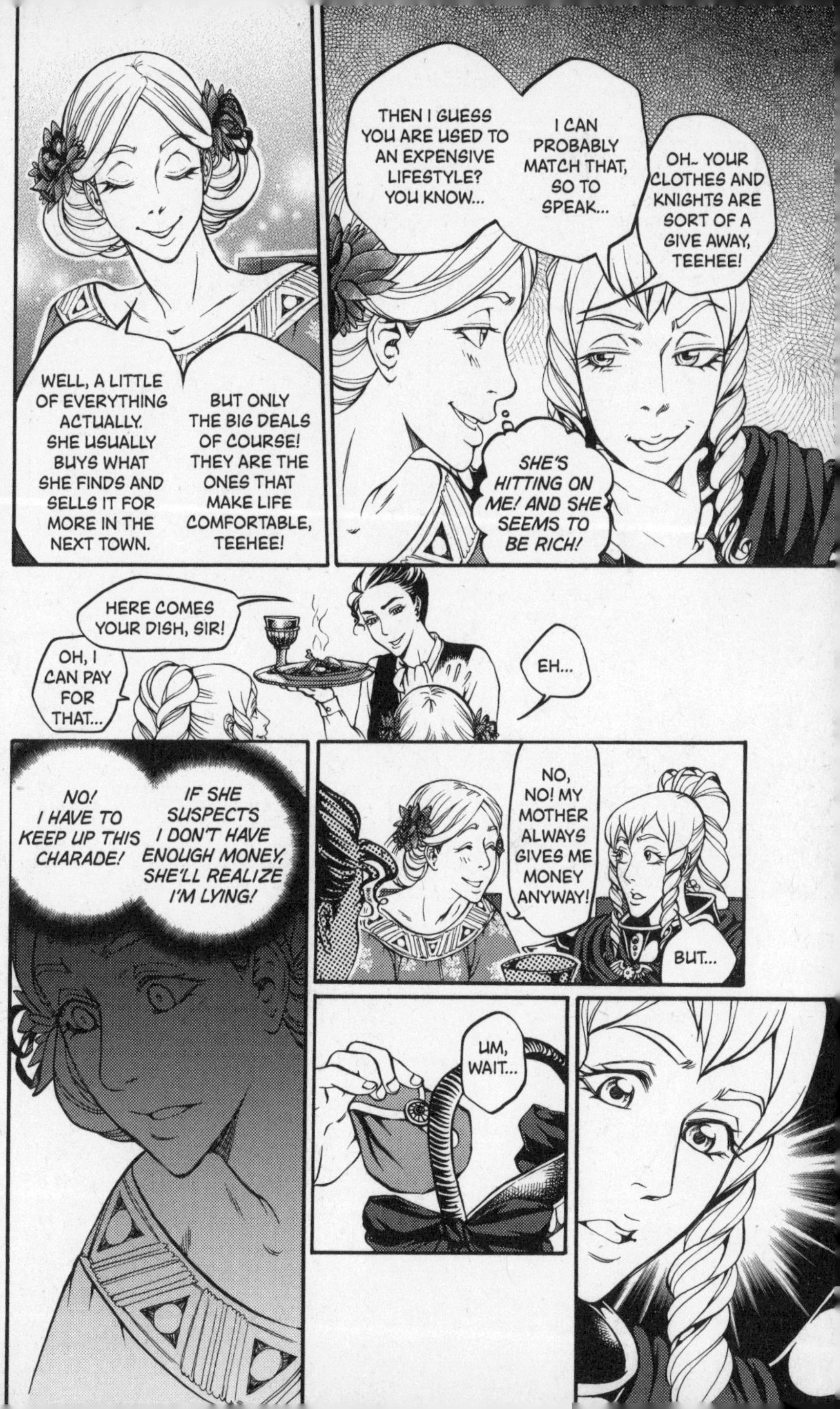
WELL, A LITTLE OF EVERYTHING ACTUALLY. SHE USUALLY BUYS WHAT SHE FINDS AND SELLS IT FOR MORE IN THE NEXT TOWN.
BUT ONLY THE BIG DEALS OF COURSE! THEY ARE THE ONES THAT MAKE LIFE COMFORTABLE, TEEHEE!
THEN I GUESS YOU ARE USED TO AN EXPENSIVE LIFESTYLE? YOU KNOW...
I CAN PROBABLY MATCH THAT, SO TO SPEAK...
OH.. YOUR CLOTHES AND KNIGHTS ARE SORT OF A GIVE AWAY, TEEHEE!
SHE'S HITTING ON ME! AND SHE SEEMS TO BE RICH!
HERE COMES YOUR DISH, SIR!
OH, I CAN PAY FOR THAT...
EH...
NO! I HAVE TO KEEP UP THIS CHARADE!
IF SHE SUSPECTS I DON'T HAVE ENOUGH MONEY, SHE'LL REALIZE I'M LYING!
NO, NO! MY MOTHER ALWAYS GIVES ME MONEY ANYWAY!
BUT...
UM, WAIT...

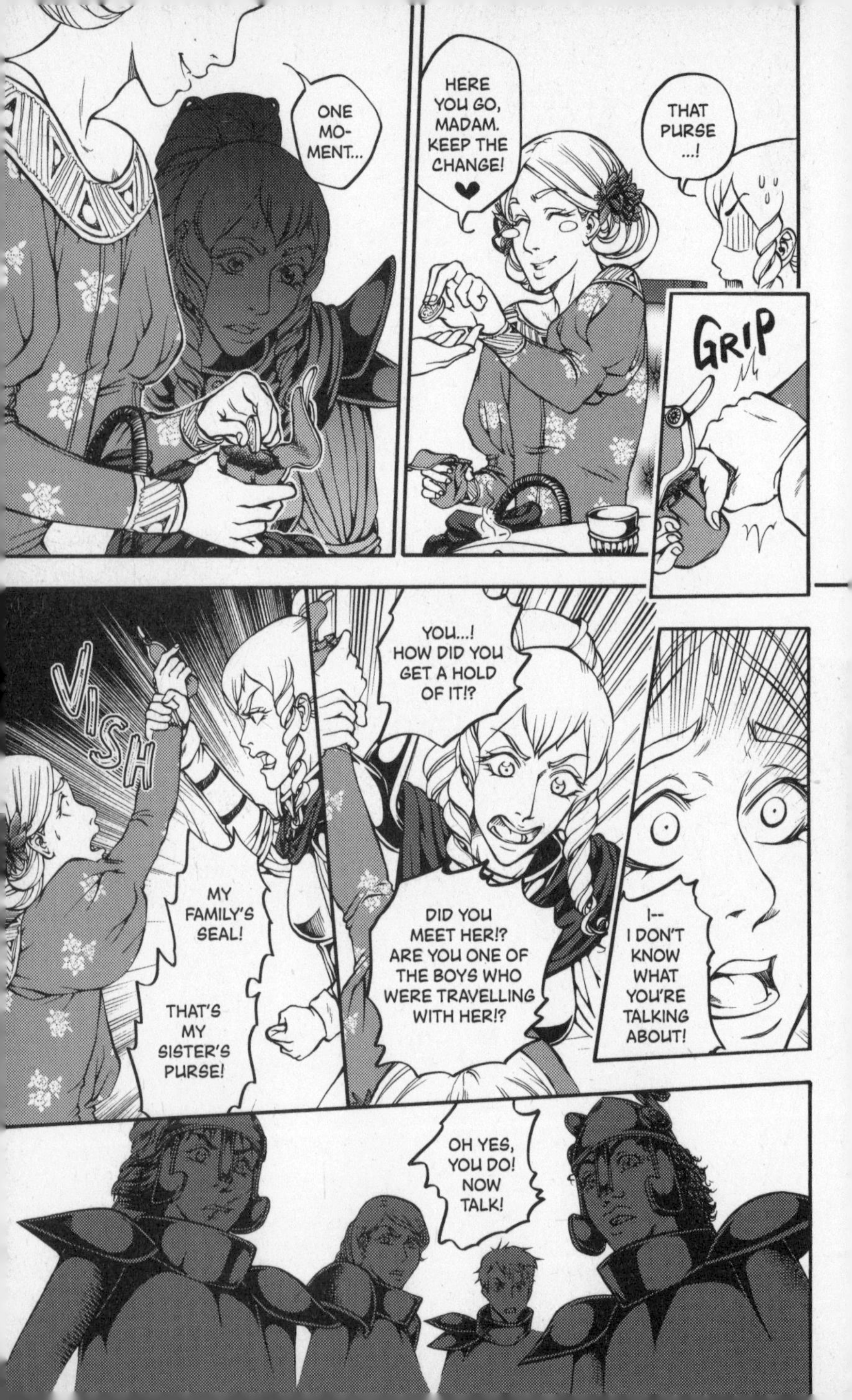
ONE MO- MENT...
HERE YOU GO, MADAM. KEEP THE CHANGE! ❤
THAT PURSE ...!
GRIP
VISH
MY FAMILY'S SEAL!
THAT'S MY SISTER'S PURSE!
YOU...! HOW DID YOU GET A HOLD OF IT!?
DID YOU MEET HER!? ARE YOU ONE OF THE BOYS WHO WERE TRAVELLING WITH HER!?
I-- I DON'T KNOW WHAT YOU'RE TALKING ABOUT!
OH YES, YOU DO! NOW TALK!

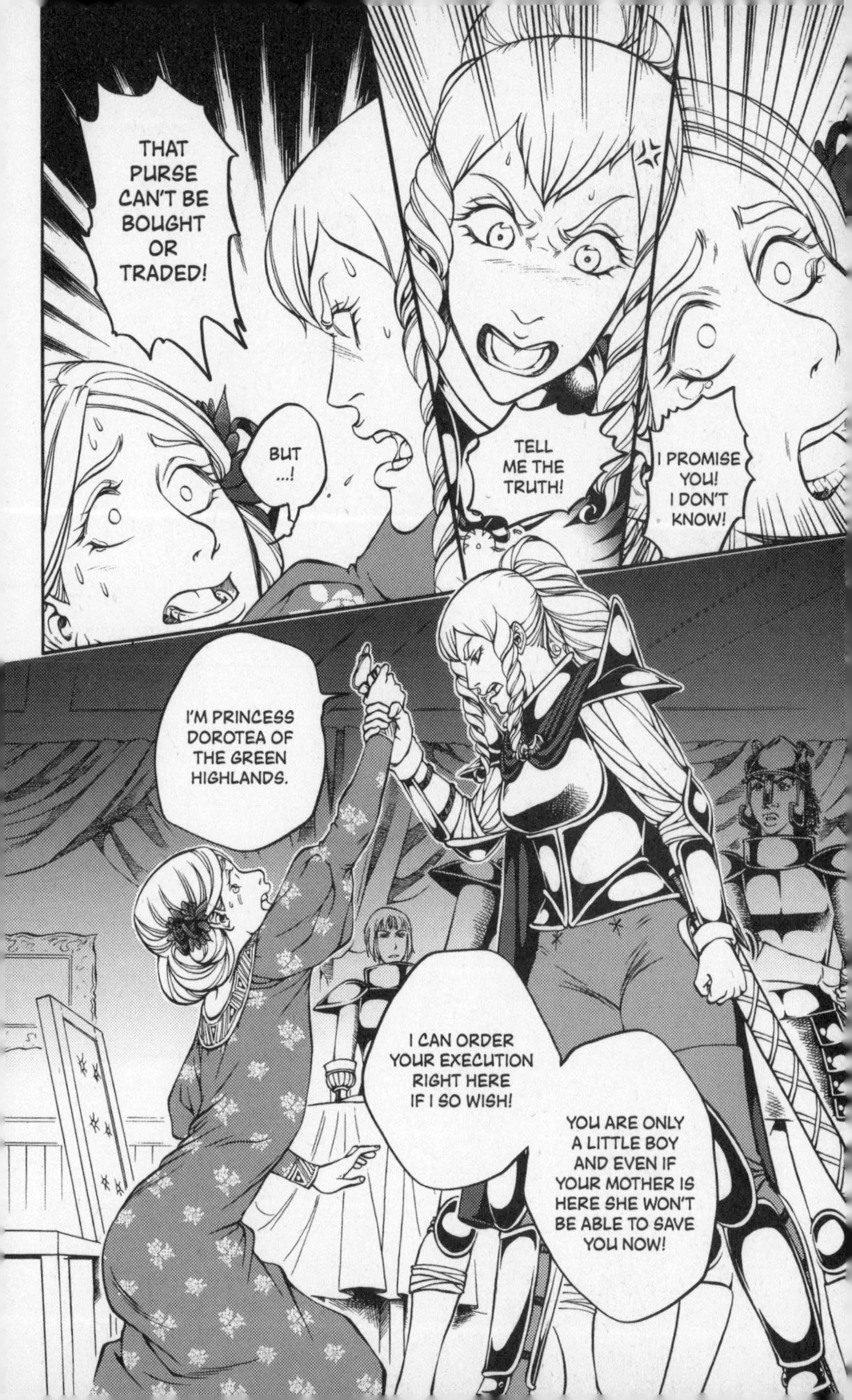
THAT PURSE CAN'T BE BOUGHT OR TRADED!
BUT ...!
TELL ME THE TRUTH!
I PROMISE YOU! I DON'T KNOW!
I'M PRINCESS DOROTEA OF THE GREEN HIGHLANDS.
I CAN ORDER YOUR EXECUTION RIGHT HERE IF I SO WISH!
YOU ARE ONLY A LITTLE BOY AND EVEN IF YOUR MOTHER IS HERE SHE WON'T BE ABLE TO SAVE YOU NOW!

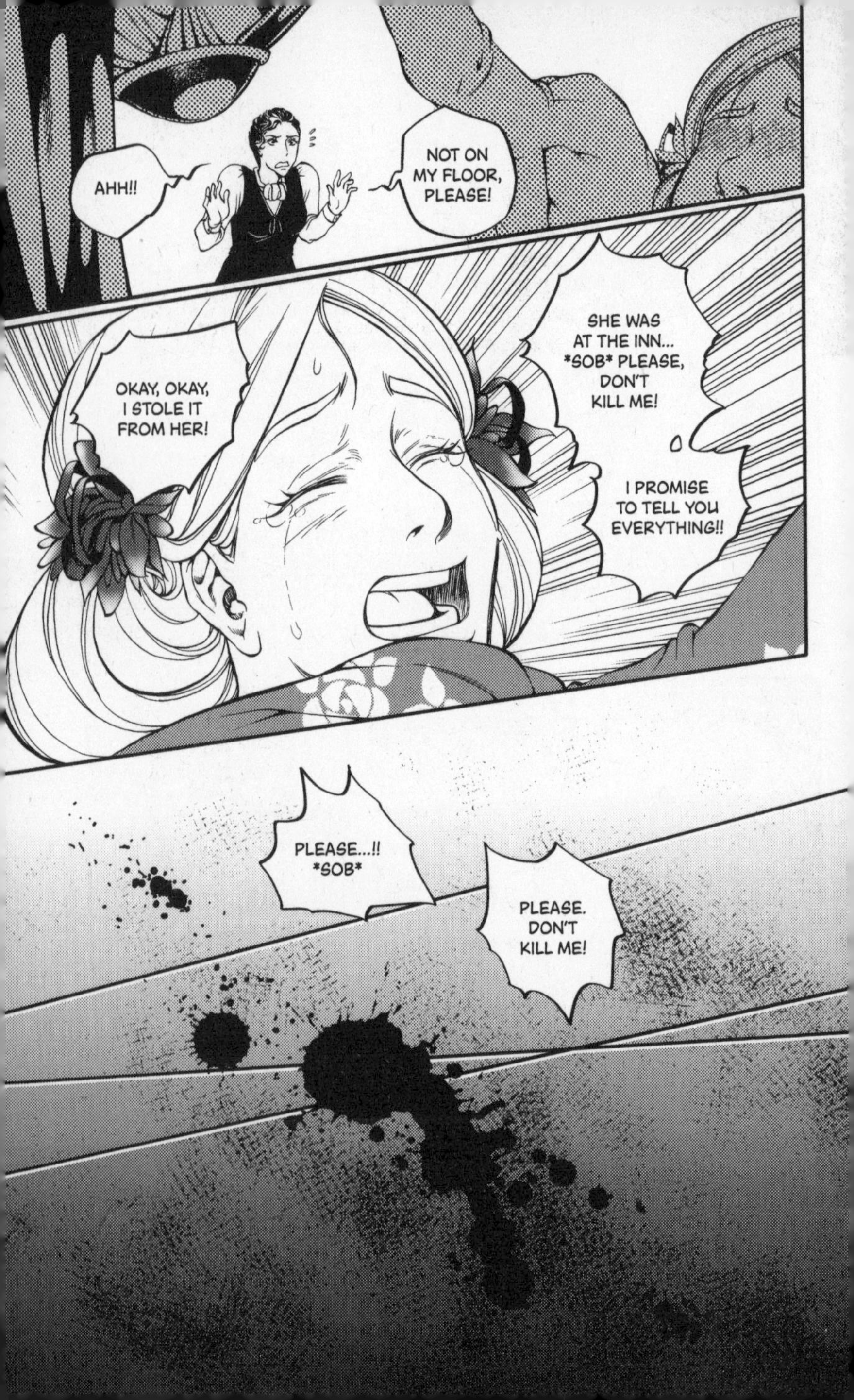
AHH!!
NOT ON MY FLOOR, PLEASE!
OKAY, OKAY, I STOLE IT FROM HER!
SHE WAS AT THE INN... *SOB* PLEASE, DON'T KILL ME!
I PROMISE TO TELL YOU EVERYTHING!!
PLEASE...!! *SOB*
PLEASE. DON'T KILL ME!

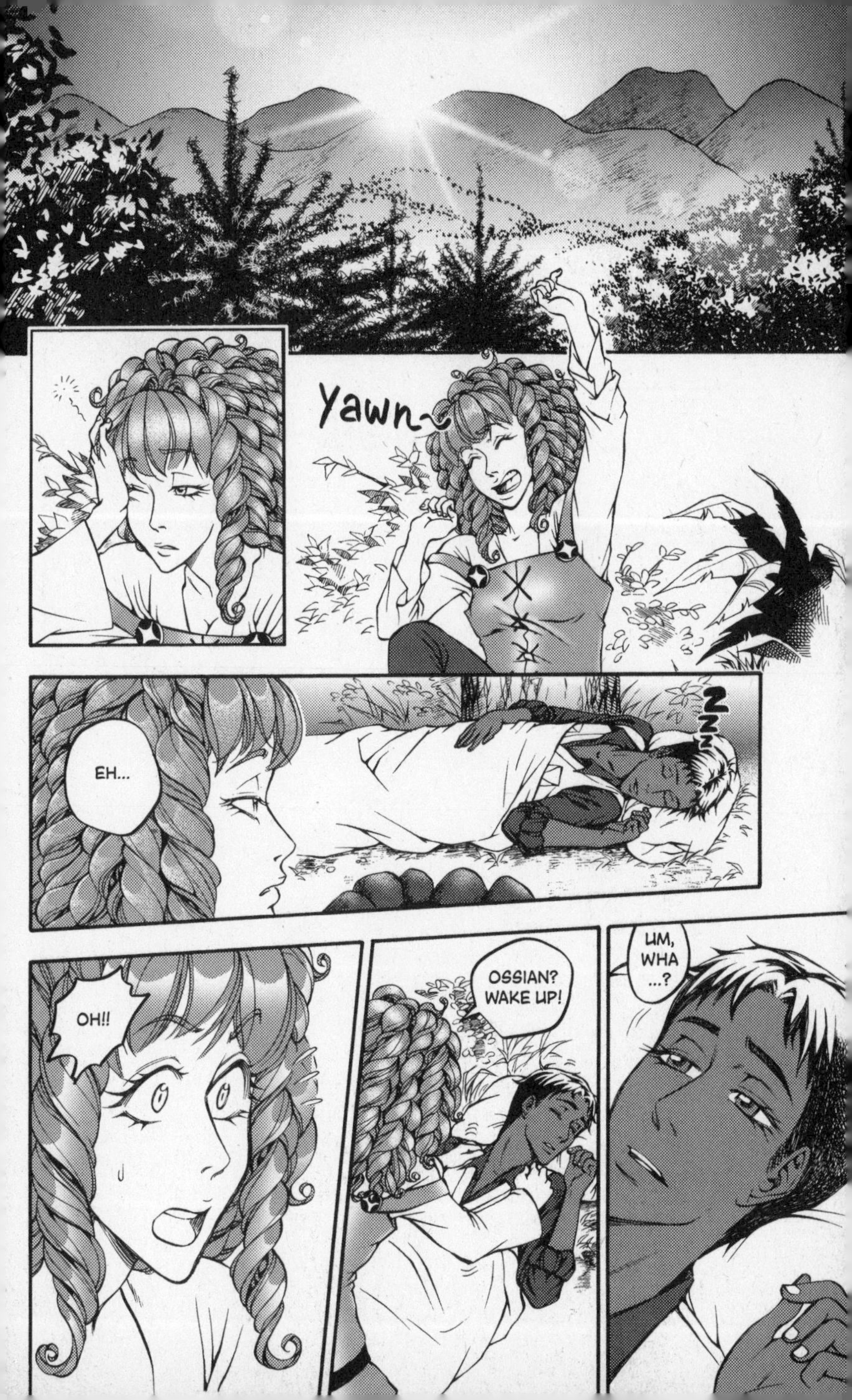
Yawn~
EH...
ZZZ
OH!!
OSSIAN? WAKE UP!
UM, WHA ...?

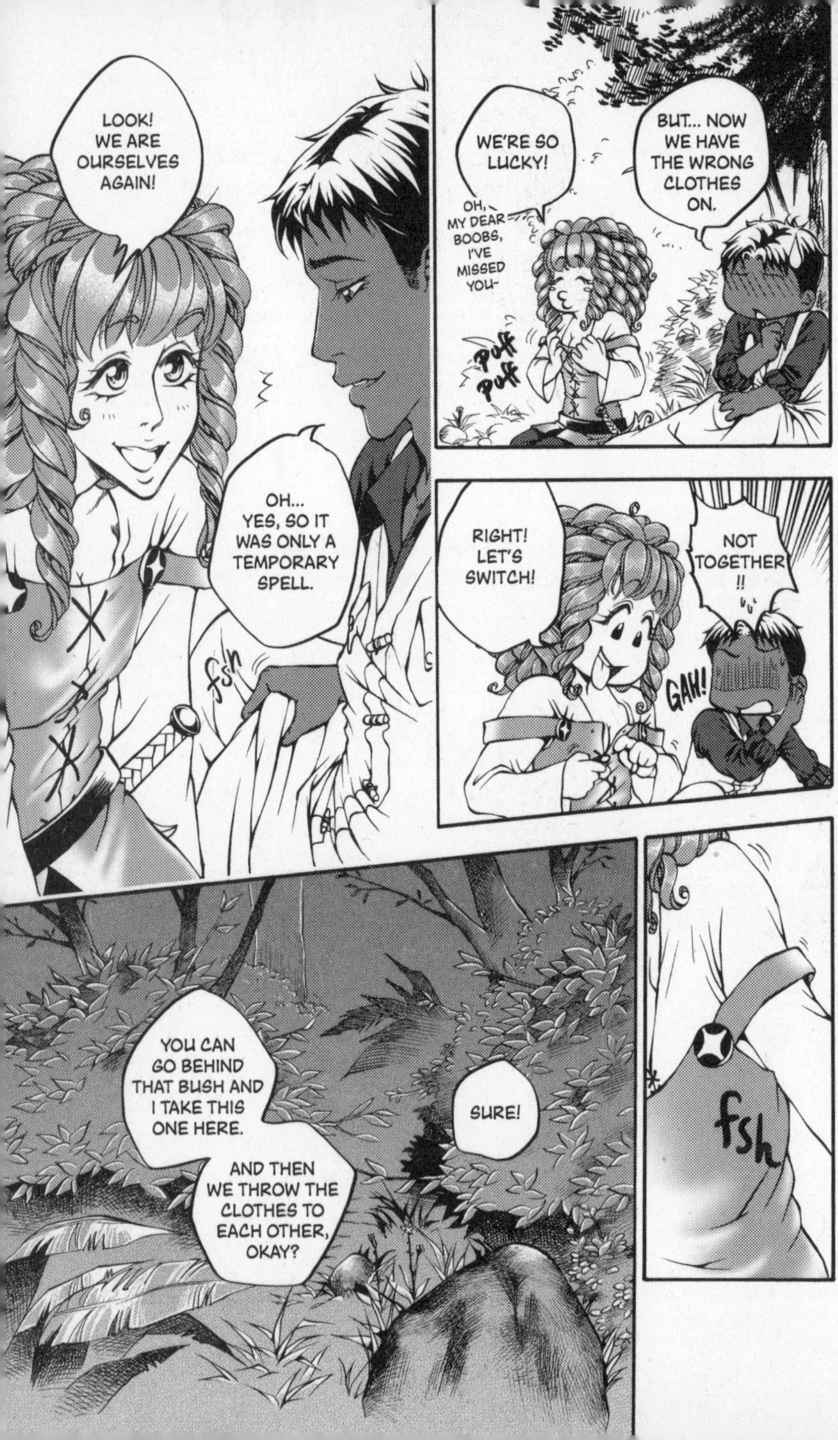
LOOK! WE ARE OURSELVES AGAIN!
OH... YES, SO IT WAS ONLY A TEMPORARY SPELL.
fsh
WE'RE SO LUCKY!
OH, MY DEAR BOOBS, I'VE MISSED YOU~
Puff Puff
BUT... NOW WE HAVE THE WRONG CLOTHES ON.
RIGHT! LET'S SWITCH!
NOT TOGETHER!!
GAH!
YOU CAN GO BEHIND THAT BUSH AND I TAKE THIS ONE HERE.
AND THEN WE THROW THE CLOTHES TO EACH OTHER, OKAY?
SURE!
fsh

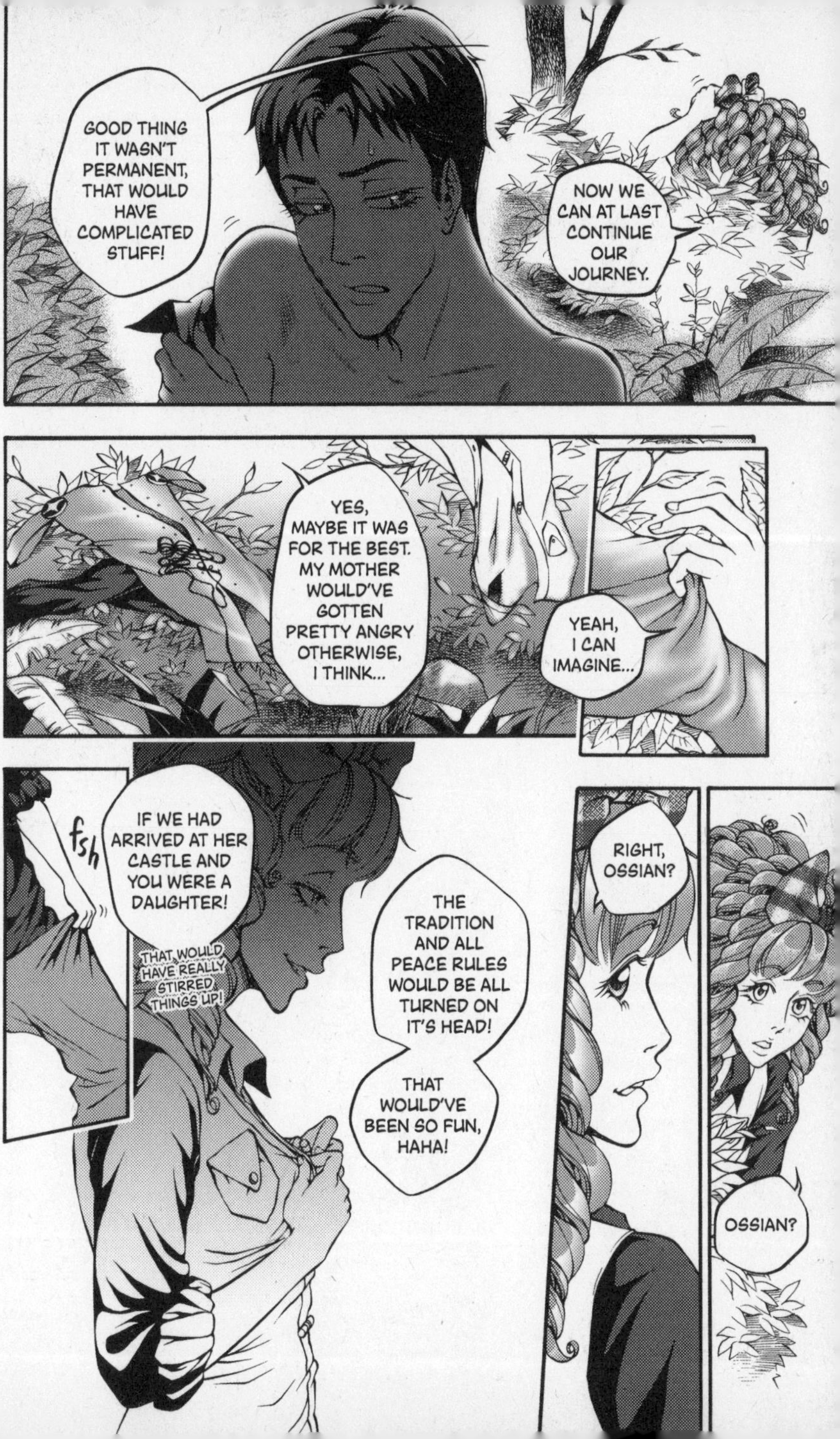

GOOD THING IT WASN'T PERMANENT, THAT WOULD HAVE COMPLICATED STUFF!
NOW WE CAN AT LAST CONTINUE OUR JOURNEY.
YES, MAYBE IT WAS FOR THE BEST. MY MOTHER WOULD'VE GOTTEN PRETTY ANGRY OTHERWISE, I THINK...
YEAH, I CAN IMAGINE...
fsh
IF WE HAD ARRIVED AT HER CASTLE AND YOU WERE A DAUGHTER!
THAT WOULD HAVE REALLY STIRRED THINGS UP!
THE TRADITION AND ALL PEACE RULES WOULD BE ALL TURNED ON IT'S HEAD!
THAT WOULD'VE BEEN SO FUN, HAHA!
RIGHT, OSSIAN?
OSSIAN?

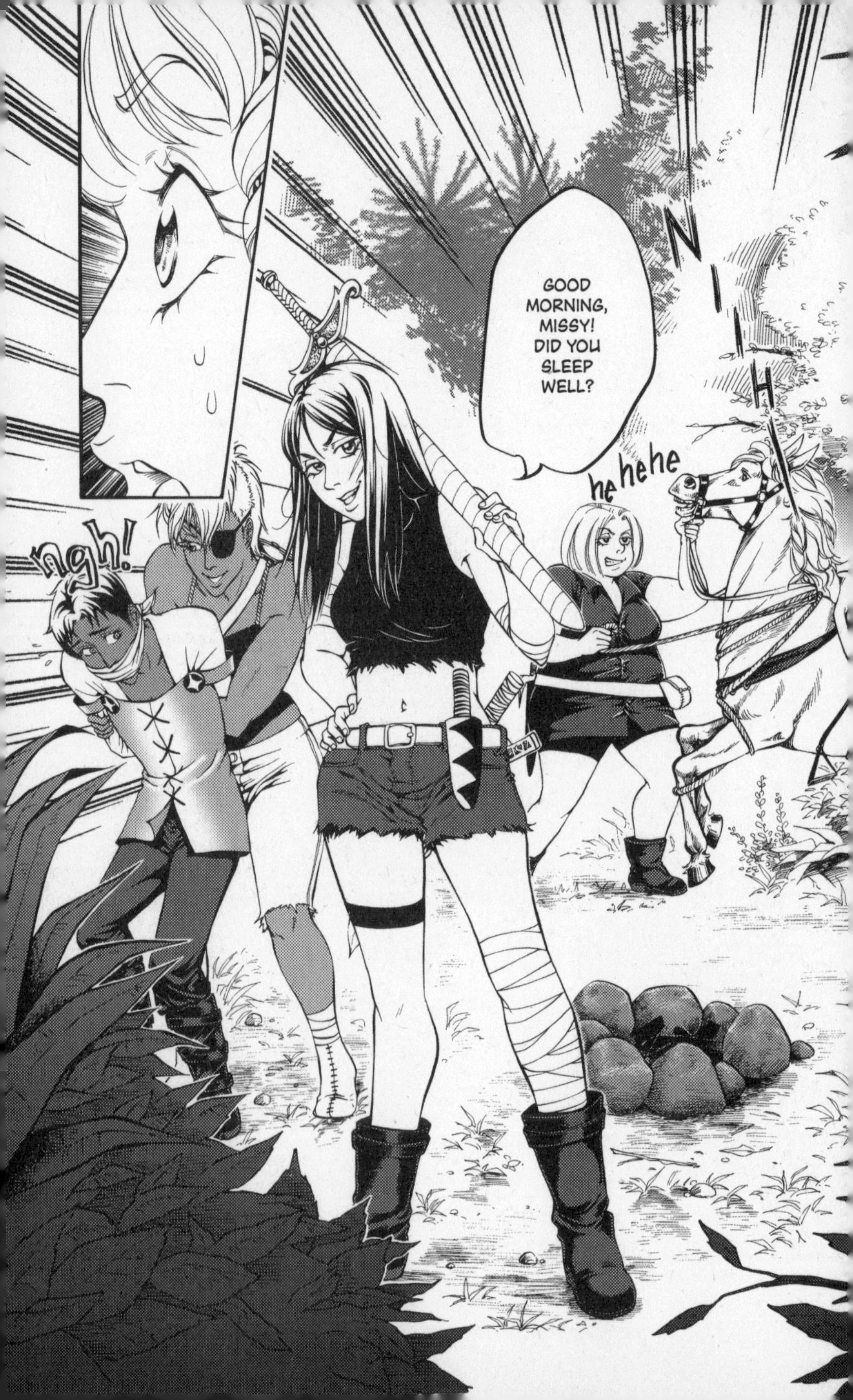
GOOD MORNING, MISSY! DID YOU SLEEP WELL?
he hehe
NIIH
ngh!

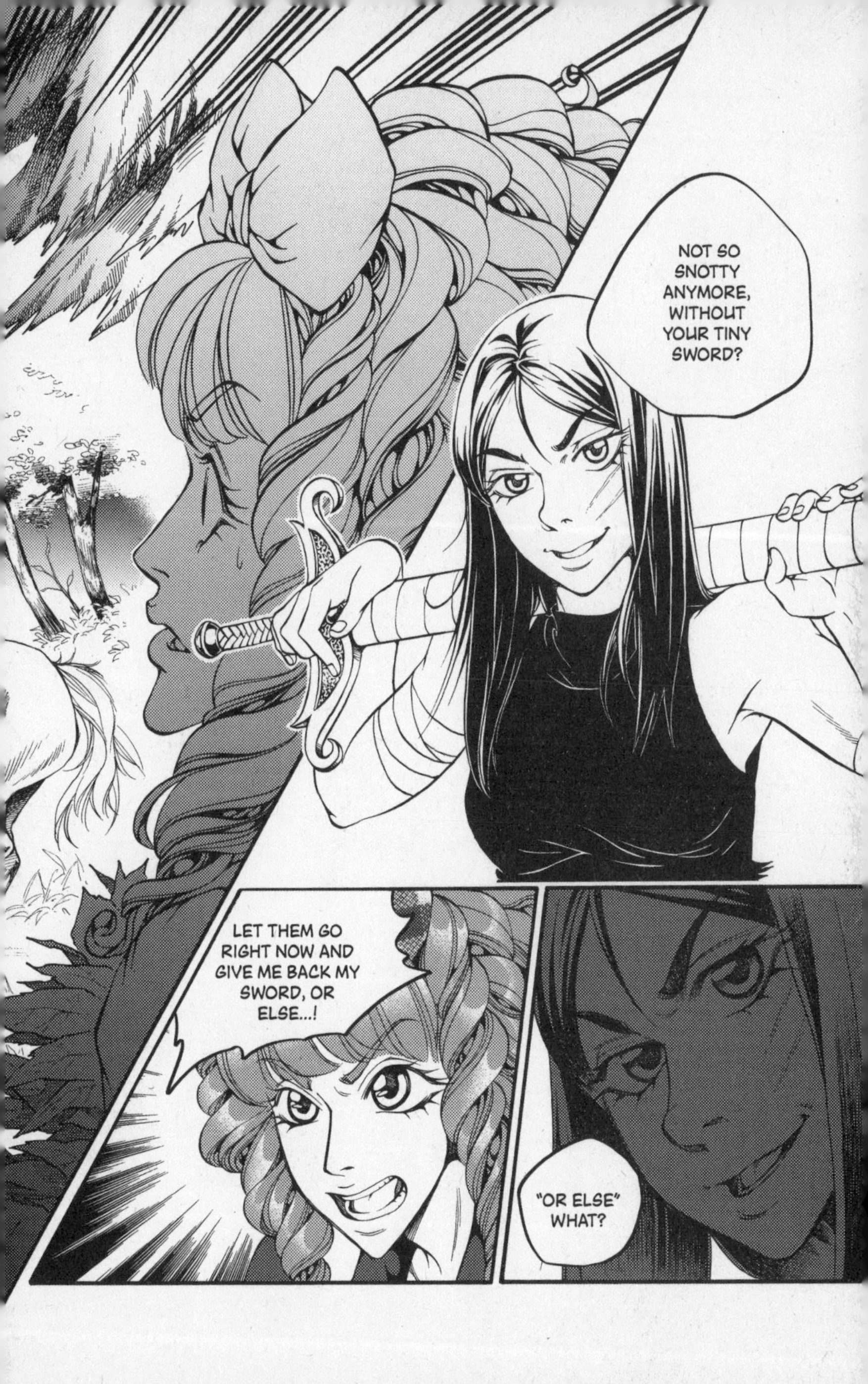
NOT SO SNOTTY ANYMORE, WITHOUT YOUR TINY SWORD?
LET THEM GO RIGHT NOW AND GIVE ME BACK MY SWORD, OR ELSE...!
"OR ELSE" WHAT?

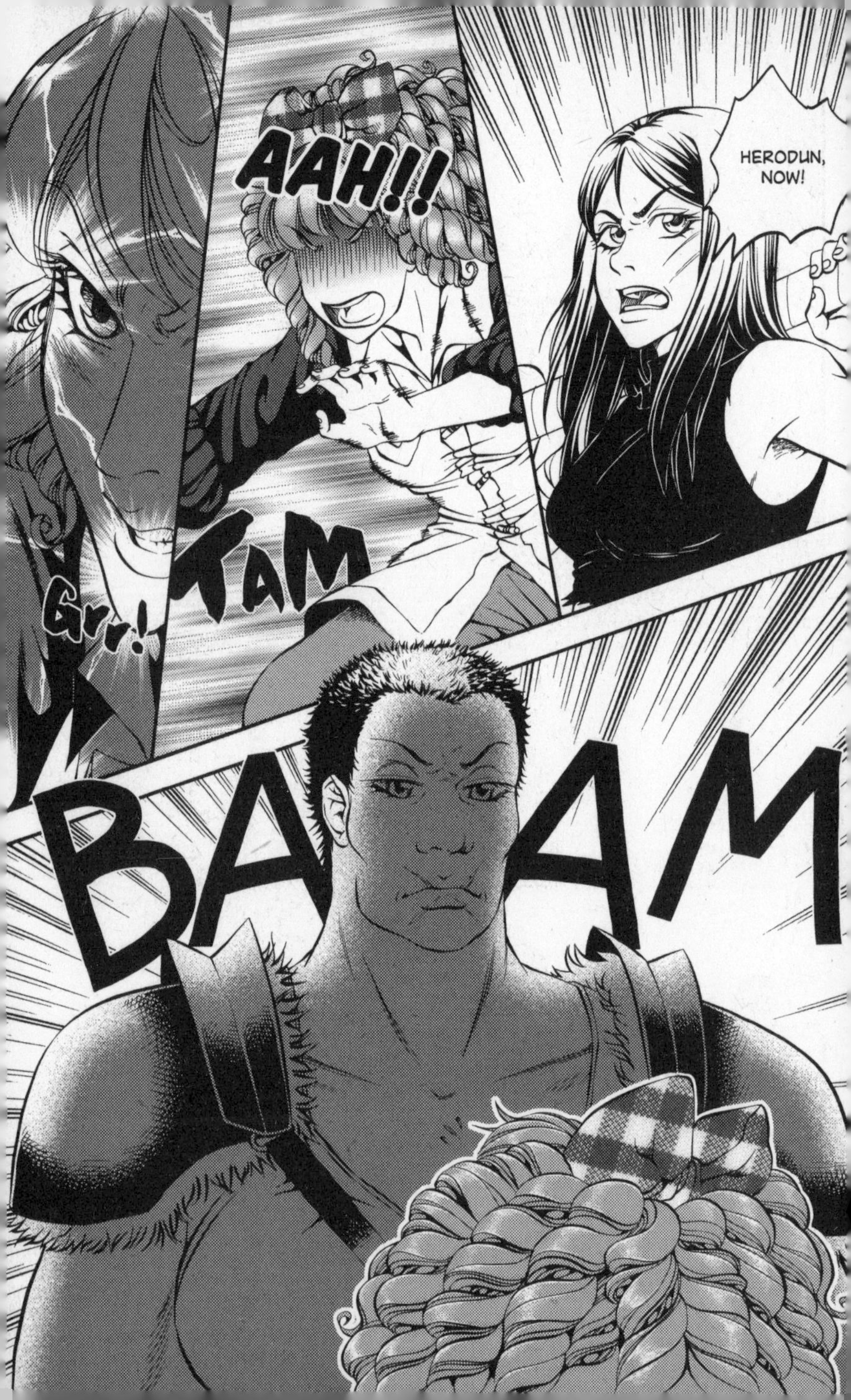
Grr..!
AAH!!
TAM
HERODUN, NOW!
BAM

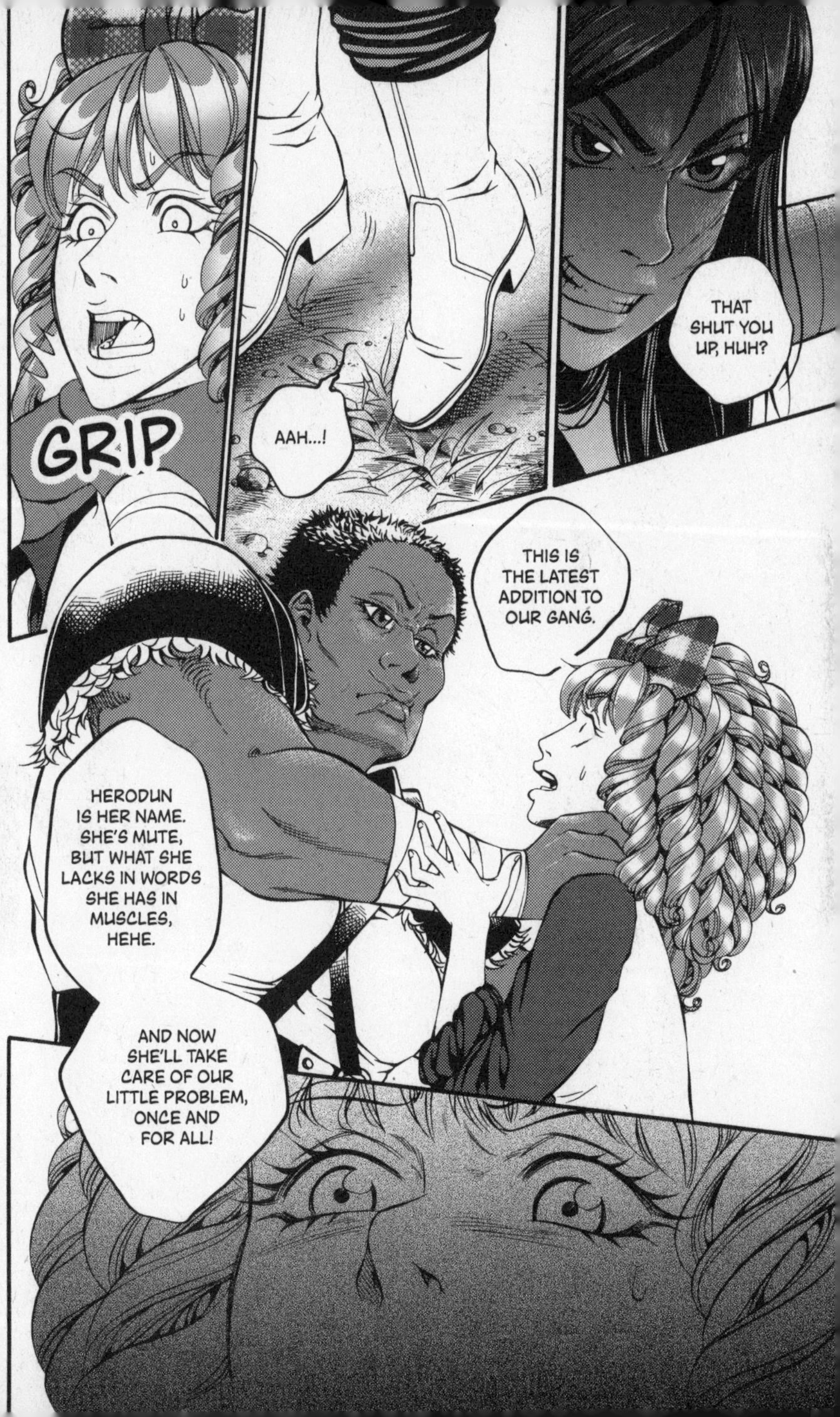
GRIP
AAH...!
THAT SHUT YOU UP, HUH?
THIS IS THE LATEST ADDITION TO OUR GANG.
HERODUN IS HER NAME. SHE'S MUTE, BUT WHAT SHE LACKS IN WORDS SHE HAS IN MUSCLES, HEHE.
AND NOW SHE'LL TAKE CARE OF OUR LITTLE PROBLEM, ONCE AND FOR ALL!

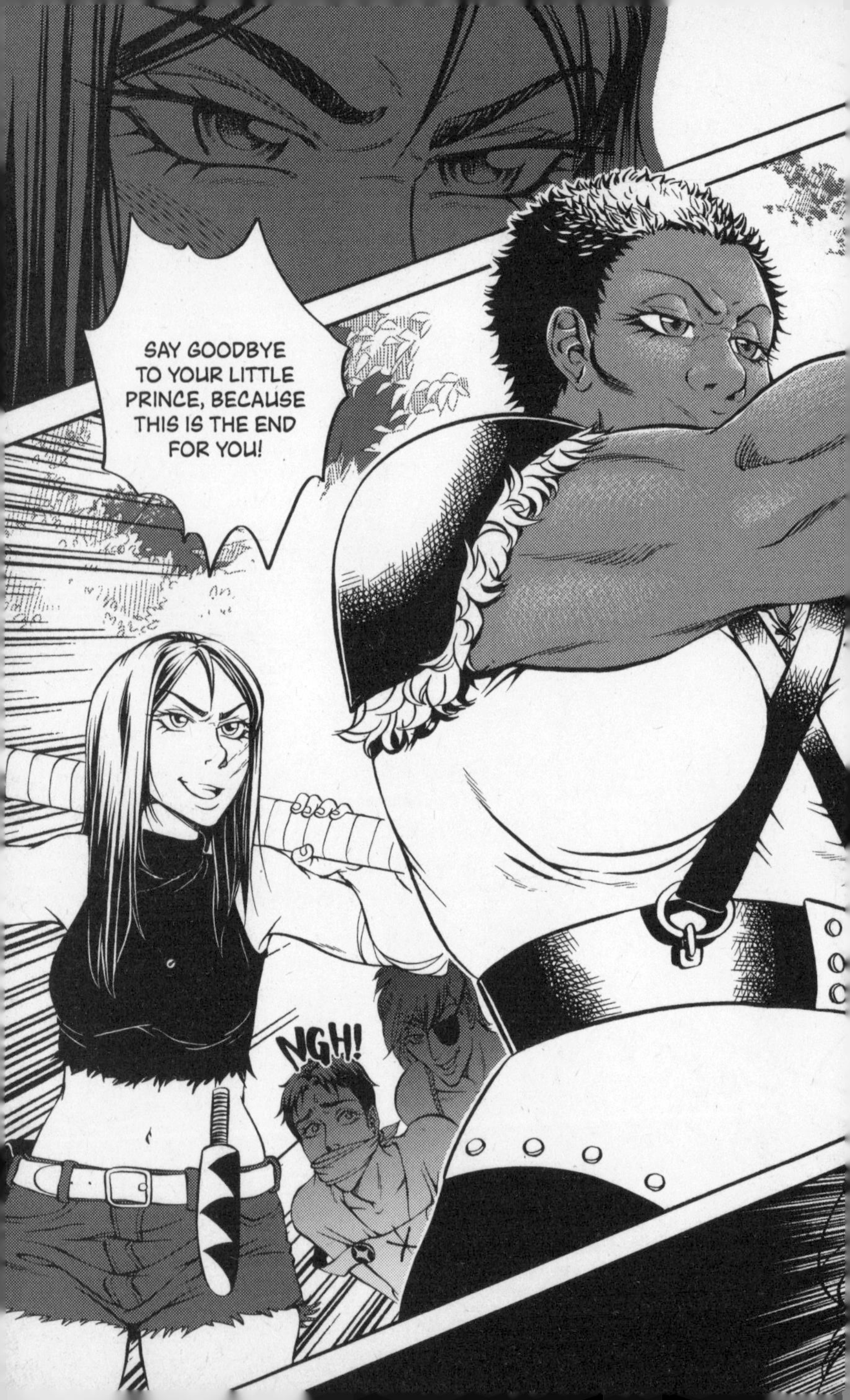
SAY GOODBYE TO YOUR LITTLE PRINCE, BECAUSE THIS IS THE END FOR YOU!
NGH!

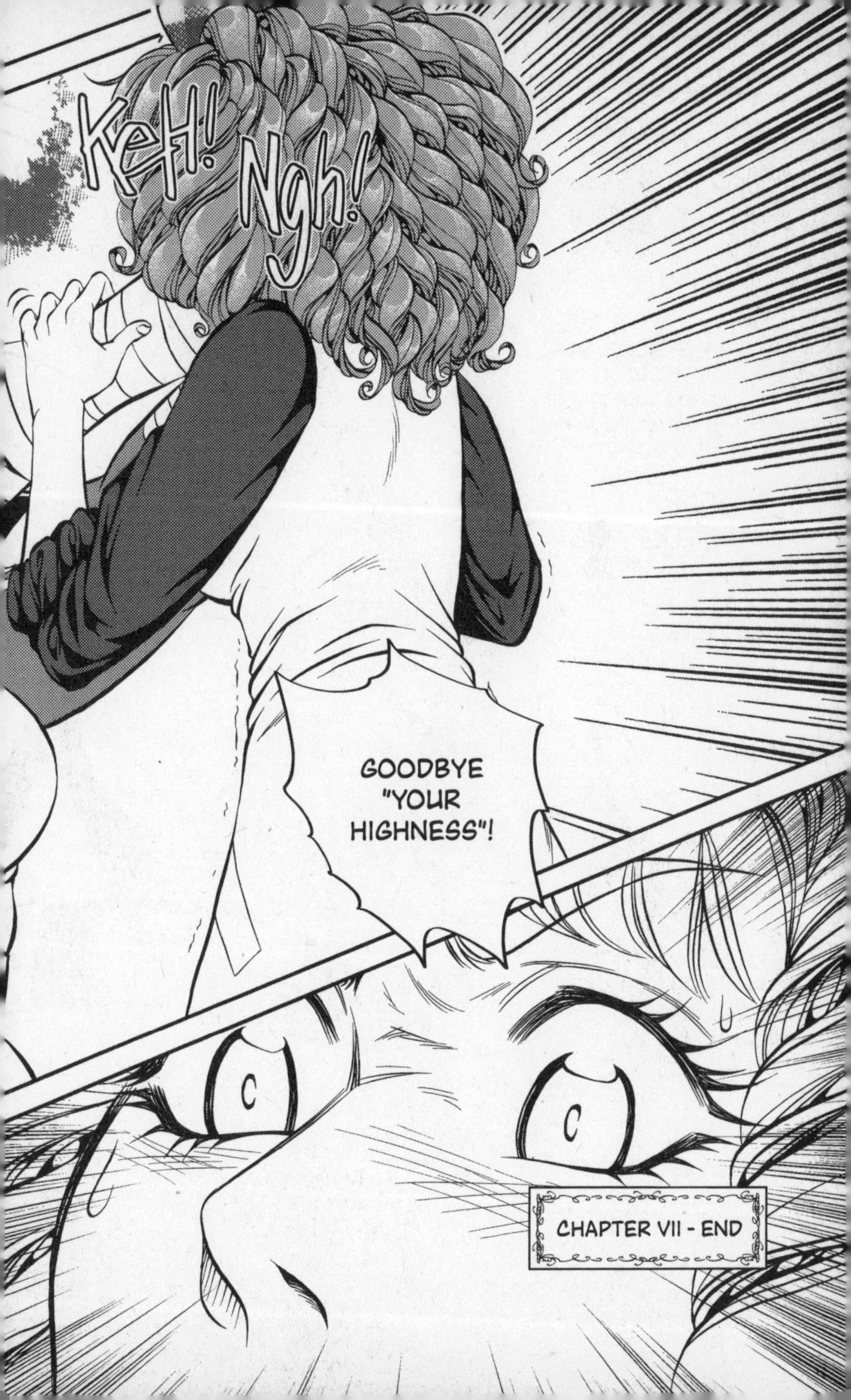
KEH! NGH!
GOODBYE "YOUR HIGHNESS"!
CHAPTER VII - END

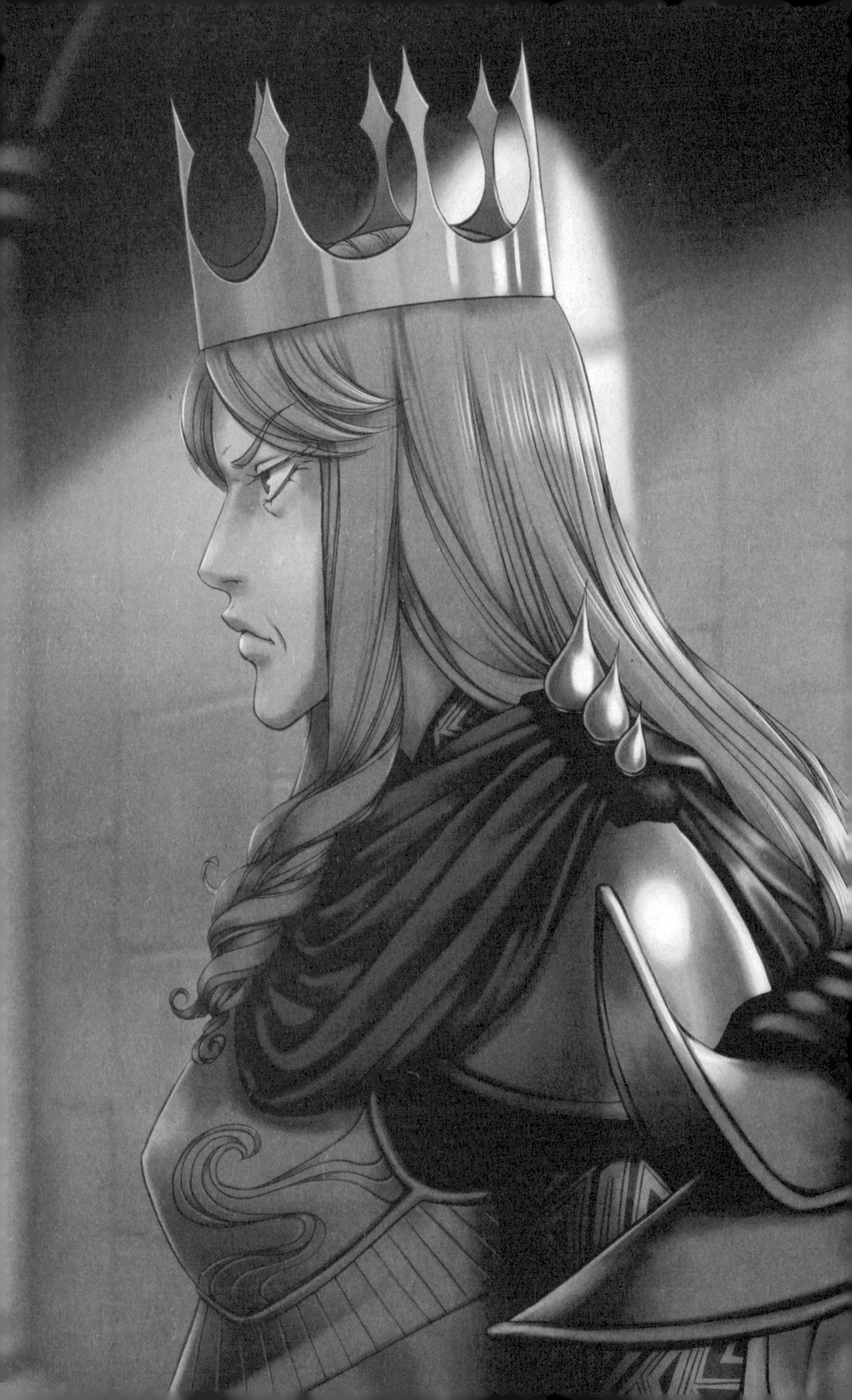

Chapter VIII

The Princess And Her Sister

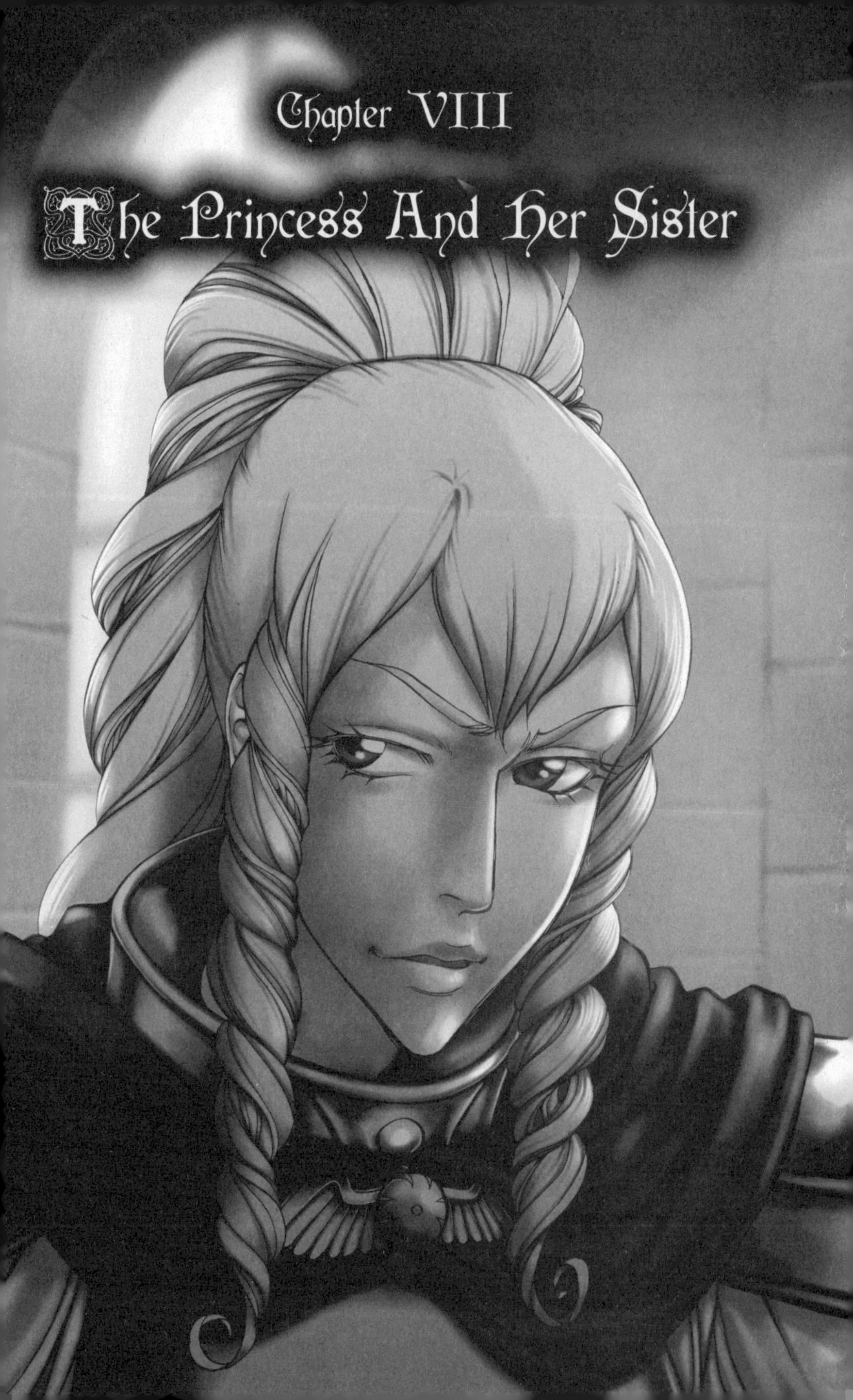

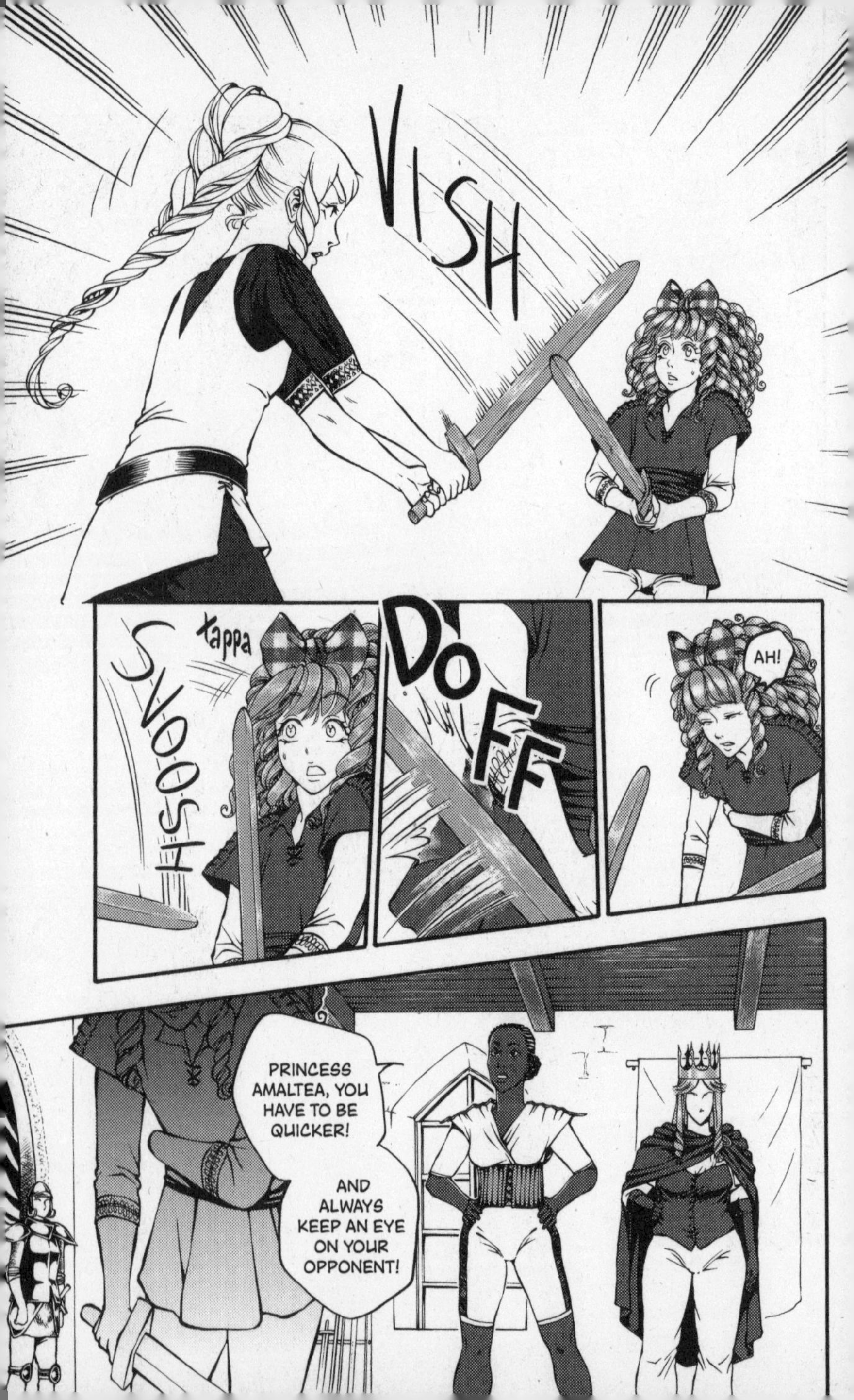
VISH
SVOOSH
tappa
DOFF
AH!
PRINCESS AMALTEA, YOU HAVE TO BE QUICKER!
AND ALWAYS KEEP AN EYE ON YOUR OPPONENT!

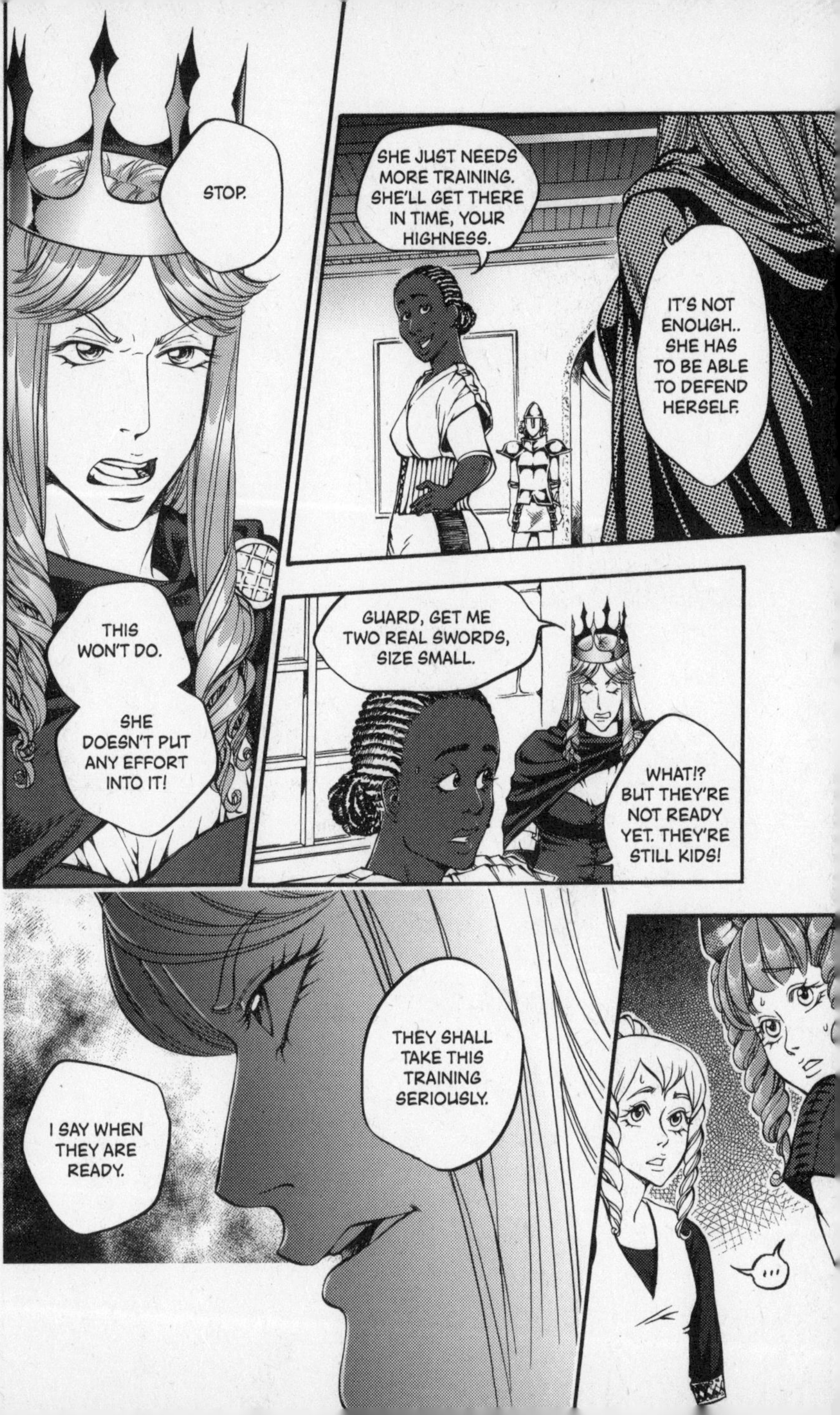
STOP.
THIS WON'T DO.
SHE DOESN'T PUT ANY EFFORT INTO IT!
SHE JUST NEEDS MORE TRAINING. SHE'LL GET THERE IN TIME, YOUR HIGHNESS.
IT'S NOT ENOUGH.. SHE HAS TO BE ABLE TO DEFEND HERSELF.
GUARD, GET ME TWO REAL SWORDS, SIZE SMALL.
WHAT!? BUT THEY'RE NOT READY YET. THEY'RE STILL KIDS!
I SAY WHEN THEY ARE READY.
THEY SHALL TAKE THIS TRAINING SERIOUSLY.
...

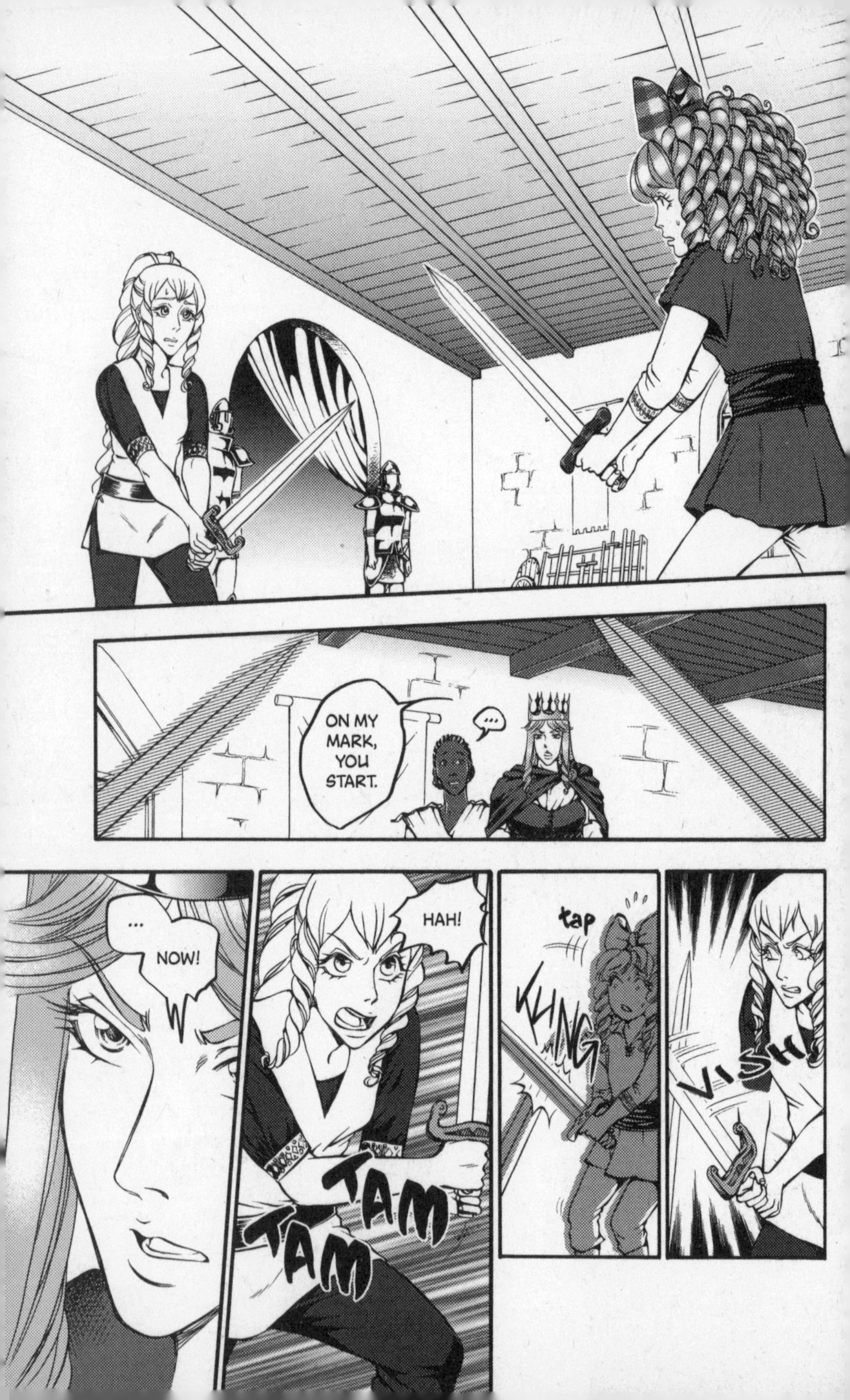
ON MY MARK, YOU START.
...
...
NOW!
HAH!
TAM
TAM
TAM
tap
KLING
VISH

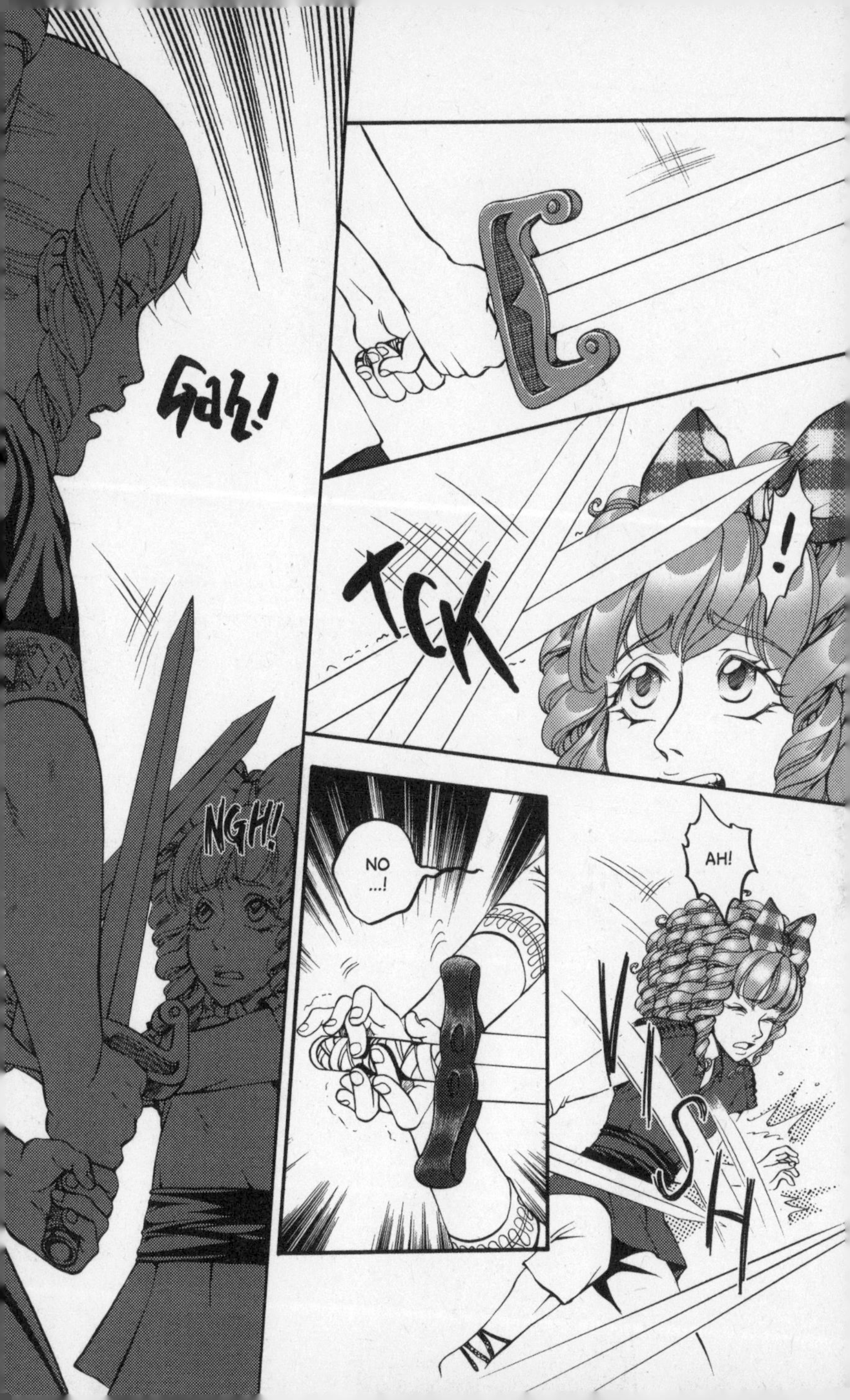
GAH!
NGH!
TCK
!
NO ...!
AH!
VISH

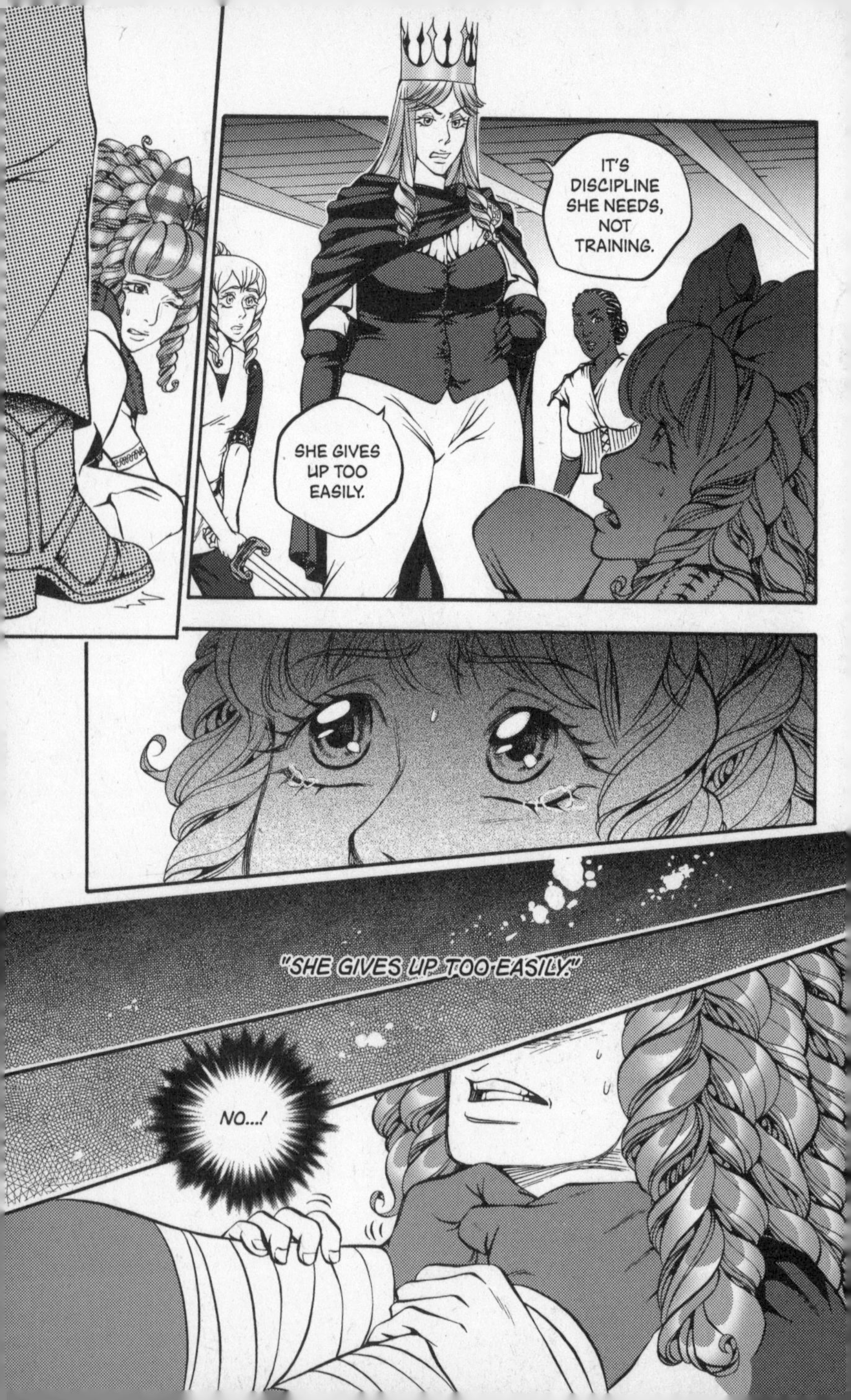
SHE GIVES UP TOO EASILY.
IT'S DISCIPLINE SHE NEEDS, NOT TRAINING.
"SHE GIVES UP TOO EASILY."
NO...!

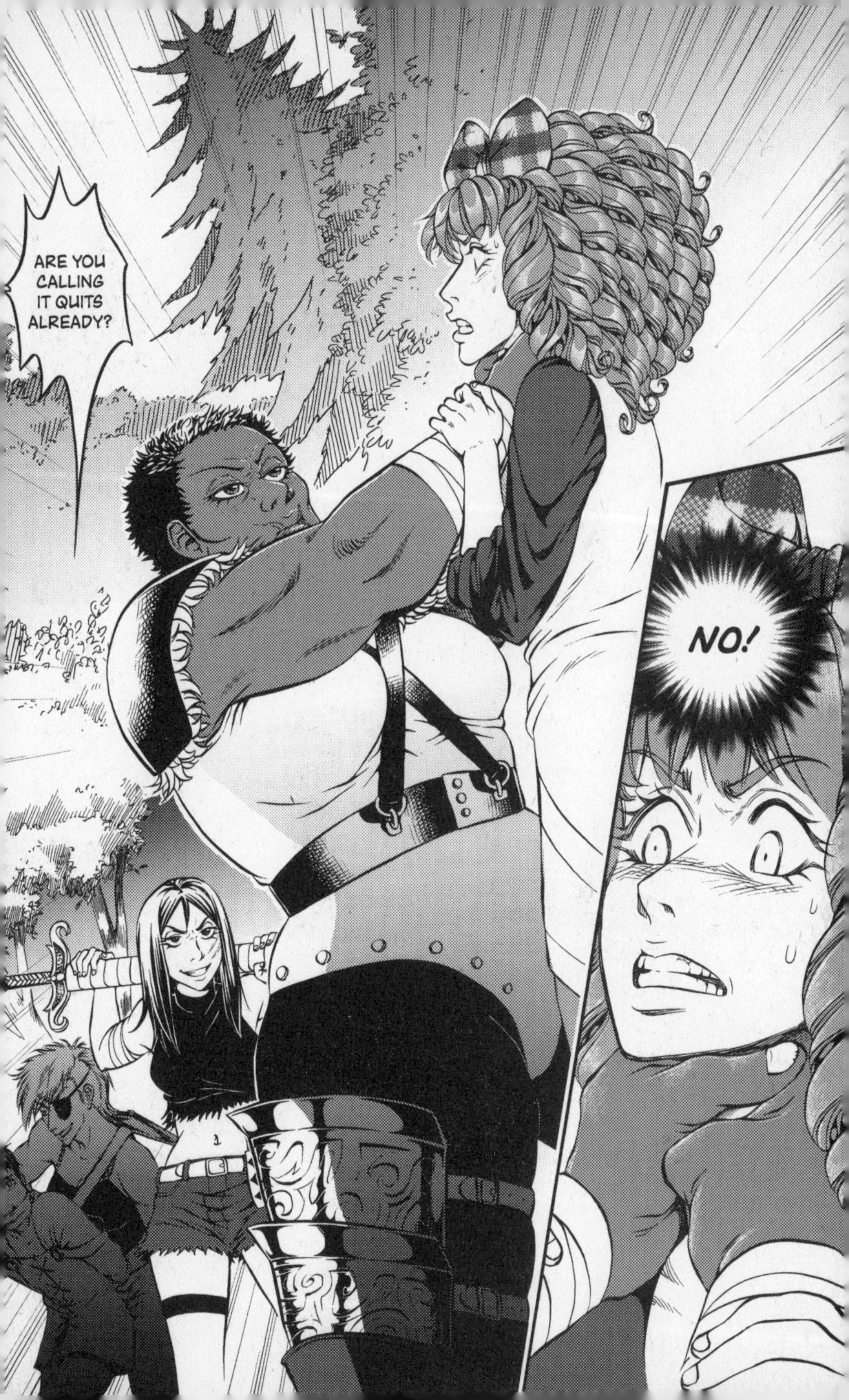
ARE YOU CALLING IT QUITS ALREADY?
NO!

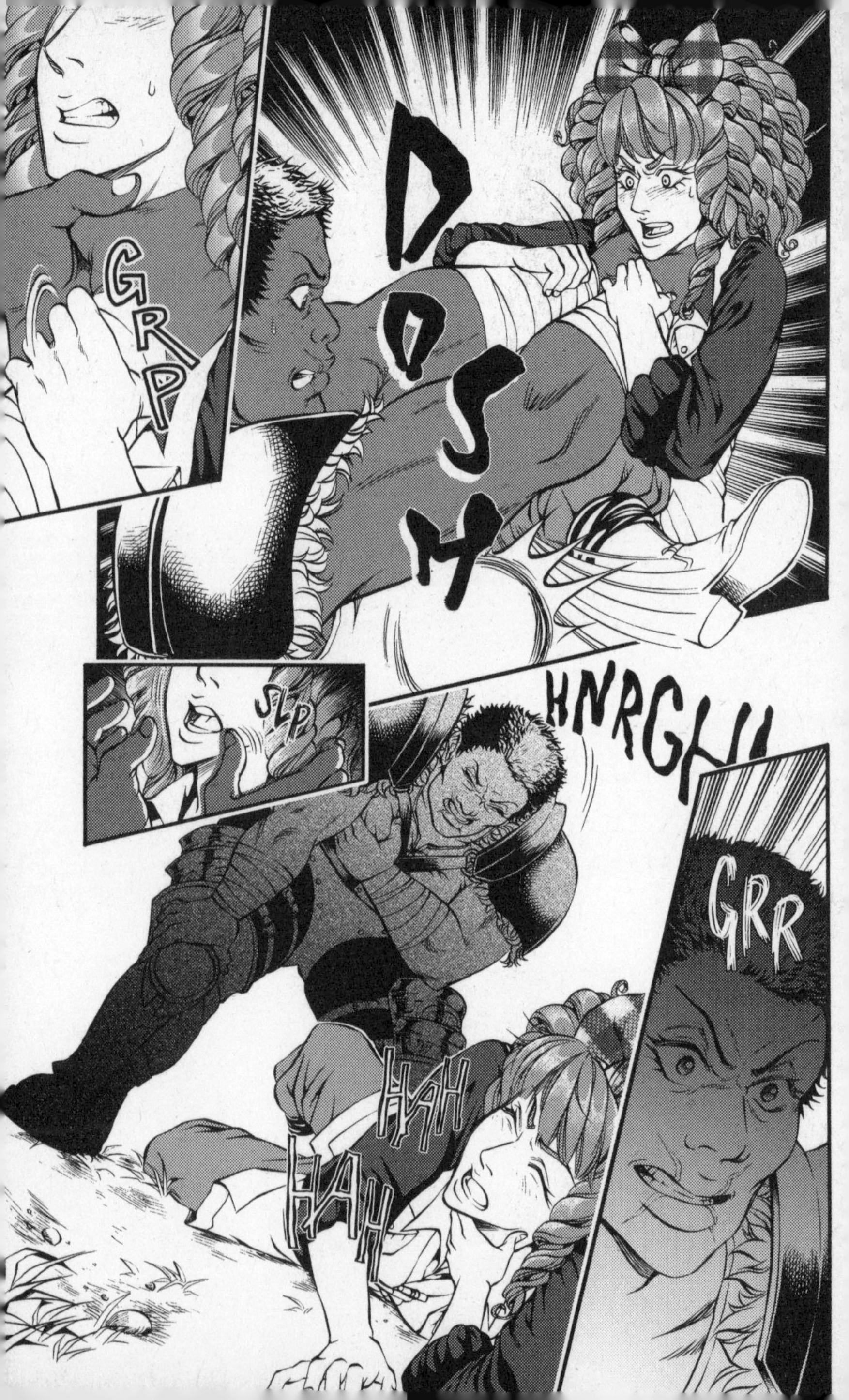
GRP
DASH
SLP
HNRGH!!
HAH HAH
GRR

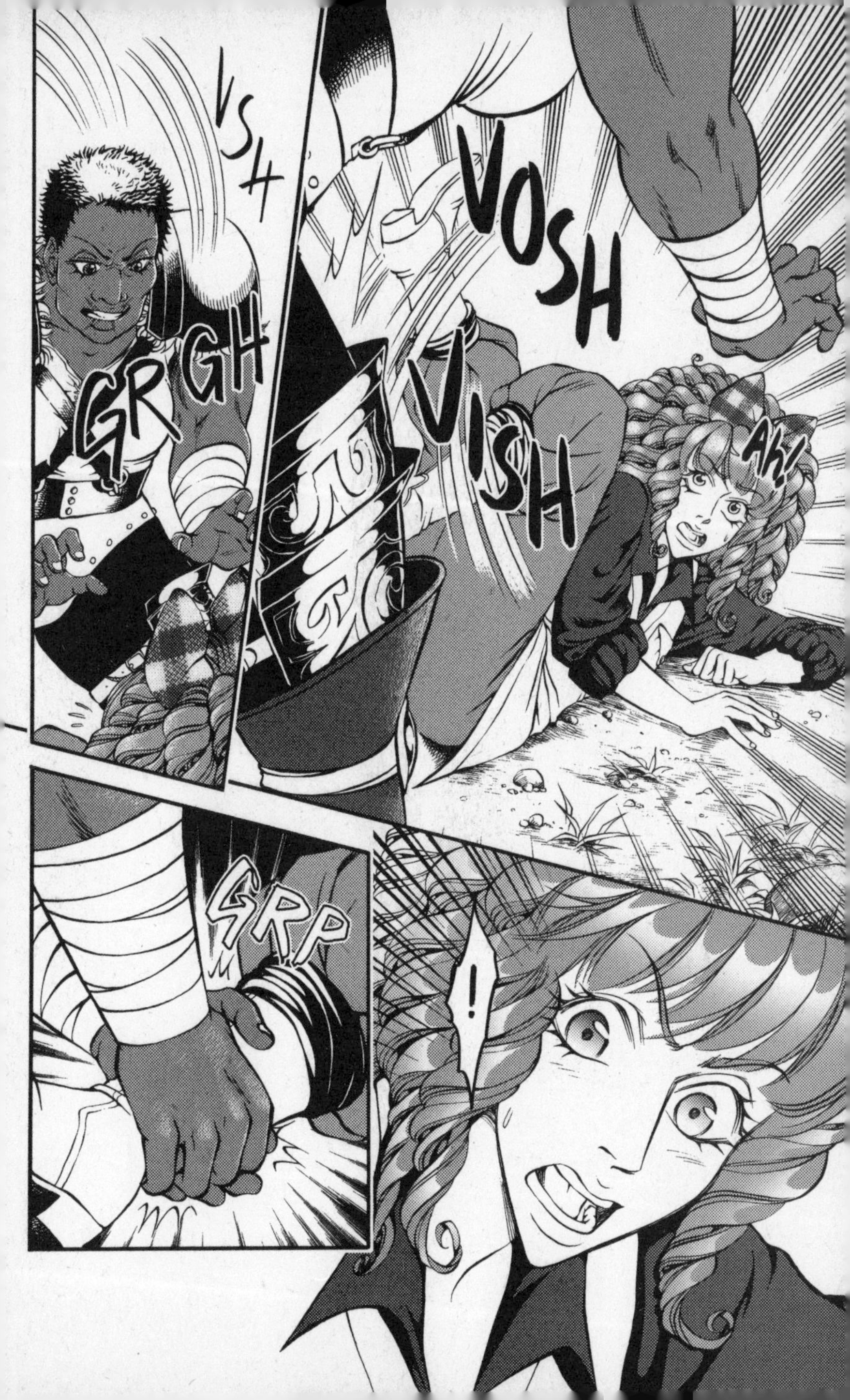
VSH
GRGH
VOSH
VISH
AH!
GRP
!

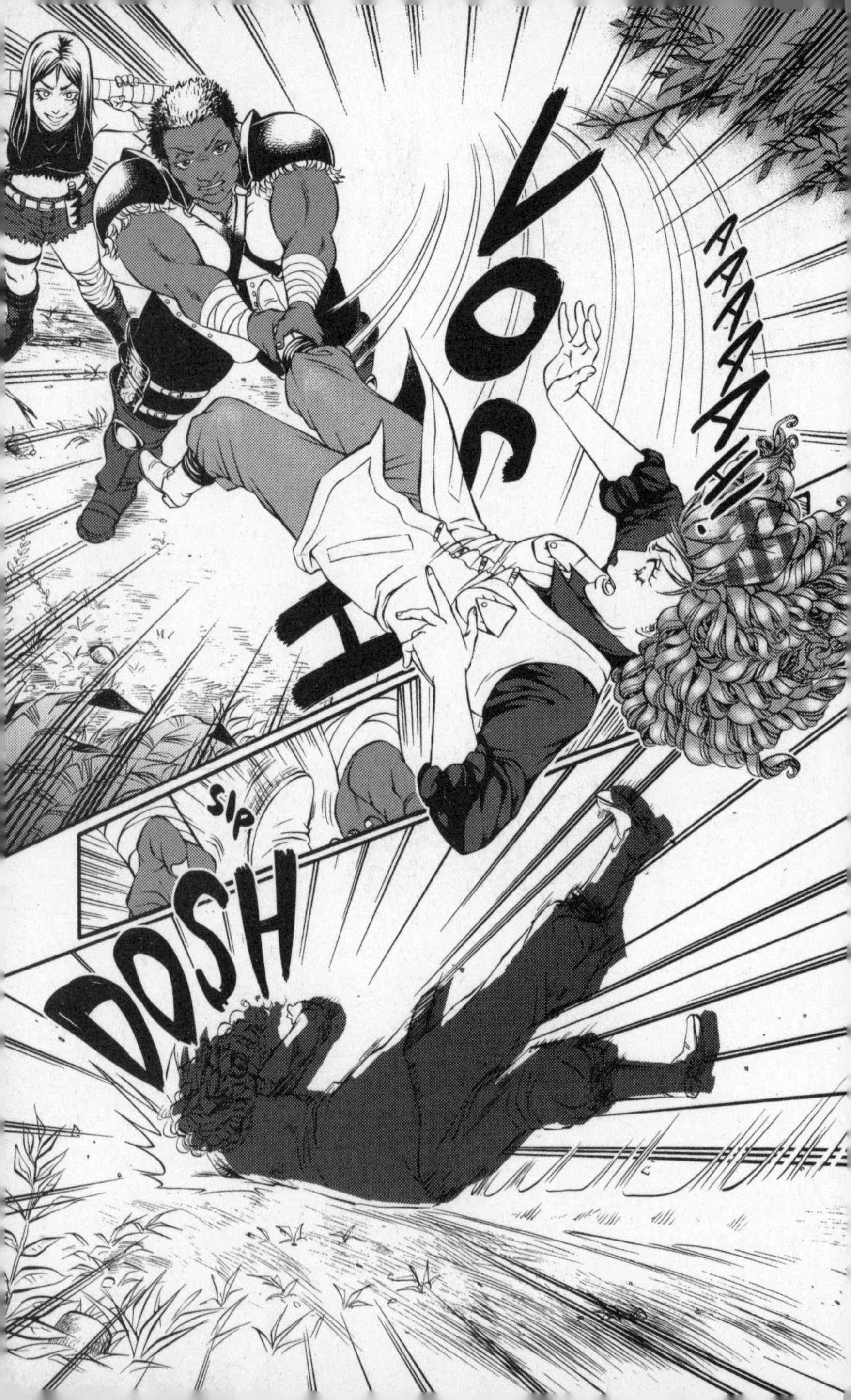
VOOSH
AAAAAAH!
SIP
DOSH

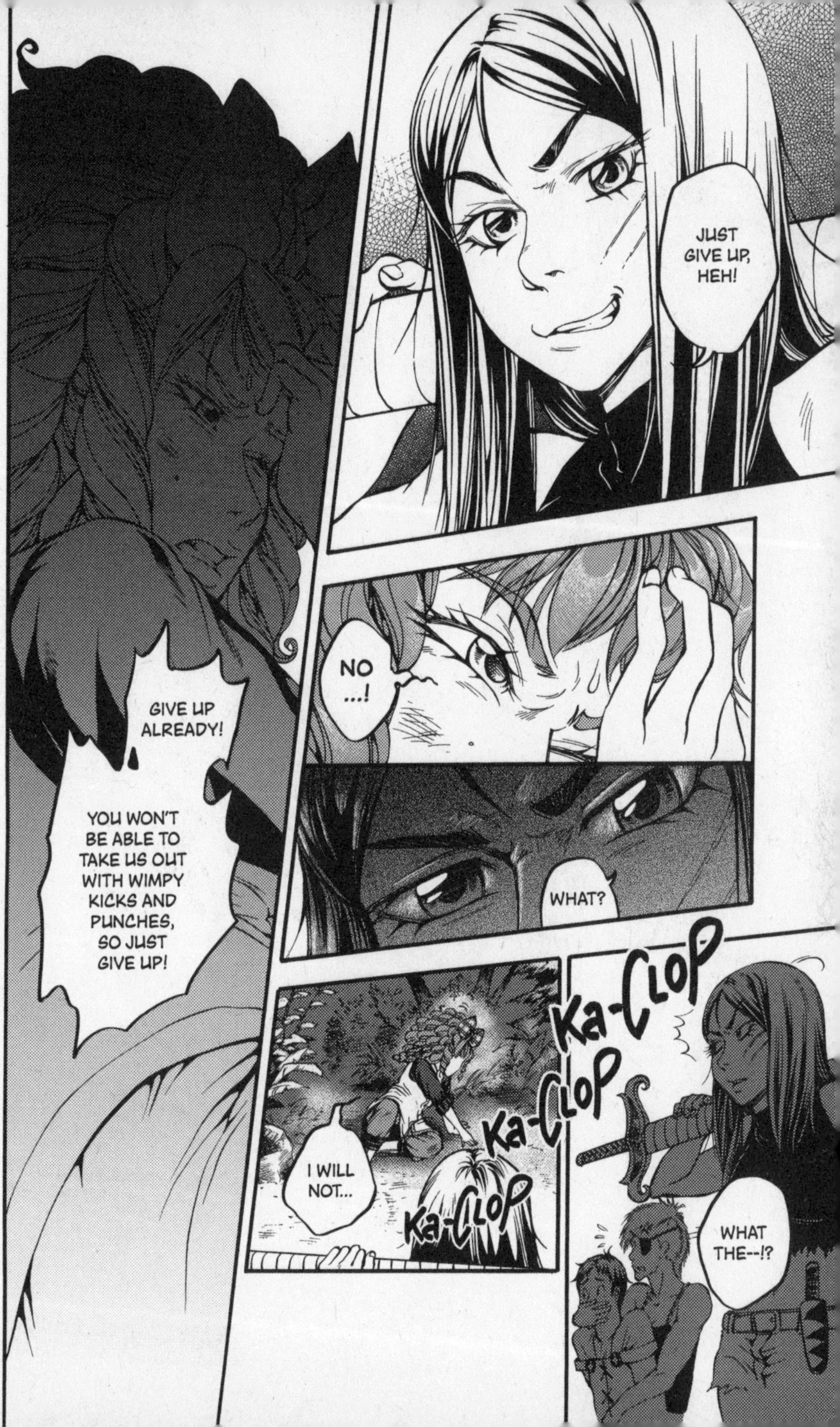
GIVE UP ALREADY!
YOU WON'T BE ABLE TO TAKE US OUT WITH WIMPY KICKS AND PUNCHES, SO JUST GIVE UP!
JUST GIVE UP, HEH!
NO ...!
WHAT?
I WILL NOT...
Ka-CLOP
Ka-CLOP
Ka-CLOP
WHAT THE--!?

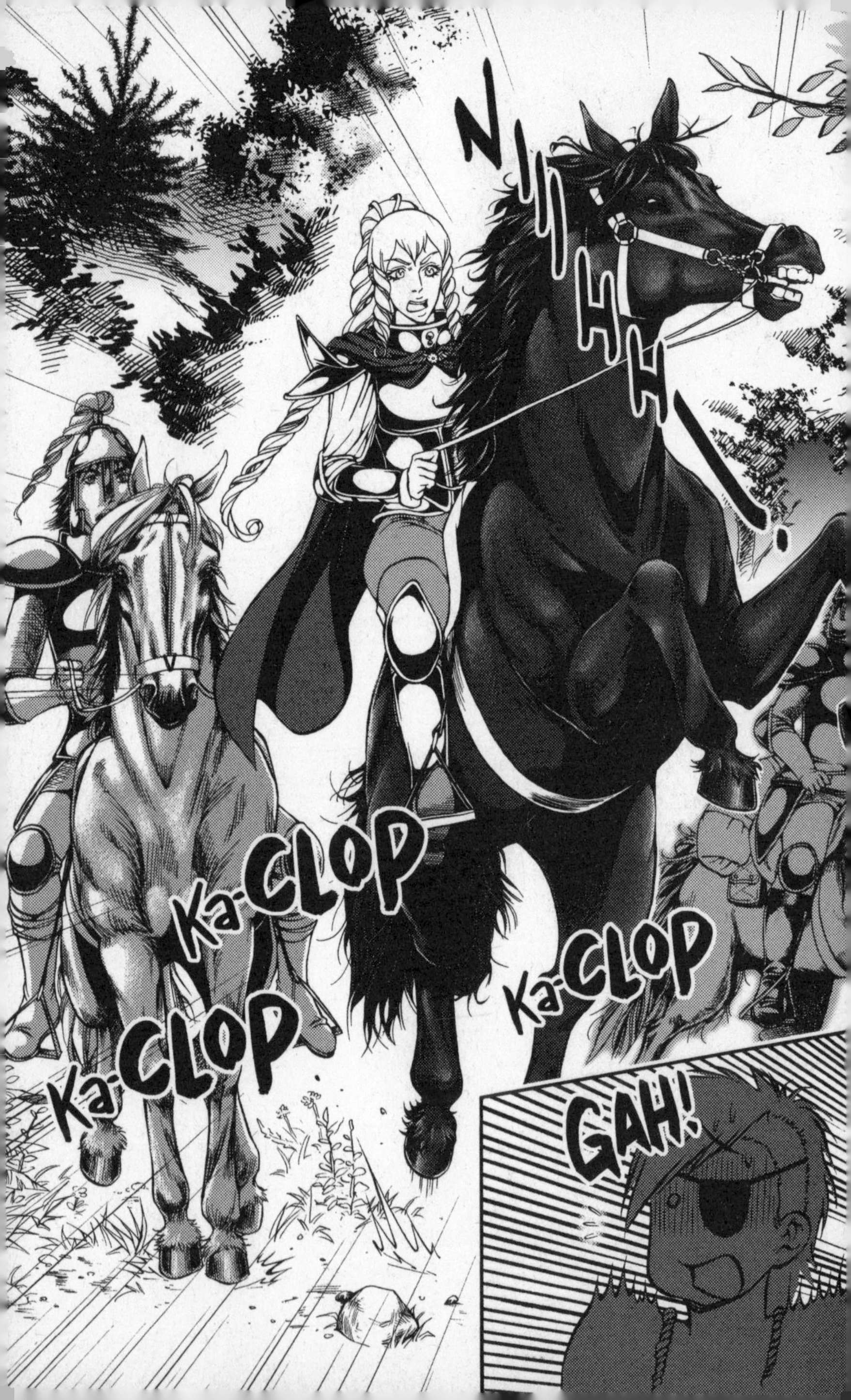
NIIIHHH!
Ka-CLOP
Ka-CLOP
Ka-CLOP
GAH!

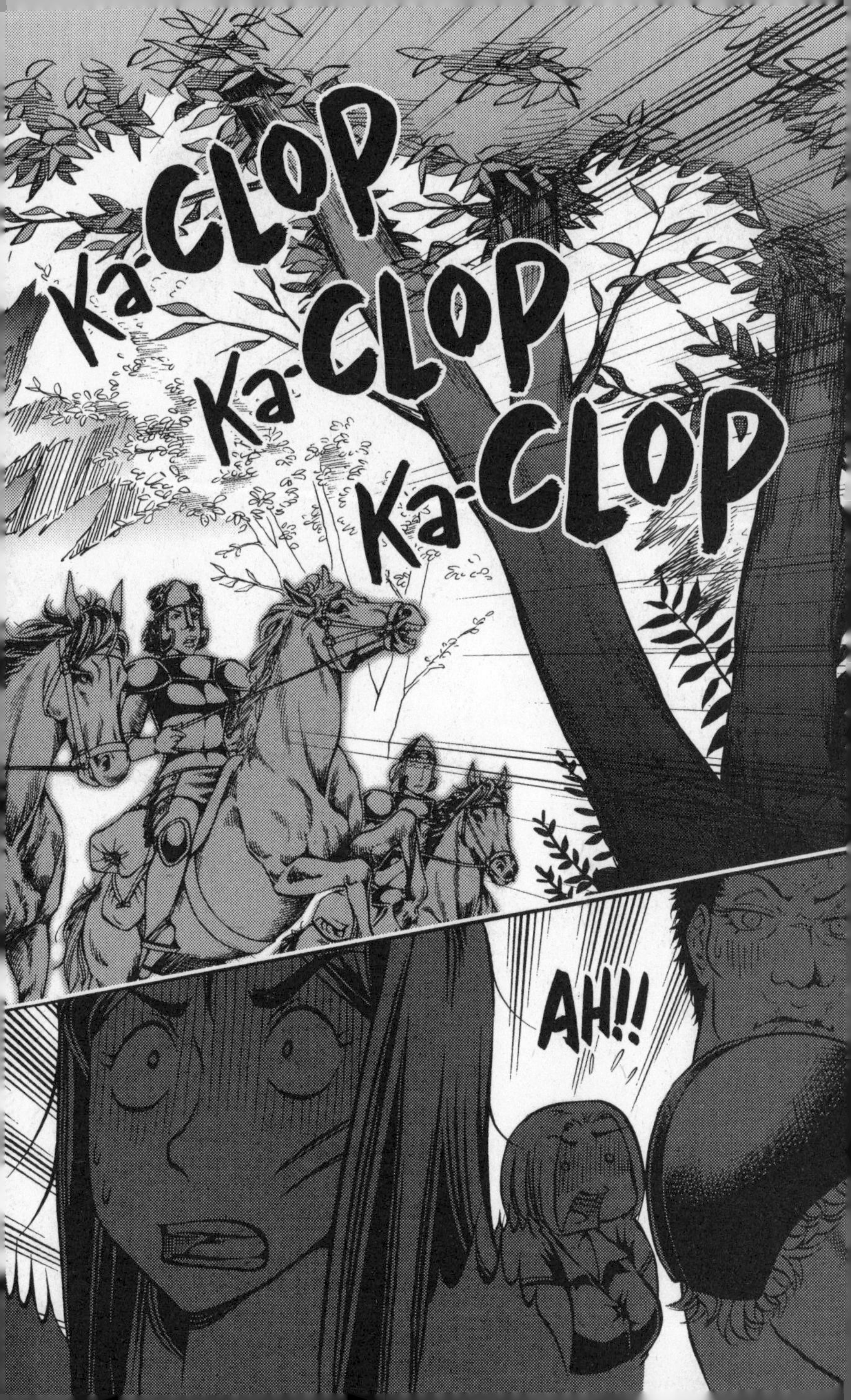
KA-CLOP
KA-CLOP
KA-CLOP
AH!!

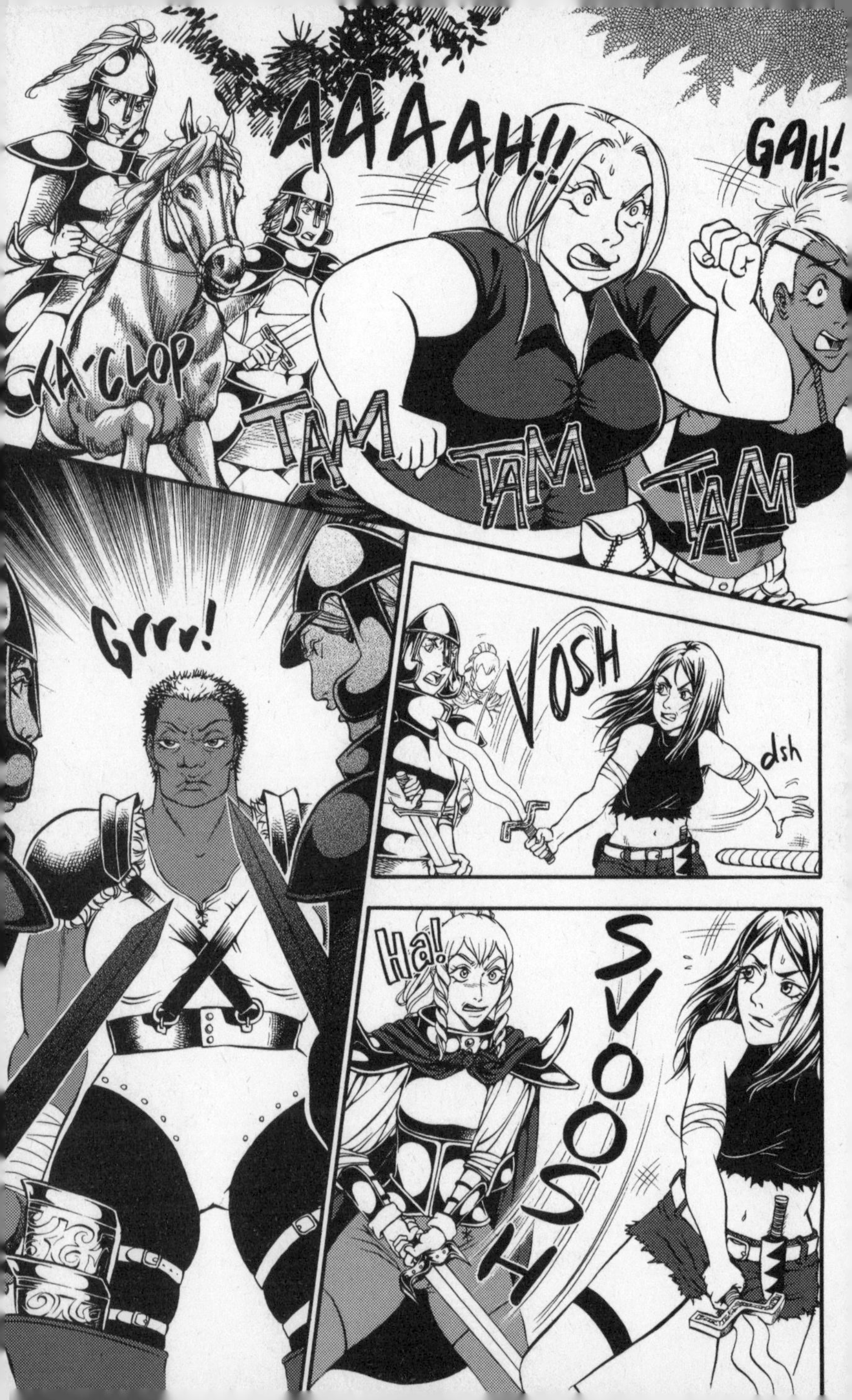
AAAAAH!!
GAH!
KA-CLOP
TAM
TAM
TAM
Grrrr!
VOSH
dsh
Ha!
SVOOOSH

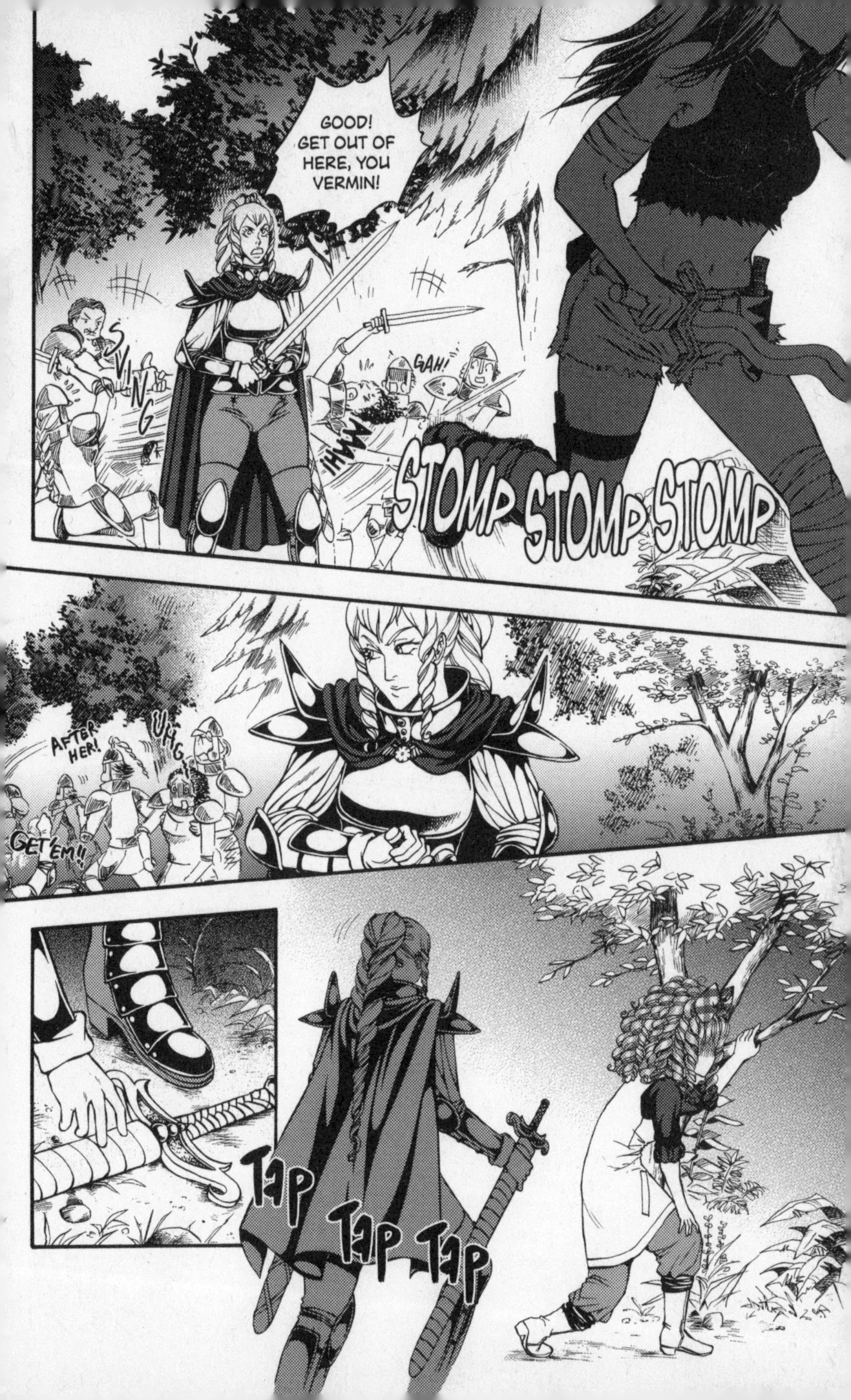
GOOD! GET OUT OF HERE, YOU VERMIN!
SVING
GAH!
WAH!
STOMP STOMP STOMP
AFTER HER!
UHG
GET'EM!!
TAP TAP TAP

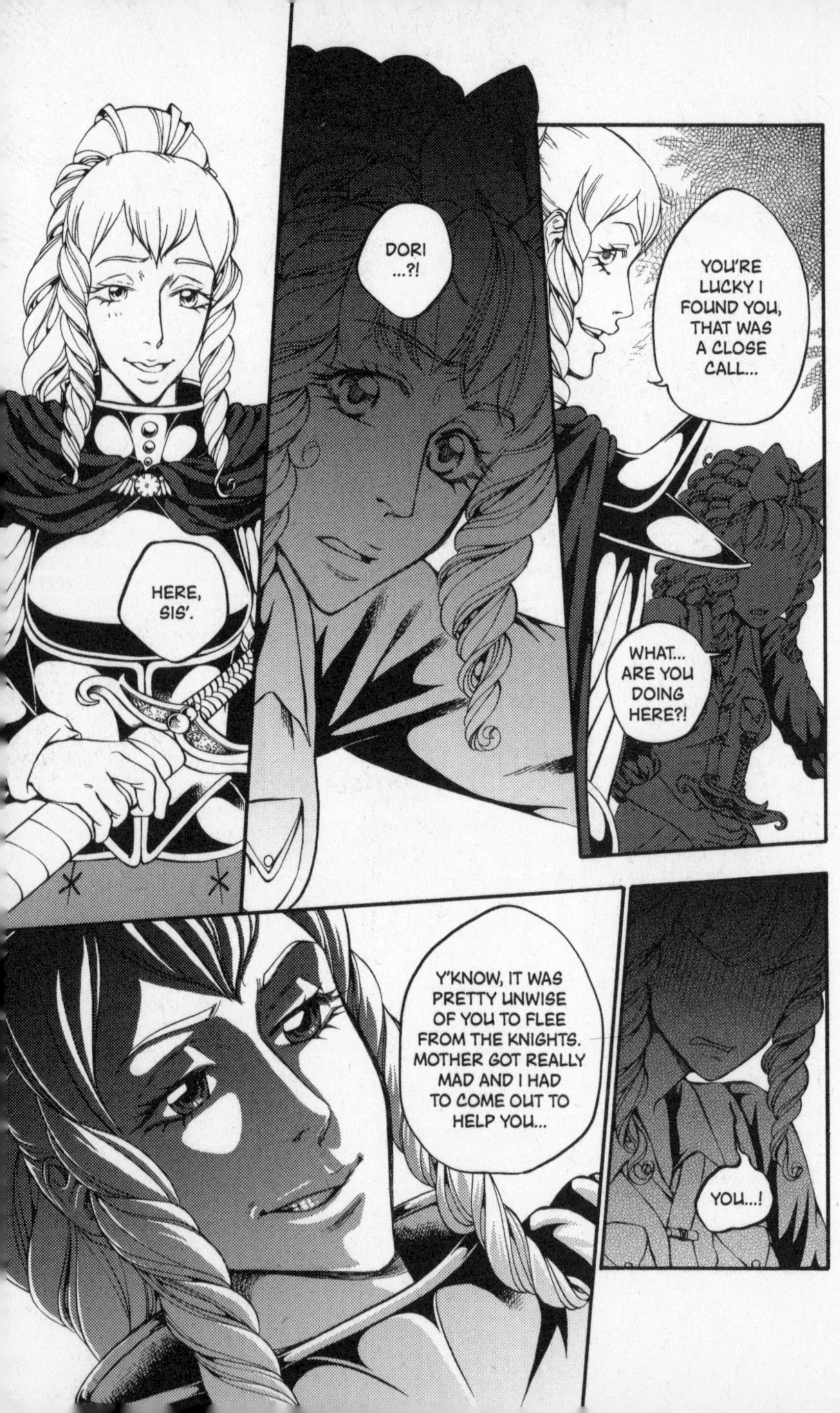
HERE, SIS'.
DORI ...?!
YOU'RE LUCKY I FOUND YOU, THAT WAS A CLOSE CALL...
WHAT... ARE YOU DOING HERE?!
Y'KNOW, IT WAS PRETTY UNWISE OF YOU TO FLEE FROM THE KNIGHTS. MOTHER GOT REALLY MAD AND I HAD TO COME OUT TO HELP YOU...
YOU...!

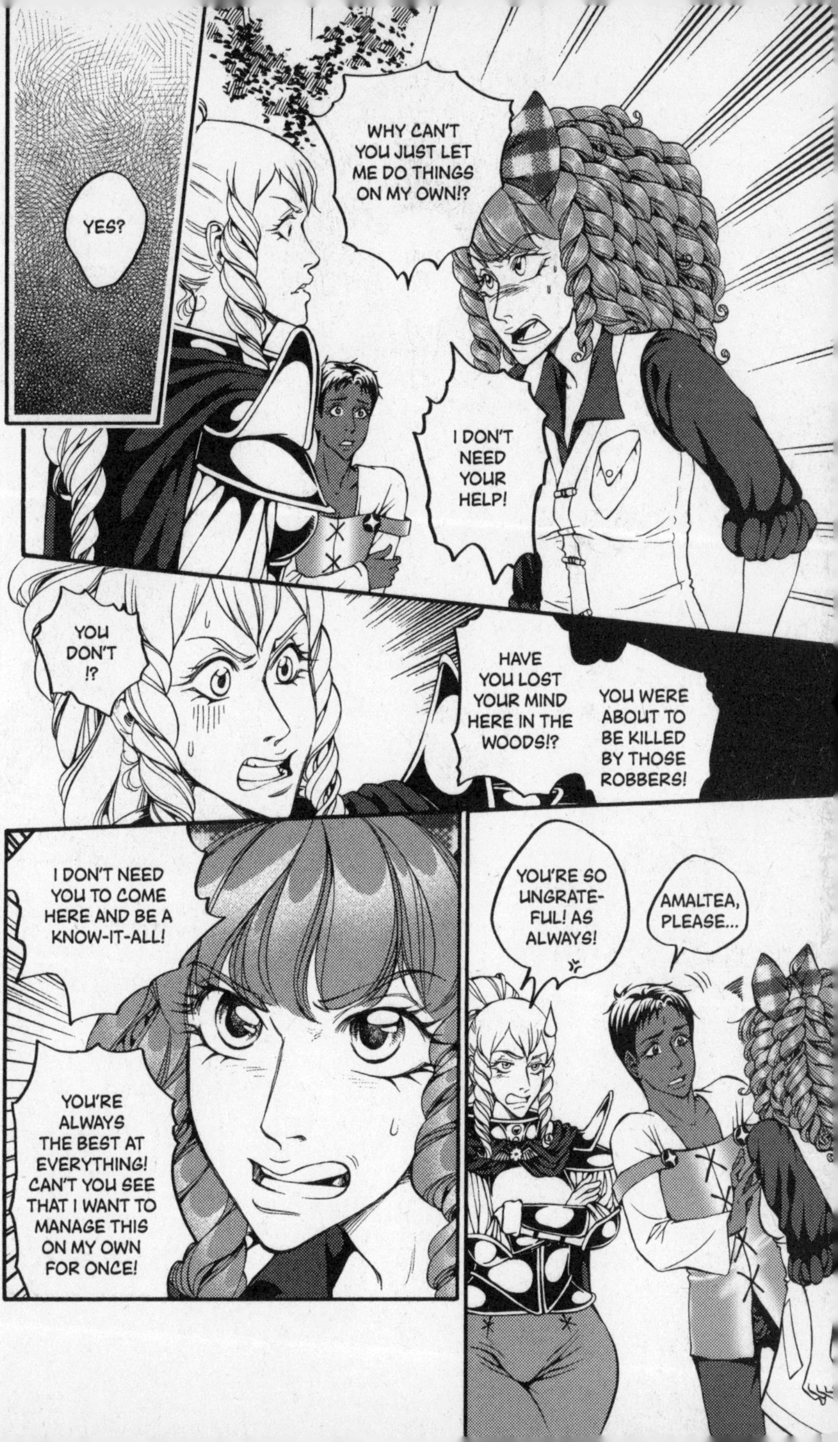
YES?
WHY CAN'T YOU JUST LET ME DO THINGS ON MY OWN!?
I DON'T NEED YOUR HELP!
YOU DON'T !?
HAVE YOU LOST YOUR MIND HERE IN THE WOODS!?
YOU WERE ABOUT TO BE KILLED BY THOSE ROBBERS!
I DON'T NEED YOU TO COME HERE AND BE A KNOW-IT-ALL!
YOU'RE ALWAYS THE BEST AT EVERYTHING! CAN'T YOU SEE THAT I WANT TO MANAGE THIS ON MY OWN FOR ONCE!
YOU'RE SO UNGRATE-FUL! AS ALWAYS!
AMALTEA, PLEASE...

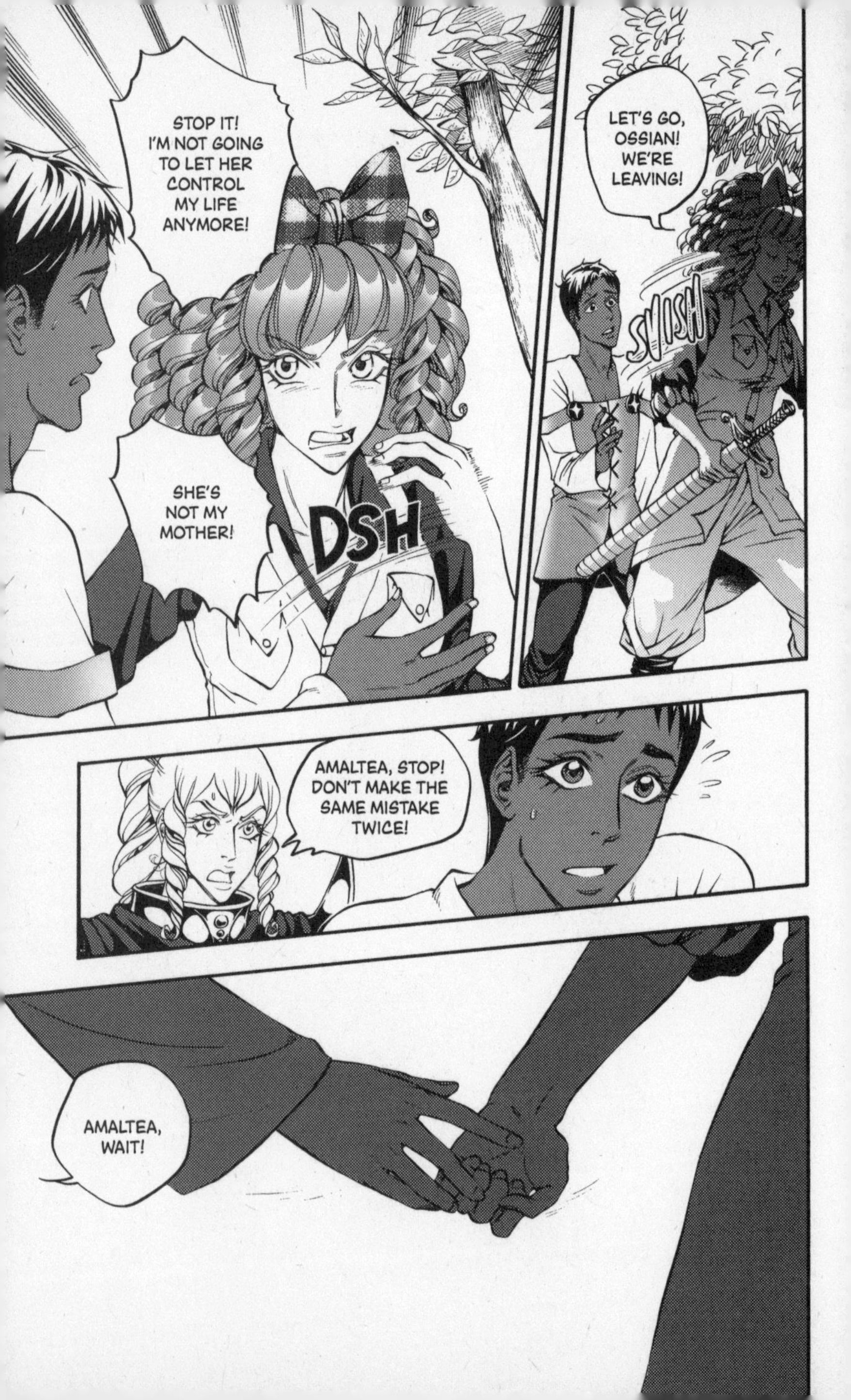
STOP IT! I'M NOT GOING TO LET HER CONTROL MY LIFE ANYMORE!
SHE'S NOT MY MOTHER!
DSH
LET'S GO, OSSIAN! WE'RE LEAVING!
SWISH
AMALTEA, STOP! DON'T MAKE THE SAME MISTAKE TWICE!
AMALTEA, WAIT!

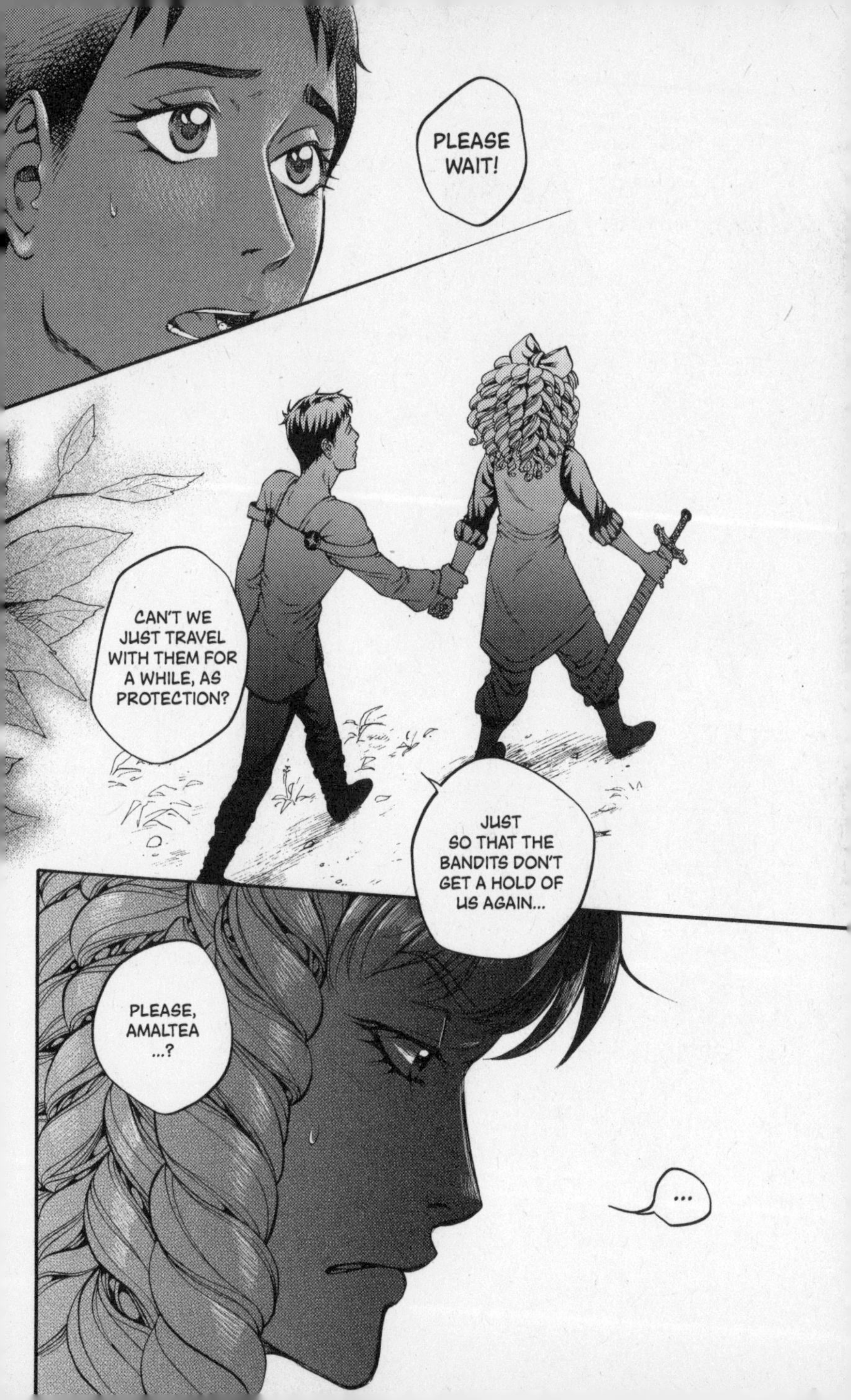
PLEASE WAIT!
CAN'T WE JUST TRAVEL WITH THEM FOR A WHILE, AS PROTECTION?
JUST SO THAT THE BANDITS DON'T GET A HOLD OF US AGAIN...
PLEASE, AMALTEA ...?
...

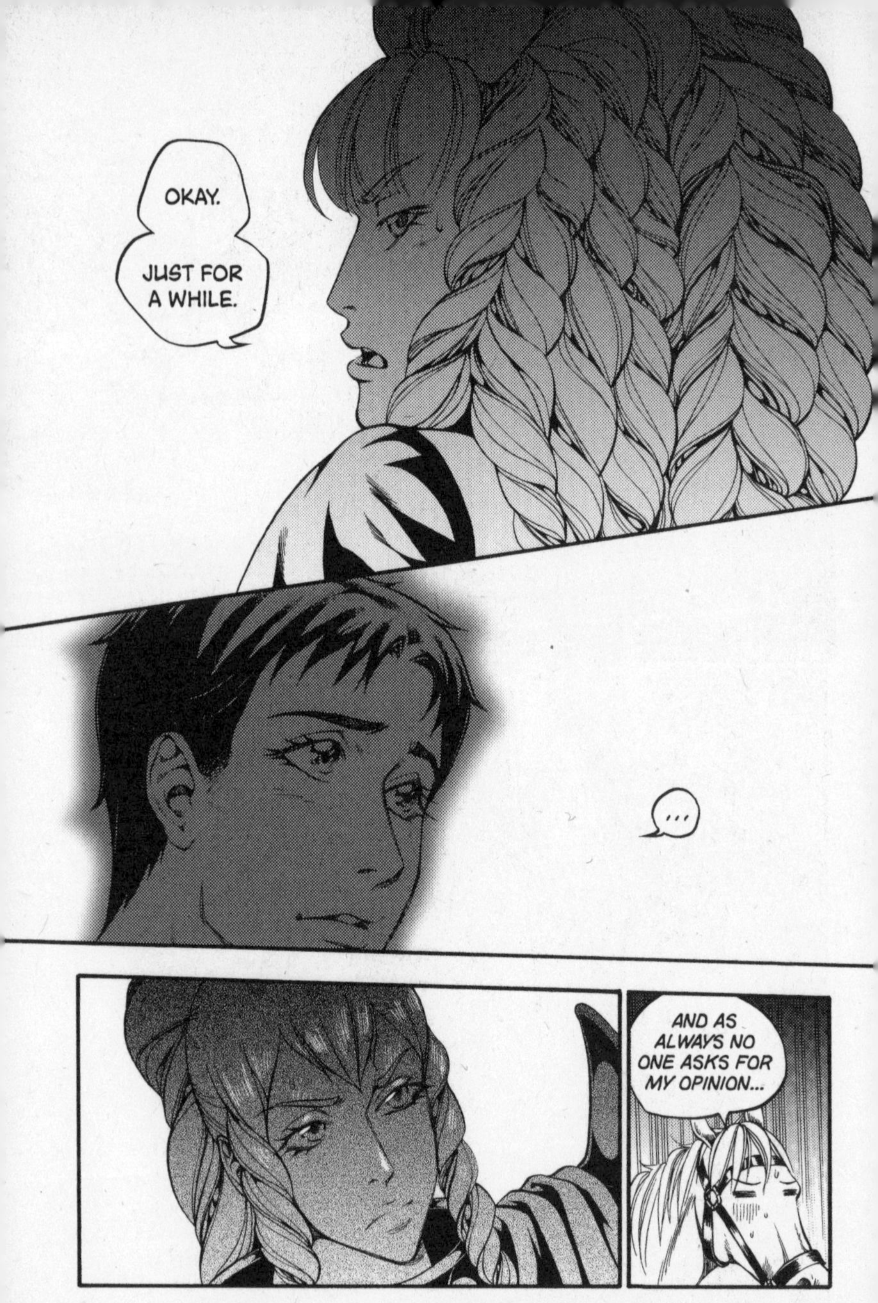
OKAY.
JUST FOR A WHILE.
...
AND AS ALWAYS NO ONE ASKS FOR MY OPINION...

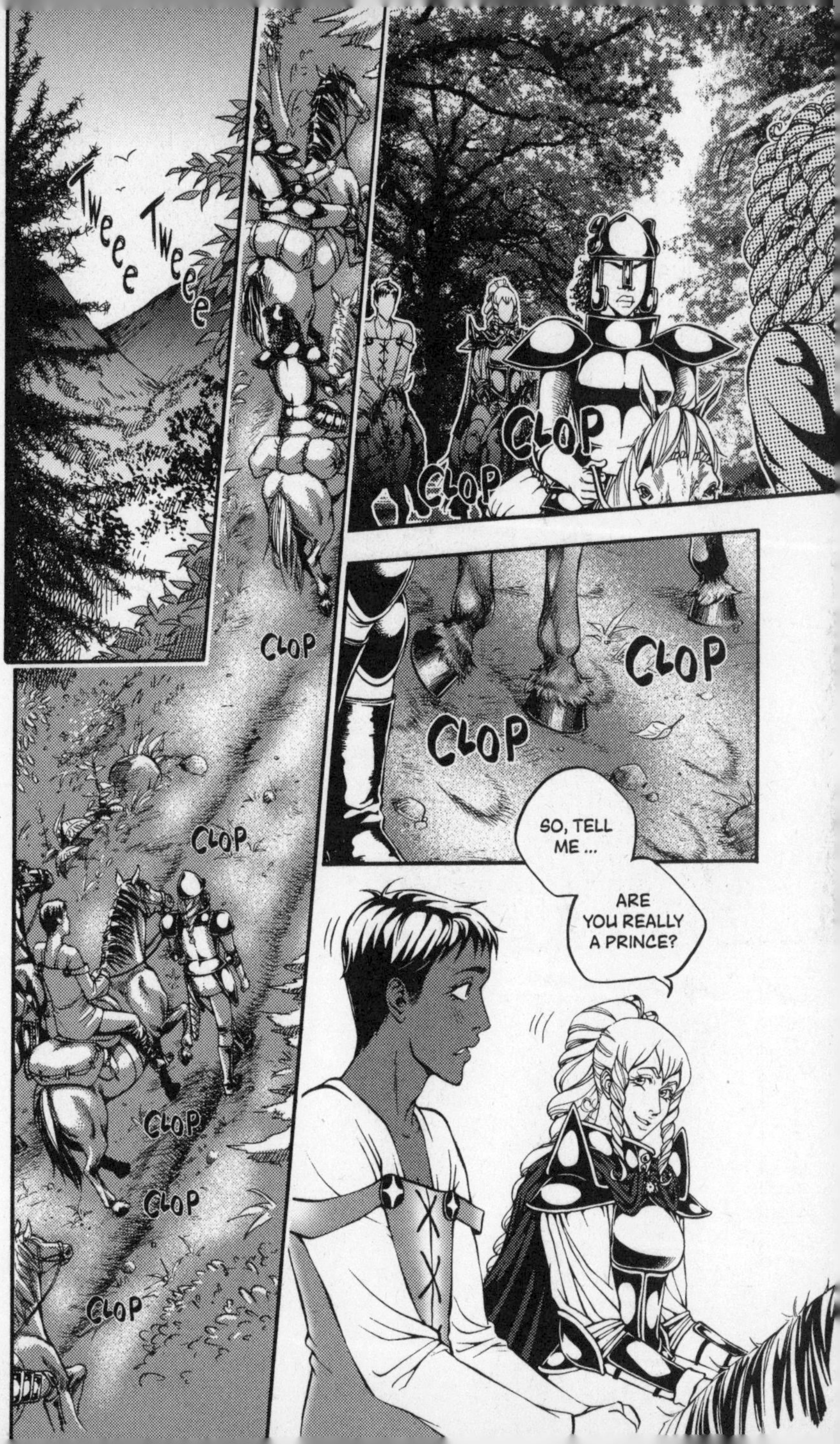
Tweee Tweee
CLOP
CLOP
CLOP
CLOP
CLOP
CLOP
CLOP
CLOP
CLOP
SO, TELL ME ...
ARE YOU REALLY A PRINCE?

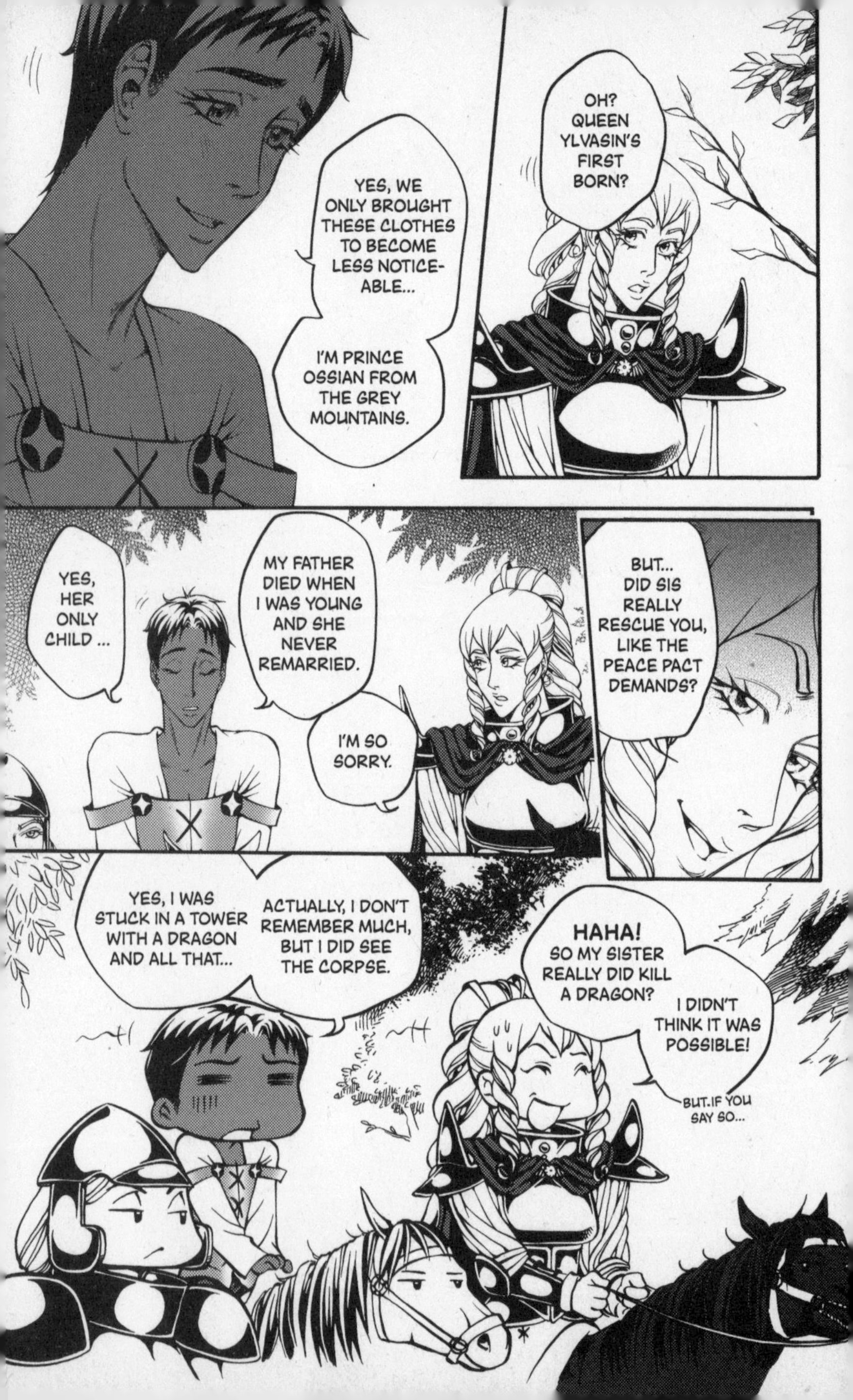

YES, WE ONLY BROUGHT THESE CLOTHES TO BECOME LESS NOTICE-ABLE...
I'M PRINCE OSSIAN FROM THE GREY MOUNTAINS.
OH? QUEEN YLVASIN'S FIRST BORN?
YES, HER ONLY CHILD ...
MY FATHER DIED WHEN I WAS YOUNG AND SHE NEVER REMARRIED.
I'M SO SORRY.
BUT... DID SIS REALLY RESCUE YOU, LIKE THE PEACE PACT DEMANDS?
YES, I WAS STUCK IN A TOWER WITH A DRAGON AND ALL THAT...
ACTUALLY, I DON'T REMEMBER MUCH, BUT I DID SEE THE CORPSE.
HAHA! SO MY SISTER REALLY DID KILL A DRAGON?
I DIDN'T THINK IT WAS POSSIBLE!
BUT.IF YOU SAY SO...

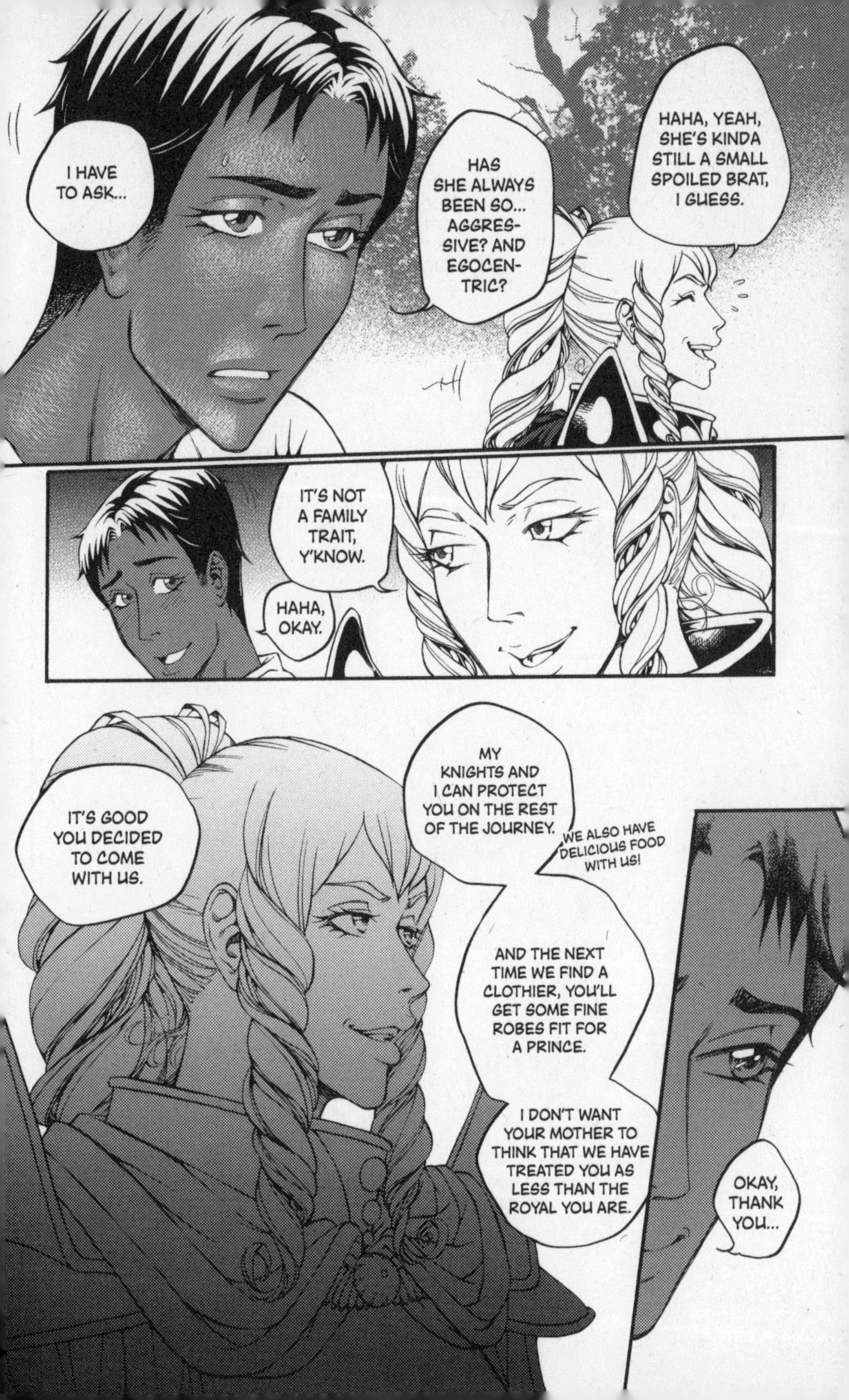
I HAVE TO ASK...
HAS SHE ALWAYS BEEN SO... AGGRES-SIVE? AND EGOCEN-TRIC?
HAHA, YEAH, SHE'S KINDA STILL A SMALL SPOILED BRAT, I GUESS.
IT'S NOT A FAMILY TRAIT, Y'KNOW.
HAHA, OKAY.
IT'S GOOD YOU DECIDED TO COME WITH US.
MY KNIGHTS AND I CAN PROTECT YOU ON THE REST OF THE JOURNEY.
WE ALSO HAVE DELICIOUS FOOD WITH US!
AND THE NEXT TIME WE FIND A CLOTHIER, YOU'LL GET SOME FINE ROBES FIT FOR A PRINCE.
I DON'T WANT YOUR MOTHER TO THINK THAT WE HAVE TREATED YOU AS LESS THAN THE ROYAL YOU ARE.
OKAY, THANK YOU...

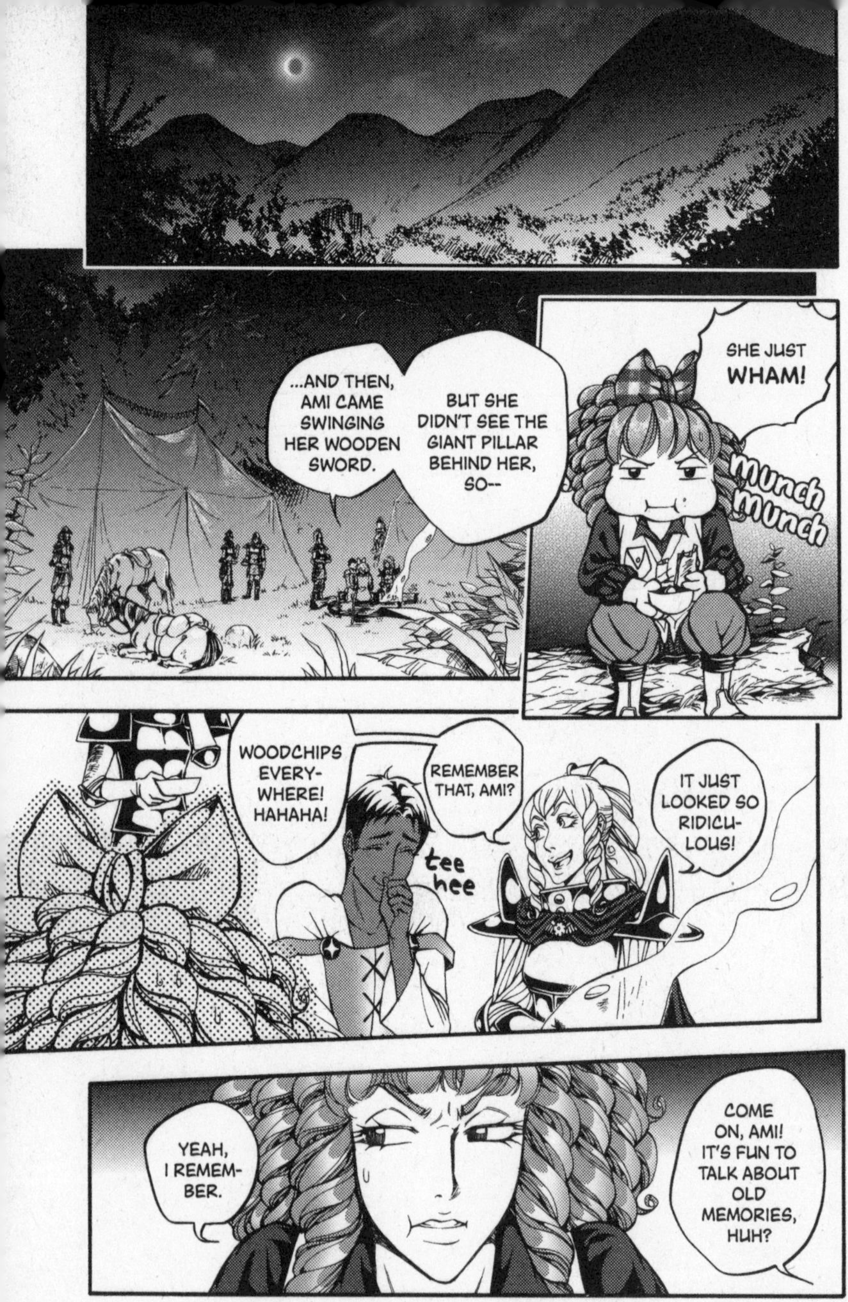
...AND THEN, AMI CAME SWINGING HER WOODEN SWORD.
BUT SHE DIDN'T SEE THE GIANT PILLAR BEHIND HER, SO--
SHE JUST WHAM!
MUNCH MUNCH
WOODCHIPS EVERY-WHERE! HAHAHA!
REMEMBER THAT, AMI?
tee hee
IT JUST LOOKED SO RIDICU-LOUS!
YEAH, I REMEM-BER.
COME ON, AMI! IT'S FUN TO TALK ABOUT OLD MEMORIES, HUH?

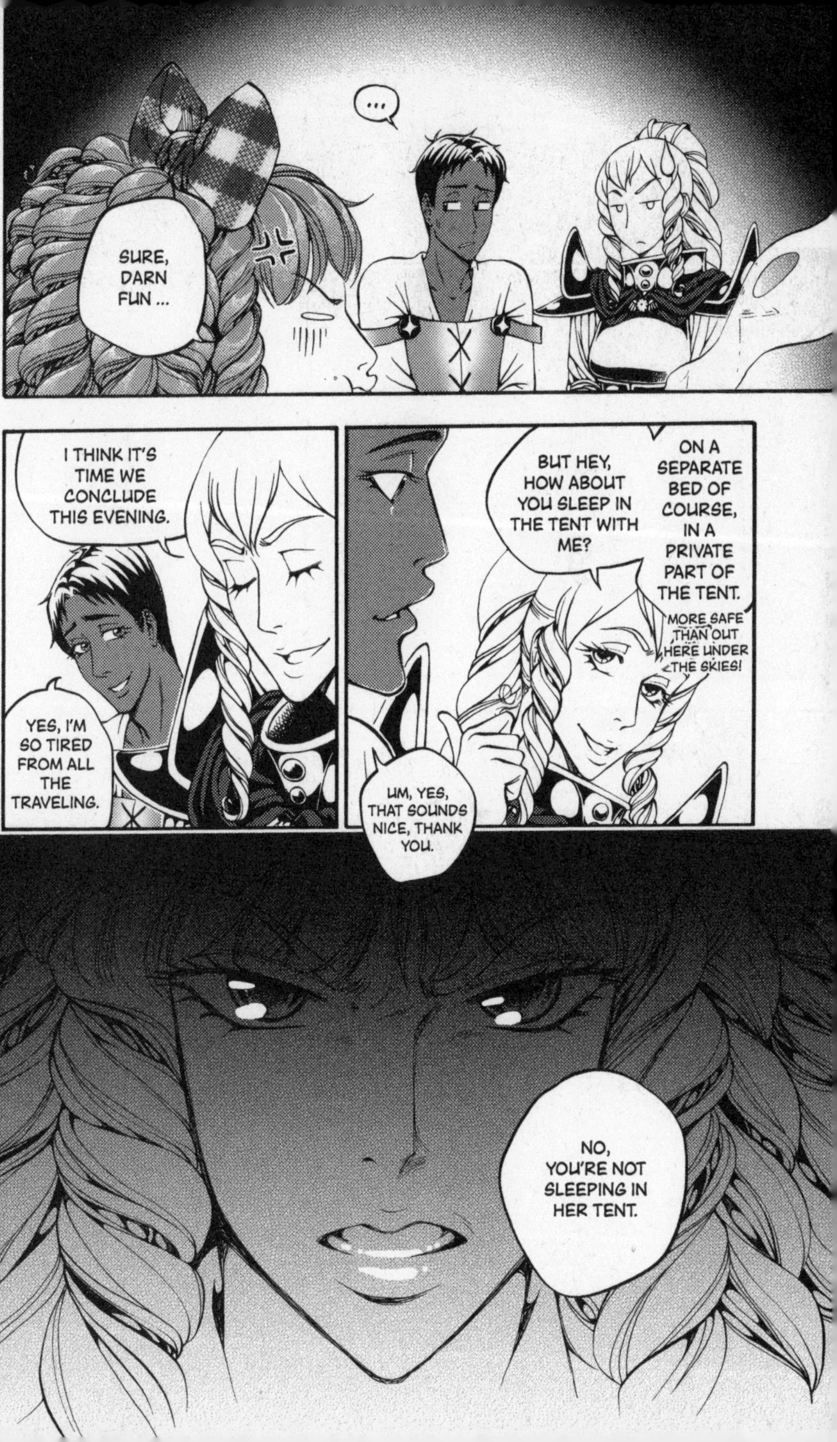
SURE, DARN FUN ...
...
I THINK IT'S TIME WE CONCLUDE THIS EVENING.
YES, I'M SO TIRED FROM ALL THE TRAVELING.
BUT HEY, HOW ABOUT YOU SLEEP IN THE TENT WITH ME?
ON A SEPARATE BED OF COURSE, IN A PRIVATE PART OF THE TENT.
MORE SAFE THAN OUT HERE UNDER THE SKIES!
UM, YES, THAT SOUNDS NICE, THANK YOU.
NO, YOU'RE NOT SLEEPING IN HER TENT.

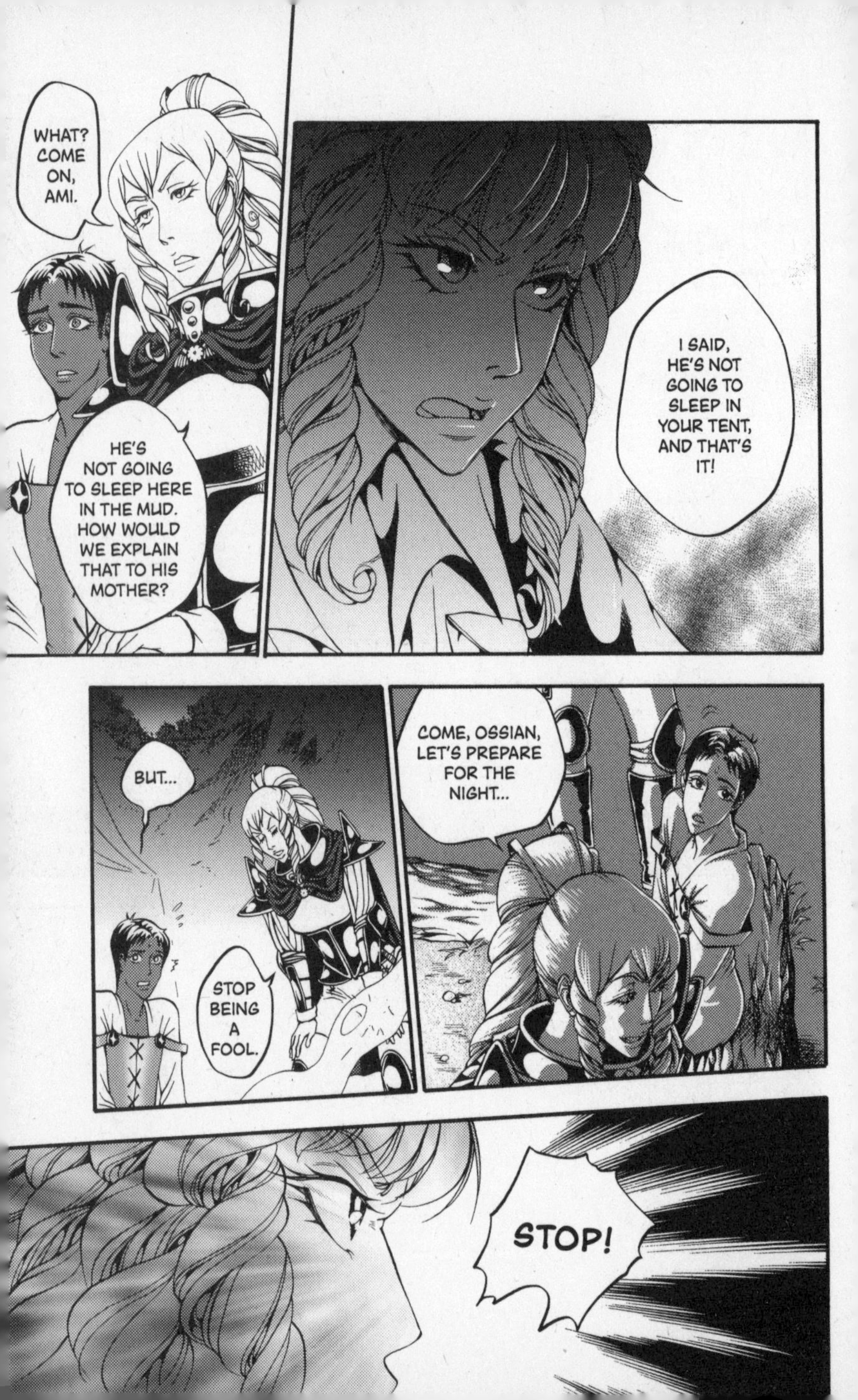
WHAT? COME ON, AMI.
HE'S NOT GOING TO SLEEP HERE IN THE MUD. HOW WOULD WE EXPLAIN THAT TO HIS MOTHER?
I SAID, HE'S NOT GOING TO SLEEP IN YOUR TENT, AND THAT'S IT!
BUT...
STOP BEING A FOOL.
COME, OSSIAN, LET'S PREPARE FOR THE NIGHT...
STOP!

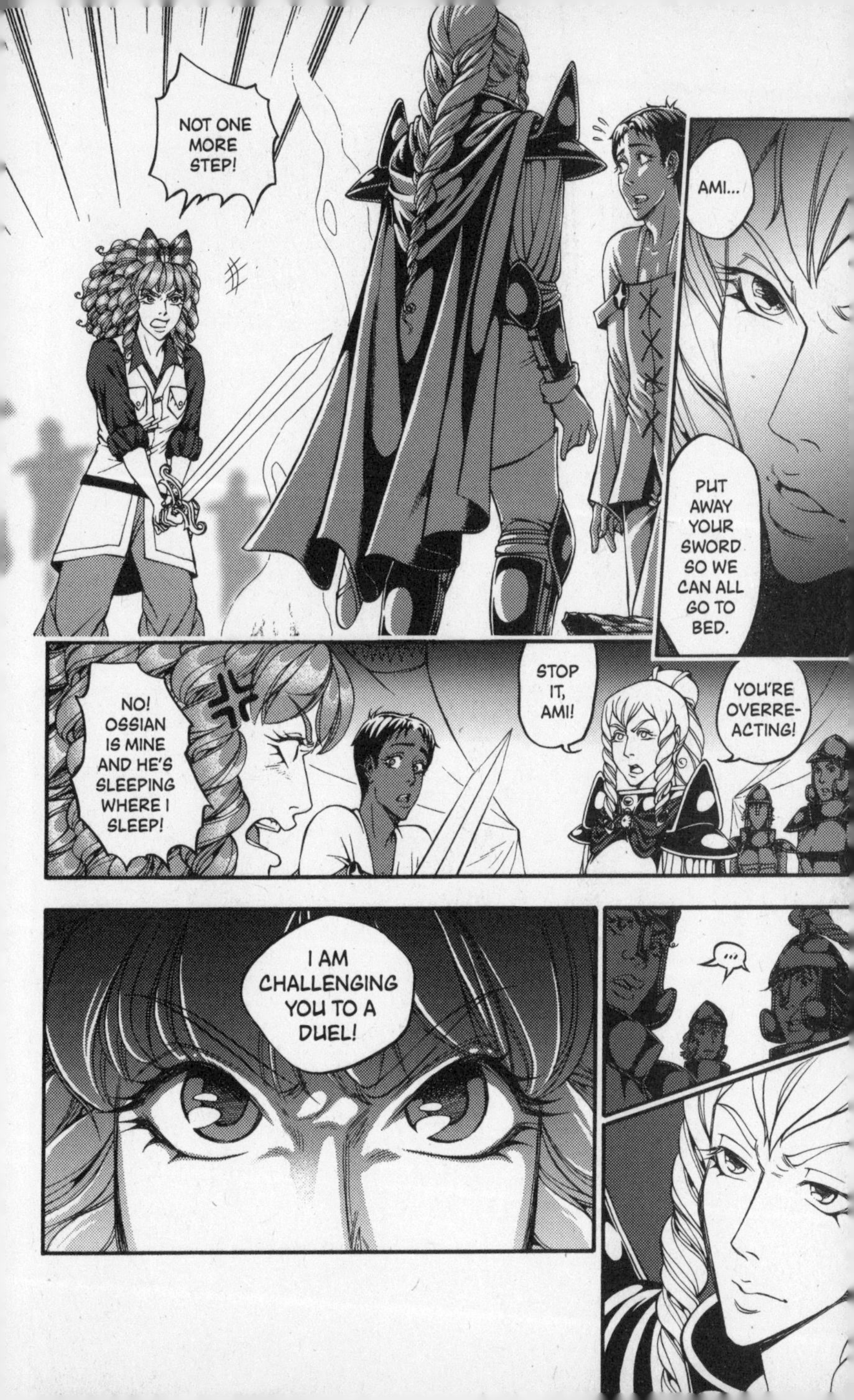
NOT ONE MORE STEP!
AMI...
PUT AWAY YOUR SWORD SO WE CAN ALL GO TO BED.
NO! OSSIAN IS MINE AND HE'S SLEEPING WHERE I SLEEP!
STOP IT, AMI!
YOU'RE OVERRE-ACTING!
I AM CHALLENGING YOU TO A DUEL!
...

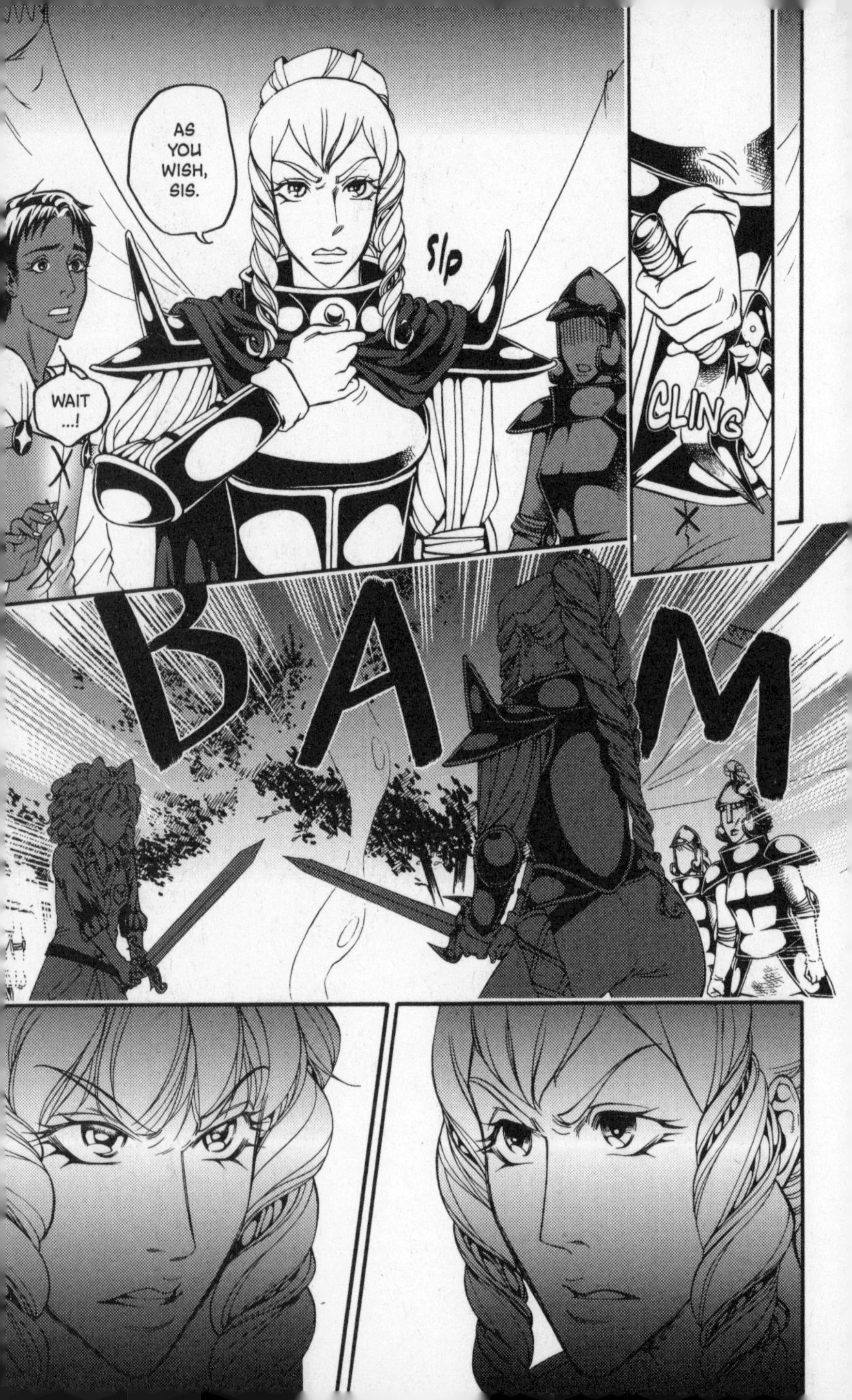
AS YOU WISH, SIS.
WAIT ...!
slp
CLING
BAM

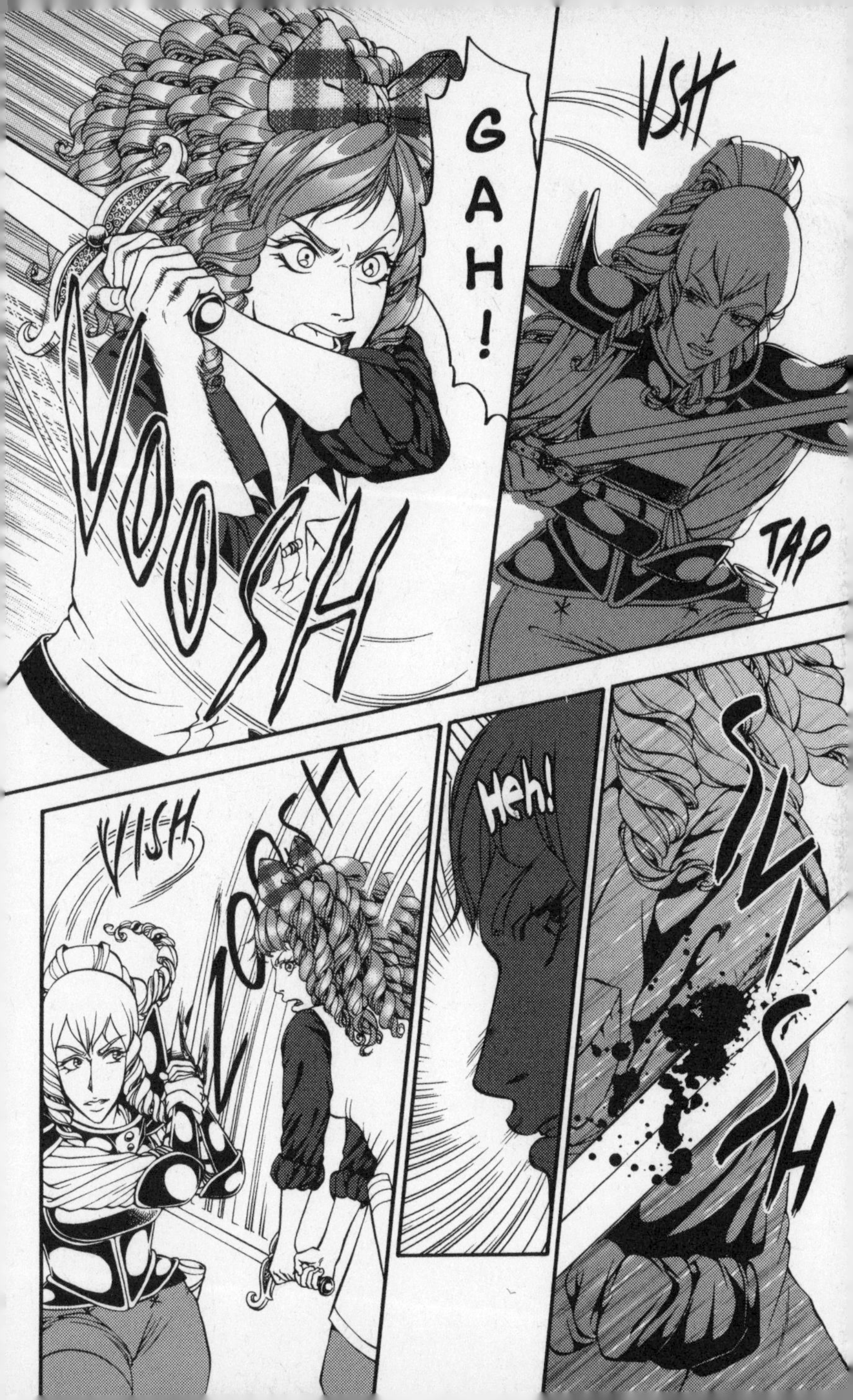
GAH!
VOOSH
VSH
TAP
VISH
Heh!
SLISH

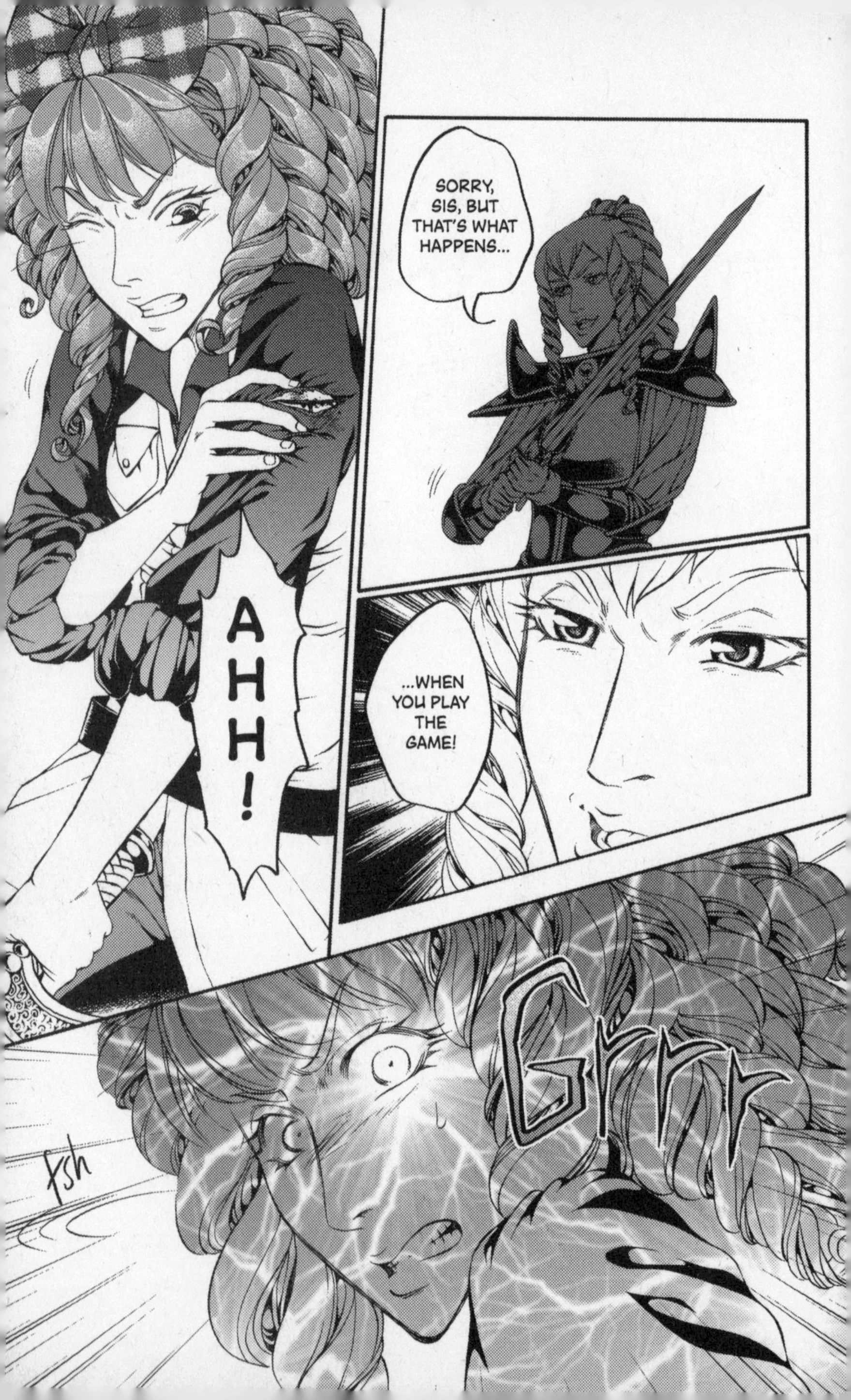
AHH!
SORRY, SIS, BUT THAT'S WHAT HAPPENS...
...WHEN YOU PLAY THE GAME!
Grrr
fsh

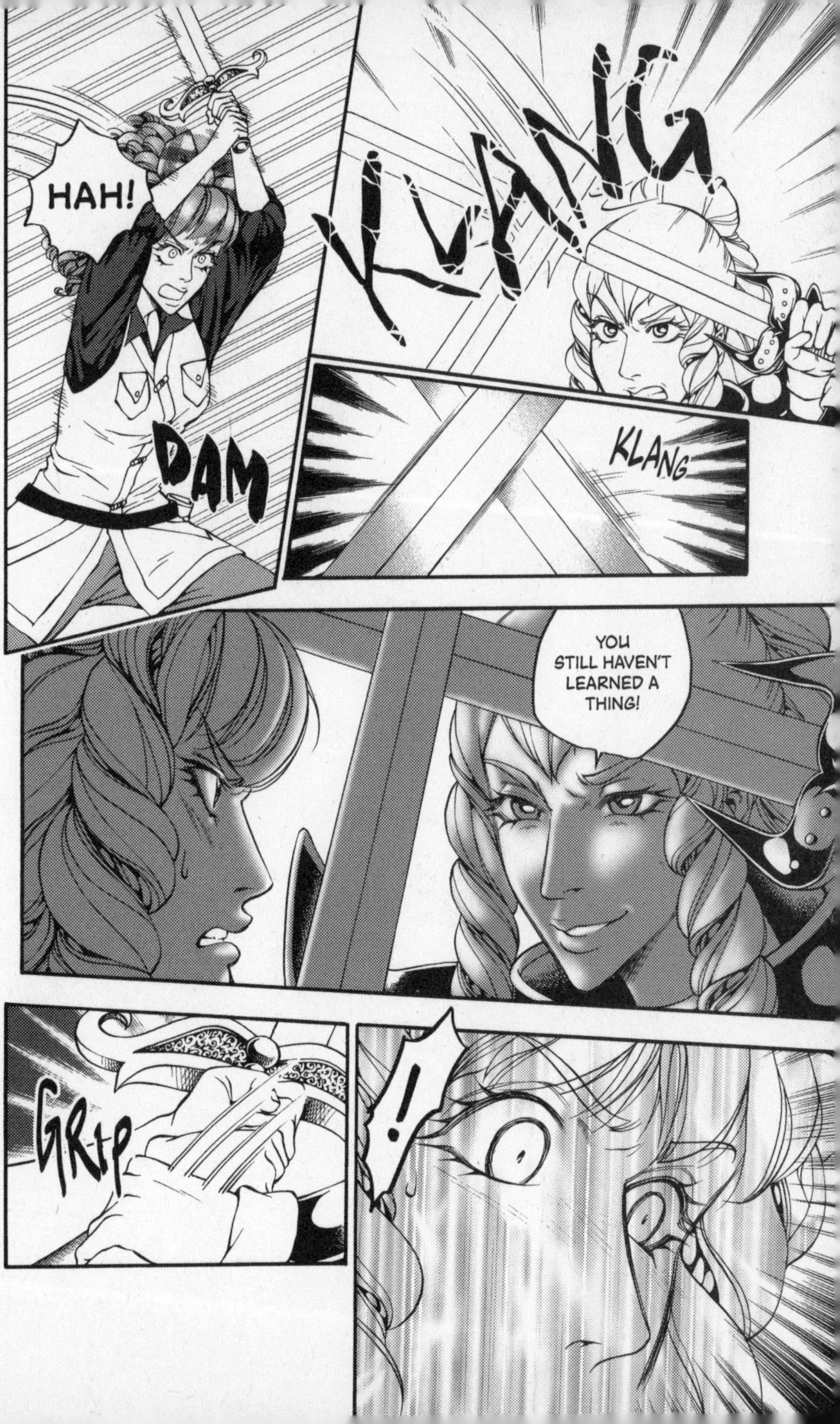
HAH!
DAM
KLANG
YOU STILL HAVEN'T LEARNED A THING!
GRIP
!

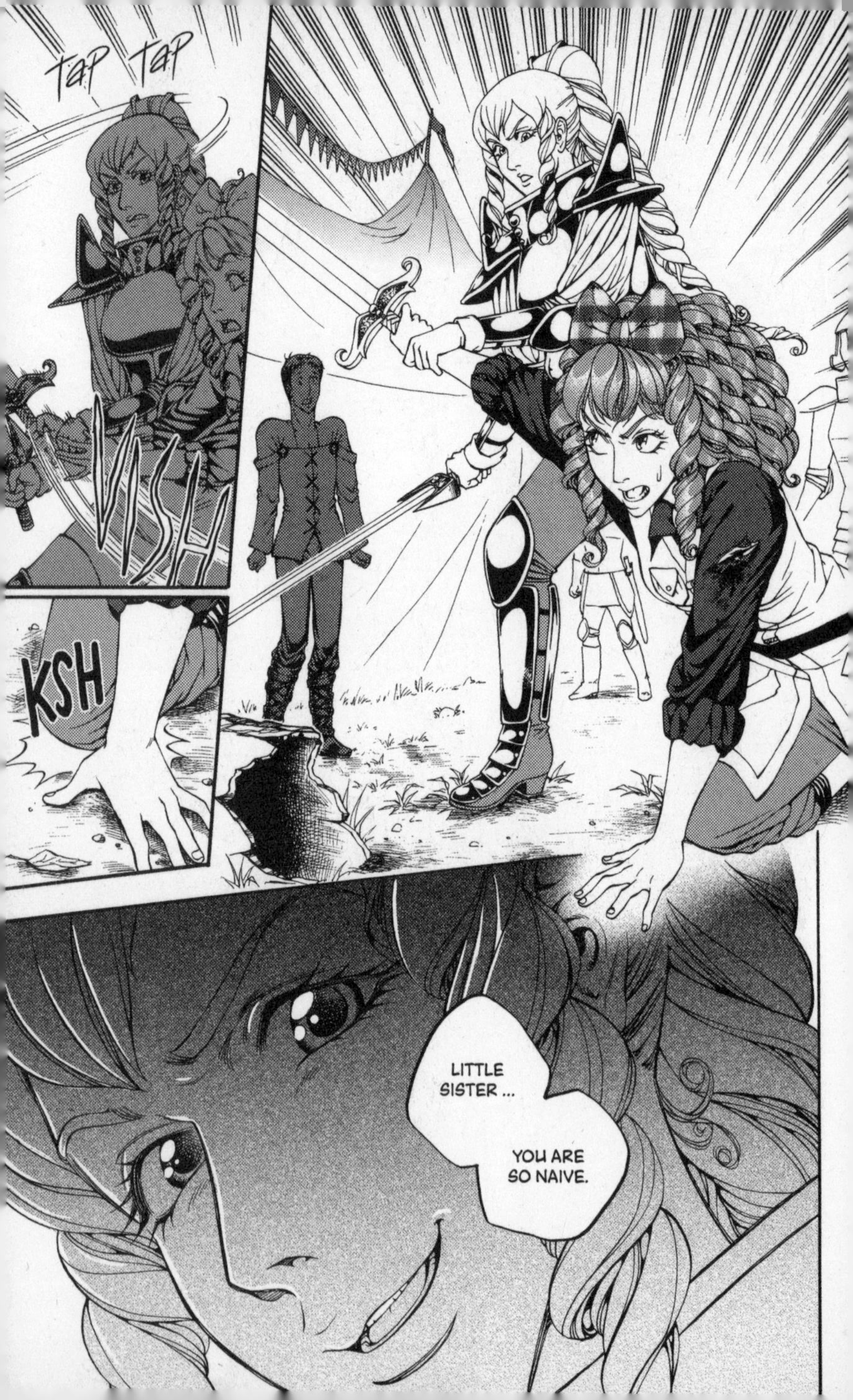
TAP TAP
VISH
KSH
LITTLE SISTER ...
YOU ARE SO NAIVE.

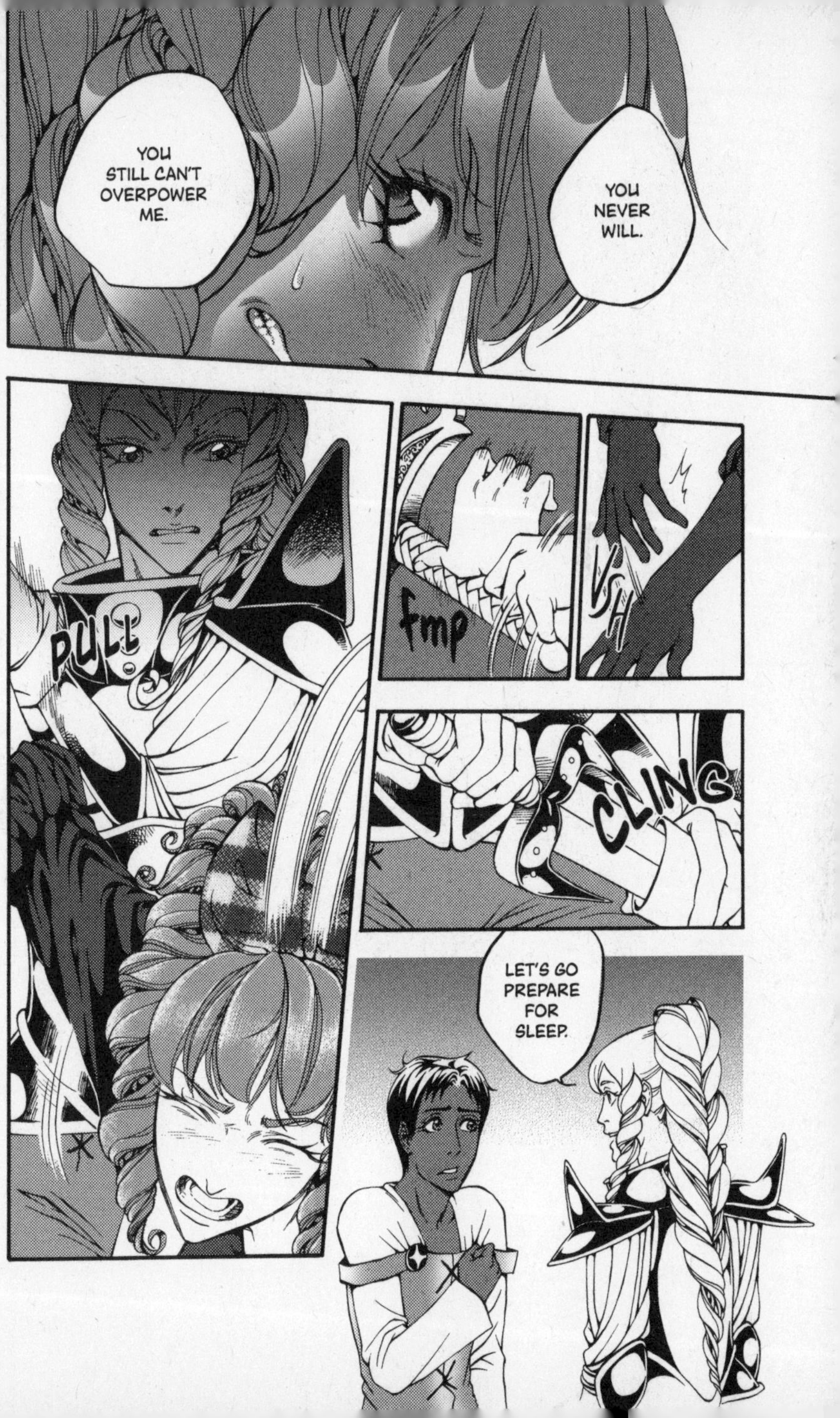
YOU STILL CAN'T OVERPOWER ME.
YOU NEVER WILL.
PULL
fmp
VSH
CLING
LET'S GO PREPARE FOR SLEEP.

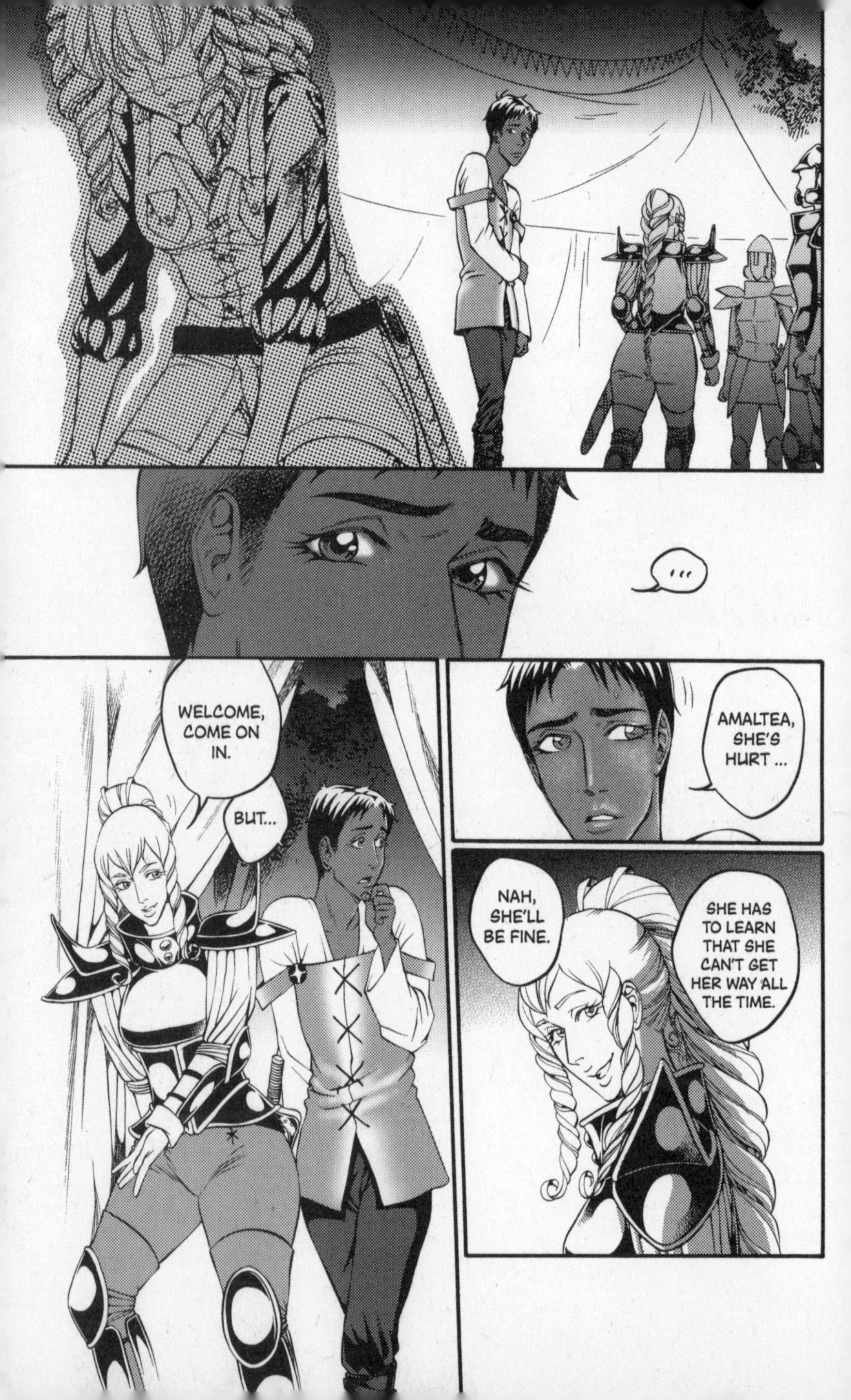
...
WELCOME, COME ON IN.
BUT...
AMALTEA, SHE'S HURT ...
NAH, SHE'LL BE FINE.
SHE HAS TO LEARN THAT SHE CAN'T GET HER WAY ALL THE TIME.

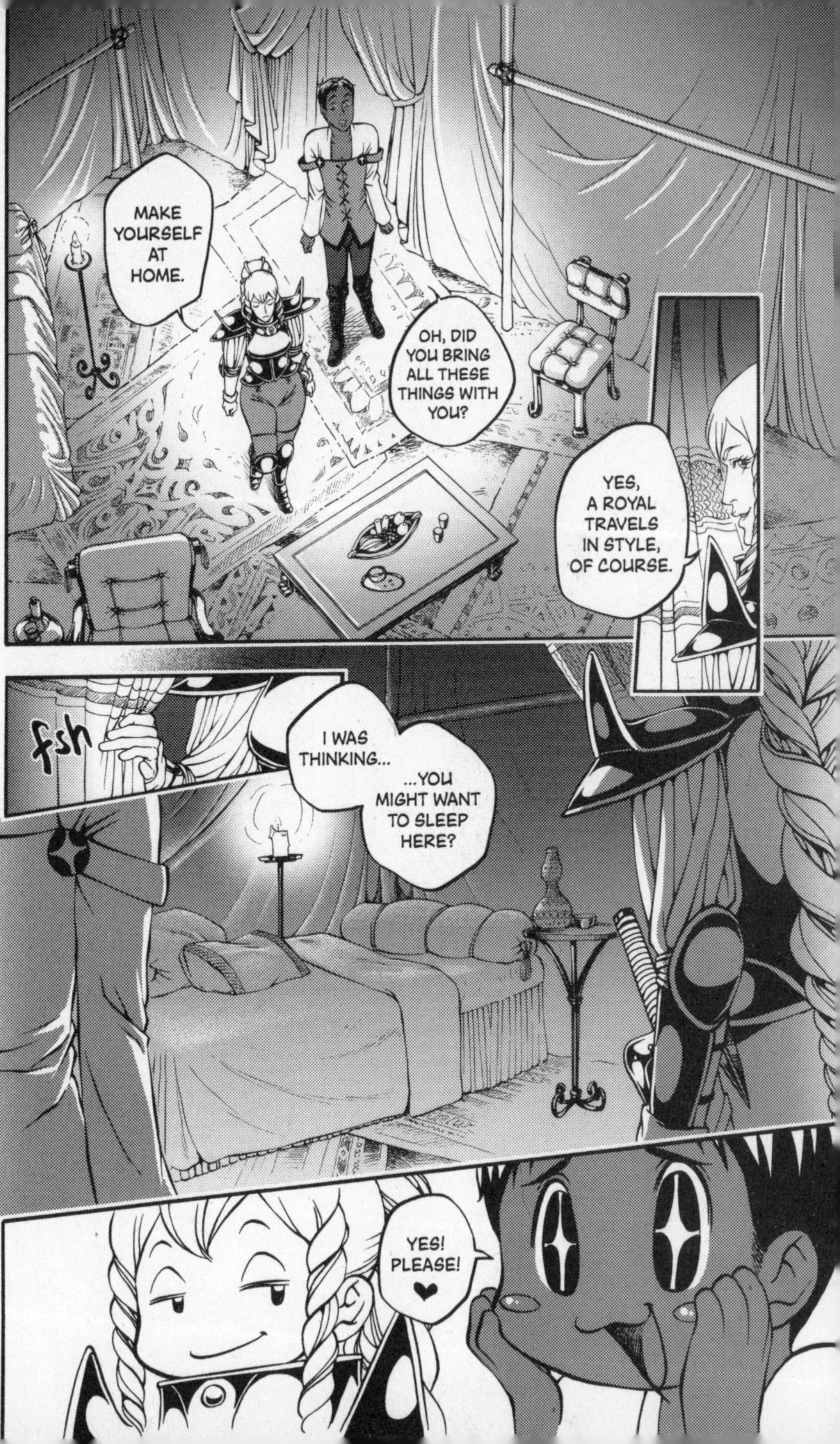
MAKE YOURSELF AT HOME.
OH, DID YOU BRING ALL THESE THINGS WITH YOU?
YES, A ROYAL TRAVELS IN STYLE, OF COURSE.
fsh
I WAS THINKING... ...YOU MIGHT WANT TO SLEEP HERE?
YES! PLEASE! ♥

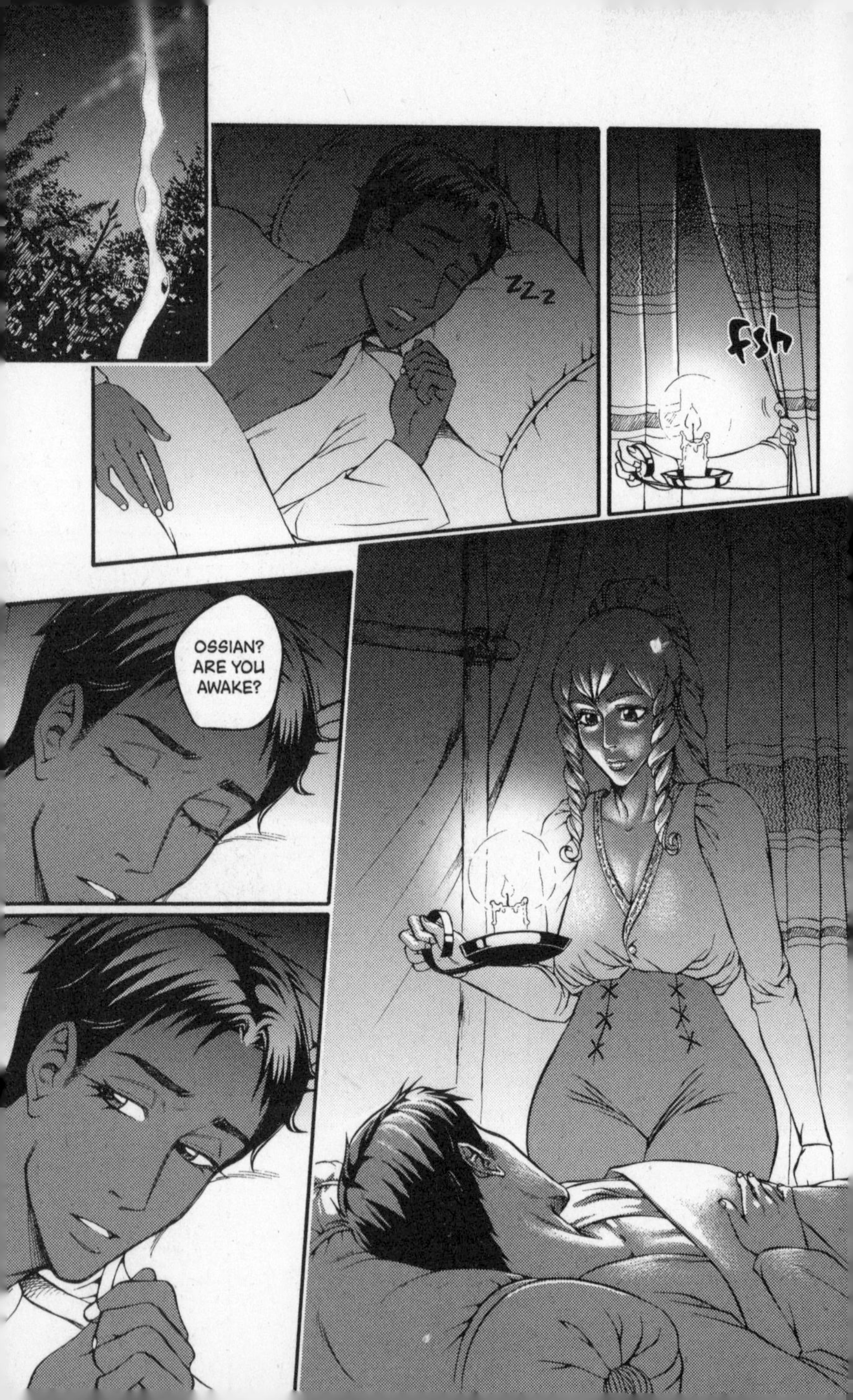
ZZZ
fsh
OSSIAN? ARE YOU AWAKE?

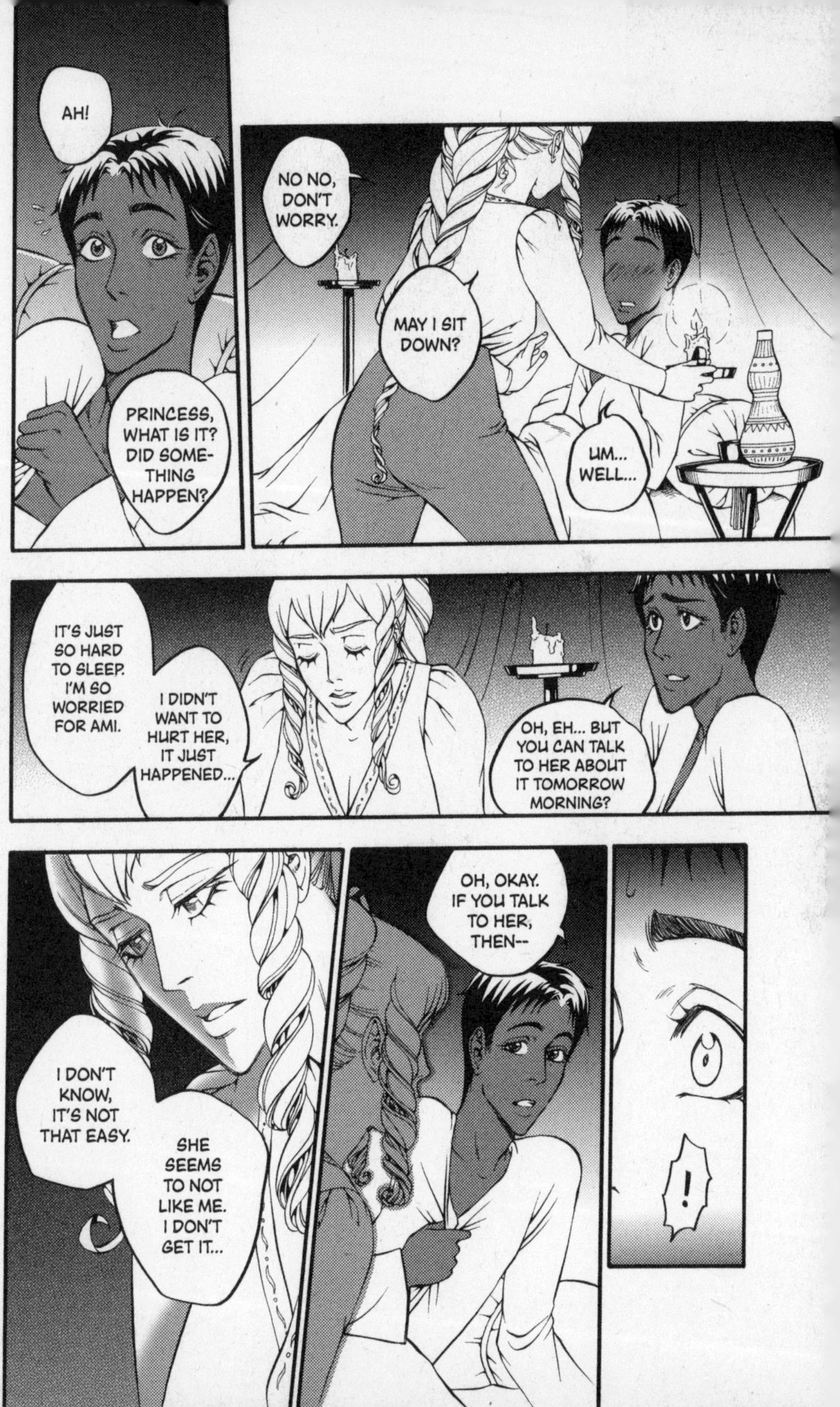
AH!
PRINCESS, WHAT IS IT? DID SOMETHING HAPPEN?
NO NO, DON'T WORRY.
MAY I SIT DOWN?
UM... WELL...
IT'S JUST SO HARD TO SLEEP. I'M SO WORRIED FOR AMI.
I DIDN'T WANT TO HURT HER, IT JUST HAPPENED...
OH, EH... BUT YOU CAN TALK TO HER ABOUT IT TOMORROW MORNING?
I DON'T KNOW, IT'S NOT THAT EASY.
SHE SEEMS TO NOT LIKE ME. I DON'T GET IT...
OH, OKAY. IF YOU TALK TO HER, THEN--
!

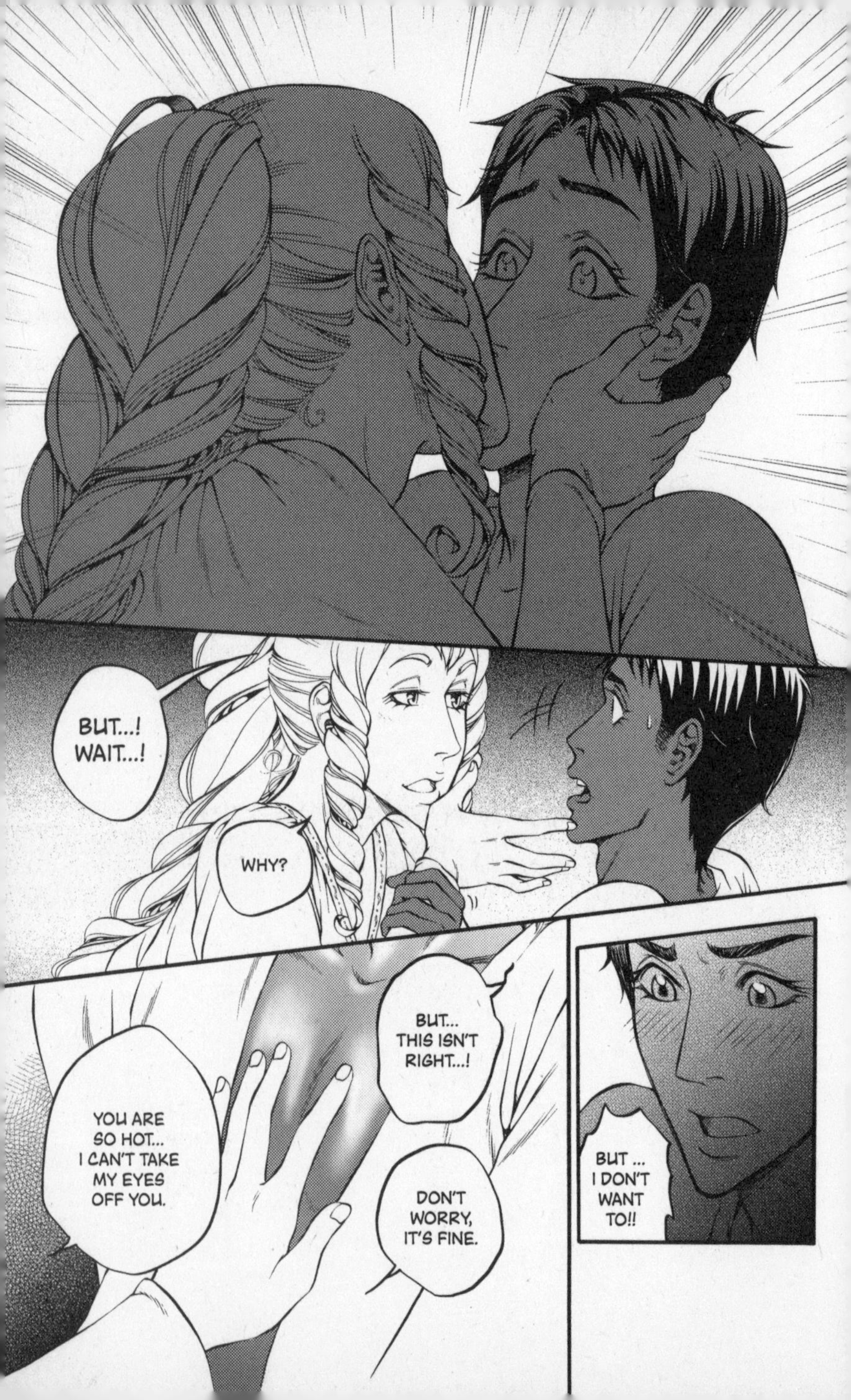
BUT...! WAIT...!
WHY?
YOU ARE SO HOT... I CAN'T TAKE MY EYES OFF YOU.
BUT... THIS ISN'T RIGHT...!
DON'T WORRY, IT'S FINE.
BUT ... I DON'T WANT TO!!

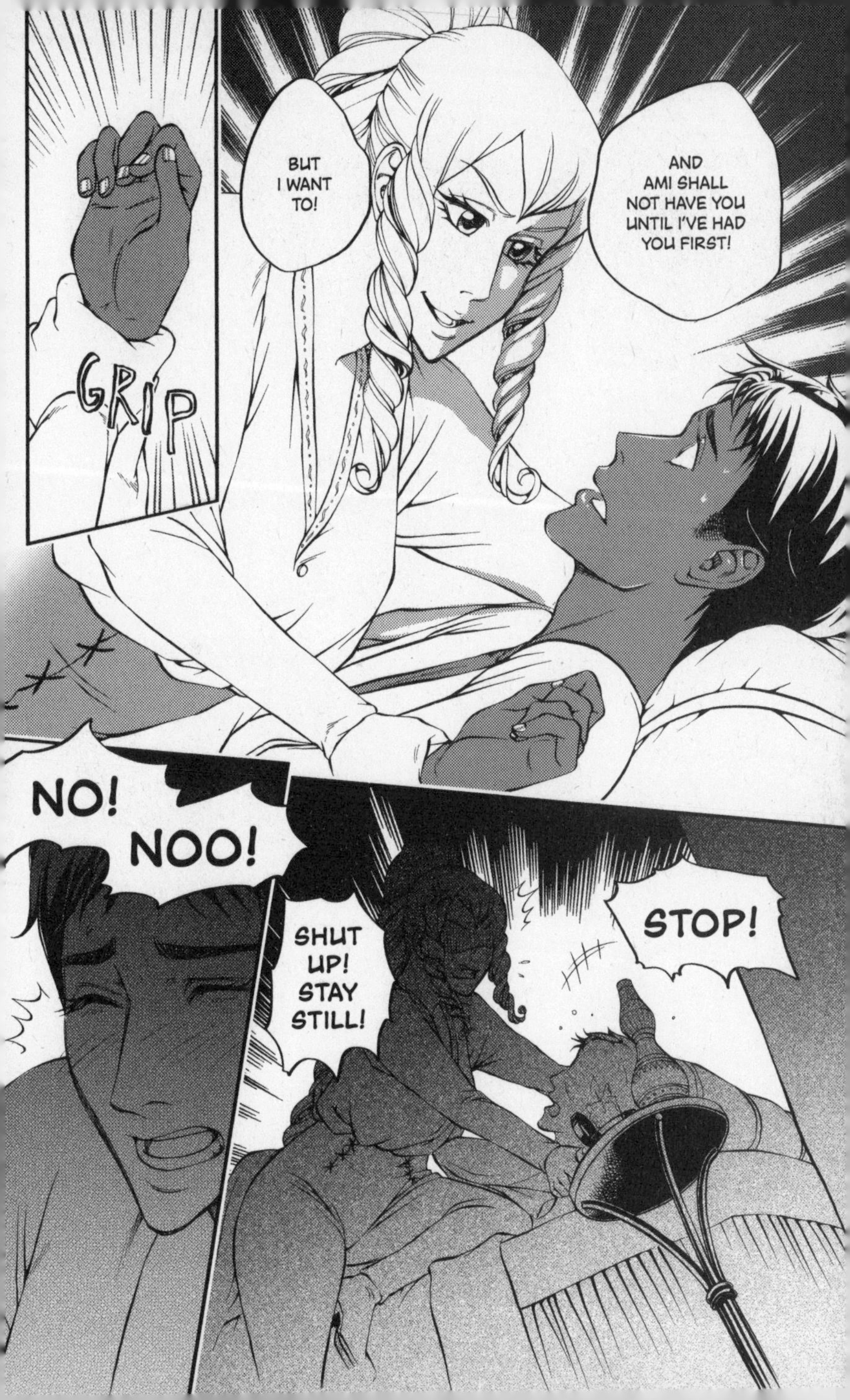
GRIP
BUT I WANT TO!
AND AMI SHALL NOT HAVE YOU UNTIL I'VE HAD YOU FIRST!
NO! NOO!
SHUT UP! STAY STILL!
STOP!

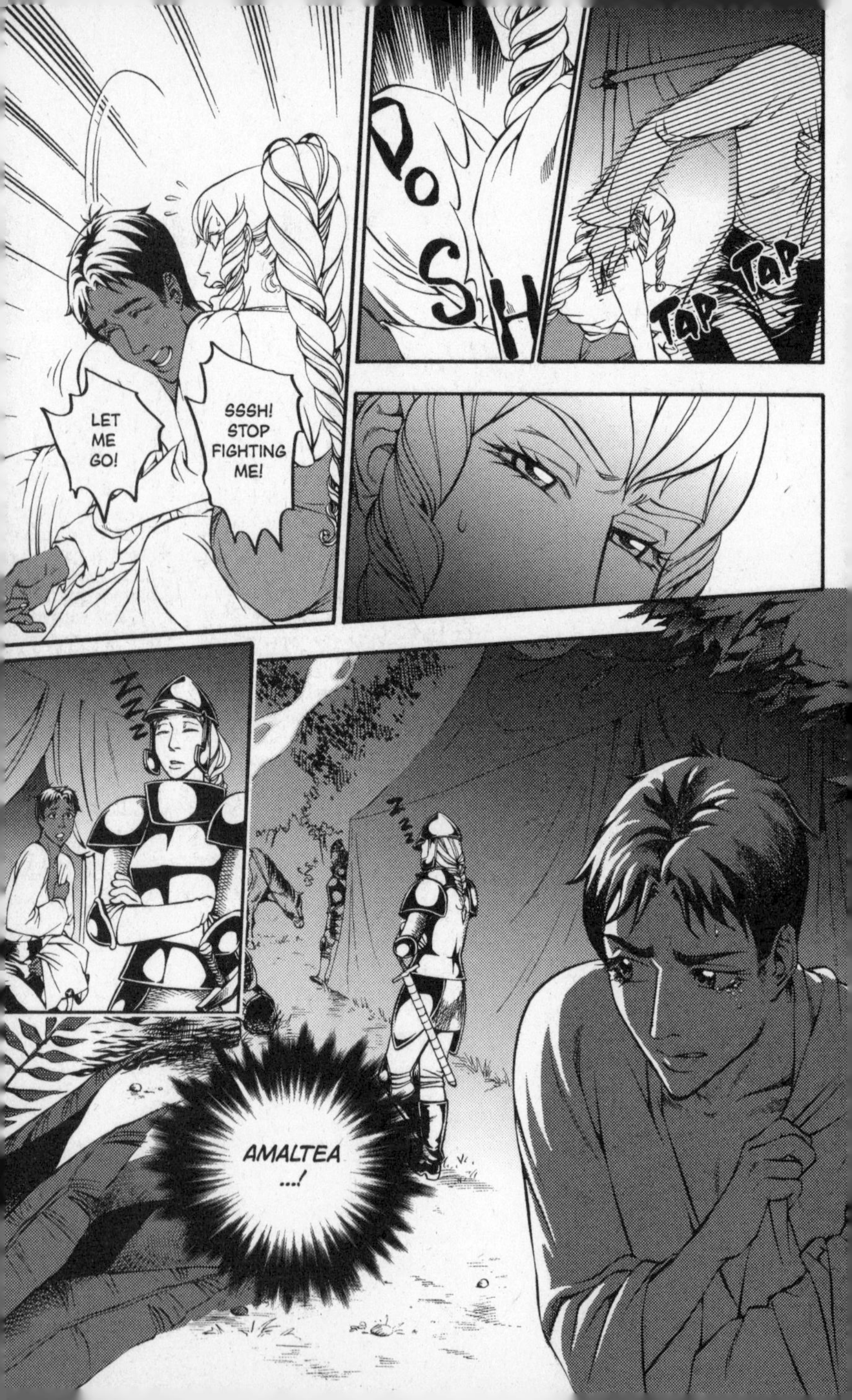
LET ME GO!
SSSH! STOP FIGHTING ME!
DOSH
TAP TAP
ZZZ
ZZZ
AMALTEA ...!

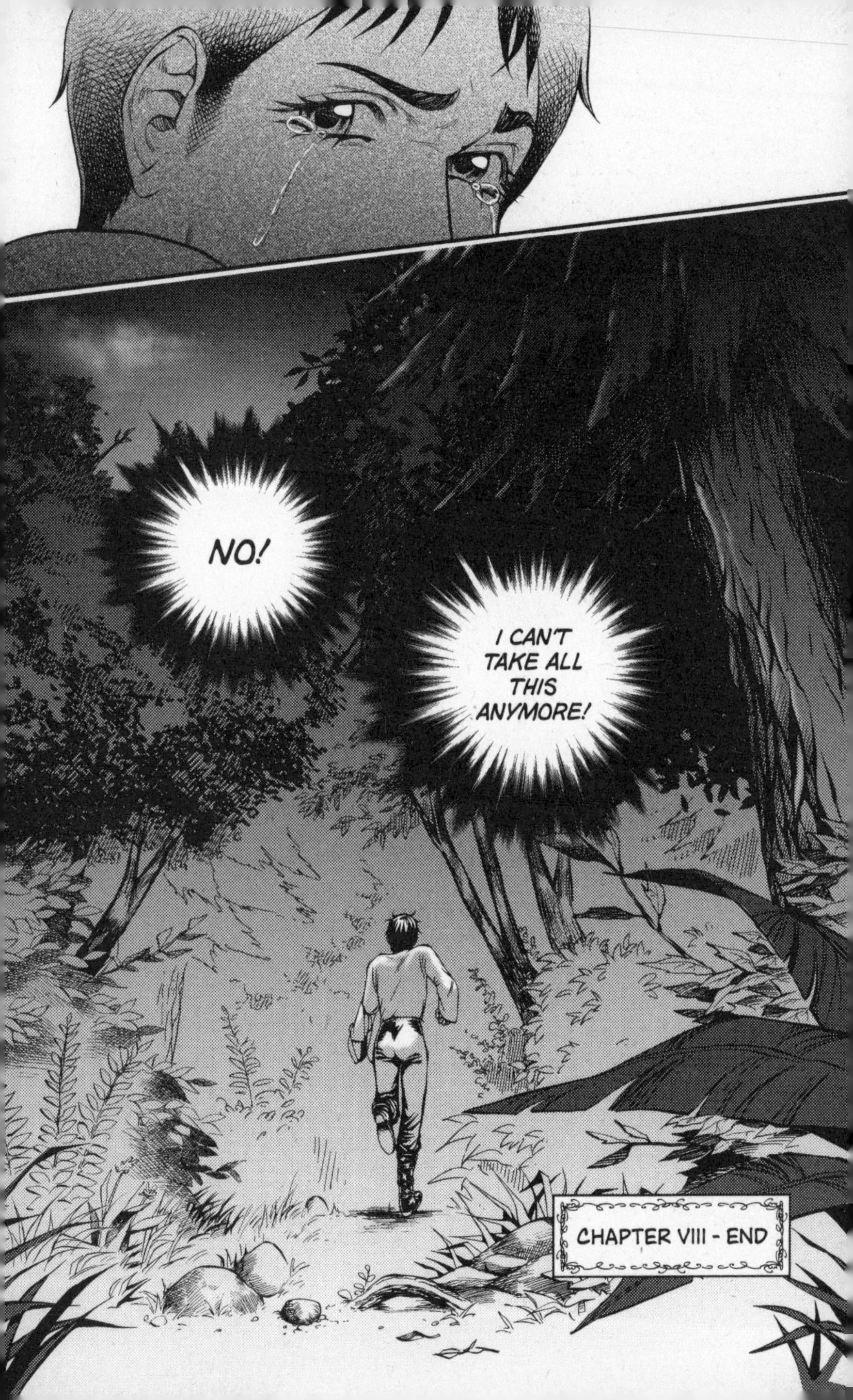
NO!
I CAN'T TAKE ALL THIS ANYMORE!
CHAPTER VIII - END

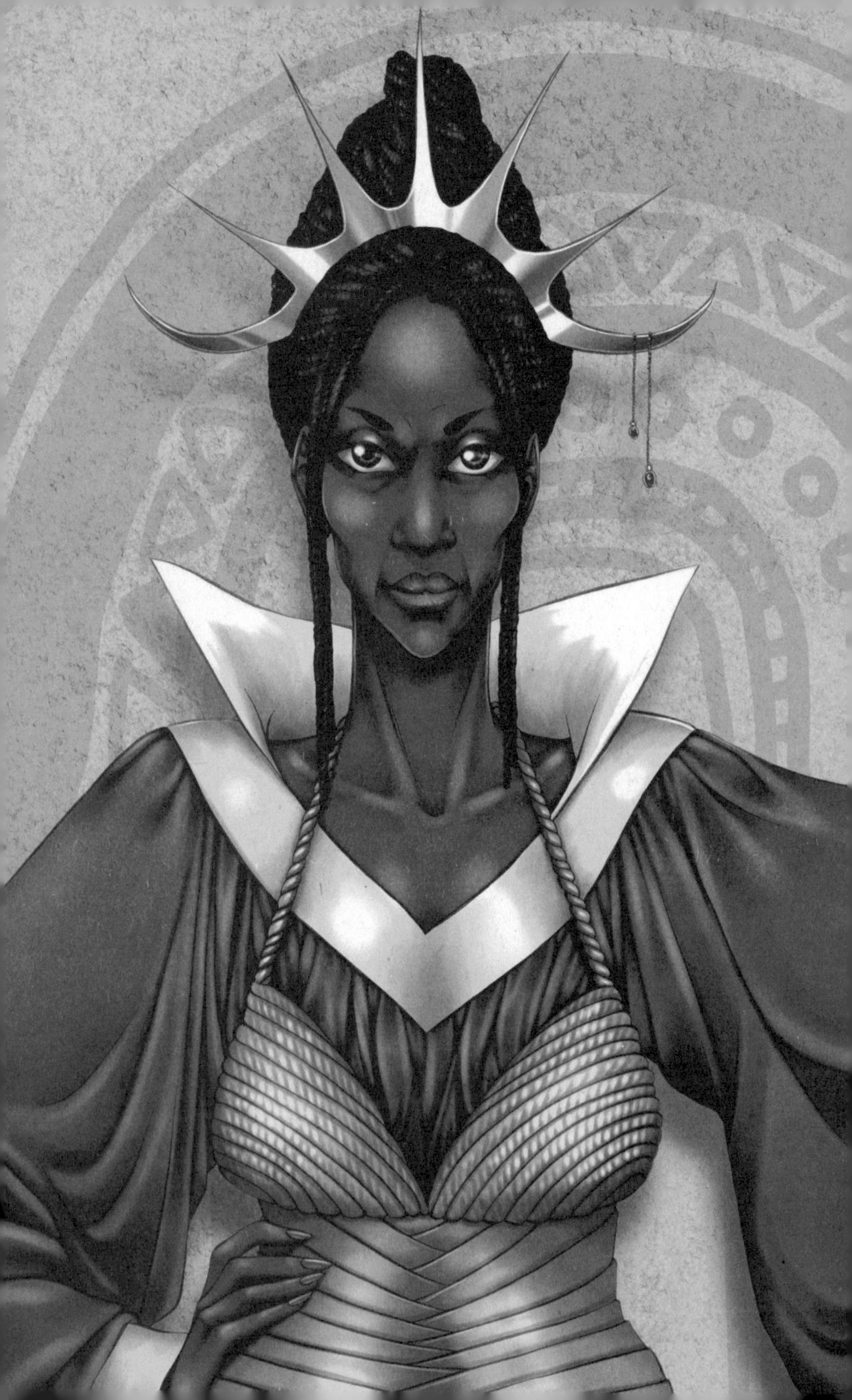

Chapter IX

The Prince And The Queen

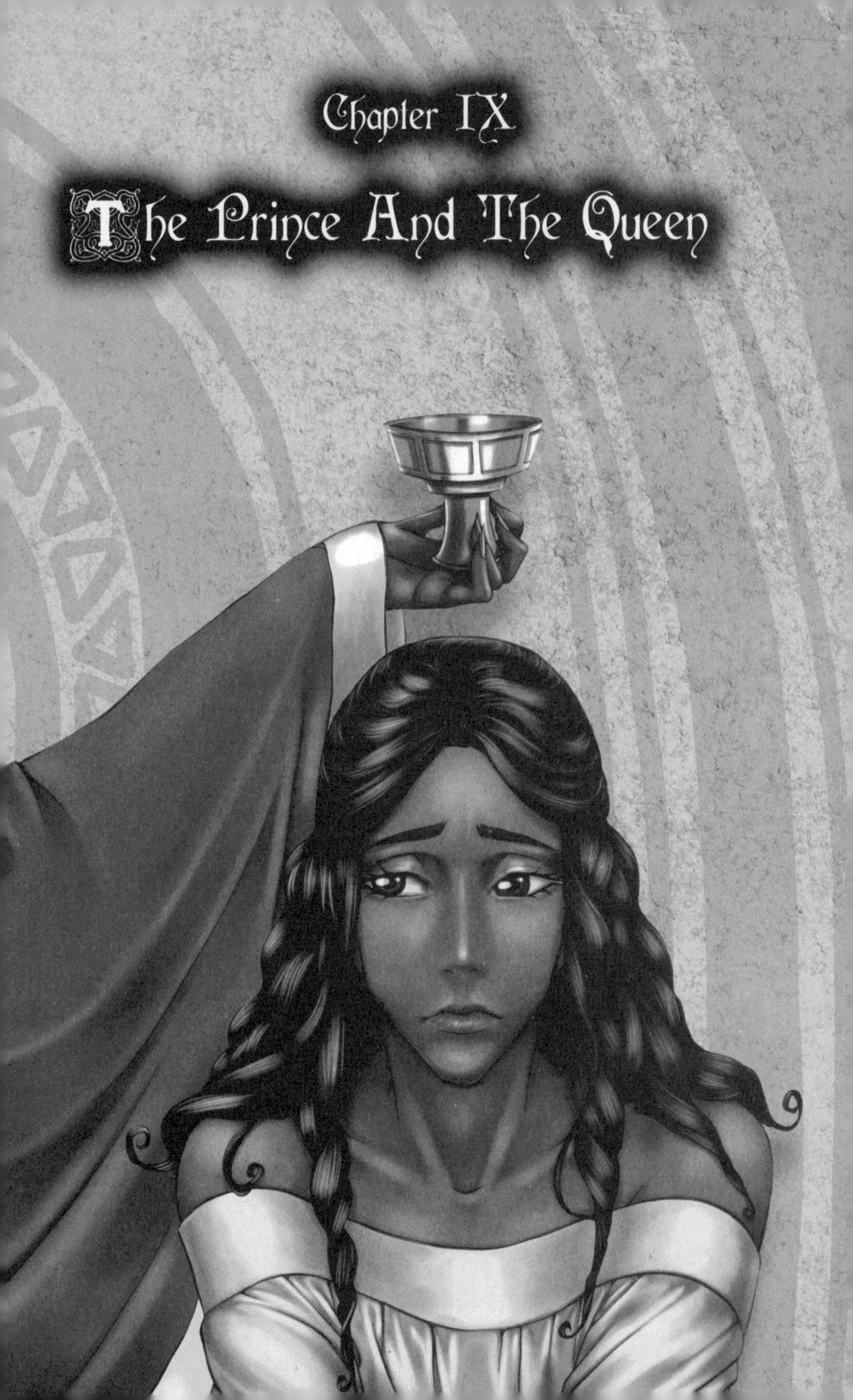

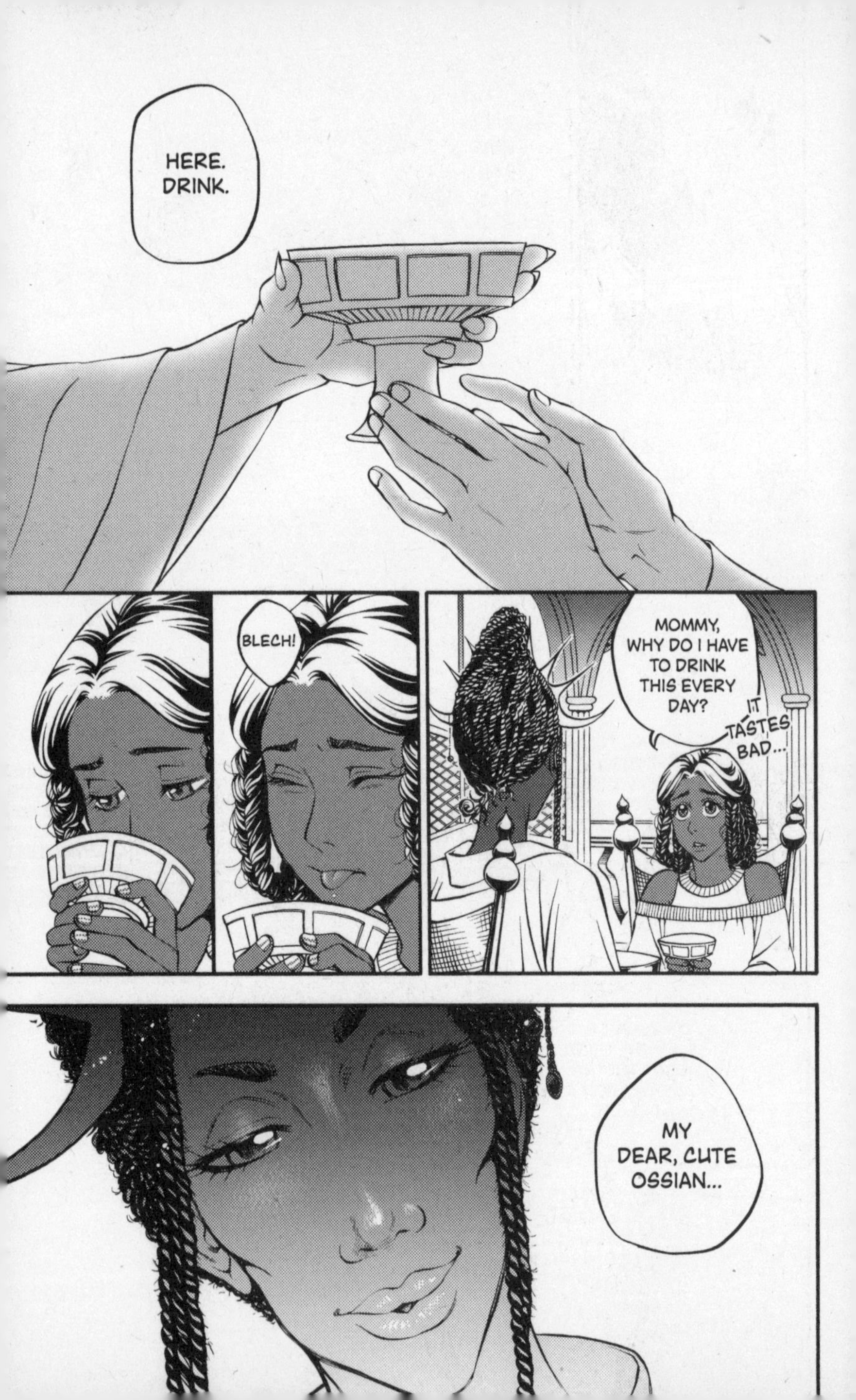
HERE. DRINK.
BLECH!
MOMMY, WHY DO I HAVE TO DRINK THIS EVERY DAY?
IT TASTES BAD...
MY DEAR, CUTE OSSIAN...

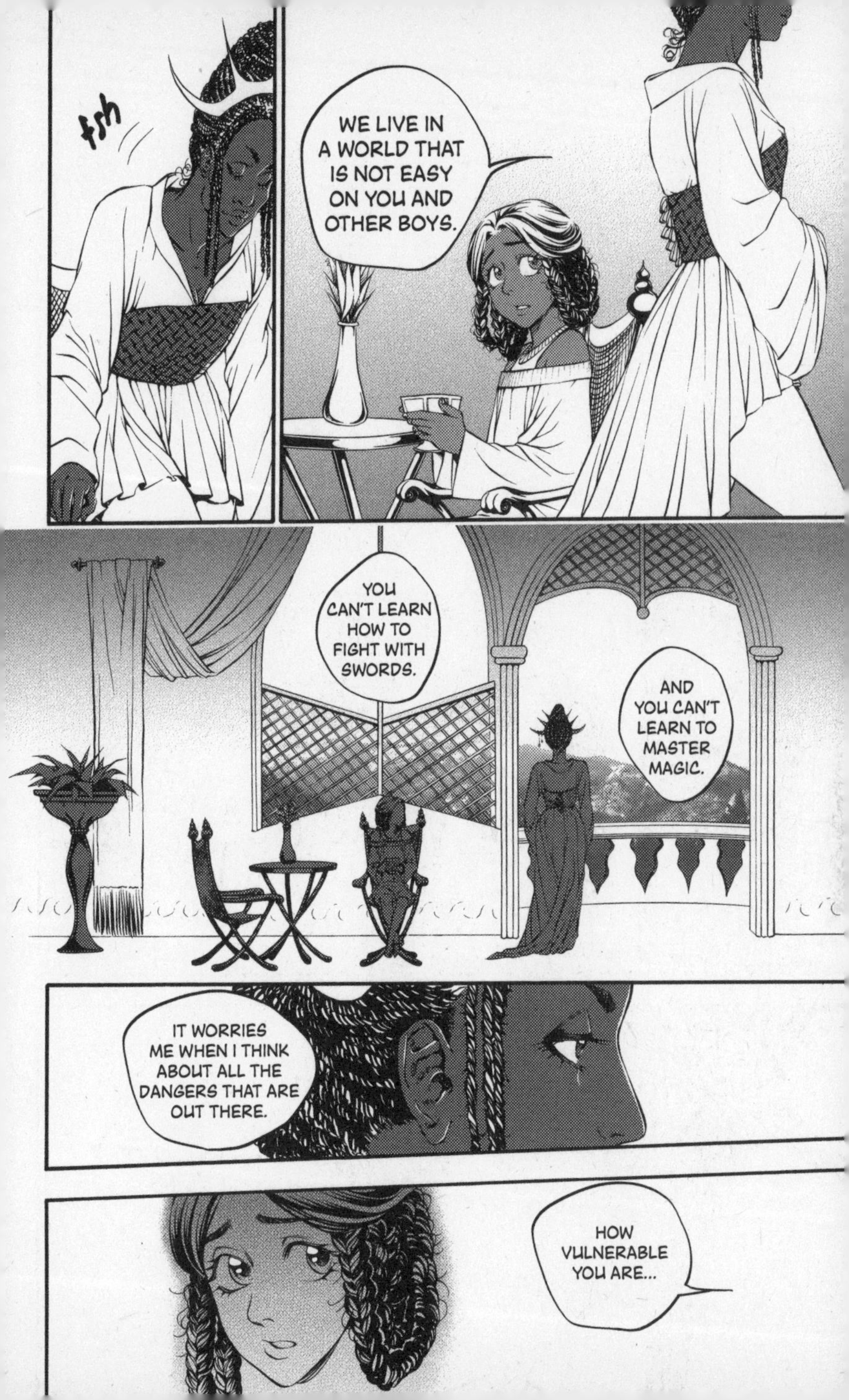
fsh
WE LIVE IN A WORLD THAT IS NOT EASY ON YOU AND OTHER BOYS.
YOU CAN'T LEARN HOW TO FIGHT WITH SWORDS.
AND YOU CAN'T LEARN TO MASTER MAGIC.
IT WORRIES ME WHEN I THINK ABOUT ALL THE DANGERS THAT ARE OUT THERE.
HOW VULNERABLE YOU ARE...

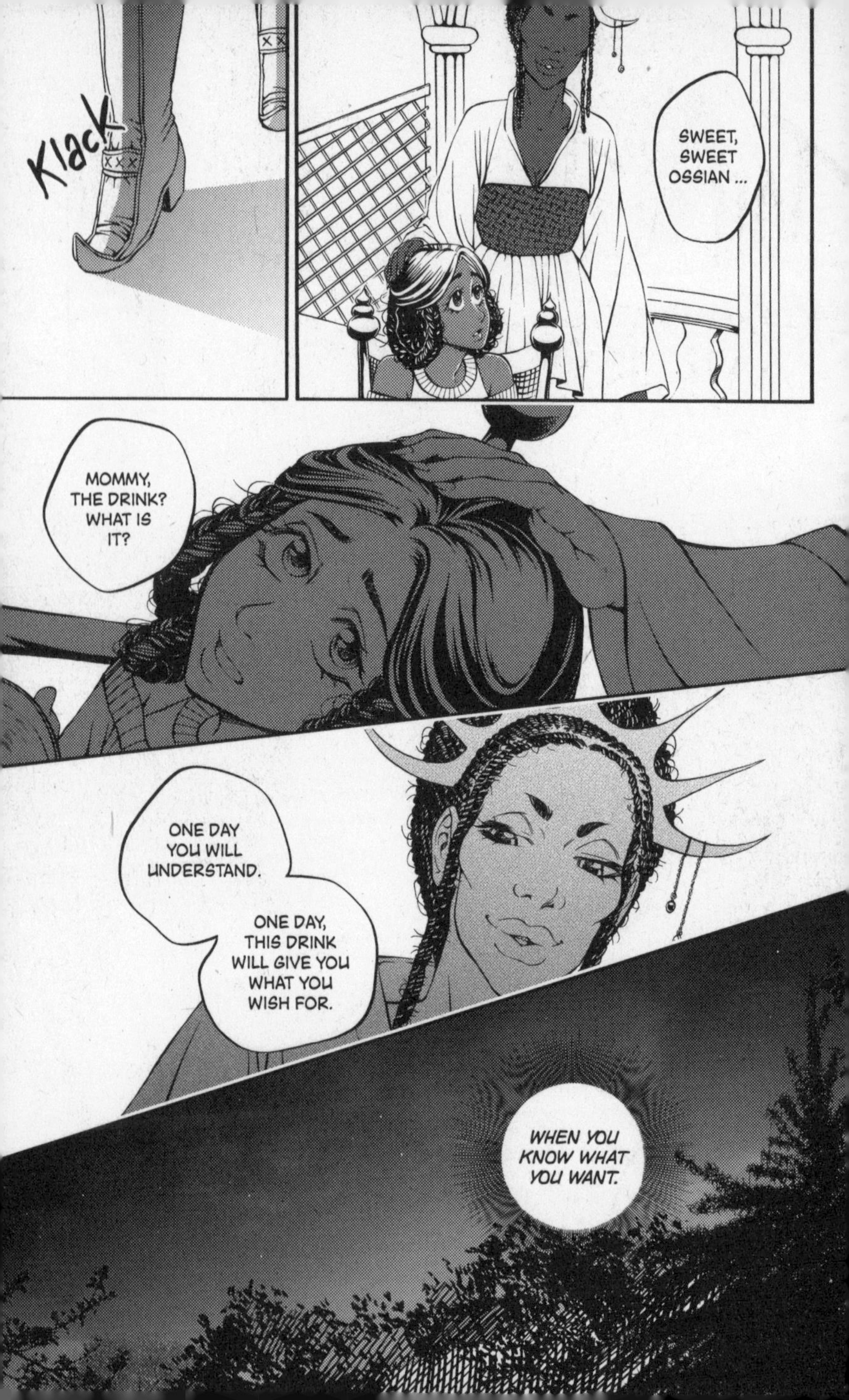
Klack
SWEET, SWEET OSSIAN ...
MOMMY, THE DRINK? WHAT IS IT?
ONE DAY YOU WILL UNDERSTAND.
ONE DAY, THIS DRINK WILL GIVE YOU WHAT YOU WISH FOR.
WHEN YOU KNOW WHAT YOU WANT.

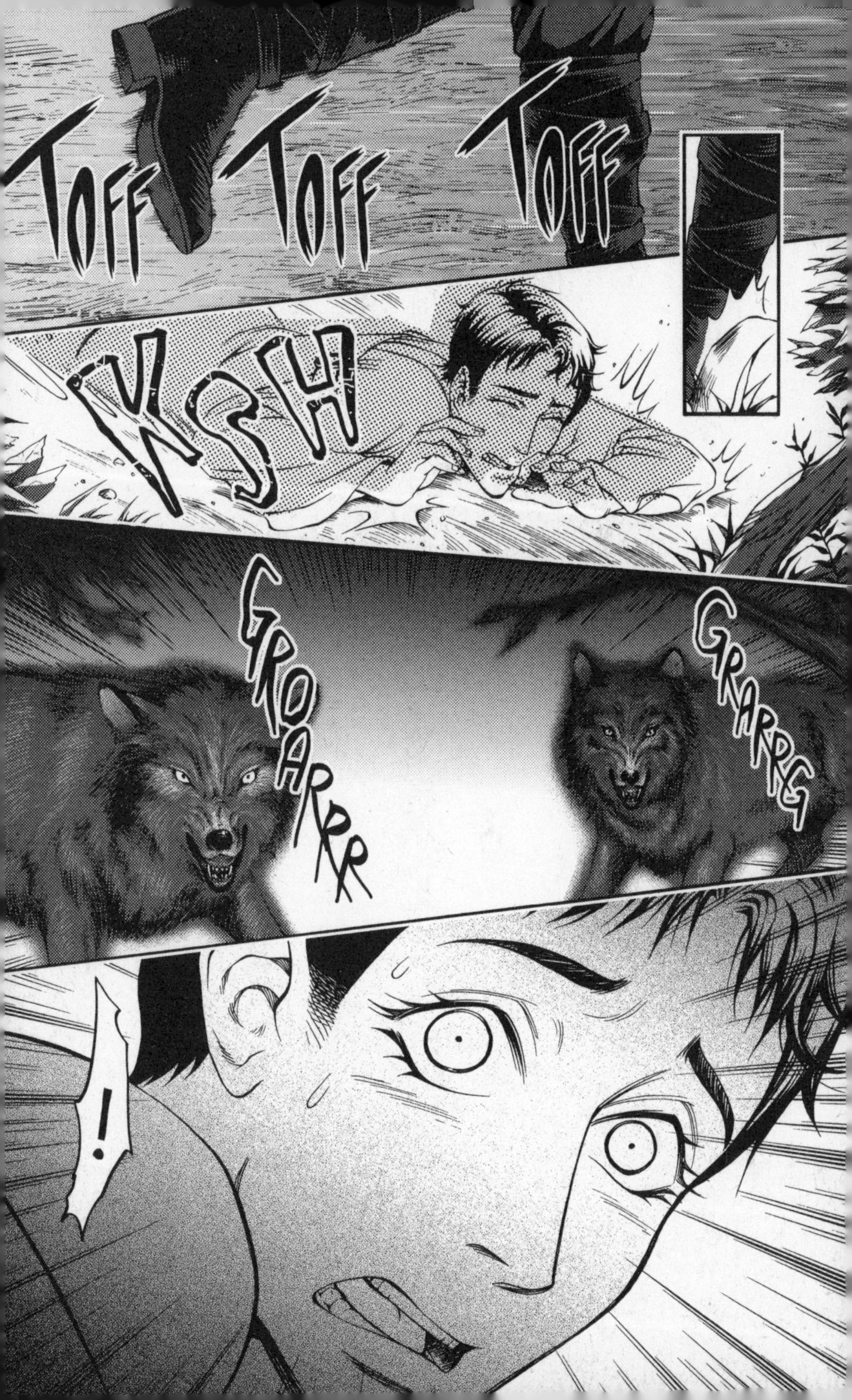
TOFF TOFF TOFF
KSSH
GROARRR
GRARRG
!

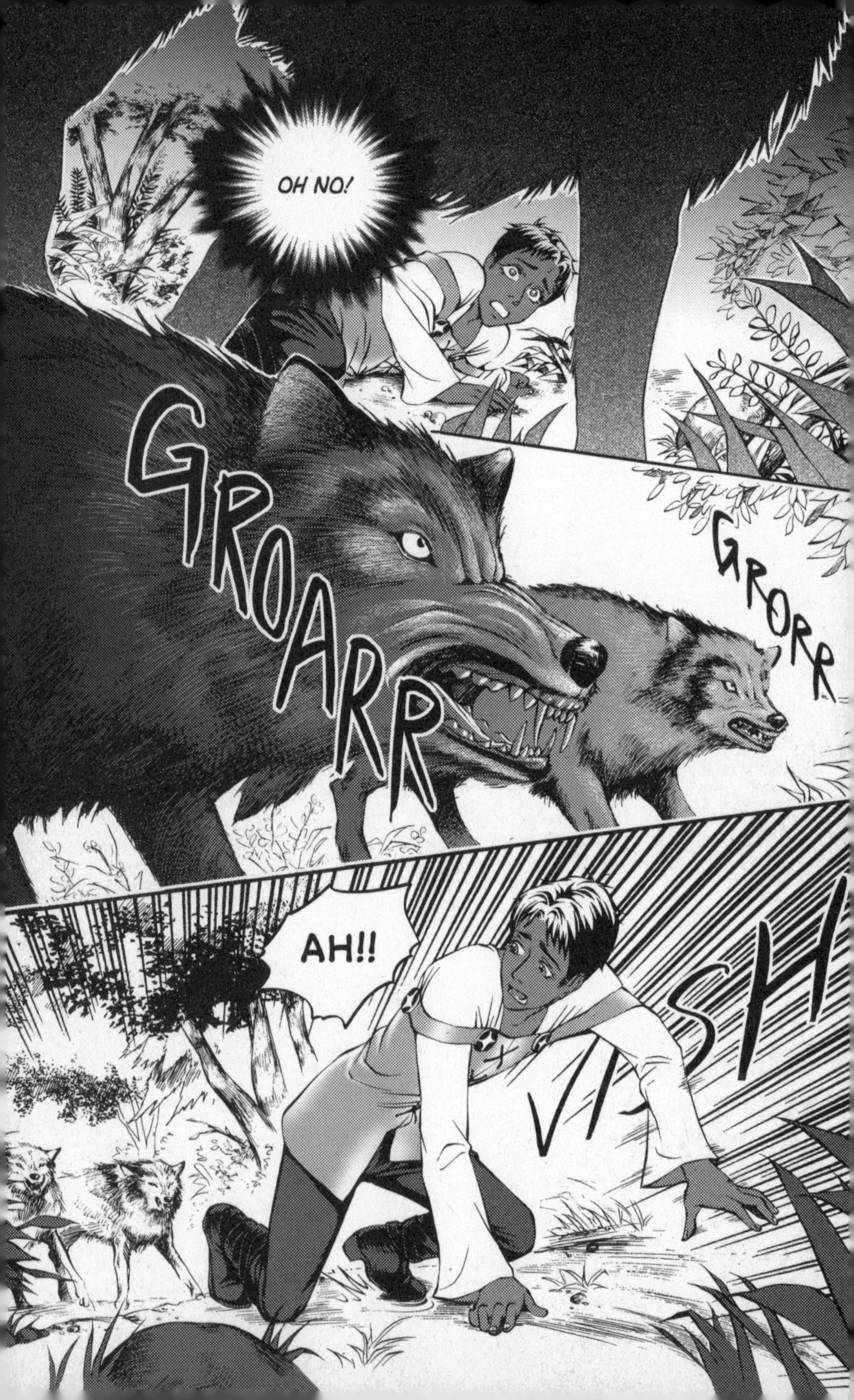
OH NO!
GROARR
GRORR
AH!!
VISH

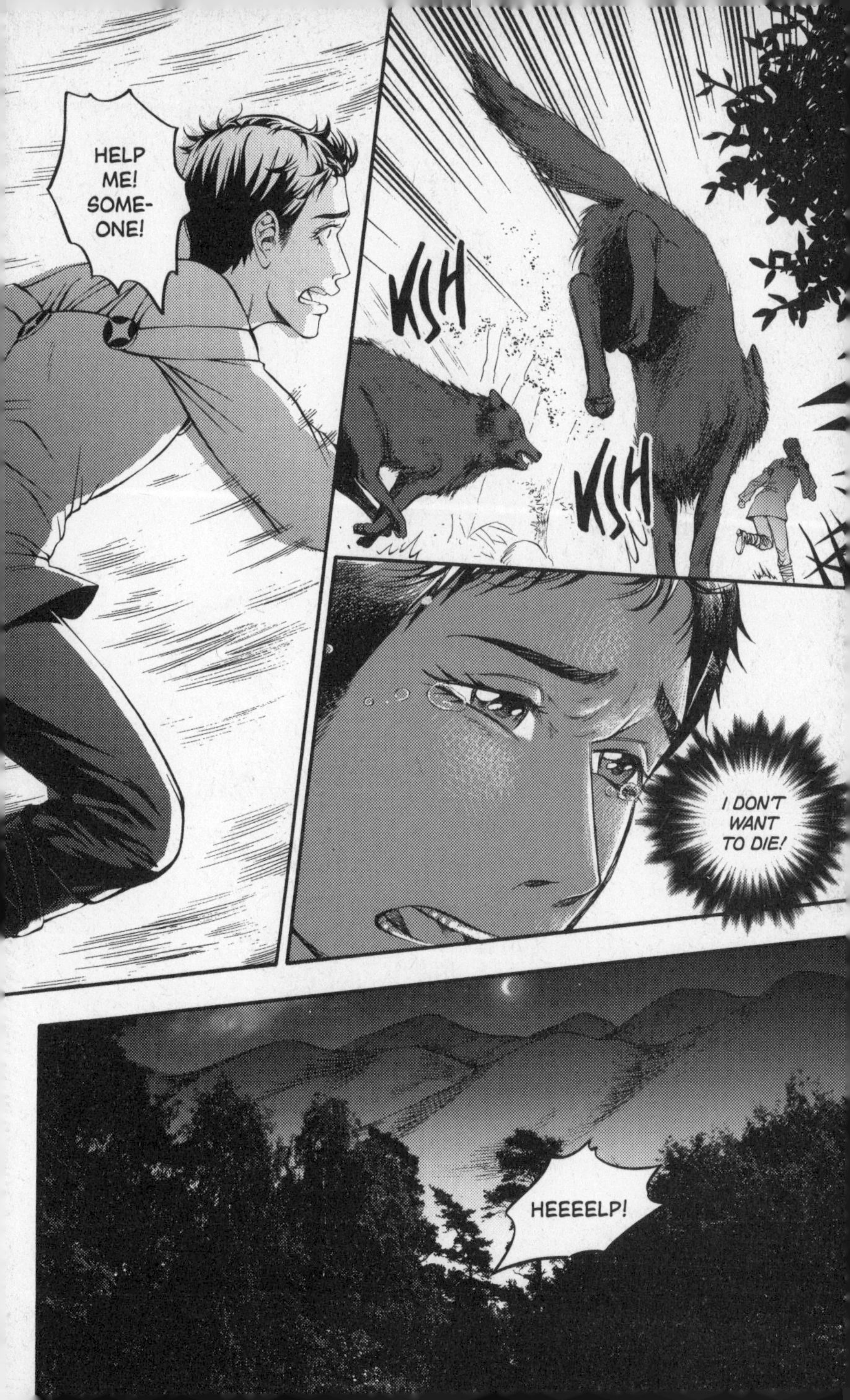
HELP ME! SOME-ONE!
KSH
KSH
I DON'T WANT TO DIE!
HEEEELP!

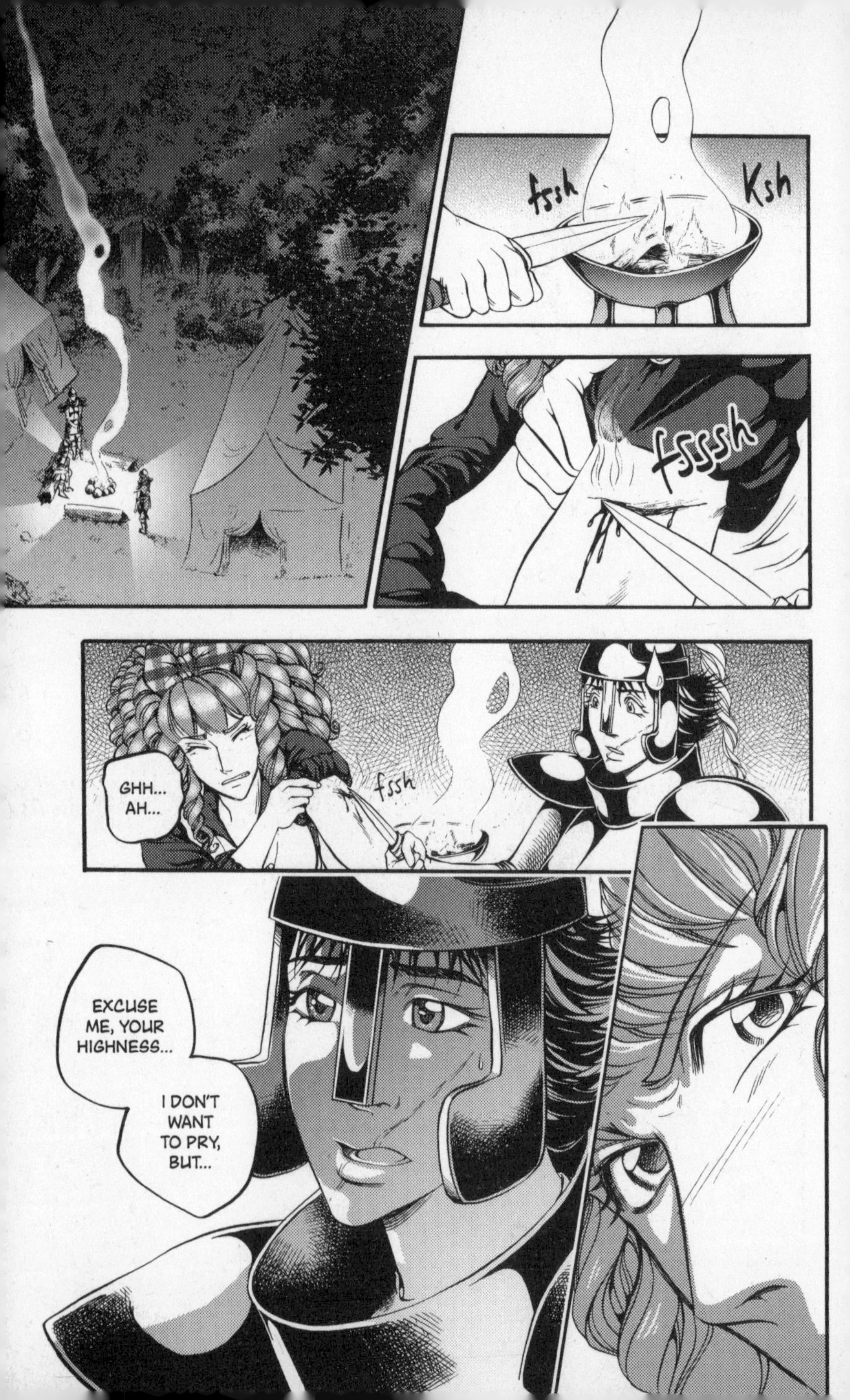
fssh
Ksh
fsssh
GHH... AH...
fssh
EXCUSE ME, YOUR HIGHNESS...
I DON'T WANT TO PRY, BUT...

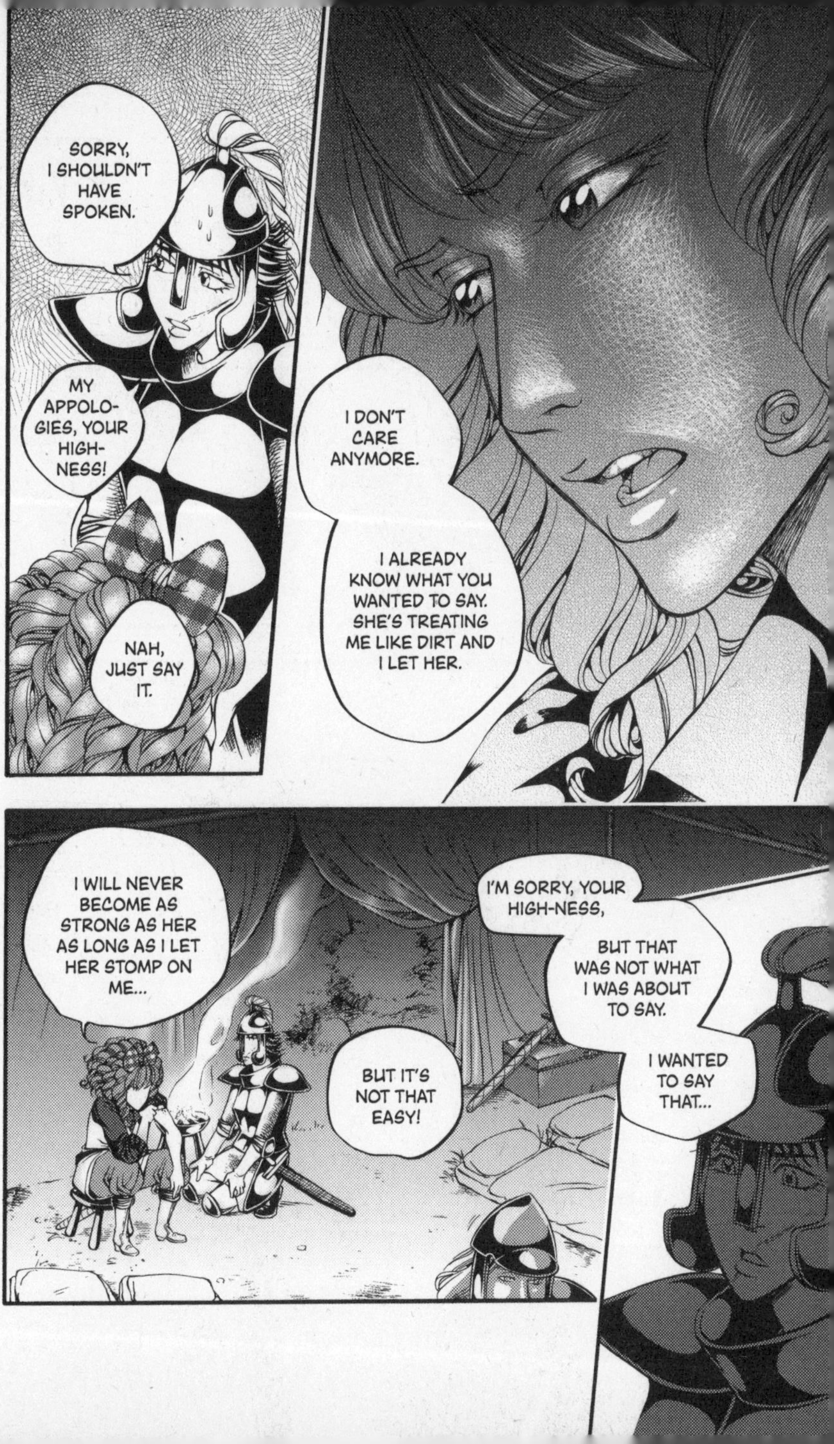
SORRY, I SHOULDN'T HAVE SPOKEN.
MY APPOLOGIES, YOUR HIGHNESS!
NAH, JUST SAY IT.
I DON'T CARE ANYMORE.
I ALREADY KNOW WHAT YOU WANTED TO SAY. SHE'S TREATING ME LIKE DIRT AND I LET HER.
I WILL NEVER BECOME AS STRONG AS HER AS LONG AS I LET HER STOMP ON ME...
BUT IT'S NOT THAT EASY!
I'M SORRY, YOUR HIGH-NESS,
BUT THAT WAS NOT WHAT I WAS ABOUT TO SAY.
I WANTED TO SAY THAT...

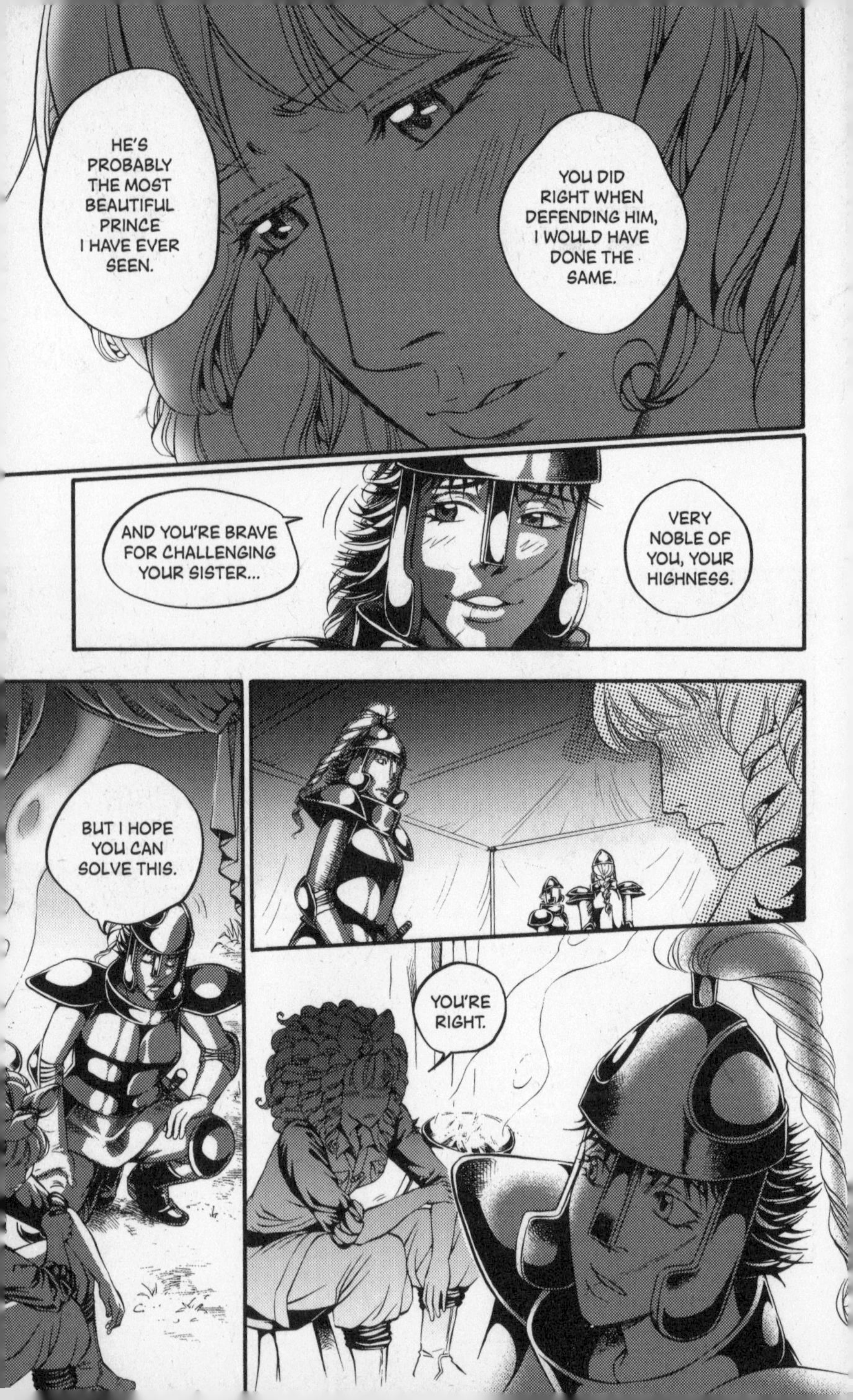
HE'S PROBABLY THE MOST BEAUTIFUL PRINCE I HAVE EVER SEEN.
YOU DID RIGHT WHEN DEFENDING HIM, I WOULD HAVE DONE THE SAME.
AND YOU'RE BRAVE FOR CHALLENGING YOUR SISTER...
VERY NOBLE OF YOU, YOUR HIGHNESS.
BUT I HOPE YOU CAN SOLVE THIS.
YOU'RE RIGHT.

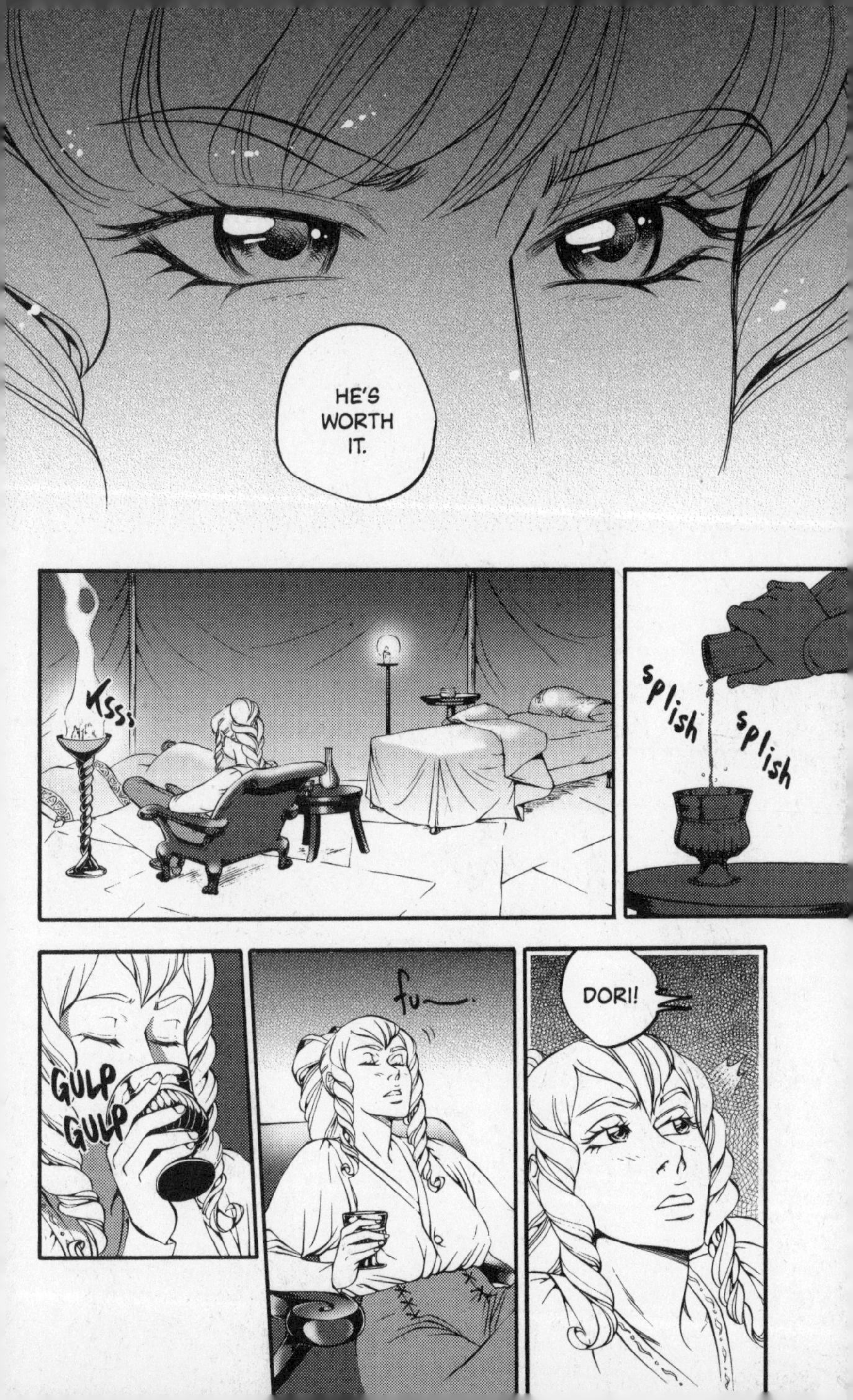
HE'S WORTH IT.
KSSS
splish splish
GULP GULP
fu–.
DORI!

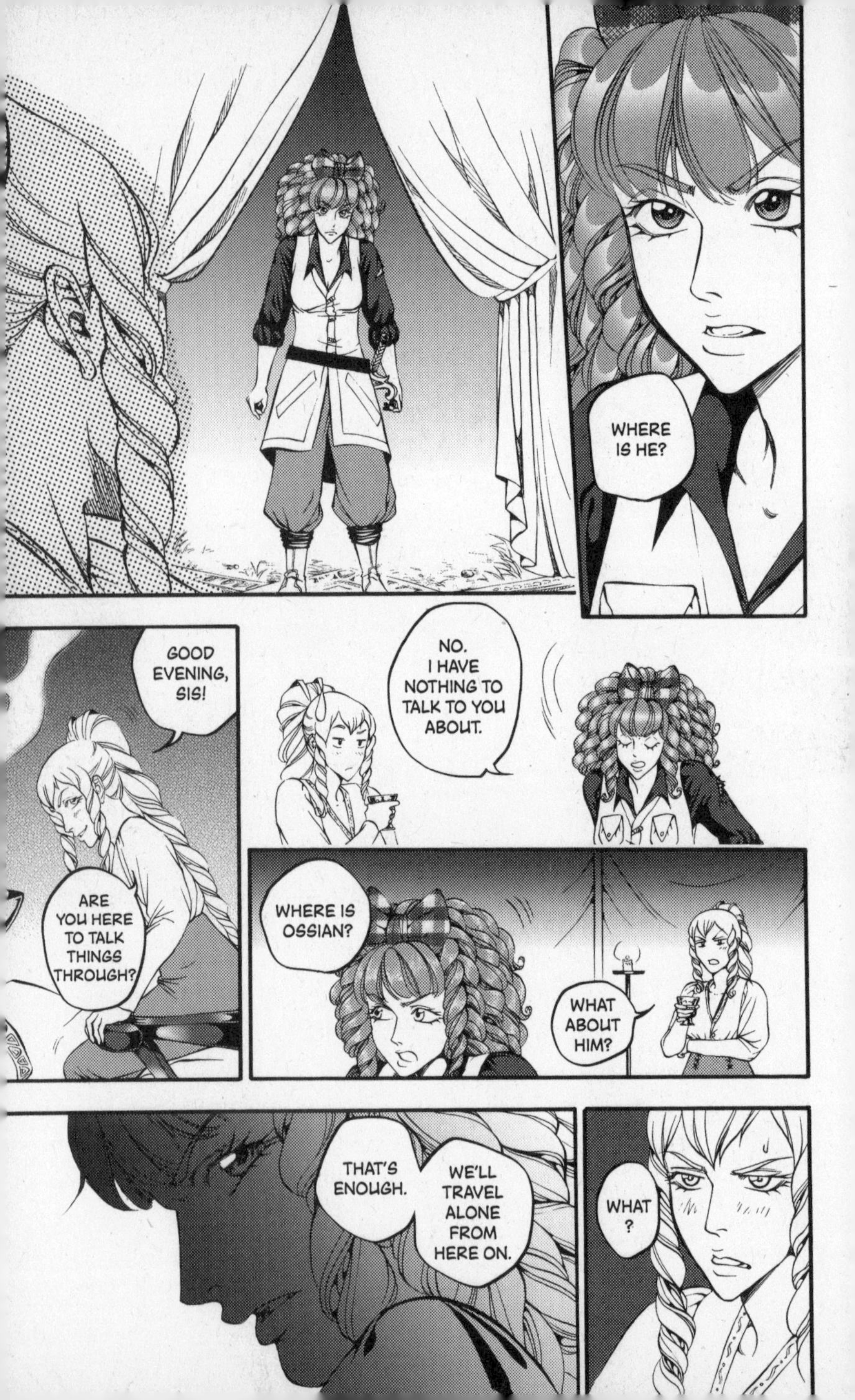
WHERE IS HE?
GOOD EVENING, SIS!
ARE YOU HERE TO TALK THINGS THROUGH?
NO. I HAVE NOTHING TO TALK TO YOU ABOUT.
WHERE IS OSSIAN?
WHAT ABOUT HIM?
THAT'S ENOUGH.
WE'LL TRAVEL ALONE FROM HERE ON.
WHAT?

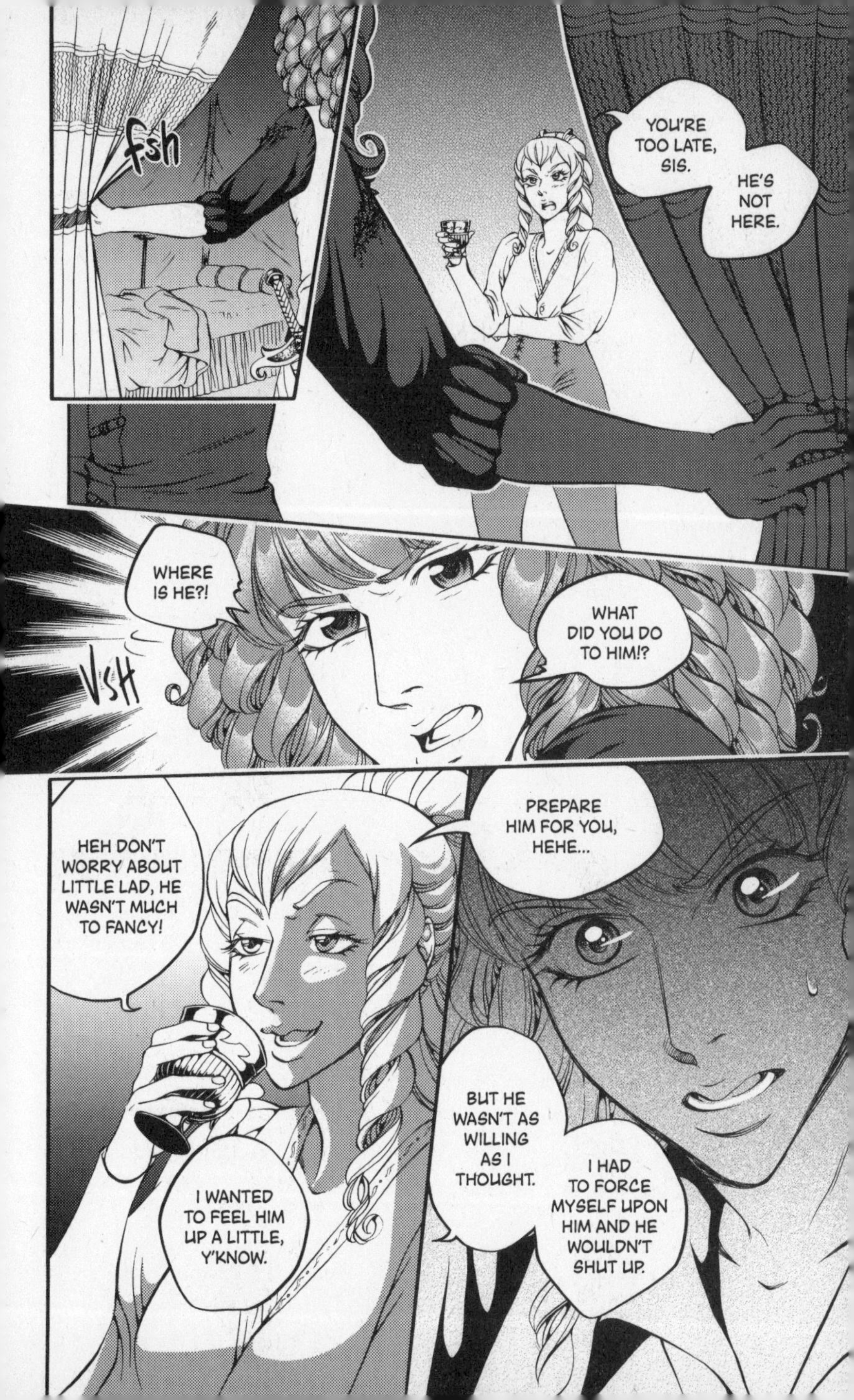
fsh
YOU'RE TOO LATE, SIS.
HE'S NOT HERE.
VSH
WHERE IS HE?!
WHAT DID YOU DO TO HIM!?
HEH DON'T WORRY ABOUT LITTLE LAD, HE WASN'T MUCH TO FANCY!
I WANTED TO FEEL HIM UP A LITTLE, Y'KNOW.
PREPARE HIM FOR YOU, HEHE...
BUT HE WASN'T AS WILLING AS I THOUGHT.
I HAD TO FORCE MYSELF UPON HIM AND HE WOULDN'T SHUT UP.

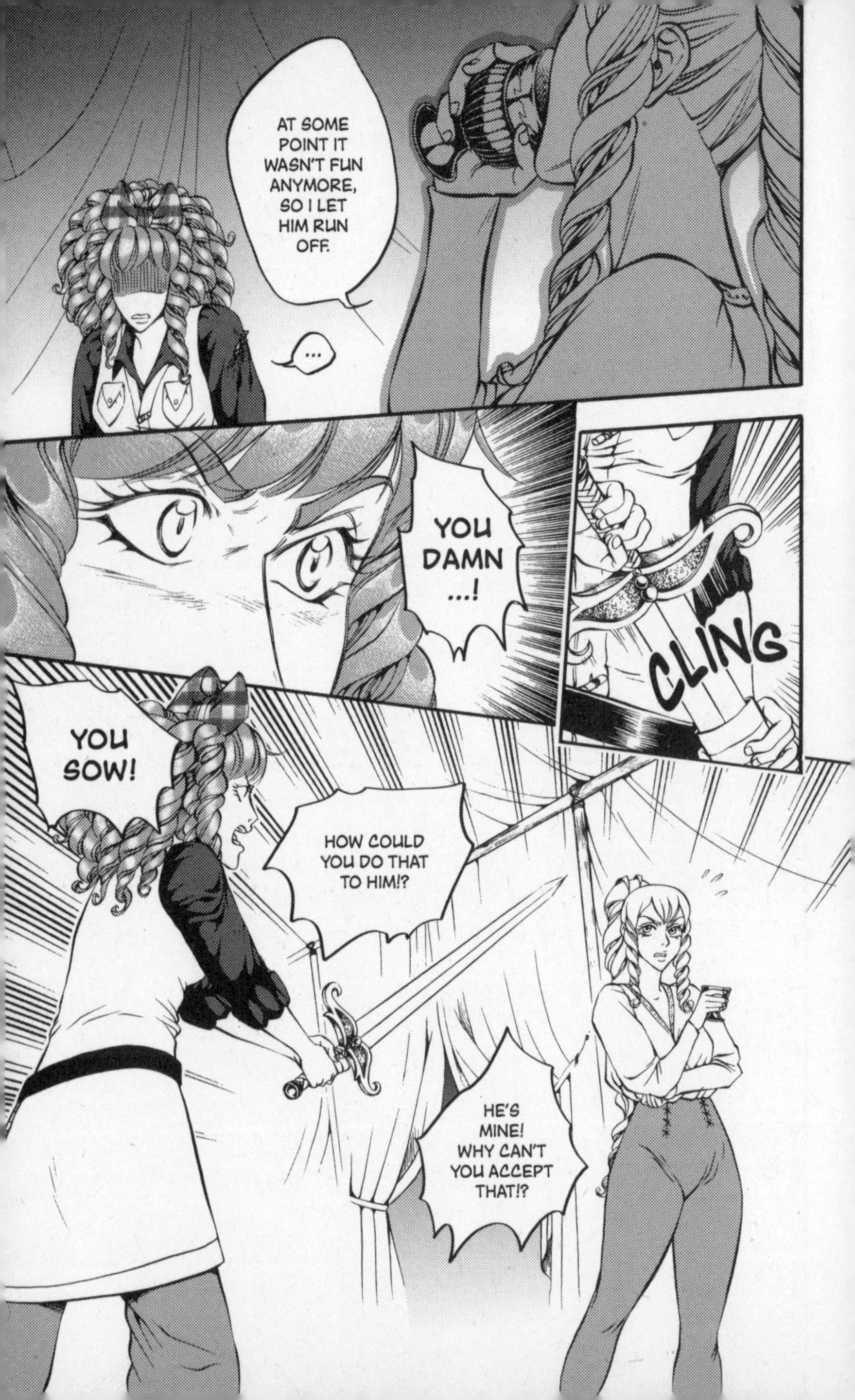
AT SOME POINT IT WASN'T FUN ANYMORE, SO I LET HIM RUN OFF.
...
YOU DAMN ...!
CLING
YOU SOW!
HOW COULD YOU DO THAT TO HIM!?
HE'S MINE! WHY CAN'T YOU ACCEPT THAT!?

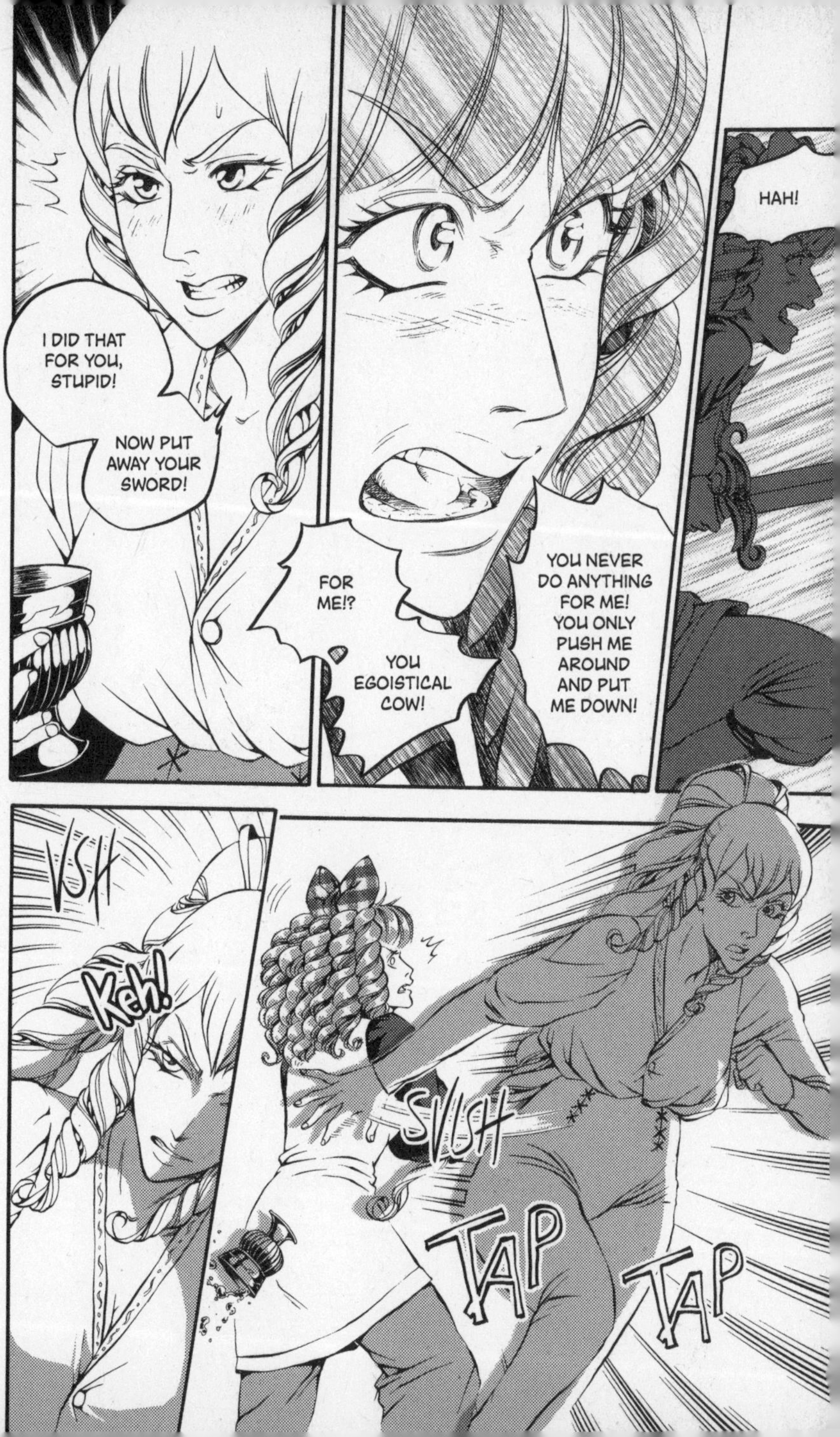
I DID THAT FOR YOU, STUPID!
NOW PUT AWAY YOUR SWORD!
FOR ME!?
YOU EGOISTICAL COW!
YOU NEVER DO ANYTHING FOR ME! YOU ONLY PUSH ME AROUND AND PUT ME DOWN!
HAH!
VSH
Keh!
SVISH
TAP
TAP

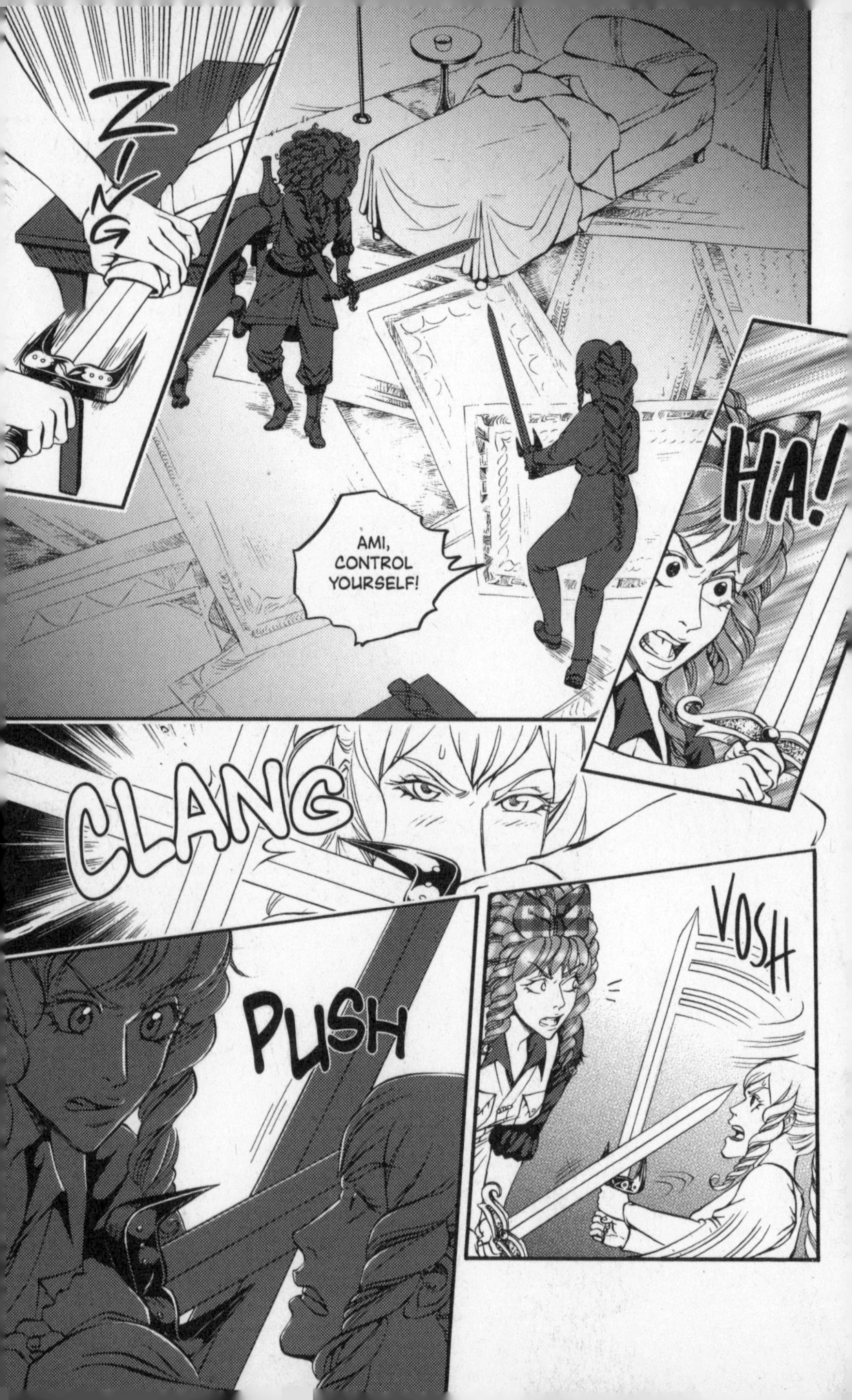
ZING
AMI, CONTROL YOURSELF!
HA!
CLANG
PUSH
VOSH

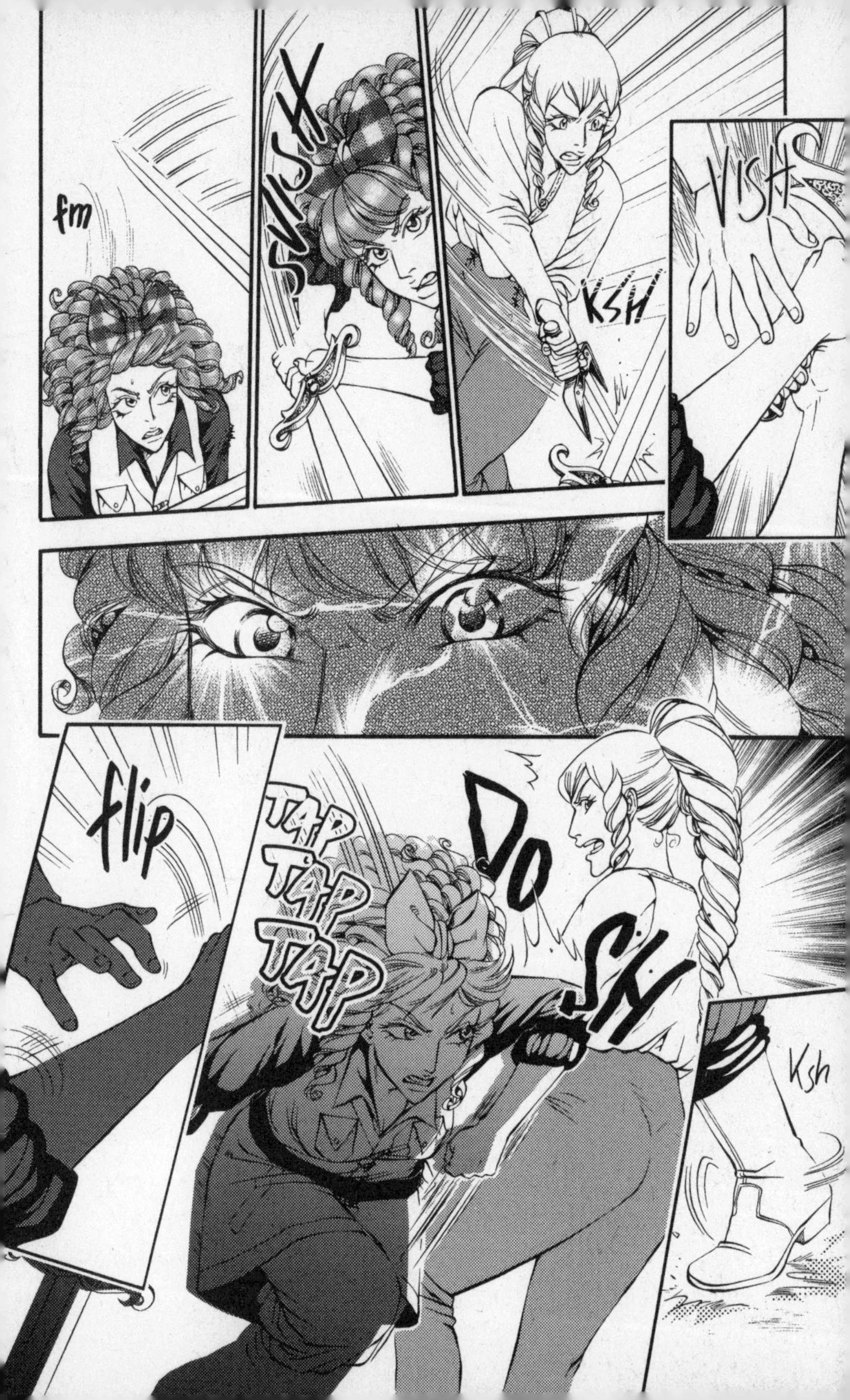
fm
SWISH
KSH
VISH
flip
TAP TAP TAP
DOSH
Ksh

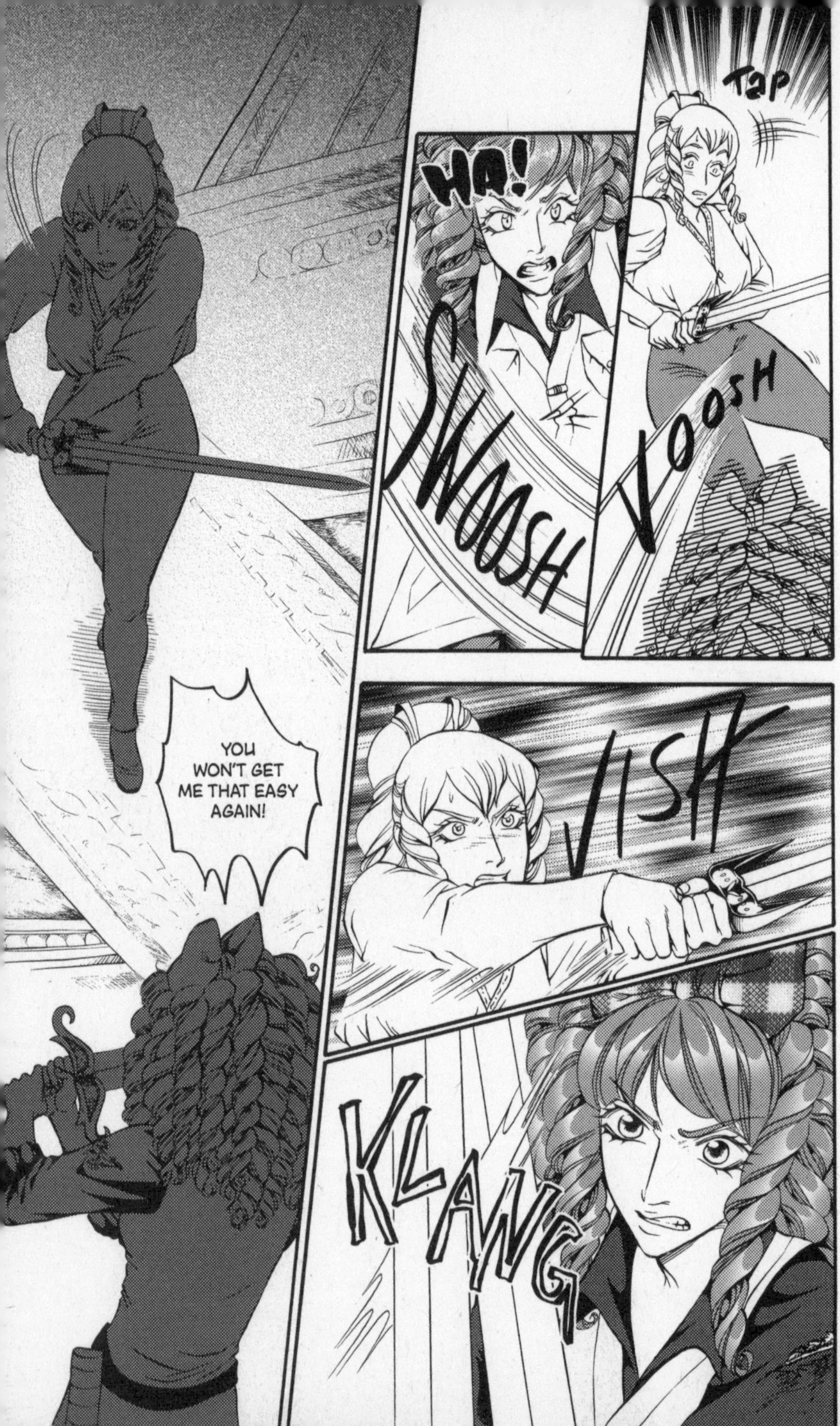
YOU WON'T GET ME THAT EASY AGAIN!
HA!
SWOOSH
Tap
WOOSH
VISH
KLANG

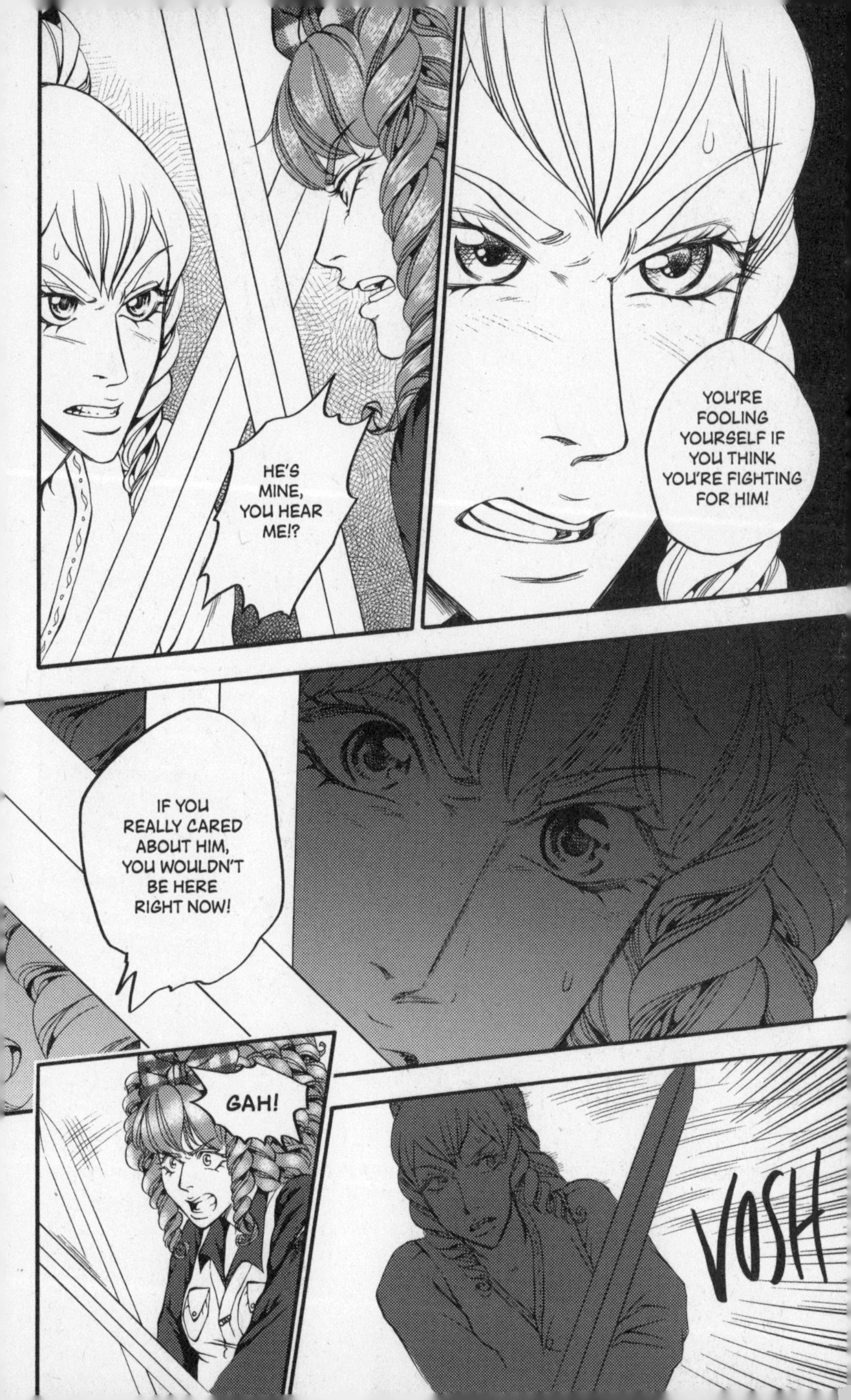
HE'S MINE, YOU HEAR ME!?
YOU'RE FOOLING YOURSELF IF YOU THINK YOU'RE FIGHTING FOR HIM!
IF YOU REALLY CARED ABOUT HIM, YOU WOULDN'T BE HERE RIGHT NOW!
GAH!
VOSH

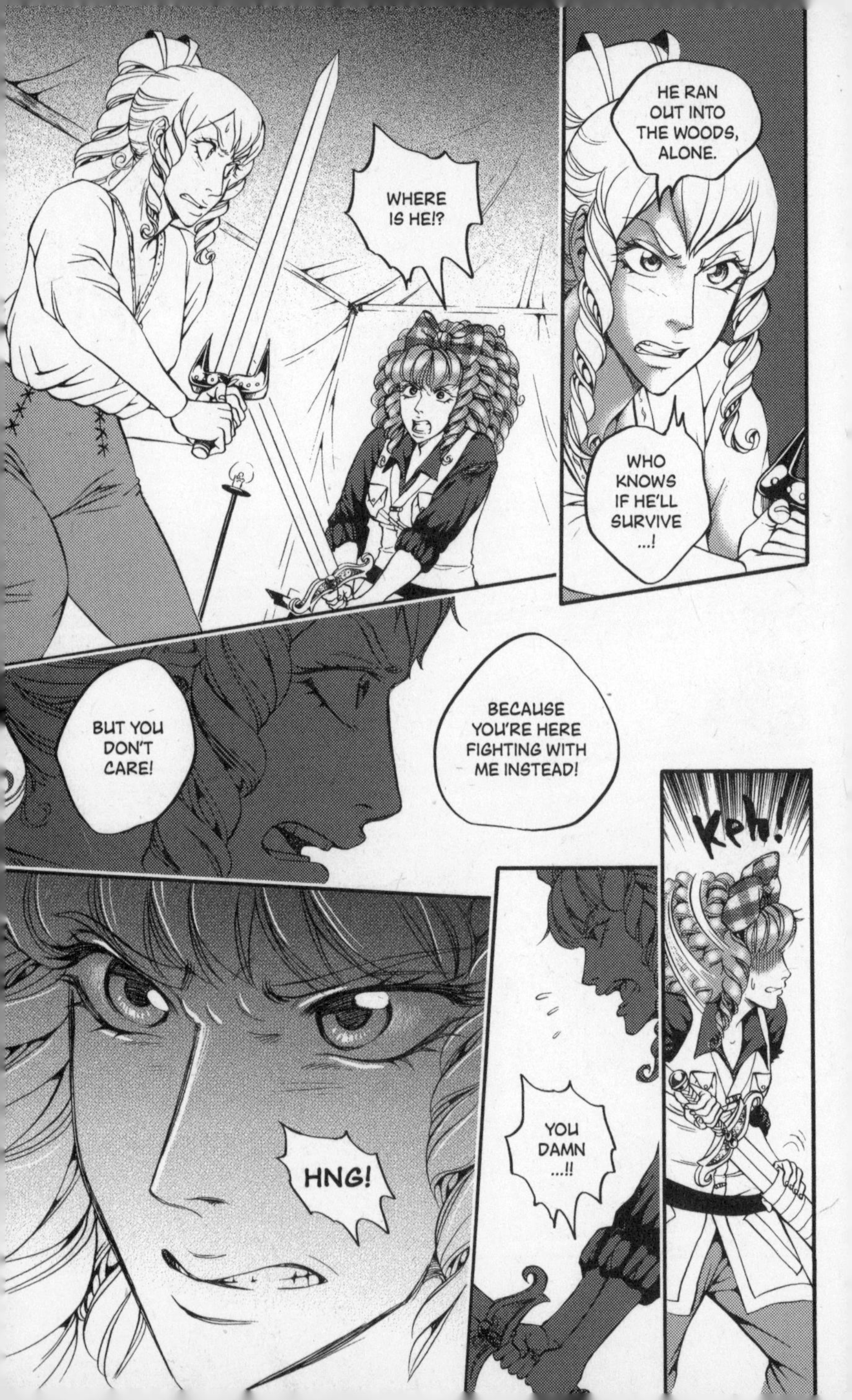
WHERE IS HE!?
HE RAN OUT INTO THE WOODS, ALONE.
WHO KNOWS IF HE'LL SURVIVE ...!
BUT YOU DON'T CARE!
BECAUSE YOU'RE HERE FIGHTING WITH ME INSTEAD!
Keh!
HNG!
YOU DAMN ...!!

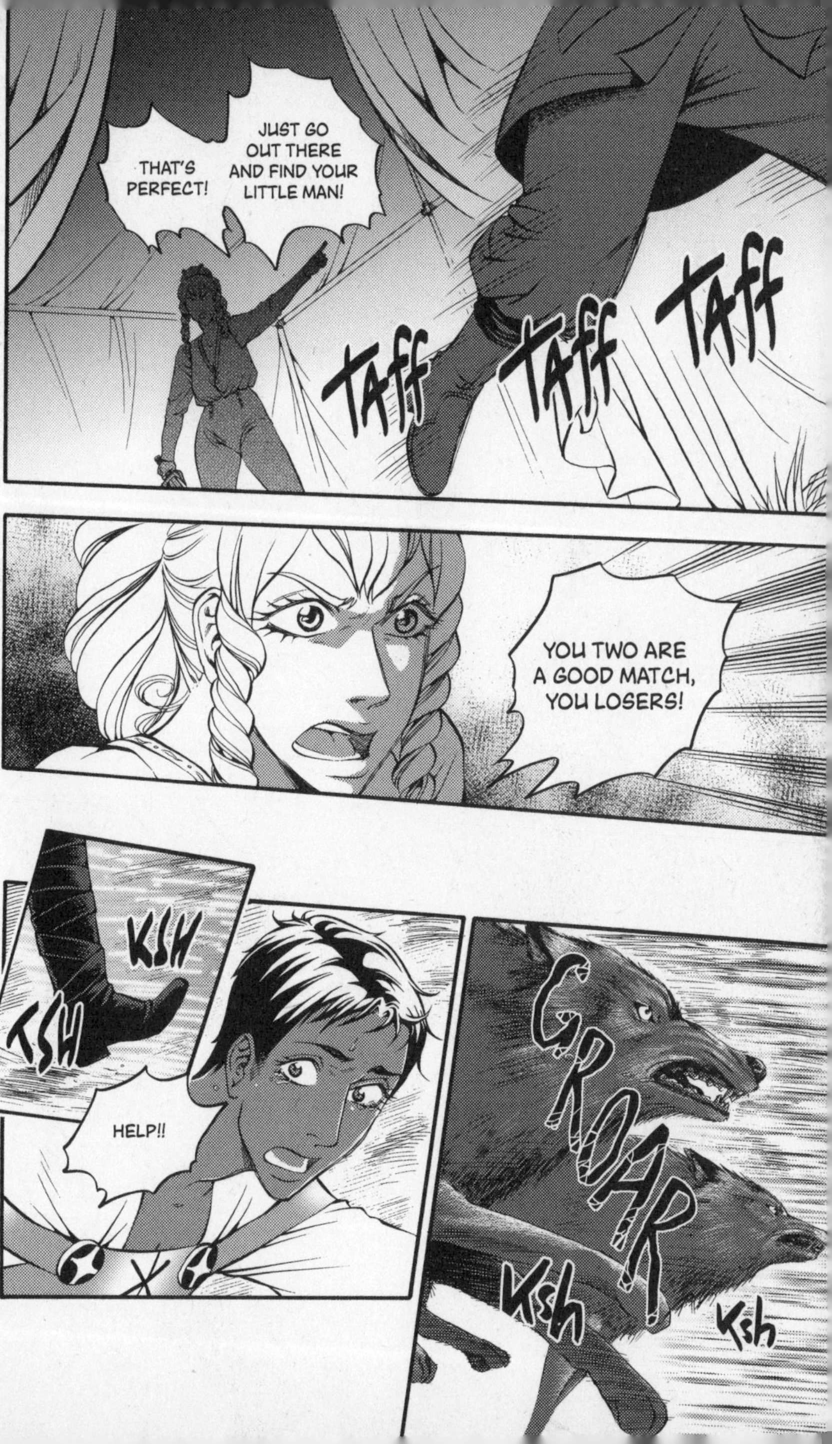
THAT'S PERFECT!
JUST GO OUT THERE AND FIND YOUR LITTLE MAN!
TAFF
TAFF
TAFF
YOU TWO ARE A GOOD MATCH, YOU LOSERS!
KSH
TSH
HELP!!
GROAR
Ksh
Ksh

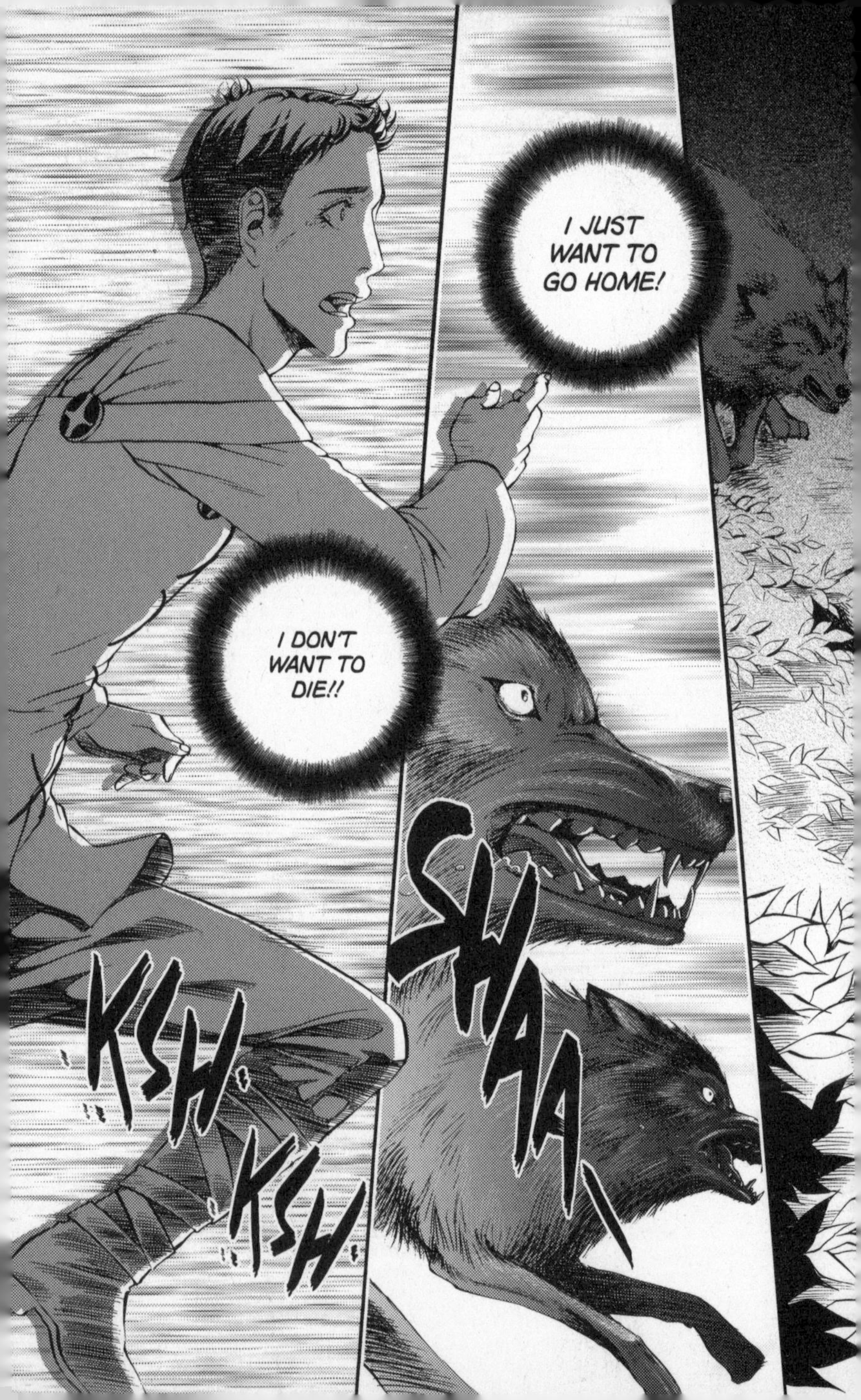
I JUST WANT TO GO HOME!
I DON'T WANT TO DIE!!
KSH
KSH
KSH
SHAA

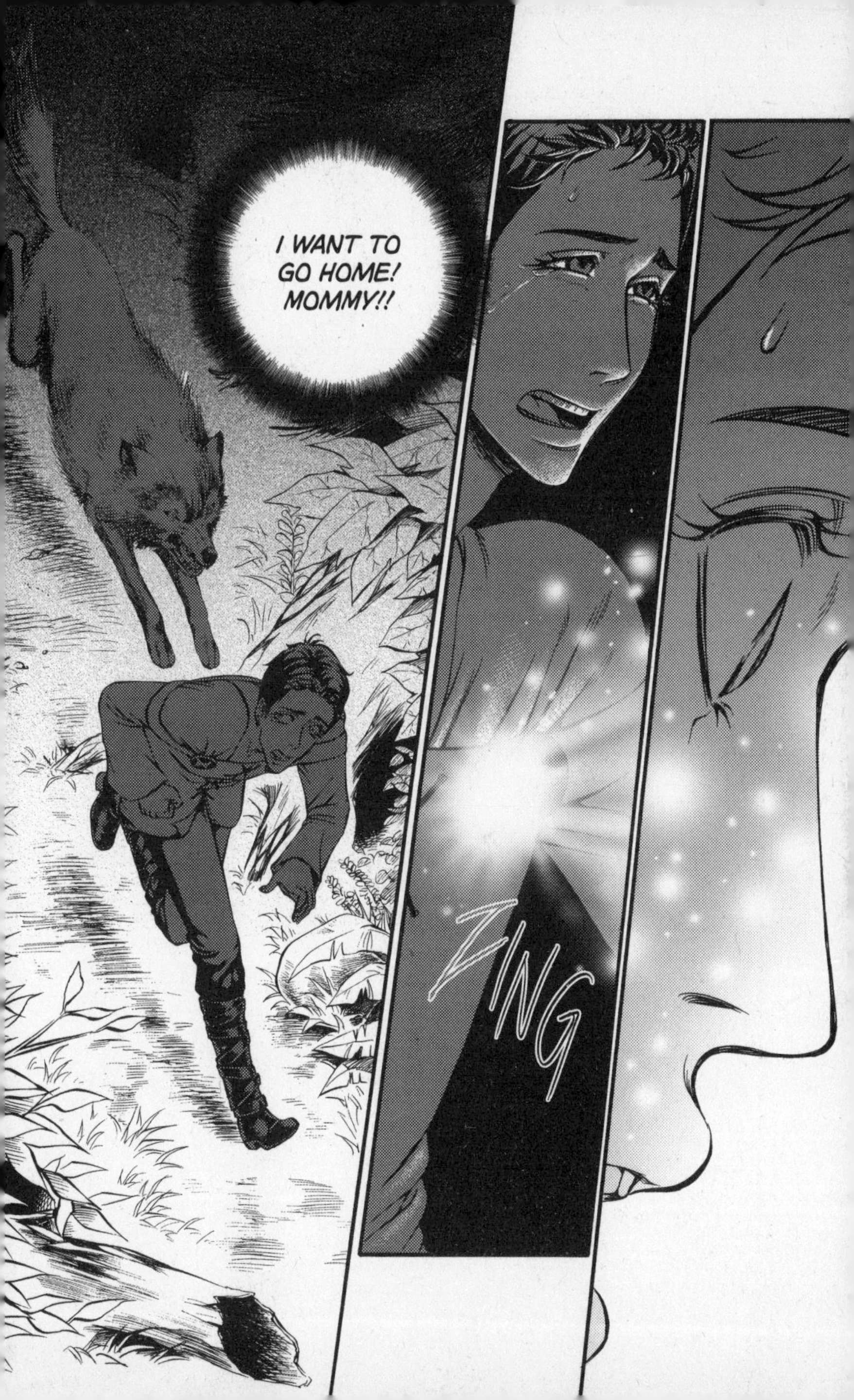
I WANT TO GO HOME! MOMMY!!
ZING

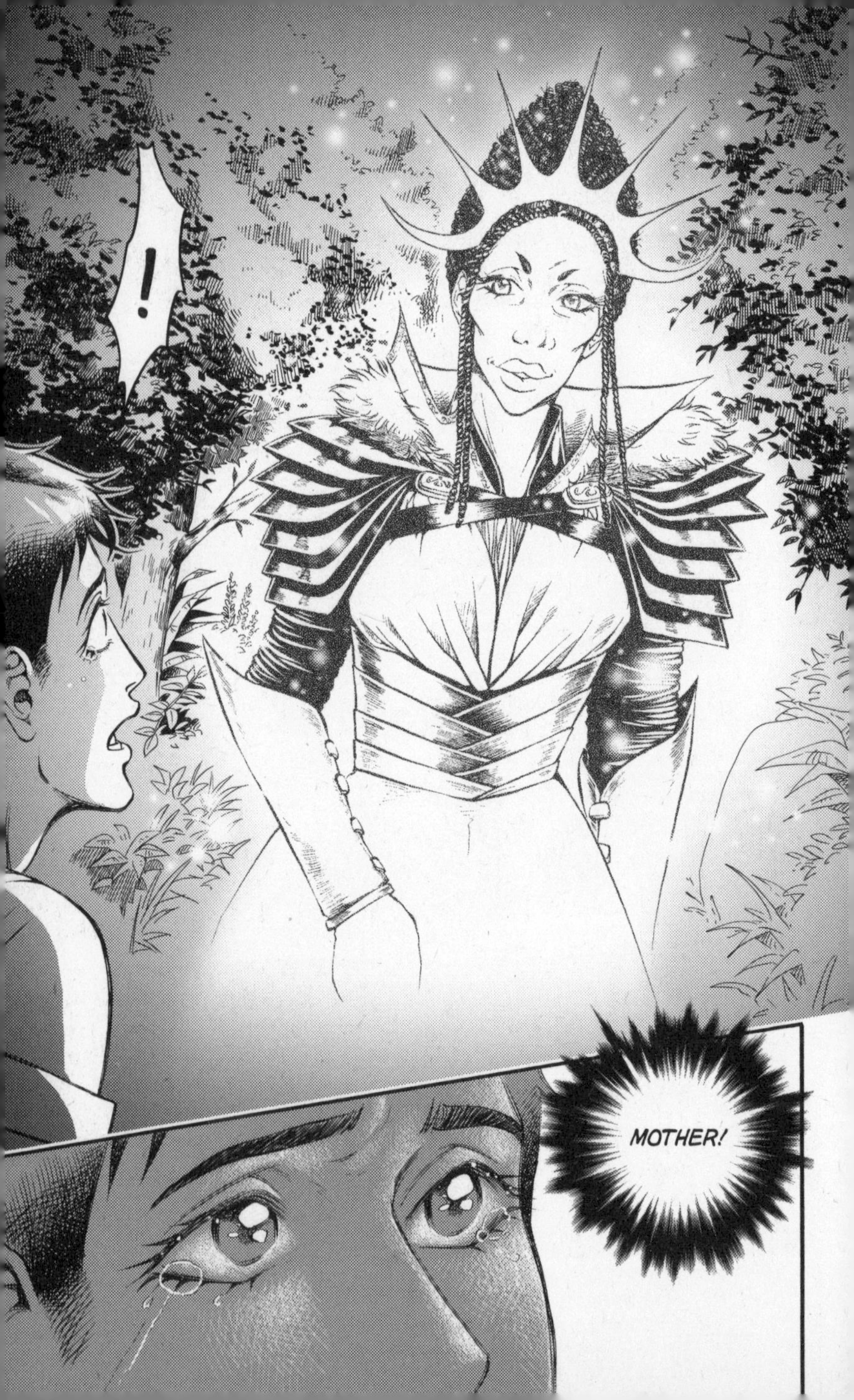
!
MOTHER!

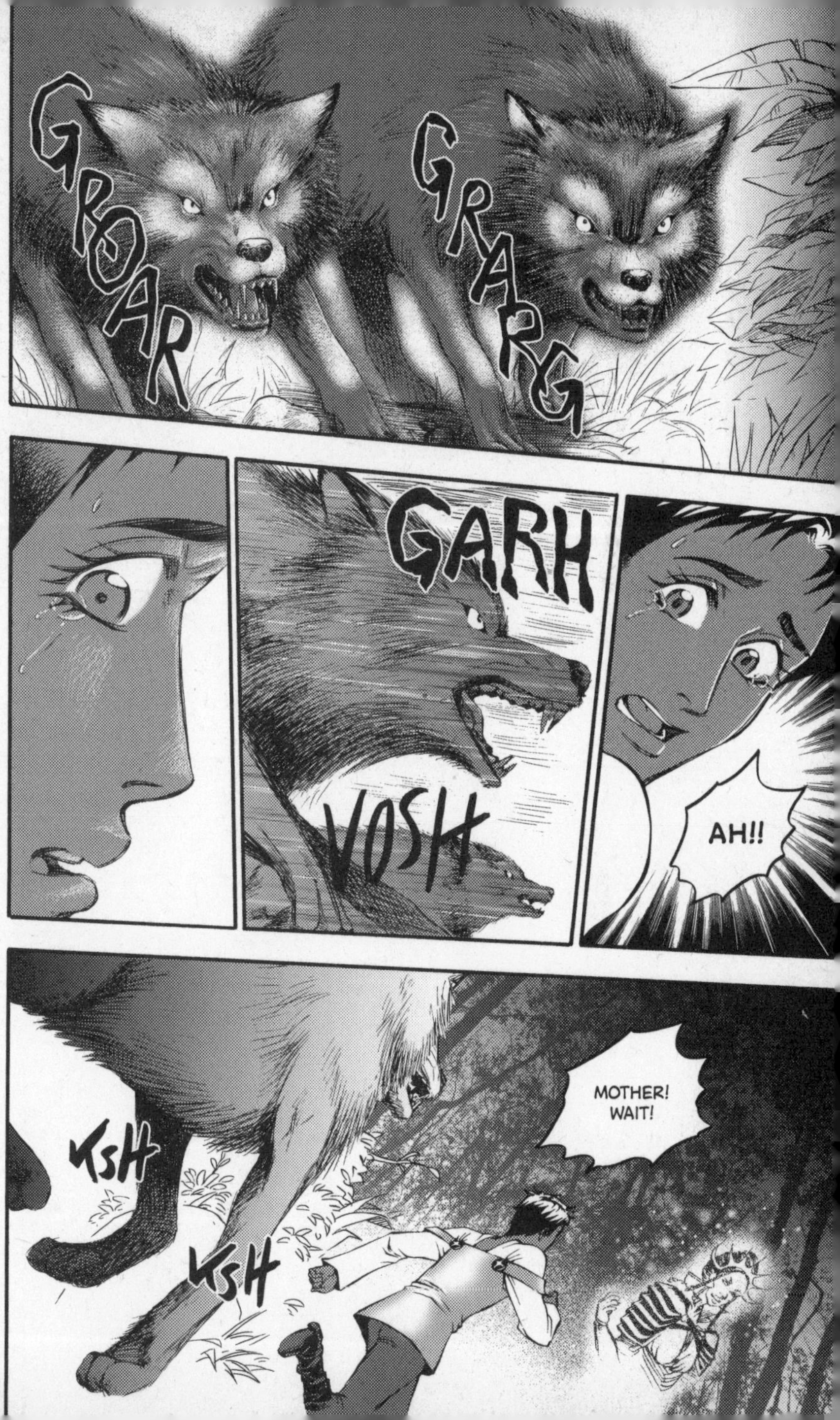
GROAR
GRARG
GARH
VOSH
AH!!
KSH
KSH
MOTHER! WAIT!

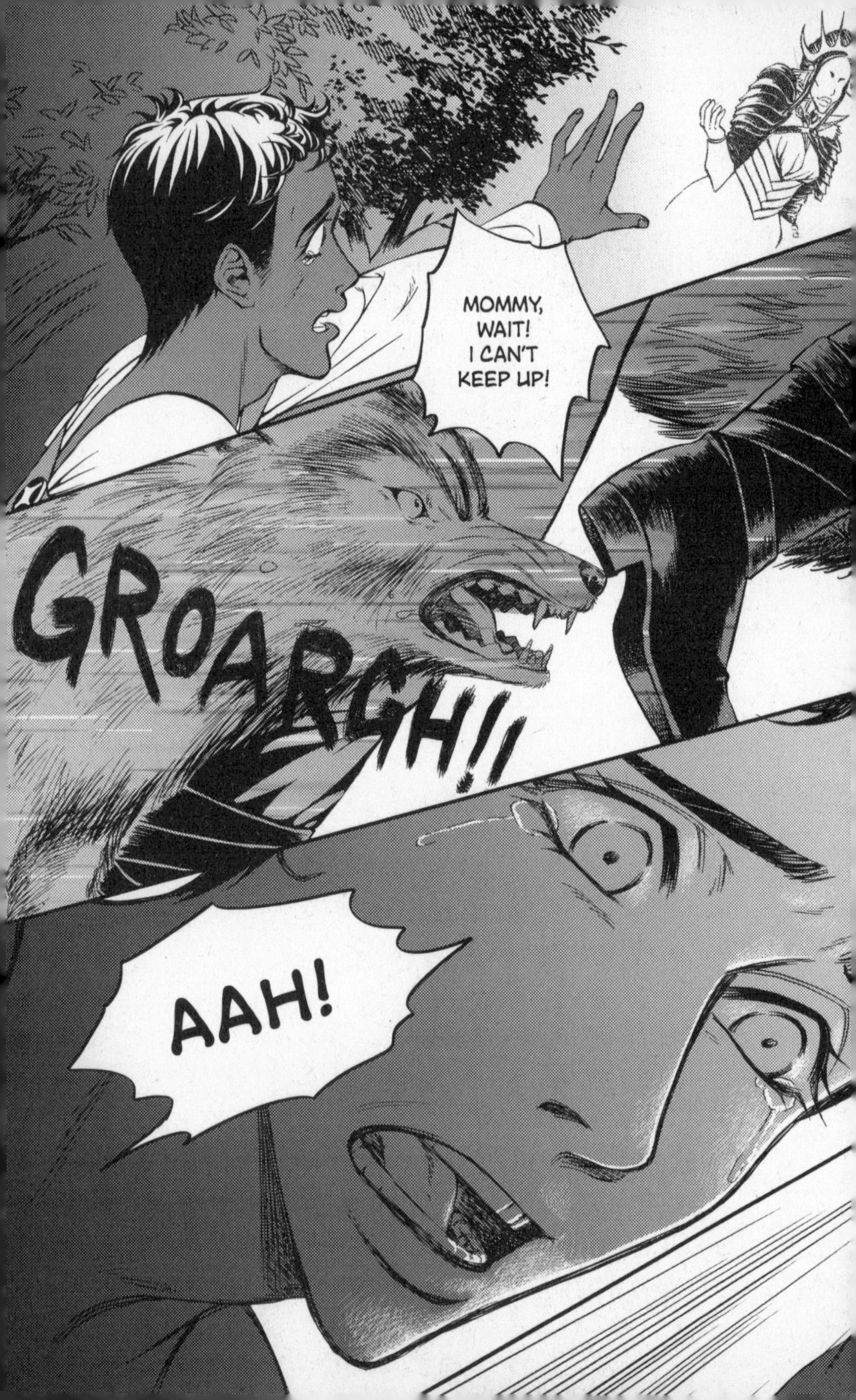
MOMMY, WAIT! I CAN'T KEEP UP!
GROARGH!!
AAH!

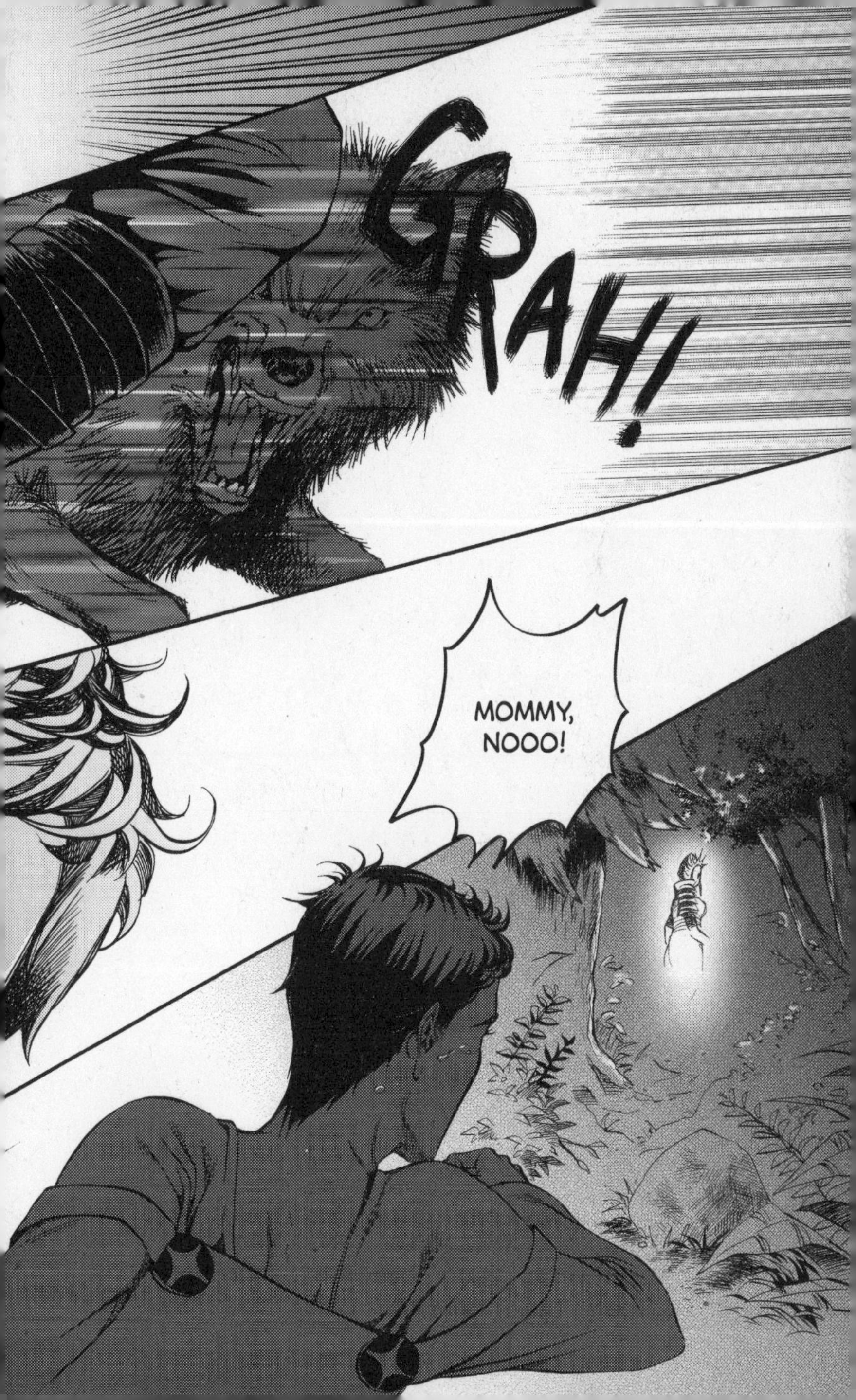
GRAH!
MOMMY, NOOO!

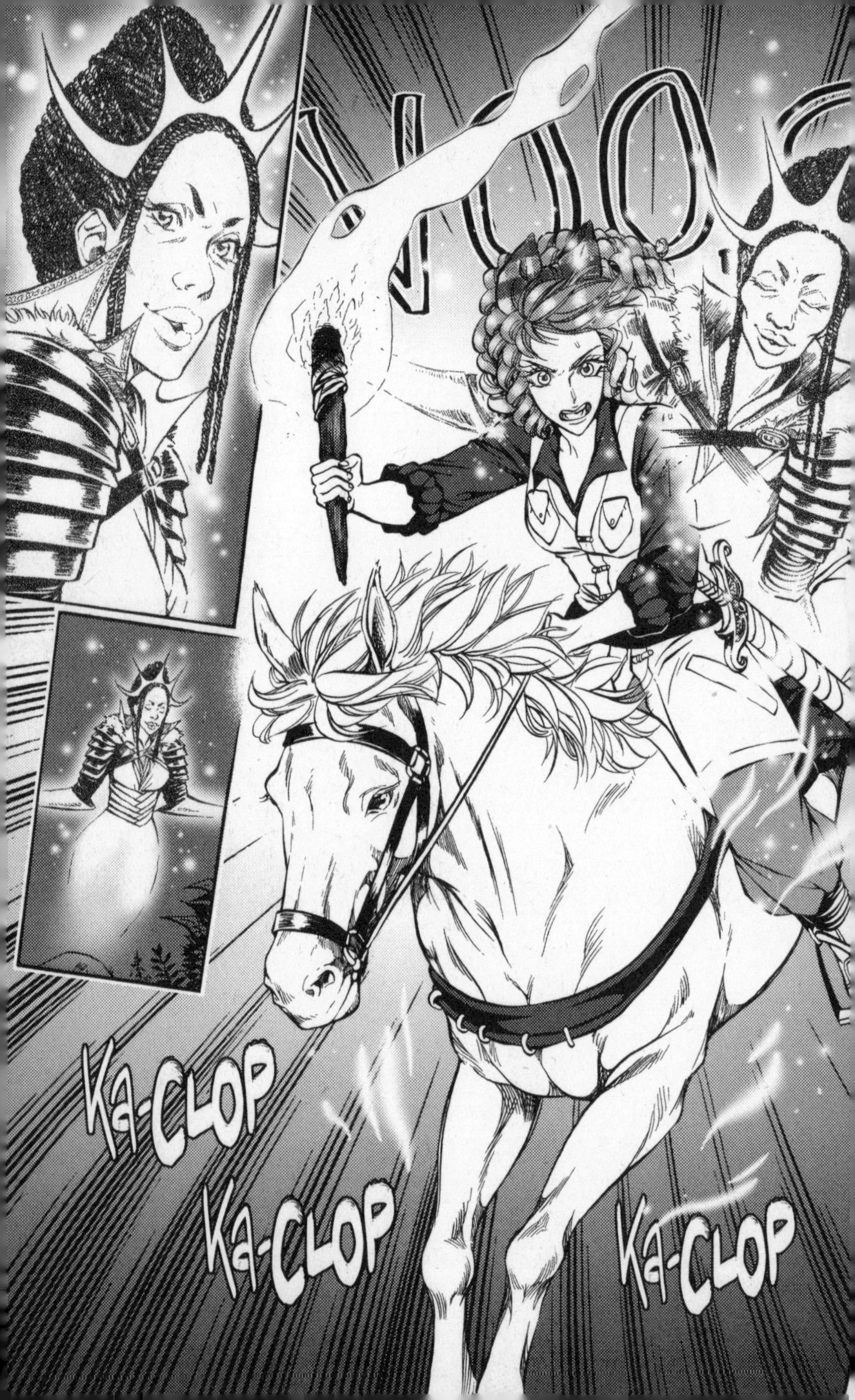
KA-CLOP
KA-CLOP
KA-CLOP

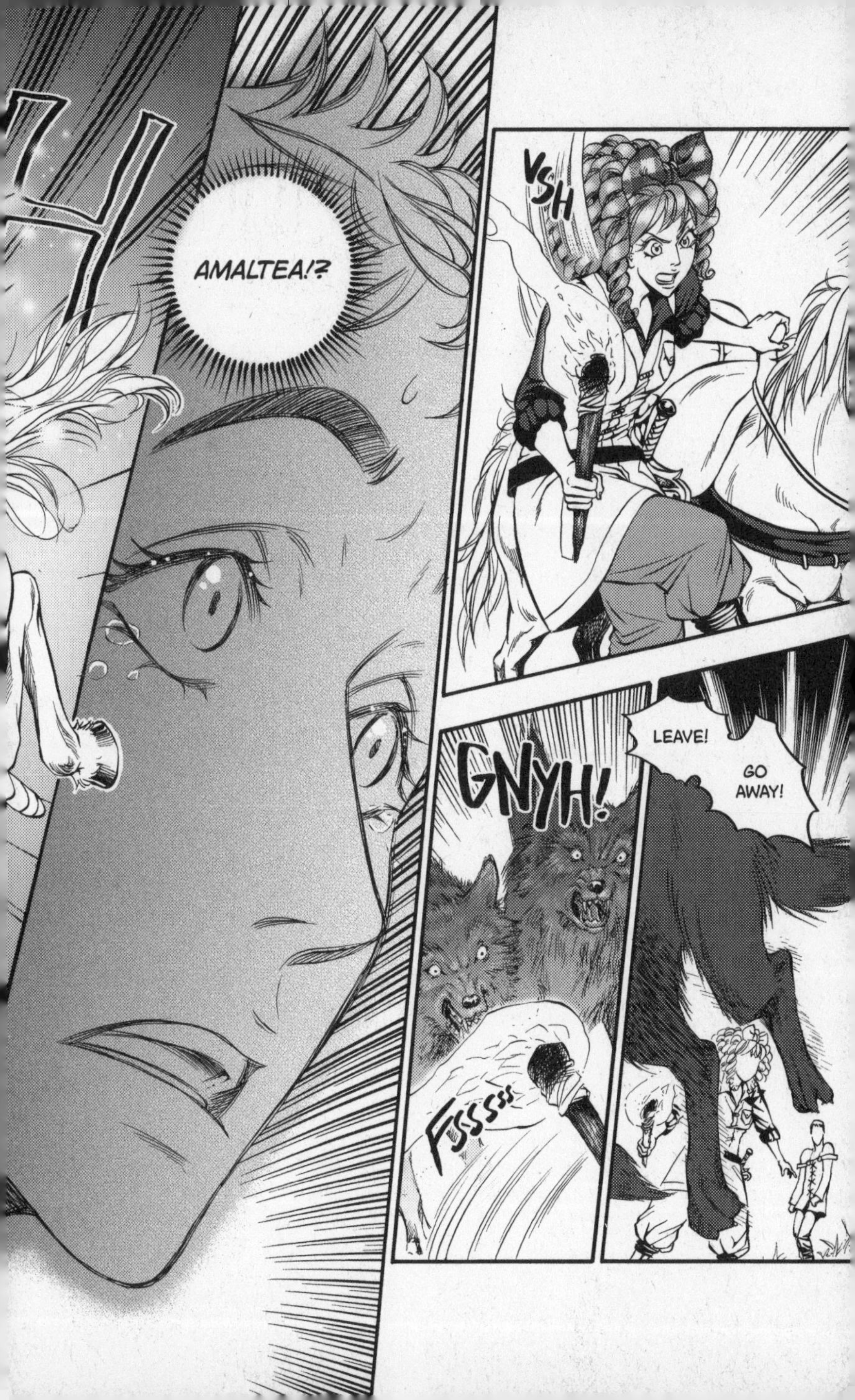
AMALTEA!?
VSH
GNYH!
FSSSSS
LEAVE!
GO AWAY!

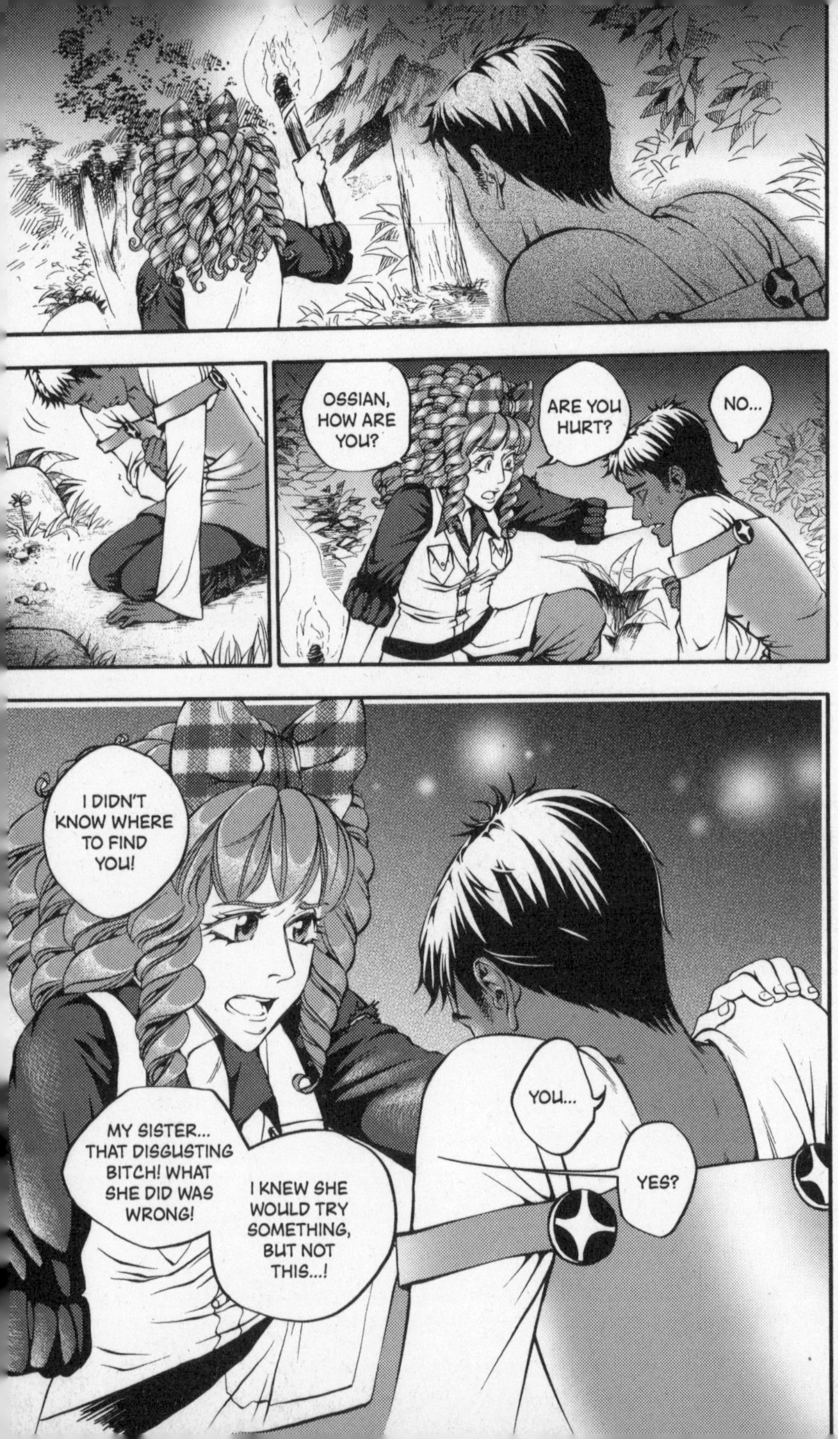
OSSIAN, HOW ARE YOU?
ARE YOU HURT?
NO...
I DIDN'T KNOW WHERE TO FIND YOU!
MY SISTER... THAT DISGUSTING BITCH! WHAT SHE DID WAS WRONG!
I KNEW SHE WOULD TRY SOMETHING, BUT NOT THIS...!
YOU...
YES?

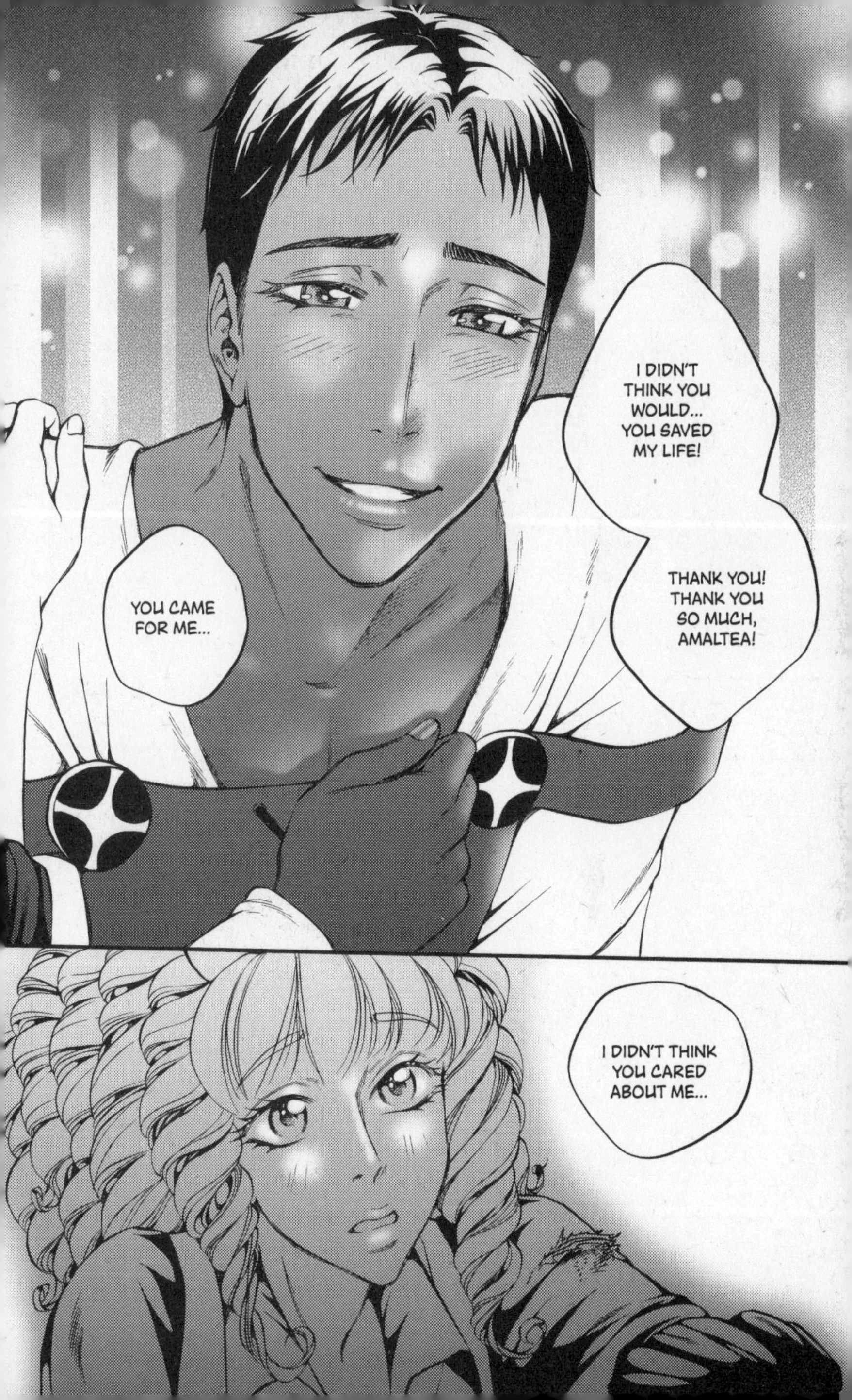
YOU CAME FOR ME...
I DIDN'T THINK YOU WOULD... YOU SAVED MY LIFE!
THANK YOU! THANK YOU SO MUCH, AMALTEA!
I DIDN'T THINK YOU CARED ABOUT ME...

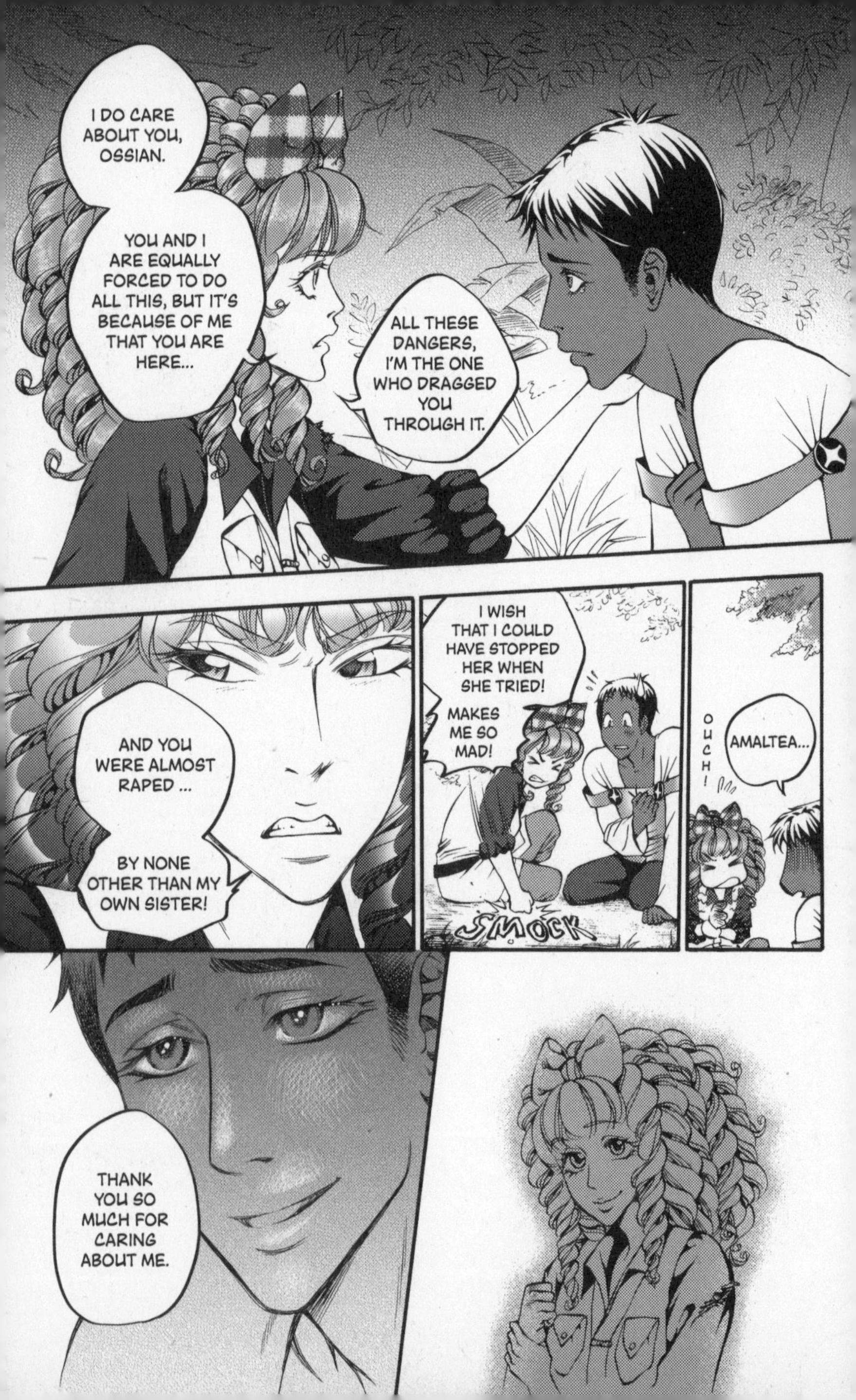
I DO CARE ABOUT YOU, OSSIAN.
YOU AND I ARE EQUALLY FORCED TO DO ALL THIS, BUT IT'S BECAUSE OF ME THAT YOU ARE HERE...
ALL THESE DANGERS, I'M THE ONE WHO DRAGGED YOU THROUGH IT.
AND YOU WERE ALMOST RAPED ...
BY NONE OTHER THAN MY OWN SISTER!
I WISH THAT I COULD HAVE STOPPED HER WHEN SHE TRIED!
MAKES ME SO MAD!
SMOCK
OUCH!
AMALTEA...
THANK YOU SO MUCH FOR CARING ABOUT ME.

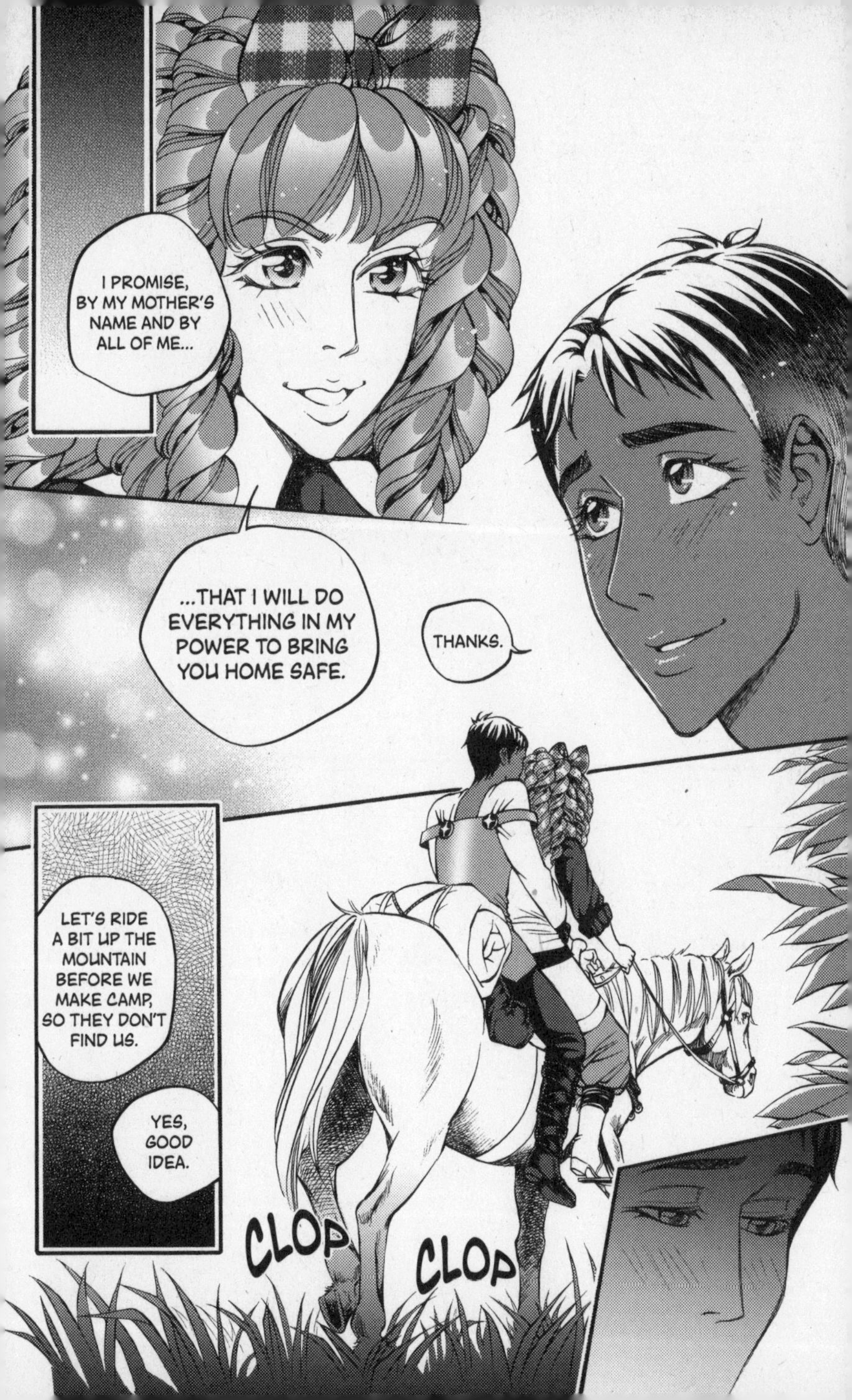
I PROMISE, BY MY MOTHER'S NAME AND BY ALL OF ME...
...THAT I WILL DO EVERYTHING IN MY POWER TO BRING YOU HOME SAFE.
THANKS.
LET'S RIDE A BIT UP THE MOUNTAIN BEFORE WE MAKE CAMP, SO THEY DON'T FIND US.
YES, GOOD IDEA.
CLOP
CLOP

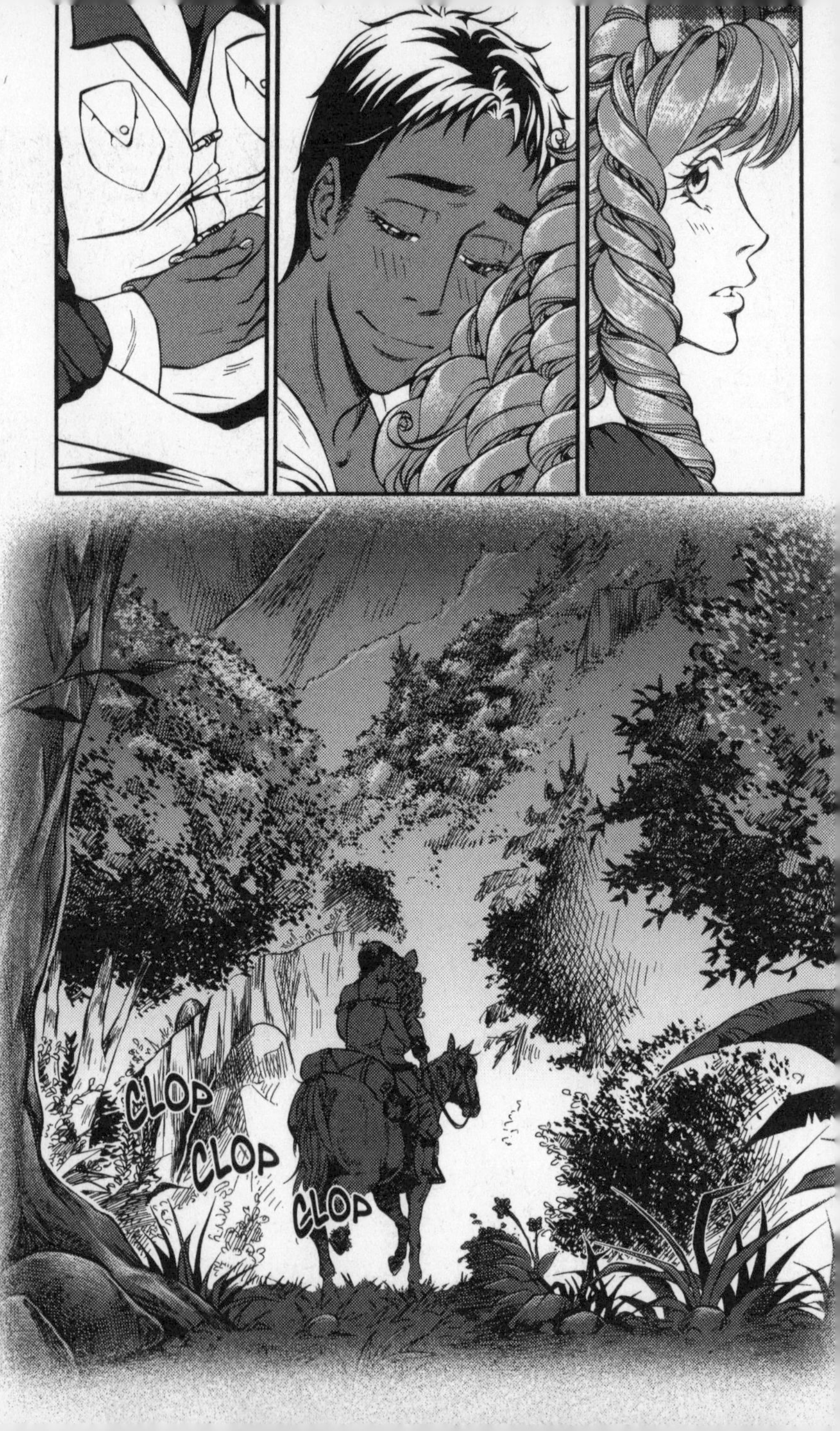
CLOP
CLOP
CLOP

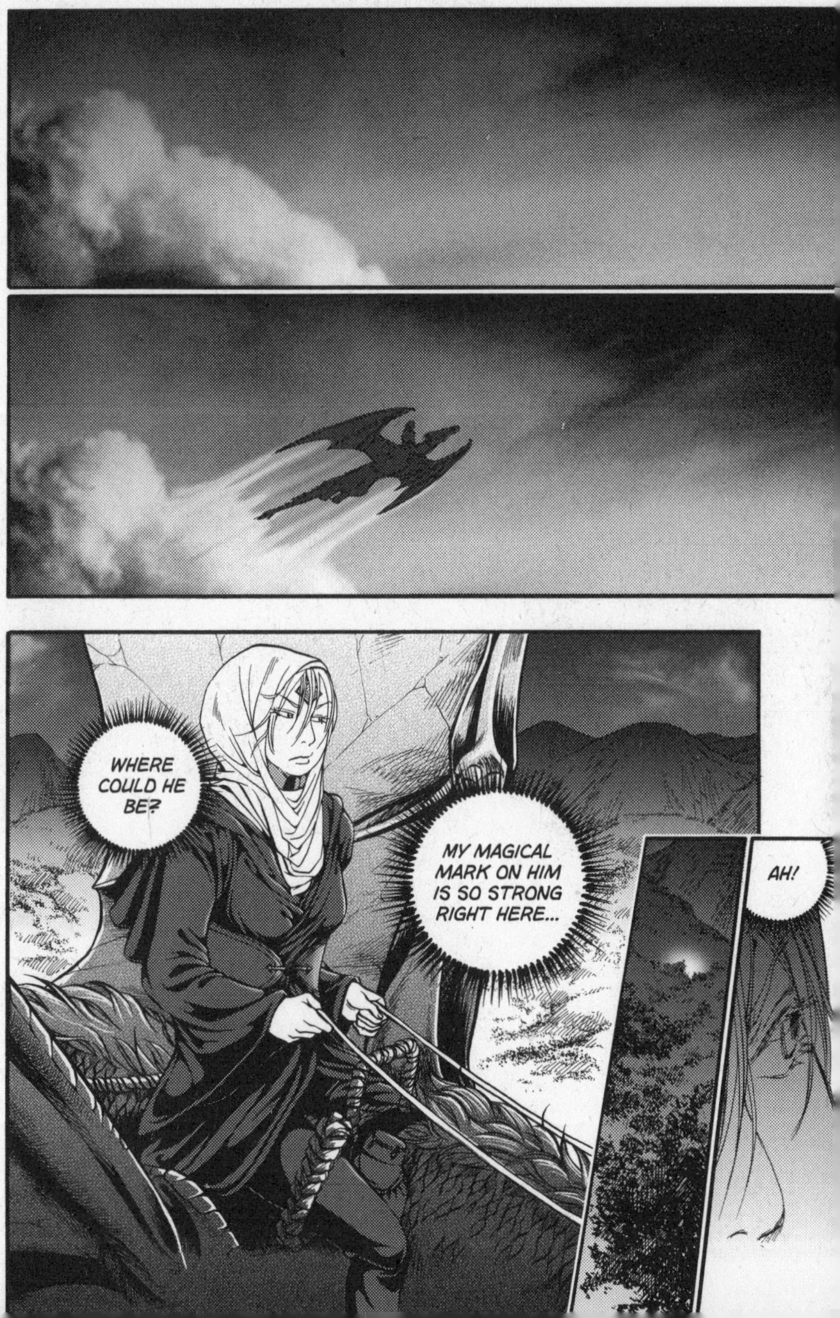
WHERE COULD HE BE?
MY MAGICAL MARK ON HIM IS SO STRONG RIGHT HERE...
AH!

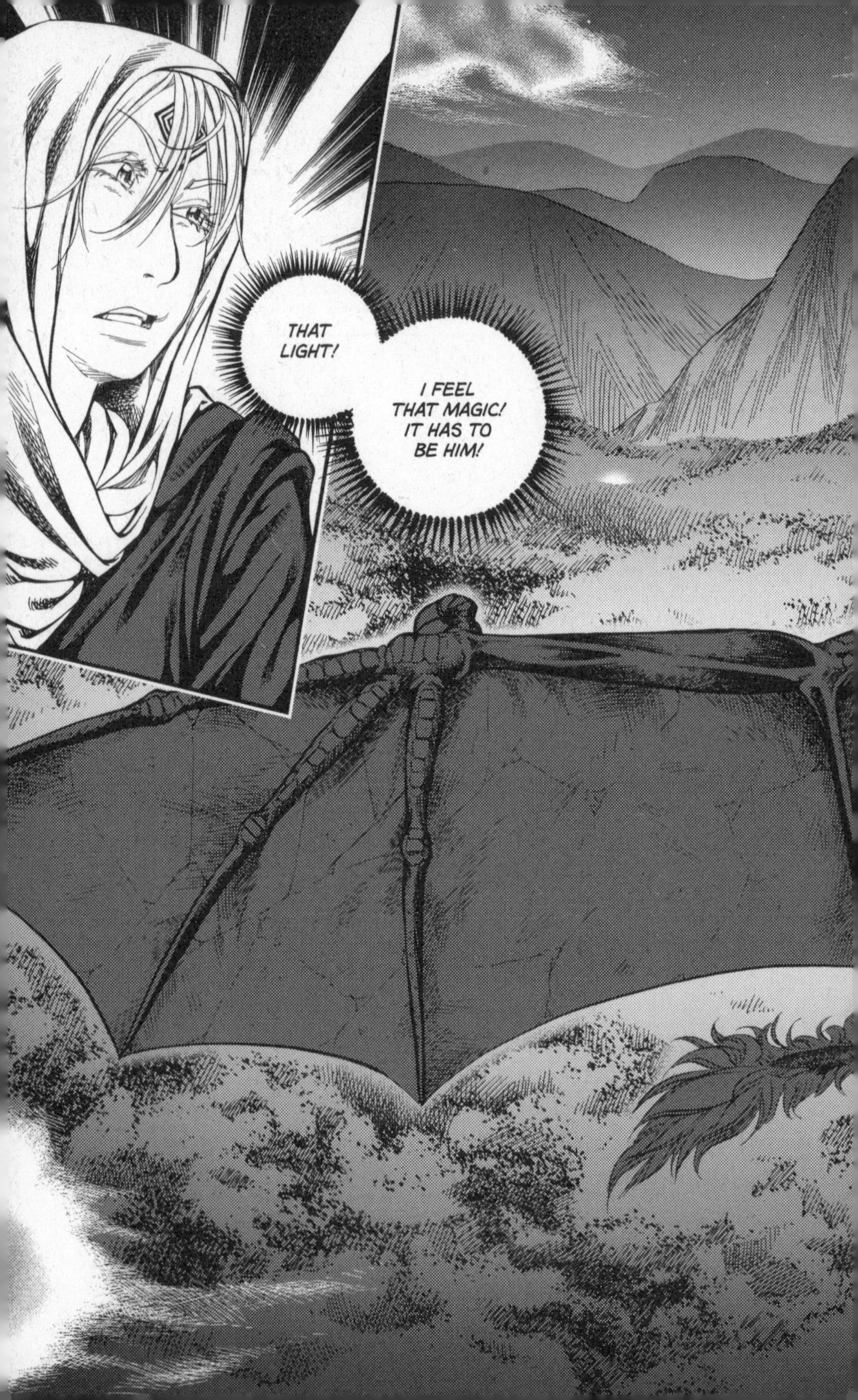
THAT LIGHT!
I FEEL THAT MAGIC! IT HAS TO BE HIM!

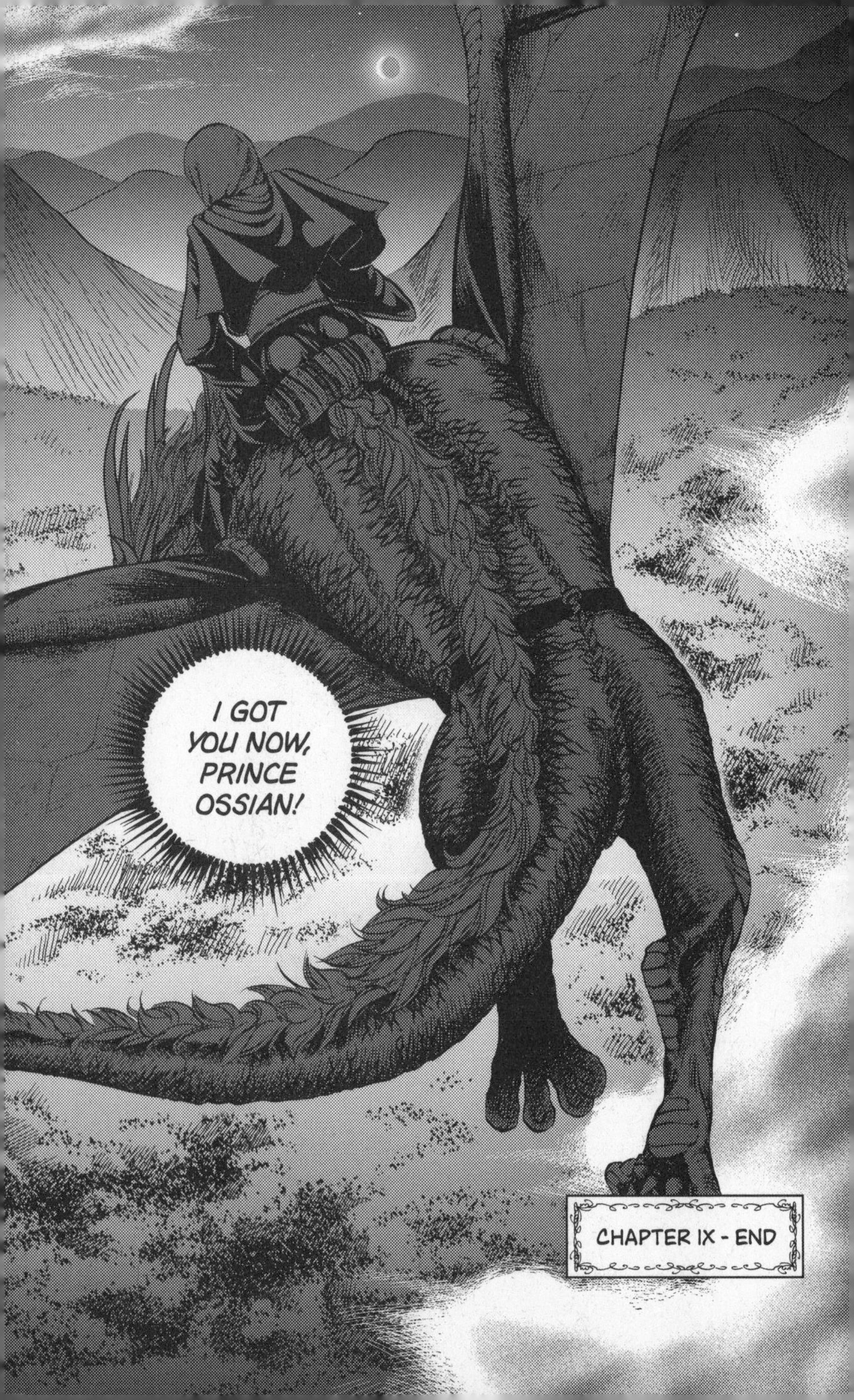
I GOT YOU NOW, PRINCE OSSIAN!
CHAPTER IX - END

IN THE FINAL VOLUME OF

TOKYOPOP
SWORD PRINCESS
AMALTEA
COVER NOT FINAL
3
Natalia Batista

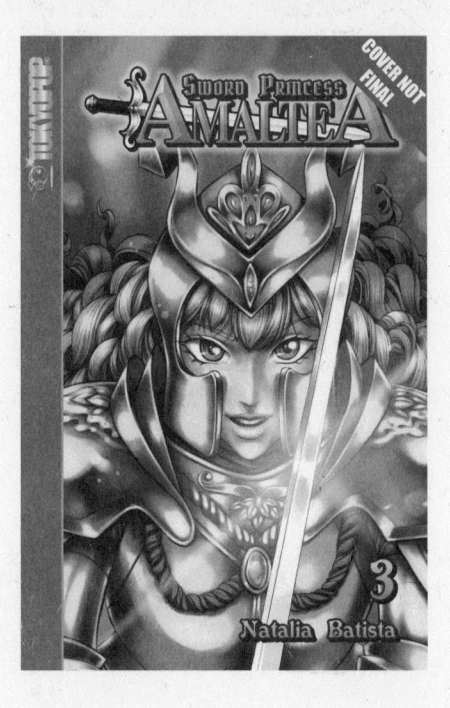

WITH AMALTEA AND OSSIAN'S FEELINGS FOR ONE ANOTHER SLOWLY BLOOMING INTO SOMETHING MORE THAN JUST A CONVENIENT PARTNERSHIP, THE APPEARANCE OF A POWERFUL CHALLENGER FROM OSSIAN'S PAST THREATENS THEIR FUTURE TOGETHER. BUT AMALTEA STILL HAS TO PROVE HER WORTHINESS AS A SUITOR AND HEIR TO THE THRONE OF THE GREY MOUNTAINS QUEENDOM. HAS SHE GROWN ENOUGH TO EARN PRINCE OSSIAN'S HAND... AND HEART?

STAY TUNED FOR THE FINAL CHAPTER IN THE HEROIC JOURNEY OF *SWORD PRINCESS AMALTEA*!

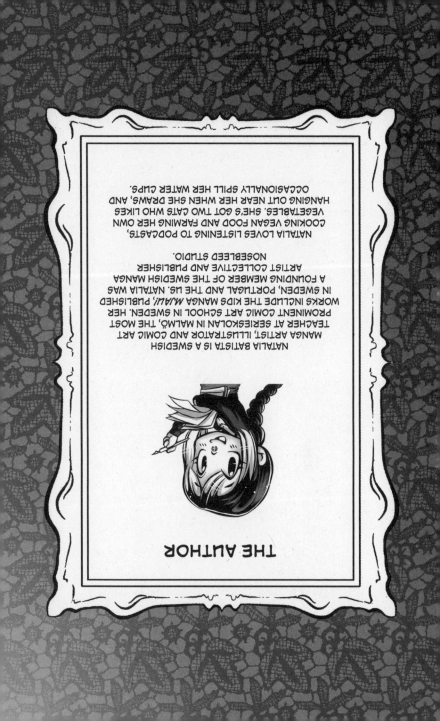

THE AUTHOR

NATALIA BATISTA IS A SWEDISH MANGA ARTIST, ILLUSTRATOR AND COMIC ART TEACHER AT SERIESKOLAN IN MALMÖ, THE MOST PROMINENT COMIC ART SCHOOL IN SWEDEN. HER WORKS INCLUDE THE KIDS MANGA *MJAU!*, PUBLISHED IN SWEDEN, PORTUGAL AND THE US. NATALIA WAS A FOUNDING MEMBER OF THE SWEDISH MANGA ARTIST COLLECTIVE AND PUBLISHER NOSEBLEED STUDIO.

NATALIA LOVES LISTENING TO PODCASTS, COOKING VEGAN FOOD AND FARMING HER OWN VEGETABLES. SHE'S GOT TWO CATS WHO LIKES HANGING OUT NEAR HER WHEN SHE DRAWS, AND OCCASIONALLY SPILL HER WATER CUPS.

ORIGINAL CHARACTER SKETCHES

2010

IN THE FALL, I STARTED DRAFTING THE FIRST CHARACTER DESIGNS. AT THIS POINT, THEY DIDN'T EVEN HAVE NAMES; I JUST CALLED THEM "THE PRINCESS" AND "THE PRINCE." I SHOWED THEM TO A GERMAN MANGA EDITOR WHOM I WAS IN CONTACT WITH BACK THEN. THE FEEDBACK I GOT WAS TO MAKE THEM LOOK MORE INTERESTING AND UNIQUE. SO I KEPT ON REVISING...

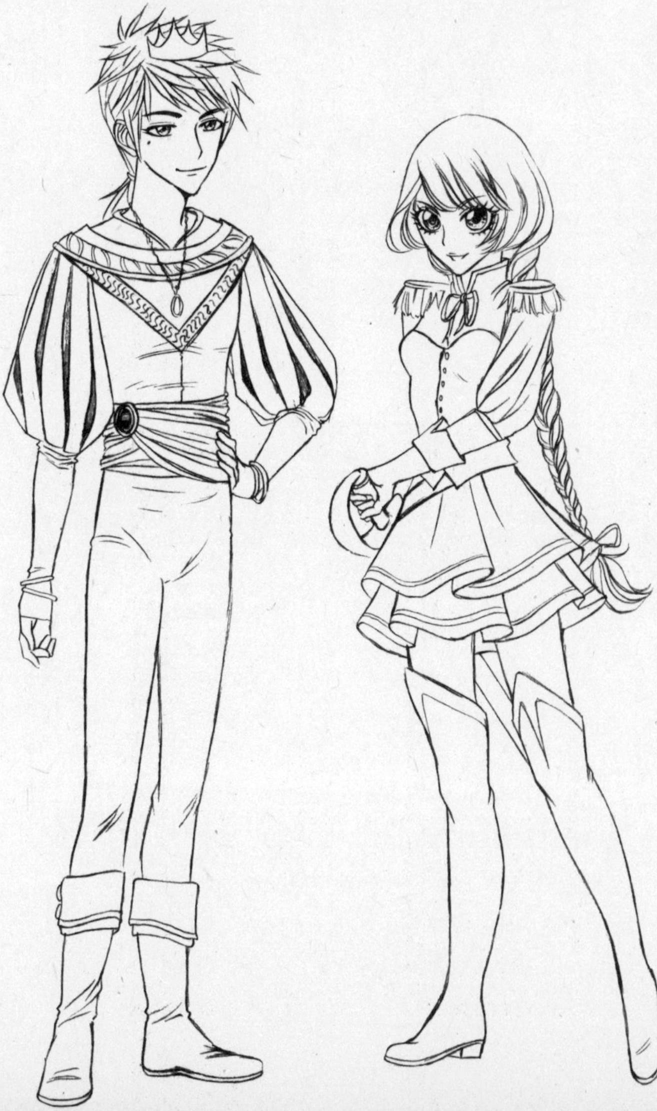

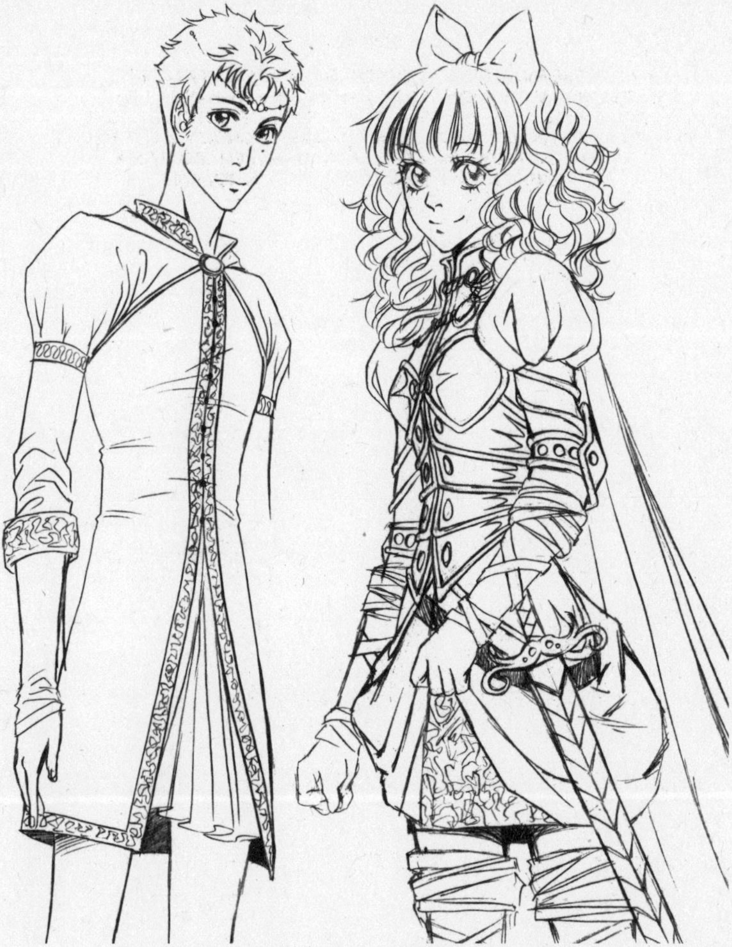

2012

AT THIS POINT, BOTH OSSIAN AND AMALTEA HAD REACHED THEIR FINAL DESIGNS. OSSIAN WAS ACTUALLY FAIR-SKINNED IN THE BEGINNING, MEANT TO STEREOTYPE THE CLASSICAL BLOND BEAUTY IN DISTRESS, BUT I LATER DECIDED TO MAKE HIM DARKER BECAUSE I WANTED TO HAVE MORE REPRESENTATION IN THE MANGA.

AMALTEA'S ARMOR DESIGN BACK THEN INCLUDED TWO BREASTPLATES. I LATER CHANGED THIS AFTER READING AN INTERESTING BLOG POST ABOUT THE IMPRACTICALITY OF DOUBLE BREASTPLATES IN BATTLE AND HOW DANGEROUS IT WOULD BE IF A WEAPON STRUCK THE WEARER BETWEEN THE PLATES. RESEARCH IS SO IMPORTANT!

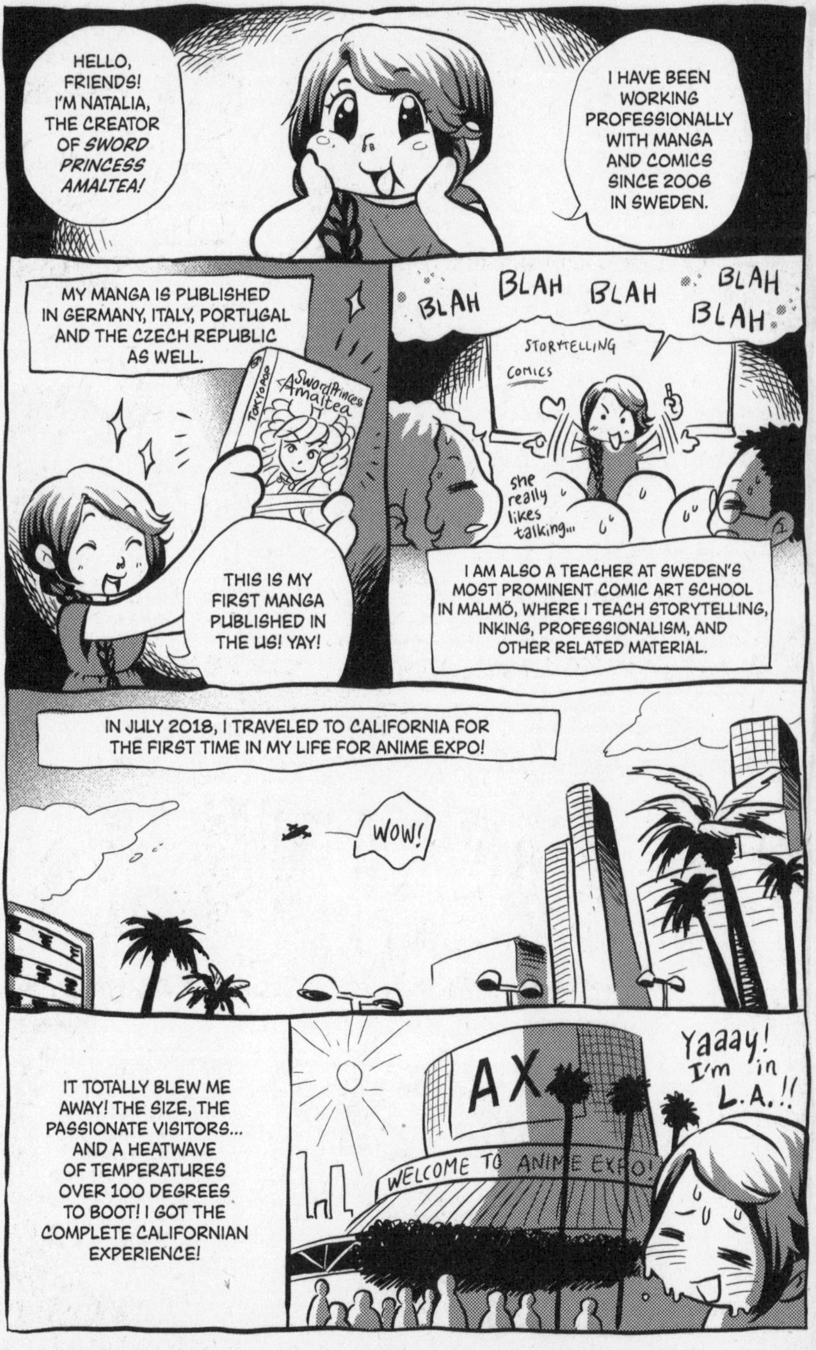
HELLO, FRIENDS! I'M NATALIA, THE CREATOR OF *SWORD PRINCESS AMALTEA!*
I HAVE BEEN WORKING PROFESSIONALLY WITH MANGA AND COMICS SINCE 2006 IN SWEDEN.
MY MANGA IS PUBLISHED IN GERMANY, ITALY, PORTUGAL AND THE CZECH REPUBLIC AS WELL.
TOKYOPOP
Sword Princess Amaltea
THIS IS MY FIRST MANGA PUBLISHED IN THE US! YAY!
BLAH BLAH BLAH BLAH BLAH
STORYTELLING
COMICS
she really likes talking...
I AM ALSO A TEACHER AT SWEDEN'S MOST PROMINENT COMIC ART SCHOOL IN MALMÖ, WHERE I TEACH STORYTELLING, INKING, PROFESSIONALISM, AND OTHER RELATED MATERIAL.
IN JULY 2018, I TRAVELED TO CALIFORNIA FOR THE FIRST TIME IN MY LIFE FOR ANIME EXPO!
WOW!
IT TOTALLY BLEW ME AWAY! THE SIZE, THE PASSIONATE VISITORS... AND A HEATWAVE OF TEMPERATURES OVER 100 DEGREES TO BOOT! I GOT THE COMPLETE CALIFORNIAN EXPERIENCE!
AX
WELCOME TO ANIME EXPO!
Yaaay! I'm in L.A.!!

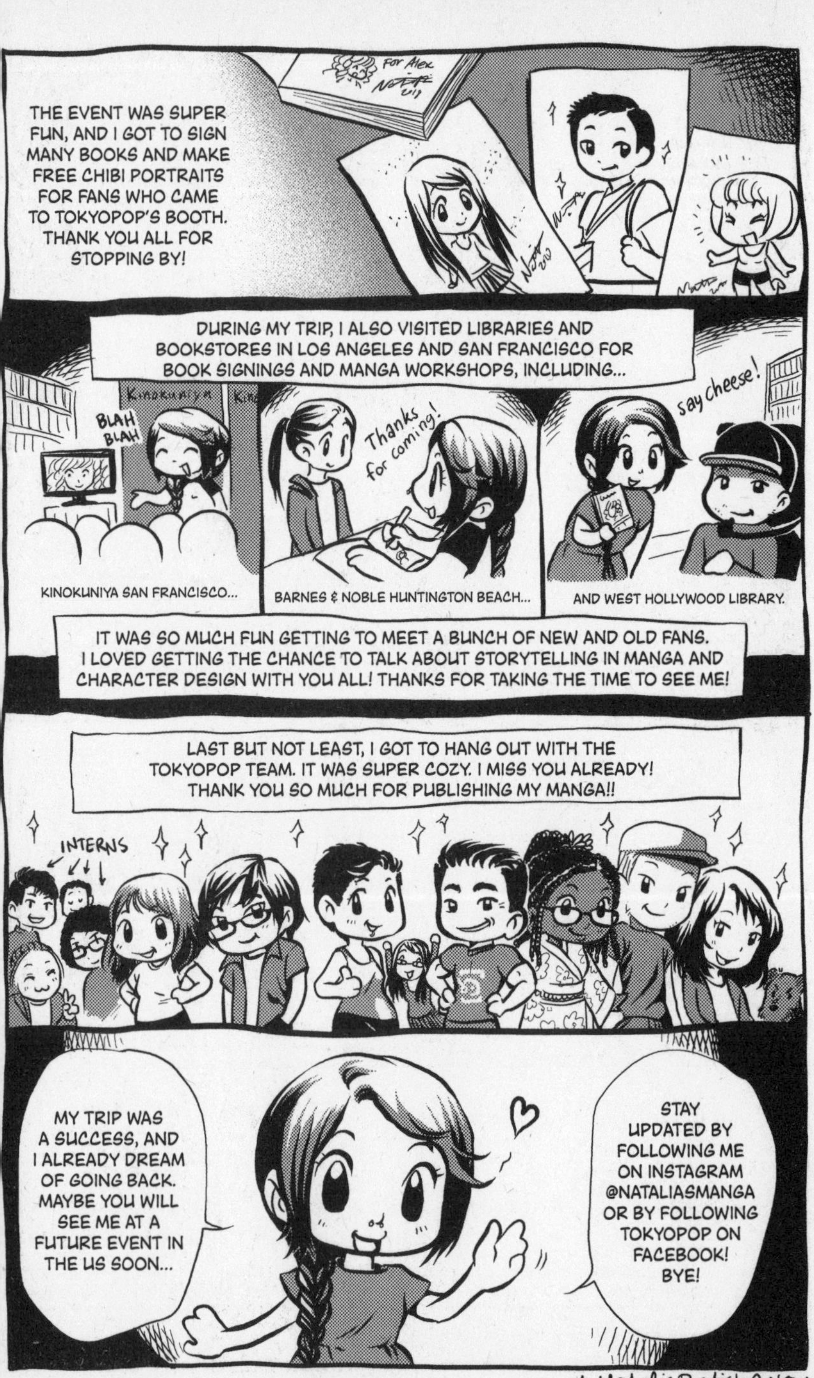
THE EVENT WAS SUPER FUN, AND I GOT TO SIGN MANY BOOKS AND MAKE FREE CHIBI PORTRAITS FOR FANS WHO CAME TO TOKYOPOP'S BOOTH. THANK YOU ALL FOR STOPPING BY!
For Alex
DURING MY TRIP, I ALSO VISITED LIBRARIES AND BOOKSTORES IN LOS ANGELES AND SAN FRANCISCO FOR BOOK SIGNINGS AND MANGA WORKSHOPS, INCLUDING...
Kinokuniya
BLAH BLAH
KINOKUNIYA SAN FRANCISCO...
Thanks for coming!
BARNES & NOBLE HUNTINGTON BEACH...
say cheese!
AND WEST HOLLYWOOD LIBRARY.
IT WAS SO MUCH FUN GETTING TO MEET A BUNCH OF NEW AND OLD FANS. I LOVED GETTING THE CHANCE TO TALK ABOUT STORYTELLING IN MANGA AND CHARACTER DESIGN WITH YOU ALL! THANKS FOR TAKING THE TIME TO SEE ME!
LAST BUT NOT LEAST, I GOT TO HANG OUT WITH THE TOKYOPOP TEAM. IT WAS SUPER COZY. I MISS YOU ALREADY! THANK YOU SO MUCH FOR PUBLISHING MY MANGA!!
INTERNS
MY TRIP WAS A SUCCESS, AND I ALREADY DREAM OF GOING BACK. MAYBE YOU WILL SEE ME AT A FUTURE EVENT IN THE US SOON...
STAY UPDATED BY FOLLOWING ME ON INSTAGRAM @NATALIASMANGA OR BY FOLLOWING TOKYOPOP ON FACEBOOK! BYE!

★ Natalia Batista 2018 ★

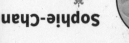

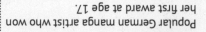
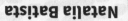